INTERVENTION STRATEGIES FOR SPECIALIZED SECONDARY EDUCATION

The Authors: David A. Sabatino received his M.A. in Speech and Hearing and his Ph.D. in Special Education Administration and Educational Evaluation and Research at Ohio State University. He has taught deaf and autistic children, has served as Associate Editor of the *Journal of Exceptional Children, Psychology in the Schools,* and *School Psychology Digest,* and has published extensively in the fields of psychology, learning disabilities, and mental retardation. Dr. Sabatino also served as a consultant for the Maryland State Department of Education, the Bureau of Correction for the Commonwealth of Pennsylvania, and the West Virginia Department of Mental Health before becoming Professor and Chairman of the Department of Special Education at Northern Ilinois University.

August J. Mauser received his M.A. and Ph.D. in Special Education at Indiana State University, Bloomington. He served as a learning disabilities consultant in the Indiana Juvenile Courts of Vigo County and as a psychological and educational consultant in the Indiana Public Schools before becoming Professor of Special Education at Northern Illinois University. He is an active member of many professional organizations, including the American Association for Children with Learning Disabilities, the International Reading Association, and the National Association for Retarded Citizens, and has served as the National Chairman for the Association of the Gifted. Professor Mauser has also published numerous articles on mental retardation, education of problem adolescents, learning disabilities and reading education.

INTERVENTION STRATEGIES FOR SPECIALIZED SECONDARY EDUCATION

David A. Sabatino
Northern Illinois University
August J. Mauser
Northern Illinois University

ALLYN AND BACON, Inc.
Boston • London • Sydney

Library of Congress Cataloging in Publication Data

Main entry under title:
Intervention strategies for specialized secondary education.
    Includes bibliographies and index.
    1. Problem children—Education. I. Sabatino,
David A. II. Mauser, August J. III. Title.
LC 4801.I56   371.9'3   77–28683
ISBN 0–205–06024–2

*This text is dedicated
to the generations of secondary school
educators who have "made a difference"
with kids that others felt weren't worth it.*

We, the editors, gratefully acknowledge the time, energy, and personal and family sacrifice made by the contributors of this book. And a special acknowledgment to Dr. Barbara Ford, Stephanie Lyons, who proofread, Mark Hill and Aileen Gormley, our workaholic graduate assistants, and Ms. Cheryl Jones, manuscript typist.

contents

chapter 3

chapter 4

chapter 5

Behavior Related to Suicides,
Runaways, Alcoholism, and Drug Abuse

chapter 6

Developing Reading Strategies
for Youths with Educational Handicaps

chapter 7

chapter 8

preface

This book reviews the current state-of-the-art in instructional use, curriculum delivery, and behavioral management techniques. It is intended for prospective and practicing special educators interested in adolescents. The material is equally applicable for correctional educators, psychologists, counselors, administrators, and regular educators. We have attempted to accomplish two objectives in this text, and at times they appear to run at cross purposes. But, if the reader understands our intent from the onset, that understanding will probably eliminate any confusion. Some of the chapters are purely reviews of current educational practices. When possible, accountability or validity will be specified when comparisons between instructional program components, characterizing efficiency, or effectiveness is noted. Other chapters are more how-to-do-it approaches. We have attempted to be careful with the latter because we do not want to recommend one approach over another. Therefore, some blending or attempts to review and provide specific information on instructional procedures has generally been accomplished.

In our related book, *Specialized Education in Today's Secondary Schools,* the characteristics and diagnostic means for ascertaining the traits of norm-violating and chronic disruptive youths was thoroughly discussed. If you have read this related book first, you will note *Intervention Strategies for Specialized Secondary Education* is sequential, continuing that discussion into the program and service aspects used to modify school related norm-violating, disruptive behavior, and educational handicaps. The stated purpose of *Specialized Education in Today's Secondary Schools* was to review the characteristics of adolescent norm-violators, and describe the best practice for diagnostic procedures. The implied purpose was to provide an informational competency base, which might alter attitudinal misconceptions, concerning youth who are classified as adjudicated; delinquent; norm-violating; chronic disruptive; mildly physically, socially, or mentally disabled; or display educational handicaps. It was the belief of the authors that a advocacy has not been created for secondary school age youths who fail to interact successfully with the academic curriculum and/or social rules. If we were successful in obtaining our objectives with *Specialized Education in Today's Secondary Schools,* we created an appetite for other information, which is a natural step beyond establishing or describing characteristics. We would, in fact, create the desire for information on educational programs, instructional interventions, and behavioral management strategies.

Chapter 1 is a review of specific programs used to prevent or remediate truancy, dropouts, vandalism, disruptive aggression, and traditional special education. This chapter does not examine any instructional procedures per se, only the program delivery of a curriculum. Chapter 2 discusses the career and vocational programming necessary for chronically disruptive youth. Reviews of and procedures for altering behaviors are found in Chapters 3 and 4. Chapter 5 addresses the frequently swept out of sight issues of runaways and suicide. This chapter then enters into a very serious discussion of drug education.

Chapters 6 and 7 review reading strategies, reading recognition, and reading comprehension skills, respectively. But the highlights of this chapter are its specific procedural steps to assist the teacher in integrating remedial, clinical, and developmental reading for nonreaders and functional readers. Chapter 8 attempts to accomplish a similar objective to the reading chapters with mathematics education.

We realize we have not exhausted our topic. We also are aware that this book places heavy demands on the reader. But, as our capabilities permit, we hope that you now have in your hands the best single review of education programs and services for adolescents in trouble in schools that is currently available. To you, the reader, we have worked to produce something worthy of your time and energy expenditure. It was our alternate objective to assist you in your advocacy, by providing you useable information. Thank you for being an advocate of secondary kids needing assistance.

David A. Sabatino
August J. Mauser

1

programs for youths in trouble

MICHAEL H. EPSTEIN, SHARON G. ROTHMAN, DAVID A. SABATINO

The attitudes and accomplishments of most secondary school students are positive and a rich source of reward for both teacher and student. However, there are some students whose school careers are filled with frustration and disruption. These youths are a part of our educational responsibility, and as educators, we shall continue to provide intervention strategies to combat the difficulties they face.

Chronic disruptive or norm-violating youths experience many profound personal crises and tend to meet academic and social competition unsuccessfully, facing reoccurring underachievement in practically all subject areas. These unrewarding social and academic experiences are released through unacceptable behavioral acts such as vandalism, truancy, aggression, and dropping out of school. It should be noted that members of the traditional special education group are not inherently involved with such activities, and yet at the secondary level, behaviorally disordered, learning disabled, and mentally retarded students have accumulated histories of school difficulties. School problems are expressed in overt attention-getting or passive attention responses, causing the secondary handicapped student to look, act, or appear to be indistinguishable from the chronic disruptive or norm-violating youth.

The multiplicity of factors involved with (not necessarily causing) chronic disruptive behavior breaks have blended into a mosaic of syndromes. Many external factors such as economics, peer influence, and family background while outside the school, shape the view of the youth toward authority. Therefore, the school must assume its share of the responsibility in coping with these students, specifically their in-school behaviors. Chronic disruptive youths present problem behaviors to the school, the courts, child welfare, various juvenile divisions, mental health centers, and the community at large. A general call for interagency liaison is necessary, and the communication needed to initiate this liaison between school and community agencies is vital.

A review of the parameters of the problem underscores the need of urgency. It has been conservatively estimated that vandalism costs our nation and schools half a billion dollars a year. School assaults and battery cases are up 58% since 1970. School robberies are up 117% for the same period. In 1973–1974, out of every 100 persons 17 years of age, 25 did not graduate. These youths in trouble are a financial loss and a psycholgical detriment to the foundation of a democratic society. The school must deal seriously with the lives and welfare of these students to ensure a normal school program and quality education for all children.

This chapter provides the reader with alternative delivery systems in secondary schools, with particular emphasis on dropouts, truants, vandals, staged and unstaged aggressive outbreaks, and special education programs. Actual programs are referred to, some of which have been tested, others tried, while some remain purely speculative. As will be noted throughout the chapter, intense future direction and development is needed in the secondary schools for youth experiencing social and educational handicaps.

PROGRAMS TO REDUCE TRUANCY

There is an acute absence of substantial corrective programming directed primarily at attenuating truancy. If the truant's behavior is not critically alarming he is either ignored, counseled by a teacher, or at most, referred to the school counselor or pupil personnel consultants. If the truant evidences more severe conduct behavior he is placed in programs for the behaviorally disordered youth. If he crosses over the line and becomes a dropout, or an adjudicated delinquent, then he is no longer viewed, of course, as a mere threat. Truancy is a major symptomatic problem that means the youth needs assistance.

Of the 50 states 47 have compulsory school attendance laws (Splaine, 1975), and it is interesting that all 47 states specify the ultimate penalty as incarceration. How severe is the problem of incarceration following non-school attendance? Statistics from the Department of Juvenile Services, Annual Reports, 1970–1974, Baltimore, Maryland, reveal that 341 children were committed to incarceration and 52 were detained. Additionally, 2,699 school-age youth were committed because they were considered to be "children in need of supervision." That label captures truants, runaways, and unmanageable children. Most states recognize that when a young person is not in school he may be headed for trouble in the streets. On the other hand, if the school officials and courts request a youth to attend school and he refuses, what options are available to the courts? Incarceration seems like an obvious alternative. The problem with incarceration is that the child is removed from those settings which are responsible for education and socialization: the school and community. What does the truant do after initial incarceration? He now has a 75% chance of returning to an incarceration setting. Moreover, the reason for this return will not be truancy, it will be "harder crime."

Currently, few programs focus exclusively on truancy, and the majority of the programs which do exist were established within the last half decade. The recent program development in this area is indicative of a new concern for the syndrome known as truancy. However, the truancy programs which are being implemented are without validation through empirical study. Truly creative program development, especially that which would prevent truancy, has not yet been developed. Generally, the programs being conducted fail to recognize the truant as possessing any distinct social/personal problems which entitle him to unique program considerations and/or treatments. A review of the existing truancy programs is included in this section.

In 1963, The Chicago Public Schools initiated IMPACT—a program for the Improvement of Attendance and Curtailment of Truancy. In each of Chicago's 27 districts (each district has approximately 2,500 students), two classrooms were established for boys 7 to 13 years of age who required special placement because of truancy problems. A trained, experienced male teacher was assigned to each class to work with 5 to 10 students. During a six year period, 80 boys were referred to the IMPACT classes, of which 52 were eventually transferred into the program. Of the 36 boys who went through IMPACT for at least one or more years, 10 are enrolled in high school, 19 are in regular elementary schools, 2 went to state institutions, 2 are gainfully employed, and 3 are in vocational-guidance schools.

Brooks (1975) used a contingency management model in his study with 40 high school truants. They were evenly assigned to experimental and control groups. The experimental program incorporated a number of behavior modification techniques including a token economy system, contingency contracts, and group guidance meetings with the truant students. A comparison of the groups on the number of days truant favored the experimental group. Of the experimental group 95% showed a reduction in the number of days truant, whereas only 20% of the students in the control group decreased truancy. An important variable which must be noted was the effect that style of teacher responses had on the subjects' rate of school attendance. Specifically, students were encouraged to elicit positive comments from the teachers and were given additional tokens for these positive teacher comments. The writing of positive comments by the teachers may have set in motion the conditions whereby the teacher began to have a positive attitude toward the student. This reciprocally positive reaction for both student and teacher may possibly have resulted in an increase in school attendance behavior on the part of the student.

Grala and McCauley (1976) worked with 32 male chronic truants between the ages of 13 and 17. The authors compared the effectiveness of threat or promise and personal school counseling for truants as a factor in returning them to regular school attendance. Interesting differences between verbal commitments to refrain from truant behavior and an actual decrease in truant behavior were noted. Half the truants received threats about the negative consequences of truancy from a community center counselor, a former dropout and drug user, who descriptively outlined the limited possibilities further truancy assured. Of the truants who received this program 70% reported intentions to return to school. The second group of truants received individual talks on the benefits of regular school attendance (optimistic appeal). Of these students, only 9% reported a change in their intentions concerning school attendance. In addition to the different appeals, half the truants in each group received individual counseling including supportive instruction on the problems of returning to school and personal academic tutoring through the community center. Interestingly, a greater proportion of subjects who received this supportive counseling actually returned to school compared to the truants who received no counseling.

Washington (1973) incorporated the idea of supportive individual counseling in his recommendations toward a solution of truancy. He described a pupil-teacher study development program which would prepare the truant for the academic and social rigors of school life. A program of this nature would provide the truant with instruction on how to study, how to prepare assignments and reports, how to use the library and references properly, as well as academic tutoring. Individually, the program would help the student develop an understanding of his own interests in order to further personal adjustment to school situations. The counseling would establish grounds for the individual's more profitable use of free and leisure time. A second recommendation advocated by Washington concerned the development of a placement center for part-time employment. State employment bureaus, local business groups, and community social and religious organizations could provide vocational and occupational information beneficial to the truant.

What are the options for curtailing truancy? The primary option is prevention, which is not an easy task for several reasons. An initial difficulty is that truants are students with many problems, only one of which is not attending school regularly. Problems range from family or home crises to total frustration with school to lack of academic success. The lack of homogeneity within the group of adolescents labeled as truants impedes progress in developing prevention programs. Additional problems which greatly exaggerate the issues of truancy are that prevalence increases diametrically in intercity environments, and increases disproportionately again when ethnic minority and non-English language factors are included.

Public education is highly valued in white middle-class America as having a perfunctory task of sustaining middle America. It is little wonder that truancy increases dramatically with minority groups. Dysinger (1975), working with intercity American Indians, identified three important program elements: a more meaningful education experience that was culturally related, direct family support, and work experiences. Hanks (1972) found that Alaskan children would not attend school regularly unless a family-home structure was developed. As it were, neither the youth or parents felt school was important. Several studies with Spanish speaking groups (DeGracie, 1974) indicated that study centers, early identification processes, and career education programs with work-study experiences have been effective means of deterring truancy.

There has been a great deal of concern about the substance of preventative programs. Should prevention programs strive to promote student conformity to existing norms through counseling, behavioral modification, remedial activities, and parent involvement? Or should they attempt to modify norms by changing the school environment? In a comprehensive review of the current research and literature, Mertens (1972) reasoned that preventative efforts should be directed at modifying the individual's behavior and attitudes. Mertens review illustrates once more that truancy is a symptom, a request for help. After it has become chronic then a different program structure is needed. The youth, at that point, should not return to a situation he was ill equipped to handle or where he could not achieve success for a number of reasons. All in all, Kohler (1976) advocates that as of yet there is no one means of successfully fighting truancy. The best prevention is early detection and rapid follow-up reaching beyond the doors of the school into the home and community. Truants need help, the school must recognize it as a symptom, and supply that assistance.

While these programs are limited by their scarcity and unvalidated by their recency, they are nonetheless positive indications of our schools' conviction to deal conscientiously and completely with our youth's social growth and needs. From the programs reviewed, four components of a program to reduce truancy appear necessary.

1. The awareness of teachers to the problem of truancy is essential. Teachers must be able to recognize the early signs of truancy and make prompt, accurate referrals to the school counseling program. Furthermore, the teacher should recognize the student as a person, providing him with a personal relationship which conveys respect.

2. The school must be aware of the factors precipitating truancy. The school must offer a varied curriculum and new approaches, such as career education or outdoor education, to provide students with reason to attend school.

3. The parents must be aware of their responsibility to the problem of truancy. Often the truant does not accept parental direction or explanations, but the parent must repeatedly emphasize the importance and their own personal regard for education.

4. The student himself must be aware of the consequences of truancy.

PROGRAMS DESIGNED TO CURB DROPOUTS

The dropout rate is definitely influenced by socioeconomic factors, pressures students feel for achievement, and adolescent peer culture. These three broad cluster phenomena, each with a number of contributing variables, are significant in driving a youth out of school. While many of these causes are external to the school milieu they dictate in part what happens to the student. And, it must be recognized that dropping out of school is rarely a cure for any of these causes.

Generally speaking, programs directed at preventing or retaining dropouts which have attempted to deal with widespread and diverse reasons have failed. The so-called comprehensive dropout preventative efforts have demonstrated only modest success over a brief period of time. These programs evidence early success which levels off rapidly and then returns to the pre-program rate after the program has terminated. Conversely, the programs which report reasonably supportive field test data have been limited in focus, concentrating manpower and other school and community resources on one symptomatic consideration. It is not our intention to be critical of any effort directed at reducing dropout rates. Indeed, anyone thinking of developing a program directed at preventing or intervening with youth who are contemplating dropping out of school should consider the specific program objectives they wish to accomplish, and therein, define the target group they wish to aid. There is little logic in the assumption that a program will assist youth when the reasons for leaving school are so vast that it is difficult to discern the characteristics of the group known as dropouts.

Three specific dropout programs are reviewed: an alternative high school, a job corps center for dropouts, and a junior high school dropout prevention program. The alternative school was an inner city daytime school placed in a housing development, where educators worked with selected dropouts on remedial and vocational training. The job corps was essentially a prevocational classroom and on-the-job training program. The prevention program stressed teacher reactions, attitude, and remediation integrated into the curriculum in an on-going junior high school.

Dauw (1970) reported a high school dropout program in the Pontiac, Michigan, schools directed at reducing the relatively high 17.1% dropout rates among disadvantaged students. Two hundred fifty high school dropouts from the Pontiac Public School District were encouraged to apply for entrance in the program. Of these, a total of 20 students responded to this invitation. The records of these students, along with those recommended by teachers and administrators were examined. Students were scheduled for interviews until 45 youths were selected. A daytime academic remediation and vocational training program was provided for these students in an inner city housing project. The students were characterized by prior poor school attendance, low academic achievement, and behavioral and/or socio-psychological problems.

The underlying concept of this alternative school was an individualized instructional program. The program components included a nonschool atmosphere, a controlled (size) setting, reduced pupil-teacher ratios, dependence on programmed instruction, individual counseling, and structured group interaction. The curriculum focused on providing training in academic remediation and vocational training. The academic curriculum was ungraded and afforded students the opportunity to express themselves creatively. The commercial materials used were the Mott Basic Language Skills, Litton Programmed Material, and a variety of materials prepared by the Science Research Associates (SRA) Corporation. Vocational awareness and training was also an integral component of the program and was conducted in a number of sites in Pontiac, Michigan. Some students participated in a work-study program, others worked in the local Neighborhood Youth Corps, and still others received career training in local industries.

The alternative Pontiac High School program was evaluated on seven variables: (1) school attendance; (2) student achievement; (3) dropout potential; (4) dropout rate; (5) student self-concept; (6) student opinions;

and (7) personal characteristics related to teacher adequacy. Data were obtained for each of these variables between the youth in the program and a group of 36 regular school attenders. Dauw (1970) reported the following results:

1. *Attendance.* Attendance of the students in the alternative program significantly improved in comparison to the matched sample group. Teachers consistently worked toward creating an atmosphere of belonging to the school program, both by their actions and by encouraging students to take part in various activities. Constant attempts were made to instill a sense of belonging through phone contacts, home visitations, or transporting students to and from school. For the first time, students acknowledged that teachers actually cared about them and cared whether or not they attended school. Furthermore, students were encouraged to establish this sense of belonging by actively involving themselves in classroom planning, organization, and decision-making.

2. *Achievement.* Academic achievement was evaluated through subtests of the California Achievement Test: reading comprehension and reading vocabulary. Seventeen students in the alternative program evidenced reading comprehension grade placement scores of 2.0 or better, in academic achievement growth; whereas only 7 of the matched sample attained this level. On reading vocabulary, an increase of 2.0 in academic achievement growth was scored by 24 of the students, in comparison to only 13 of the control group. The individual instructional program curriculum, as part of the alternative school program, emphasized reading through the use of high-interest, low vocabulary reading materials. The inclusion of these materials may have accounted in part for the improvement of the experimental group in relation to the control group.

3. *Dropout Potential.* The Cottle School Interest Inventory was used to ascertain dropout potential. The higher the score on the 150-item test, the greater the dropout potential. On the Cottle inventory, a score of 30 is generally considered the *critical point* in determining dropout potential. An analysis of the scores from both groups indicated that participation in the alternative program significantly reduced dropout potential. By decreasing the likelihood of a student leaving school, the program may have increased school holding power for the adolescents. The average score of students in the experimental group was 29.4, while the average of the control group was 34.7, which exceeded the critical point.

4. *Dropout Rate Variable.* On the dropout rate the alternative school program was compared to statistics for two Pontiac high schools. The students' dropout rate was obtained by dividing the number of dropouts who had attended ten days or more of the alternative program by the total enrollment. Using this procedure the dropout rate for the program was 14.9%. In comparison, the dropout rate (for the two Pontiac high schools) during the same time period was 17.1% for grades 10 through 12. The

overall effect of the program has resulted in a 2% decrease in the dropout rate for the total Pontiac School System. Over the course of the program, 33 students have graduated from the alternative program and received high school diplomas.

5. Self-Concept. A version of the Self-Esteem Inventory, developed by Coopersmith, was used to assess student self-concept. The mean difference of the groups was not significant which indicated that participation in the program had no effect on student self-concept.

6. Student Opinions Variable. A student opinion questionnaire was developed to assess students' perceptions of the alternative program. The high response items were divided into three categories which may be regarded as the main ingredients of the alternative school program as perceived by the students. The three categories were:

  a. Teachers and methodology. The teachers were viewed by the students as being more understanding, as fostering the students to express their own opinions, and as caring less about grades and more about the students as individuals.

  b. School atmosphere. As a result of the alternative high school the students appeared to like school better, were more relaxed, felt less pressure to succeed, and enjoyed coming to school.

  c. Students' self perceptions. The students felt their peers at the alternative high school were a good group, whom they were close to, and that more alternative high schools would be helpful to more students if they had the chance for enrollment.

7. Personal Characteristics Related to Teacher Adequacy. The personality characteristics of teachers in the alternative program were compared to teachers in the control group. The purpose of this evaluation was to ascertain if any significant teaching differences were present. If the personality characteristics differed in favor of the experimental group teachers, it would imply that a special type of teacher would be necessary to implement the alternative school program. The Minnesota Teacher Attitude Inventory was given to both groups of teachers and no significant differences were apparent.

Besant (1969) described an occupation training program at the Rodman Job Corps Center, in New Bedford, Massachusetts, where nearly 85% of the youths who attended two levels of successful study completed a high school equivalency exam and qualified for a high school diploma. The Rodman Center was established on observations that were made on teaching dropout youths. Dropouts have a deep sense of school inadequacy which is partially supported by a prior record of failure. If dropouts are to succeed as students in any preventative or remedial program they must experience early success in school. Characteristics of effective teaching are to present instruction in concise brief units which ensure constant evaluation and reward progress. Failure should be quickly identified and checked by recycling the student through the units that were not mastered. Initial instruction must be verbal with a gradual shift to written material as the student's reading ability increases. Counseling of students for personal and vocational reasons plays an important role. Individual and job related counseling must be intensive, highly personal, and realistic. Inexperienced teachers and counselors trained on the job under careful supervision are often successful because they are not bound by established patterns of teaching.

Learning some of the above principles permitted the staff to build a curriculum that provided maximum aid to students in minimum time. Besant (1969) found that "six to nine months of classwork and concurrent on-the-job training were sufficient to qualify the average 17- to 22-year-old trainee for an entry level job in a range of office skills" (p. 52).

The academic skill level of adjudicate youth (Berman, 1975) has been demonstrated time and time again to rarely exceed a fourth grade achievement level. The problem as Berman points out, is that the basic reading, writing, spelling, and arithmetic skills (tool subjects) are so inadequate that they are unusable for daily living purposes. More importantly, reading vocabulary is so weak that skill deficiencies actually decrease as the youth grows older.

That conclusion was borne out by the finding that at the eighth grade level, achievement in the disadvantaged areas was relatively lower than it had been in the fifth grade. Concommitantly, the dropout rate in predominantly black, urban high schools was two-thirds that of the entering ninth grade class and twice the city-wide rate. The reading and writing level of students in the disadvantaged areas was far too low for them to either advance in school or to function effectively in society. As direct consequences of this illiteracy, welfare problems, unemployment, poverty, and social and political isolation are important variables in a dropout program.

Douglass (1969) developed a junior high school dropout prevention program based on the premise that youths drop out because of their inability to learn to read and consequent failure in other subject areas. The major points covered by Douglass in preventing school dropouts were: (1) improve pupil-teacher interpersonal relations; (2) increase remedial work at the junior high school; (3) offer special study habits and skill building guidance centers of classes; (4) improve counseling relationship with an eye toward dropout systems; and (5) increase the number of work-study programs.

The issue faced by the school is simple: dropout prevention and career guidance are more effective than attempts to return youths to school. Once a youth has left school it is exceedingly difficult to persuade or entice him to return. Dropouts frequently want to return to school, but are stifled by the prospect of attending classes where they cannot achieve competitively with younger students. Alternative schools, especially those with evening classes and work-study coordinated programs, are a promising prospect which needs greater attention.

More than any other issue affecting dropouts, however, are the poorly aimed instructional objectives they receive. Issues, such as sex, marriage, vocational preparation, and consumer economics must be provided and presented in a meaningful manner. Teacher-student conferences should be more a direct dialogue rather than a didactic lecture or textbook oriented course. The adolescent in trouble needs answers to questions, especially questions he cannot get the answers to because he does not read, does not want to read, or does not know where to find the necessary materials.

Schooling, Miller and Woock (1970) contend the school does afford meaning to the dropout. It is, in their words, the "mechanism through which group and individual characteristics are transmitted into social status" (p. 27). The payoff for attending school is that:

> The child begins at a given socioeconomic level and with a specific academic ability level; these interact to influence his early level of school achievement and his aspirations for both more education and future occupation; by high school, his previous academic attainment and influence of significant others influence still further his decisions for more schooling and future occupation.   (p. 27–28)

Millions of dollars and over a half century of programmatic concern have been expended, and yet the dropout problem remains. Various proposals have been brought forth as solutions to the problem, including on-the-job training, Career Education, relevant curricula, and abolishing compulsory schooling laws. As school personnel confront the issue today it would benefit them to keep in mind the fact that school is not a panacea. In fact, as the evidence suggests, it has been anything but that for lower socioeconomic class children. Accordingly, while attempting to improve the quality of schooling for all of America's children, educators should refrain from misleading promises and inaccurate statements. Furthermore, educators should consider the possibility that, at least for high school age pupils, school might not be the best place. Above all, school personnel should never engage in a campaign against dropouts which results in social stigmatization. Dropping out of school may be said to be a symptom of preexisting problems, rather than a problem itself. In the opinion of many authorities the source of that problem may well be in the fiber of our society, of which our schools are an integral part. Programs that will work must be one of attitude; if the school reinforces the feelings of inadequacy and continues to deny success, the youth's options dwindle to but one. A few concerned teachers and an overworked counselor will make a small difference. If leaving school is viewed as a community problem which must be addressed by all parties, courts, stores, employers, service agencies, and the schools, effective measures for prevention and the job of returning dropouts can commence.

PROGRAMS DIRECTED AT VANDALISM

Throughout the country the cost of vandalism is skyrocketing and it is difficult to recap. In a national survey, Furno and Wallace (1972) noted that only 5.3% of damage incurred by vandals had been recovered. School officials have directed significant energies to develop programs to reduce the level of vandalism. A review of the programs to curtail school vandalism indicates three major categories: (1) structural adjustments; (2) parents and communities; and (3) group and individual therapies.

Structural adjustments may include either the use of technological equipment or changes in the architectural configuration. Schools have incorporated such technological equipment as television cameras, radar systems, intercom systems, and floodlights. In Dallas, Texas, at the T. W. Browne Junior High School, the administrators installed a closed-circuit television system. A surveillance system of 16 cameras were placed in strategic locations in school corridors and classrooms. Immediately following the installation, 80% of the school-hour vandalism incidents were reduced. In Parma, Ohio, a radar alarm system was installed, not to assist in the apprehension of vandals, but rather to alarm the vandals, thereby reducing to a minimum the physical damage to the building. The radar system included a microwave alarm that triggered a series of sirens accompanied by flashing lights that could be seen both inside and outside the school building. School officials considered the program successful where, in a one year period, damages were reduced to amounts of no more than $300 to $400, with only one illegal entry being recorded. An intercom receiver system was used in the Jefferson County, Kentucky, school system to monitor hallways and rooms after regular school hours. Intercom receivers identified unusual noises (such as shattering glass) which triggered an alarm device and relayed a message to a central system. Prior to the installation of the system, vandalism cost the district approximately $150,000 a year. In 1973, one year after the system was in operation, the cost was reduced to $33,000.

Perhaps one of the most sophisticated technological systems of aiding school vandalism control was a program developed in a cooperative venture between Kennedy High School (Sacramento, California) and the Jet

Propulsion Laboratory, California Institute of Technology. The anti-vandalism program combined a unique alarm program (Private Alarm Signaling System, PASS), and an attendance register system (Automated Attendance Accounting, AAA). PASS employs an ultrasonic transmitter the size of a fountain pen which, when activated, sends a signal to a central location. Within minutes, a patrolman, monitor, or administrator can be at the scene. The AAA uses digital electronics or data transmission technology, and a mini-computer to complete a print-out of attendance for an entire school. AAA can provide almost minute-by-minute information as to where students are—or are not. According to school authorities, the dual program has significantly reduced the rate of vandalism.

Architectural structures have also been studied to minimize vandals' destruction. In a national survey (Nations Schools, 1968), 69% of the school administrators acknowledged that window damage was a major problem of school vandalism. Harvard architect Zeisal (1973) found that large, empty hardtop surfaces, roofs with easy access, and hidden alcoves were poor school designs which invited damage. Architects, in an attempt to reduce the problem of window damage, have investigated the use of window substitutes, including such resistant materials as acrylic plastics and wall finishes which are less susceptible to damage.

Pablant and Baxter (1975) compared high vandalism and low vandalism schools in Houston, Texas. Schools were matched on such variables as neighborhood income level, ethnic backgrounds, school size, and elementary vs. secondary buildings. The authors found that the use of fences, lighting, and electronic alarm systems had no relationship to the level of vandalism. However, a significant relationship was noted between vandalism rates and aesthetic quality and level of preservation of school property, regardless of age or architecture of building. Pablant and Baxter suggested that minimal or no vandalism will occur at schools which have an open view, aesthetic school property, and high populations which use the building for sundry activities. In support of Pablant and Baxter's findings was a program developed by the Baltimore City Public Schools (Lloyd, 1968). The school district added multi-unit relocatable buildings and placed these units on the grounds of existing schools built with conventional brick and mortar. These air-conditioned buildings had exterior walls made of bright-colored and beautifully finished porcelain-enamel steel paneling and colored plexiglass windows. While the permanent buildings were heavily vandalized, the new relocatable units, which were situated only yards away, were hardly damaged. Apparently, the aesthetic integrity and colorfulness of the new buildings aroused genuine community pride.

The second category of programs for reducing school vandalism involves parents, children, and community groups. Some communities have organized their own neighborhood patrols. In Akron, Ohio, a program called The Youth Vacation Vigil conducted an intensive campaign against vandalism during the summer vacation months and on Halloween (Underwood, 1968). The program was staffed by high school juniors and seniors, most of whom were outstanding students or well-known athletes. These students were trained by the highway patrol, the local police force, and the school board. Later, area captains met with students in each school in their district at an assembly program or in individual classrooms to explain the program and its aims. These students were the main force in the youth-to-youth effort to prevent vandalism. The long range goal of the program was to garner as many students as possible to acknowledge pride in their school and recognize their responsibility toward the school. Following the 1962 campaign, vandalism damage in Akron (estimated to be $10,000 for 1961) was reduced by 15%, and in 1964 total damage was below the $5,000 mark.

In Washington, D.C., the Walker-Jones School has directed its efforts toward the student body by increasing student pride to curb vandalism. Student awareness was heightened by educating students on the importance of conservation and beautification in the school and community. Accomplishments of the program included: (1) fewer broken windows; (2) more responsible students; (3) student pride in being a Walker-Jones pupil; (4) awareness of the need to maintain the program; (5) desire to extend beautification further in the community; (6) student willingness to work on projects that help keep the school beautiful; and (7) greater zest for working in groups on a purposeful activity.

In California, two schools looked to the students to alleviate this costly problem. South San Francisco Unified School District initiated an incentive program called "$1 per ADA," which involved a special school fund that students could allocate for their purposes at the end of the school year. For each act of vandalism a corresponding amount of money was subtracted from the fund. In 1972–1973 this program reduced the districts' vandalism costs 82.5%. The program gave the students concrete experience with the cost of vandalism. One theory involved with "$1 per ADA" is that students can influence the behavior of other students. This program has encouraged students to inform officials of acts of vandalism which has led to restitution payments by students and parents.

Neighborhood awareness and participation promoting community pride and responsibility can be established and used in turn to reduce vandalism. Accurate public awareness is often cultivated to attenuate vandalism. The purpose of the awareness programs is to reeducate the community on the importance of a school to the community. In Brooklyn, New York, a pamphlet was published illustrating recent acts of vandalism and their costs in terms of educational materials and equipment. Since 1963, Alpena,

Michigan, has been involved in a project known as Community Schools. The Community Schools program is aimed at even broader goals than the elimination or control of vandalism. According to McConnel, superintendent of schools, the project "is striving to involve all citizens, from preschoolers to senior citizens, in a variety of programs designed to meet their educational, cultural, and recreational needs" (Buchner, 1968). Police officials cited a 12-month decline in vandalism cases since the program's inception.

State and local municipalities, in an effort to lower the cost of vandalism, have enacted laws whereby parents are being held responsible for the actions of their children. According to the National Education Association, in 1972, 38 states enacted parental responsibility laws, and by 1975 some 46 states had enacted parent liability statutes (Severino, 1972). The Los Angeles Juvenile Court (1973) sponsored a program called Prevent School Vandalism Project. The court publicized that damage suits may be filed against parents of young vandals and that the court would assist schools with information to file these law suits. A school security director in Florida supported this notion: "Parent restitution programs should have lots of follow-up. The pay-off isn't necessarily recovering more damages. It's that by dogging parents hard, you upset them enough to put pressure on their kids to behave in the future" (Grealy, 1974, p. 35).

Legislatures, in addition to the courts, are also becoming involved in this growing problem. The Florida legislature directed a frontal attack against vandalism by enacting a Safe Schools Act, whereby funds were provided for county school systems to develop programs emphasizing positive educational alternatives for disruptive youngsters and for protective measures to provide physical safeguards for school property, students, and faculty. In the federal sphere, Congressman Jonathan Bingham of New York (1974) introduced a bill known as The Safe Schools Study Act. The bill required the Department of Health, Education, and Welfare to conduct a full and complete study to determine the extent of the problem of crime in our nation's schools and evaluate the most practical and effective solutions to school crime.

Both structural and community programs treat vandalism exclusive of causative factors. The final category of programs directed at vandalism focuses on the presumed underlying causes of vandalism. Group and individual therapy are advocated by these individuals who view vandalism as a symptom of some unresolved personal problems. Some therapy is preventative in nature and aimed at the entire student body or identified potential vandals. Problem situations or feelings are discussed before they occur, which theoretically yields more rational decisions and socialized behavior. The work group or work-study group directed by a high school counselor has been shown to be a useful therapeutic tool (Newman, 1967).

The therapeutic milieu is a relatively new approach to working with vandals. The strategies of the counselor and/or therapist have not been fully explored to provide any definitive answers. These programs, however, exist as an alternative approach, particularly in the area of prevention.

In summary, the structural programs (technological or architectural) described are aimed at the prohibition and elimination of vandalism through suppression or isolation of disruptive behavior. Such programs have been termed *coercive programs*. Coercive programs may very well be the first step toward controlling vandalism, but stricter security and/or tougher law enforcement alone merely builds the vandals' antiauthoritarian feelings. It must be remembered that our final interest and responsibility lies with the student, not the school building. Coercive programs must be followed by supportive programs, such as the therapy processes and the programs immersing students with parents and communities that have been described. These programs have a positive quality to keep the vandal performing in an acceptable manner and persuading the vandal to return to conformity, when necessary. These programs move toward modifying the behavior and changing the attitude of the vandal. Vandalism is generally conscious and organized. Therefore, programs to minimize school vandalism must also be conscious, organized, and rational. Short term, haphazardly planned programs may only stimulate vandalism in the long run.

AGGRESSION: A CRISIS IN TEACHER-STUDENT INTERACTION

Aggression, when displayed appropriately in certain settings as anger, hostility, or frustration is certainly a normal human expression. Conversely, when inappropriate models, peer pressures, frustrations, anger, or anxieties inhibit the controlled, prosocial, rule regulated expression of aggression, then frequently antisocial, criminal, and/or a full array of norm-violating behaviors result. It is those sets of aggressively displayed behaviors that attracts the attention of educators. In this section, the programs for norm-violating aggressive behaviors are addressed. However, since the sum of this book is directed toward various approaches of managing aggressive behavior, this section focuses directly on the teacher, as it is the professional educator who must act when confronted with inappropriately expressed aggressive behavior.

The teacher: the primary dispenser of reinforcement

The teacher is not only a dispenser of reinforcers, but his or her presence is a reinforcer, a model, and advocate for prosocial behaviors. Thus, it is axiomatic that teachers and other school personnel are instrumental in changing student behavior. Unfortunately, such a basic truth is not so obvious, as many educators seemingly have lost the faith, or indeed never had it. The secondary public school is an achievement-oriented academic arena of departmentalized curricula, where teachers tend to view pupils as good or bad, and sense their roles as behavioral change agents as minimal. Reality would dictate that most educators have never changed global behavioral output to the degree which they desired. Certainly, as a profession, education has observed that the impact on the behaviors of truants, dropouts, vandals, and aggressors is minimal. These are not isolated behaviors, but behavioral complexities representing many ill-defined variables.

Aggression is invariably displayed in violation of rules and conduct unbefitting to the situation and remains as the ultimate test of the human relations aspect of teaching. The expression of aggressive acts implies conflict, confrontation, manipulation, and rebellion. Human beings are constructed with the mechanism to express anger, hostility, frustration, disappointment, and despair. The school as a social institution seldom considers these expressions appropriate in the classroom or corridor and fails to condone such acts. Teachers, principals, counselors, and other school personnel are positioned to support school rules. Similarly, many schools have social organizational pressures which dictate that rules be enforced at all costs. These rules do, in fact, establish the norms for acceptable and unacceptable behavior. A youth who needs attention generally desires to strike out or back at the adult world. By merely breaking a rule an adolescent has tested and manipulated the status quo. When a youth addresses another youth through verbally aggressive abusive language in a study hall, he breaks several rules, putting teachers in a position where they are forced to intervene at the time of crisis. Is it possible that the relative position of defining behaviors as good or bad, rather than describing behaviors, seriously limits the range of responses or the alternative mode of responses available to a teacher?

The most common but unsatisfactory response to verbally aggressive behavior is to counter with verbal threat. For example, an adolescent threatens a peer and the teacher counters with a threat to the adolescent. Psychologists and educators consider threats as *noise* which has virtually no effect on behavior. Behavioral observations of teacher-student and student-student interactions confirm the belief that threat simply has no effect on lessening the strength of the aggressive response (Fink, 1972). The following vignette, recorded by Bushell (1973), underscores the problems inherent with repeated teacher threats.

	"David, the next time you're going to see the principal."
Ten minutes later	"David, if you do that again, you're going straight to Mr. Jones."
Five minutes later	"Stop that, David."

One-half hour later   "David, the next time you do that I will
                           march you right down to the office."

Obviously, David is successfully manipulating the teacher. The mistakes are
many and serve to perpetuate the encounter. Most obvious of the mistakes
is that the teacher enforced no consequences for a given behavioral
response. Second, a target behavior was not identified because the boy, not
the behavior, was being referenced. Through the repeated use of the term
that, the actual behavior remains a mystery. Third, if the youth in question
was deriving increased peer status or was desirous of teacher attention,
teacher threats may have inadvertently reinforced his inappropriate acts.
Finally, the teacher offered no concrete plan to the youth for his consideration to reduce, eliminate, or modify behavior. The road to eliminating undesirable aggressive behaviors is paved with good intentions. A rule which
educators must remember is that realistic consequences must be derived for
each student's behavioral response which will in turn stengthen or reduce
that response.

     For a teacher at the secondary school level to maintain classroom
control and a therapeutic environment the task remains complex. Specific
teaching attributes such as fairness, honesty, and rule establishment
enhance the teachers capacity to be effective with adolescents. A reputation
for fairness is constructed by keeping promises, assisting students in
regulating overt behavior, upholding rules, and handling broken rules in a
consistent manner. It is indeed an absolute that the teacher must maintain
and regulate rules which are ideally established or agreed upon by the
students. A teacher who is tardy to class cannot expect her students to
perform in a more superior fashion. Above all, adolescents respect honesty
and avoid entrusting personal questions to teachers who respond in a
flippant manner or condemn and generalize on the basis of little evidence.
The adolescent is conditioned to suspect adult values and perceives the
hypocrisy in a dual value system which adults accept so freely. If the consequences of behavior are to be understood, the rules regulating those behaviors must be simple and readily understood. Rules must be made in relationship to a particular environment, their relativity must be explained, since it
cannot be understood.

     There are no simple cookbook solutions which transfer from situa-
tion to situation concerning eliminating aggressive behaviors. There are
times to be firm and demanding, but not rigid or sarcastic in expecting compliance with rules. There are times that students should be singled out and
told what is expected in most certain terms, with a line firmly drawn. There
are times when the approach should be softer and the issue addressed as an
individual variation in response to an array of behavioral possibilities, one
of which the student should have selected. Aggressive acts may frequently
be reduced or eliminated when the teacher has made the classroom a secure

place for students to express themselves in a normal voice, relating personal issues, knowing that the teacher is their advocate, and is supporting them personally.

In the previous section the importance of the teacher as a behavioral change agent was highlighted. The purpose was not to talk specifically about changing any particular behavior or suggesting a specific behavioral modification approach, since that topic is well addressed in Chapters 6 and 7. The intention was to identify specific adult behaviors that may reduce or eliminate aggression. The teacher is the single most important instructional and behavioral change agent in the classroom. If aggression flares, the problem belongs to the teacher. Conversely, if aggression is never felt in the presence of good classroom management, the teacher has performed a commendable job. The classroom is an unreal, sometimes contrived environment where the teacher assumes many roles. Those roles that promote the teacher as an arbitrary and capricious rule maker, benevolent despot, judge and jury, are destined for continuous manipulation and limit testing by the students. Additionally, if a teacher desires an adviserial relationship with students to fulfill power needs or for many other reasons, aggressive behaviors may be triggered. Once aggression is triggered in a school environment it may spill over into the next class where the teacher is unprepared, inexperienced, and the unsuspecting recipient of aggression. It is not good enough to address the issues of consistent rules for a classroom. Optimally, the principal, counselors, department heads, and other teachers need to address rules across classrooms into corridors.

The classroom: a human arena

The school fails youth in several ways, namely a lack of commitment to help low performing students; antiquated methods and materials which fail to address cultural, language, and motivational differences; failure to teach realistic personal, social, and job survival skills; and the inability to provide alternative behaviors to displace persistent aggressive and disruptive behaviors. Finally, there exists an attitude that if a youth evidences aggressive-disruptive behavior in school he will drop out or be expelled, thus ends the problem. The failure of school personnel to understand that aggressive-disruptive behavior in school transfers to delinquent behavior in the community has not been well accepted by educators.

In studies on classroom interactions, aggressive behavior has been related to teacher attributes, the physical structure of the classroom, and the type of instructional materials. In an early study on teacher personality, Anderson, Brewer and Reed (1946) found that a dominative teacher's style incited dominative behaviors by students, and an integrative teacher's style promoted integrative student behavior. In essence, the verbal behavior displayed by teachers has a direct influence on pupil attitudes toward the class, anxiety levels, achievement, and amount of disorderly behavior displayed by the students. Similarly, if teachers verbal behavior has an effect on student behavior then also should the physical environment. The ecology of the classroom environment determines, in part, the role played by the actors. If a classroom is disorganized and the lesson preparedness of the teacher loose, the youths' performance will be representative. A number of authorities in the field have established the importance of the physical-environmental setting on aggressive outbreaks. Teachers have recognized the importance of seating patterns, size of classes, and the means by which instructional material is delivered as major considerations in establishing a healthy, expressive atmosphere. In several studies, Hewett, Taylor and Artuso (1967) and Gallagher (1972) disruptive behavior was studied as related to increased range of action and movement space in the classroom. The data suggests that when, as an alternative to the large group setting, students are able to self-select activities within a smaller group appropriate to the discussion, project, or other activity, disruptive behavior was sharply reduced. Experienced teachers have emphasized the technique of using smaller groups for project activities within a self-directed curricula theme for a number of years. It would appear that this teaching practice now has empirical validity.

If the environmental setting has a direct impact on aggressive classroom behavior what influence does instructional material or media have? The nearest approximation to empirical evidence on such influences comes from the controversy over TV violence and the effect on the viewer. The Surgeon General's Scientific Advisory Committee on Television and Social Behavior investigating the relationship between televised violence and disruptive behavior reviewed several studies. The relationship between televised violence and observation of such programming was expressed accordingly:

> When we ask about the effects of the mass media, we must not phrase the question in terms of whether the media have an effect, but rather how much effect on what kind of [people], and under what circumstances will the effects be exhibited.   (Maccoby, 1968, p. 120)

> Apparently, the nature of the viewer, the nature of the stimulus, and the nature of the situation interact in such ways that exposure to mass media may *either facilitate or* inhibit the [actual] expression of aggression.
> (Wrightsman, 1973, p. 146)

> . . . violence can serve as a catalyst for social change as when alienated sectors of the population take recourse to violence and aggression to overcome blocks to social economic achievement.   (Larson, 1968, p. 116)

From the accumulated empirical data two findings were outlined in the Surgeon General's report: (1) the viewer reacts to televised aggressive violence although the parameters of that reaction depend upon the individual person, and (2) there is no data yet available to support any conjecture that aggressive portrayal has any widespread effect on the behavior displayed by the viewing audience. It would appear that modern day teachers must perform three functions with instructional materials, particularly in the presence of television and the movies. First, teachers should assist youthful audiences in exploring their own feelings as they read, hear, or view the actions and sense the feeling of others. Next, adolescents should be cognizant that they are accountable for their behavior. Finally, teachers must instruct adolescents that the purpose of written and televised media is to assist the reader or viewer to express internally his or her feelings, not display them overtly.

Classroom management strategies that teachers adopt, maintain, develop, or modify to control aggressive behavior are not important as strategies, but in creating a classroom climate. What teachers do before (antecedent events) or after (consequent events) behavior directly influences the climate in the classroom. In a review of antecedents of aggressive classroom behavior, Redl (1968) described aggression as an interaction of the psychological dynamics an individual imposes on self. If long term planning is to be implemented to dispell aggression the teacher must recognize the precursors of aggression. Redl hypothesized three such factors.

1. Carry over aggression from the home, community, or playground which is brought with the youth into the school.
2. Explosive aggression from pent-up feelings, emotions, or desires, frequently associated with emotional disturbance.
3. Aggression engendered by the classroom, teacher, or youth.

Redl delineated two suggestions for managing aggression in the classroom: cutting the contagion chain and signal interference. These strategies were viewed by Redl as the means of getting the youth "off the hook" before aggression spilled over into the classroom. In the former approach, cutting the contagion chain, the *timing* of the teacher intervention is underscored. As Redl noted in the following vignette:

> Take Joe, for example. He's sitting over there shaking imaginary dice, and at the moment you're not too bothered. You catch his eye and he stops, but only temporarily. After a while everbody else gets interested. You want to cut that contagion chain now, because if you wait another five minutes, you'll have a mass problem on your hands.

> If you interfere too early, everyone thinks you're a fusspot, a dope, or chicken, and you only aggravate things. If you don't interfere at the right time, you'll have trouble. Getting Joe *off the hook* at the right moment will stop his behavior without a big scene, and the rest of the group will not be too heavily afflicted. This skill of cutting contagion chains without making too much of a mess is, I think, one of the most important for anybody who deals with groups.   (Redl, 1968, p. 31)

The issue of the teacher as a possible stimuli (or stimulator) of aggression is addressed by Redl. Aggression can be caused in any individual by any other person; by producing discomfort in that person through fear, threat, hate, annoyance, or frustration. And, it is possible for the teacher's own hostility or aggression to show, making matters worse. Teachers have feelings, anger is normal, and occasionally everyone has the right to express it, or at least express the fact, "I am angry." But, the professional behavior which reduces aggression is that which is expressed in a nonprovoking aggression reducing manner.

A second practical approach Redl described was signal interference which is the process of "nipping misbehavior in the bud." The teacher must learn the preaggression signals and be conscious of their occurrence. There are a number of physiological and gestural signals which precede aggressive outbreaks. Facial expressions, excessive daydreaming, voice fluctuations, and restlessness are but a few behavioral patterns specific to individuals which signal disruptive behavior. Redl provides the reader with an example of signal interference.

> A kid is sitting stiffly at his desk, obviously determined that he "ain't gonna do *nothing*." The teacher walks over to him, pats him on the shoulder, and says: "Now, how about it? You don't feel so good, huh?" And he doesn't say anything. What does she do then? She says: "OK, I'll come back in a while. Maybe by then you'll feel better." That's all. She doesn't push him. ("Why don't you . . .? What's the matter with you? What kind of family do you come from, anyway?")
>
> She uses her judgment, and sooner or later he's over the hump. His face clears up; his posture is relaxed. Then she comes over and puts the pencil in his hand and he starts working.   (1968, p. 31)

Hartocollis (1972) described the management of aggressive youth in a psychiatric hospital setting; the staff rigidly intensified their activity level due to an inability to cope with their feelings toward, or concern for, controlling the adolescent patient at hand. This is interesting to read and note because it is so vividly portrayed. What Hartocollis is saying is that the belligerent-aggressive adolescent can produce a loss of self-esteem by challenging a professional person. When adolescents sense that challenge, they are reinforced, and continue to reissue the threat at will. The problem is the initial inability for staff to be tougher, smarter, and more agile on their feet than the adolescent. The trap is to become rigid, interpreting inflexible rules which tend to place a professional in a defensive position with a defensive attitude.

Adults in decision making capacities often believe they are setting the limits when in actuality they are administering punishment to enforce their will. The fear of physical confrontation causes teachers consciously or unconsciously to react to rebellious adolescents by restricting their movements and limiting their decision making freedom. Youth respond to this loss of personal freedom by decreasing their desire to act appropriately.

In addition, the adolescent fails to develop a sense of respect for the rights of others as he attempts to dominate the affective stage upon which he plays. Frightened by this play for power, professional educators react to the rebellious adolescents by increasing the limitation they have already imposed on the youth, further reducing their personal freedom. This cycle happens so quickly that the deterioration in human interaction is rarely sensed.

Punishment is one of the oldest and least understood methods of classroom control. When applied consistently and appropriately, punishment is the most effective strategy to attenuate behavior. Unfortunately, punishment is rarely used in a correct manner in schools and the effects can be devastating to the punished youngster. In light of the fact that many teachers emphasize punishment as a major component of classroom management some of the shortcomings are discussed.

Holland and Skinner (1961) describe punishment as either (1) the withdrawal of a pleasant reinforcer; or (2) the presentation of an aversive stimuli. Generally speaking, the use of punishment in school signals that the situation is out of the teacher's control. In short, there is no longer an interaction between student and teacher promoting a human relationship growth phenomena. Punishment will stop a behavior from occurring, but it does not direct the development of a more acceptable alternative response. Teachers must have the option to punish, but they must recognize that punishment is injurious to an increased appropriate behavioral response repertoire.

The effects of verbal punishment on inhibition of aggression was examined by Hollenberg and Sperry (1951). The experiment demonstrated that verbal punishment subsequent to aggression decreased that behavior, but only temporarily. Similar findings on the transitory effects of punishment have been reported by Azrin (1960) and Reese (1966). There is some evidence to suggest, in fact, that the behavior may recur at a much higher frequency than it did prior to the punishment. The lack of permanency and the renewed frequency of the undesirable behavior clearly indicate that punishment be used sparingly, and that when necessary, be used in conjunction with more goal directed strategies.

Research has tended to center on the importance of punishment as a determinant of resistance to deviation. Resistance to deviation is defined as the ability to withstand pressure or to deviate from a behavior standard in the absence of surveillance. Walters, Parke and Cane (1965) substantiated the importance punishment plays in determinant of resistance. They have demonstrated that punishment is an effective means to internalize social rules in children. The effectiveness is a function of timing, when punishment is delivered upon initiation of the act, rather than termination. Aronfreed (1965) has shown that punishment can be effective when it is accompanied by verbal rationale. The personal attribute of the teacher also plays a role in the use of punishment. As Adams (1973) noted,

" . . . the personality of the punishment agent may be an important determinant in the effective use of punishment. Warm and friendly teachers may find that they can use punishment effectively and efficiently, while cold and distant teachers may not be able to do so. Perhaps the cognitive interpretation by the student may go as follows: the warm teacher really likes me and is not punishing me just for the fun of it, but to help make me a better person; while the cold, unfriendly teacher either does not care about me or dislikes me and is punishing me because of it.   (p. 161)

Hoffman and Saltzstein (1967) have examined three disciplinary techniques used by parents: (1) power assertion (power and authority are used to dominate); (2) love withdrawal (a nonphysical expression of disapproval); and (3) induction, which centers on the consequences of a person's acts. Induction was the only teaching method highly related to guilt feelings after transgression, as measured by such factors as confession, willingness to accept responsibility for one's own actions, consideration of others, etc. Therefore, the logical consequences, as proposed by Dreikurs and Grey (1968) in their book, may be a beneficial practice.

In logical consequences, the emphasis is placed on the resulting consequences that occur due to the child's own acts (Dreikurs & Soltz, 1964). The term *logical consequence* is used over *natural consequence* because the parent or teacher is defining the consequence in a rational and logical manner. The child is granted freedom of choice: to inhibit or terminate his behavior, or to continue and shoulder the consequences of his actions. Logical consequences emphasize the experiences that result as a function of the act. When the consequences are pleasant, the act will more likely recur; if unpleasant, the action probably will be avoided. Hence, in reality, logical consequences are capitalizing on the effects of positive and negative reinforcement that occur subsequent to an act in the social environment.

In working with adolescents an alternative to punishment is positive reinforcement of appropriate behavior. Although different reinforcement paradigms are discussed at length in Chapter 6, one method to structure a healthy relationship between student and teacher is contingency contracting. In constructing an atmosphere of mutual respect, one of the more fruitful time tested teacher practices has been to develop a written behavioral contract for a target behavior. A behavioral contract is a structured means of exchanging positive reinforcement between two persons for fulfillment of specified responsibilities. The two contracting parties may be the teacher-student, a peer group-student, or any two groups. The specific language of the contract is to specify behavior, what will be done about it, and to what degree. For example, the reduction in the use of unacceptable language, an inappropriate target behavior, will facilitate improvement in academic learning.

In general, behavioral contracts contain five essential elements:

1. A behavioral contract should specify the favorable long term consequence for fulfilling its obligations.
2. A behavioral contract should have a clearly detailed description of the contractor's obligations.
3. A behavioral contract should specify the sanctions for failure to meet its requirements.
4. Any type of intermediate reward for making some progress through time should be outlined.
5. The monitoring system and feedback system must be clearly a part of the contract, and contractual process.

A set of guidelines for school personnel who work with aggressive youth are listed.

1. Provision should be made for students to relate significant experiences to curriculum content, e.g., drugs can be incorporated into biology, chemistry, or even sociology, economics, and government.
2. Develop field curricula based on the job, survival skills, or social skills the youth needs.
3. Provide feedback into the teaching process by requiring dialogue from students, using inductive techniques, and the nurturing of critical analysis, problem solving, and the application of derived generalizations to new phenomena.
4. Consider the student as a contributor to curriculum development, evaluation, teacher selection, and teacher evaluation.
5. Involve students in decision-making; they should serve in numbers equal to the combination of teachers, administrators, and parents who serve them, particularly on school rules and required curriculum.

6. Bear with student apathy and student over-reaction as they learn to make decisions.

7. Provide "rap" sessions on topics of importance, invite parents.

8. Learn to be insensitive to relatively unimportant things such as dress and hair style and become sensitive to what the person's purposes are.

Classroom control, at least that which is necessary to deter unwanted and inappropriate aggressive-destructive behavior is one of the major, if not the major concern of secondary teachers. The existing literature supports the belief that while programs emphasizing behavioral change in secondary schools are important they do not make the major difference in behavioral change. What does make the difference? The answer is simple—the teacher. Teachers in a building should be consistent in enforcing rules that the students established and sensed would promote the good of their order. When belligerence, and even destructive aggression occurs under these conditions, the inappropriate behavior must be curtailed and the consequence of that behavioral response felt. The teacher has two responsibilities in that situation: (1) to gain control, and punish if necessary; and (2) determine, if possible, the triggering mechanisms. The question why a behavior occurs is inappropriate to ask. To ask implies that there is rational thought that guided what may appear to be premeditated action. In most cases, adolescents just react to what they frequently are not really sure. Maybe just feelings that accompany looking at the big world through only the eyes that pre-adolescent play has provided. Maybe to challenge, because they wonder what life's missions are, to threaten because they feel threatened, to test the limits of what they perceive are arbitrary rules, to fend off frustration, or to express, for any reason, what can produce anger. Does it matter?

If a triggering mechanism can be identified and eliminated, then yes. If a target behavior which reoccurs can be isolated, good. Those are real problems that can be solved. But, that is not where the teacher makes the difference. It is in the model of behaviors they present, and the interpretation of other models they provide, their reaction under the stress of being aggressed, and their maintenance in the belief that people, no matter how inappropriate their behavior, are worthy of dignified human relationships. Aggression will never stand up to a human interaction between teacher and student where mutual respect is in search of mutual reason.

The evidence is in—aggressive behavior only reinforces feelings that generate aggressive behavior. It is destructive to self and others. One salvation for all mankind is a different behavioral mode. History records that the behaviors of nations can be shaped to express kindness on one hand or aggression on the other, through culture or a ministry of propaganda, schools can produce a desired behavioral outcome. In the writing of Pogo, "I have found the enemy, he is us."

HIGH-INCIDENCE HANDICAPPED YOUTH

Special education programming for secondary school handicapped children has been characterized by benign neglect. Over the years, consistent emphasis and progress in program development has been placed at the elementary level. In a national survey, Metz (1973) reported that 75% of the students receiving special education services were at the elementary level, while only 20% were at the secondary school level. These figures are incongruent with the number of handicapped students at the elementary (55%) and secondary (40%) school levels. Obviously, the disproportionate statistics favor educational programming at the elementary school level and underscore the need for rapid program development in the secondary schools.

The number of identified handicapped children and youth in public schools provides further evidence for the need of secondary school program development. Approximately 5.9% of the secondary population evidences some type of handicapping condition. The prevalence figures for each type of exceptionality at the secondary school level appear in Table 1.1. The majority of children and youth fall into the category of high-incidence handicapped: learning disabled (1.8%), behaviorally disordered (0.9%), and mentally retarded (1.4%). Secondary school programs are more prevalent for the mentally retarded (85%) than the other handicapped groups. The learning disabled (54.8%) and behaviorally disordered (44.1%) represent underserved populations.

As indicated in Table 1.1, 5.9% of the secondary school population evidence some type of handicapping condition. Of these, high-incidence handicapped (learning disabled, behaviorally disordered, mentally retarded) account for 4.1% of the total. Although many of these youths are unserved or underserved, alternative special education services can be developed, and in some cases are in operation to assist these youths. There are services relevant to the education of high-incidence handicapped youth. In this section the services for exceptional youth as well as two curriculum models, career education and vocational education, will be discussed.

Services for exceptional children

The field of special education has as a major task the education and rehabilitation of exceptional children and youth. Over the years, the types of services and delivery systems have expanded in number and quality. The

Table 1.1. NUMBER OF PUPILS WITH HANDICAPS IN LOCAL
SECONDARY SCHOOLS, PERCENT OF ENROLLMENT,
AND NUMBER AND PERCENT OF HANDICAPPED PUPILS
SERVED, BY TYPE OF HANDICAP

Type of Handicap	Handicapped Pupils		Handicapped Pupils Served[1]	
	Number	Percent of Enrollment	Number	Percent of Handicapped Pupils
Total[2].........	1,045,000	5.9	606,000	58.0
Speech impaired...	198,000	1.1	104,000	52.5
Learning disabled..	314,000	1.8	172,000	54.8
Mentally retarded..	257,000	1.4	218,000	84.7
Emotionally disturbed.......	160,000	0.9	70,000	44.1
Hard of hearing...	50,000	0.3	21,000	41.2
Deaf.............	3,000	*	2,000	54.7
Crippled	36,000	0.2	11,000	31.3
Partially sighted...	24,000	0.1	5,000	21.1
Blind	3,000	*	3,000	93.2

[1] Handicapped pupils receiving instruction or assistance from 1 or more of the following:
separate (special) classes, special instruction from regular teachers in regular classes, individualized instruction from specialized professional personnel.

[2] The actual total numbers and percents of handicapped pupils may be somewhat less than the
figures presented because in some cases the same handicapped pupils may have been reported
in more than one category.

*Percent greater than zero but less than 0.05.

types of educational services are varied, ranging from only partial assistance
such as a resource room teacher or crisis teacher, to providing the total
educational program in an alternative setting. Dunn (1973) identified 12
alternative administrative plans for serving exceptional children and youth.
These services are categorized into four subgroups, ranging from most
integrated (least restrictive alternative) to the most segregated: (1) special education programs; (2) residential or boarding school facilities;
(3) hospital instruction; and (4) homebound instruction.

Special education programs. Since almost 9% of exceptional children and youth attend public schools, a great number of services are furnished in the day school setting. For this reason, Dunn (1973) subgrouped
these services into nine categories.

1. Special education instructional materials and equipment services are provided for students who can function in the educational mainstream with minimal support services. Supportive service is for materials or equipment, such as a braille reader for a visually impaired child or a special desk to accommodate a wheelchair for an orthopedically handicapped student.

2. Special education teacher consultants to regular teachers afford indirect service to exceptional children and youth. The regular teacher is the focal point of the consultant's service. For example, the consultant may model diagnostic teaching strategies or suggest alternative methods of instruction with a particular pupil.

3. Itinerant or special education resource room teachers provide direct service to exceptional children and youth. Tutors may spend a majority of time in one-to-one or small group instruction with students who have a special need. The remaining time is spent in a consultative role with the regular teacher.

4. In resource room programs exceptional children or youth remain in a regular class but receive direct instruction from a special education teacher. The responsibility of the special education teachers is to provide instruction and coordinate their work with that of the regular classroom teacher.

5. Part-time special classes are provided for children and youth in need of more intensive special education services. One example is a high school learning center where the student may work on biology, history, english, and math in a special learning environment, but be integrated with the other students in all other subject matter. A major objective is to facilitate the interaction between regular and special education classes, enabling the child to receive special services while participating in the educational mainstream.

6. Self-contained special education classes are designed for children and youth who experience problems when left in the regular classroom. Generally, these classes are arranged to accommodate a group of students with a similar categorical exceptionality (such as ruled mental retardation). Generally, these classes are segregated from the mainstream although students may partake in some school-wide activities, for example, music, physical education, home economics, or shop.

7. In the combination regular and special day schools, exceptional children and youth are bussed to a central location and share the facility with children from the immediate area. These youths are brought together in order that essential classroom services can be provided.

8.   In a special day school children who mainfest great difficulty in the educational mainstream may receive their complete instruction. One type of exceptionality generally comprises the total school population. Special education schools, sheltered workshops, and evening schools for the adult retarded (17 to 25 year old persons) have been designed for the severely retarded.

9.   Diagnostic and prescriptive teaching centers represent a new secondary school service. For a brief interval of time youths are scheduled into these facilities for diagnostic and instructional purposes. A team of educators and diagnosticians evaluate the child's performance and develop a remedial plan. The child then returns to his regular class where his instruction is based on the remedial teaching strategies developed in the diagnostic and prescriptive teaching centers. Such a process may include a constant recycling format where the youth is in the diagnostic and prescriptive teaching center for two weeks, the regular class for six weeks, and back to the diagnostic and prescriptive center. Diagnostic and prescriptive centers may be the wave of the future. A relatively new public law 94-142 advocates that an educational prescription shall be available for all handicapped children by 1980. That law certifies that all handicapped children or youth shall be educated in the least restrictive alternative environment. That means that handicapped youth will be integrated in regular classes and other school functions to the highest degree possible in support of their social, personal, vocational, and academic achievement and adjustment.

Residential or boarding schools.   Approximately 10% of exceptional children and youth receive educational services in residential schools (Dunn, 1973). The students are those who cannot function in a regular public school setting and are in need of an intensive twenty-four hour service. The main task of a residential facility is to remove the child from the mainstream of society to provide the intensive services required for rehabilitation, to protect him, society, or both, or to concentrate a habilitative or rehabilitative plan for a short period.

Hospital instruction.   Local school districts are required to provide educational services for children confined to a hospital or convalescent home. If the period of hospitalization disrupts education, a tutor is assigned to teach the child.

Homebound instruction.   Homebound instruction is the most segregated of special education administrative plans. The instruction is furnished by either an itinerant teacher or the regular classroom teacher. Since the child is isolated from his peers, a recent attempt has been made to decrease the number of children on homebound instruction.

The proper assignment of an individual for a particular service is influenced by many variables. Those factors which directly influence the decision are the characteristics of the child, the school, the parents, and the community (Dunn, 1973). Some of the child's variables are: (1) type and degree of disability; (2) motivation factor; (3) academic performance; and (4) behavioral characteristics. Factors included under school variables are: (1) adequacy of regular class program; (2) alternative special education facilities; and (3) competence of special educators. The parental and community factors include: (1) parental support; (2) home environment; and (3) community services.

The types of special education programs and services available to exceptional children and youth are depicted in Figure 1.1, which is adapted from Reynolds' model. It identifies programs along a continuum from least restrictive environment to fully segregated settings.

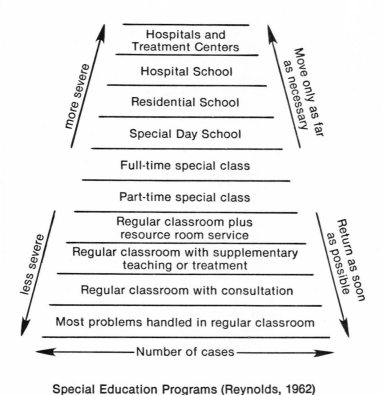

Special Education Programs (Reynolds, 1962)

Figure 1.1 Reynold's Intervention Hierarchy

In compliance with recent legislation (PL 94-142) and the trends in special education programming, a new breed of interagency and cross disciplinary programs are being developed. The dichotomies among regular education, special education, and vocational education must give way to integrated programming. Furthermore, the isolation of public school programs and community, or public and private agency programs, suggests a

Table 1.2. INTEGRATING HANDICAPPING CONDITIONS WITH REGULAR, SPECIAL AND VOCATIONAL EDUCATION

Type of Handicap	Regular Education			Special Education
	Academic Classes	Laboratory (Cooperative Home Econ., Physical Ed., Music)	Learning Center: Self-Teaching Aides	Special Classes: Self-Contained
Visually Handicapped	X	X	X	
Auditorily Handicapped	X	X	X	
Trainable Mentally Retarded				X
Educable Mentally Retarded	X	X	X	
Learning Disabled	X	X	X	
Seriously Emotionally Disturbed			X	X
Social Disruptive	X	X	X	X
Physically Handicapped (no mental retardation)	X	X	X	

new interface. The one generality that appears obvious is that the youth in trouble is the same youth who has difficulties in school and in the community. In fact, a concept of the early 1970s, Zero-reject, implies that youth will no longer be excluded from services or programs, but all will be served by programs that provide the greatest assistance. Career education is one example of a bond between special education, regular education, and vo-

Special Education		Vocational Education		
Resource Rooms: Part-time Intervention	Cooperative (work-study or work-shops)	Distributive Educ. Vocational, Consumer Info.	Career Information	Integration into job: Apprenticeship
X		X	X	X
X		X	X	X
	X	X		
X	X	X	X	
X		X	X	X
X	X	X	X	X
		X	X	X

cational education, and is detailed in the next section of this chapter. An entire chapter (Chapter 2) is written on career education. In sum, interagency interfacing shall be a dimension of great importance for the future of secondary special education.

There is one more pronounced consideration which must be understood in differentiating elementary and secondary programs. At the elementary school level, most school buildings and programs are similar. The greatest difference from school to school is contrasting the self-contained classroom structure to a totally open classroom building. However, even in these two diverse settings special education programs generally have all the usual resource rooms, special educators, teachers, consultants, and self-contained room structures. Therefore, it is a simple matter to construct an elementary special education program that can be transported from building to building and even across district lines from state to state. High schools are much more individualistic, having more components such as departments with unique disciplinary mixes, a wide range of guidance functions, well defined and fully developed vocational education to no vocational or special education. Consumer education, a course information center, distributive education, cooperative work study, a well developed pupil personnel team, and pupil appraisal teams are important dimensions which influence how a high school is administered and what decisions are made concerning the pupils. In summary, the programmatic variables and administrative structure operating in any two high schools are so diffuse that comparisons of a common special education model, except to detail its dimensions, are not practical.

Therefore, we shall attempt to detail selected program dimensions against a background of the known variables. Most certainly three proven variables are component aspects: regular classes, vocational programs, and special education programs. The other known variables are the handicapping conditions. Table 1.2 brings these two dimensions into an integrated program structure. The interesting aspect of Table 1.2 is that most handicapped youths are primarily dependent on regular and vocational education programs, with special education serving a supportive role. What then is the primary feature of high school special education programming? It simply depends on the attitude of the principal, disciplinary vice-principal or dean, guidance personnel, and teachers.

CAREER EDUCATION

Career education is presently being thrust into the educational limelight. The individual credited with spearheading the career education movement is Dr. Sidney P. Marland, Jr., former United States Commissioner of Education. As demonstrated in the following passage, Marland stated that:

> All education is career education—or should be. I propose that a universal goal of American education, starting now, be this—that every young person completing his school program at grade 12 be ready to enter either higher education or useful and rewarding employment. (1971, p. 22)

Following the leadership of Dr. Marland, the Bureau of Adult, Vocational, and Technical Education, United States Office of Education (1971) set forth the following goals of career education:

1. To provide more relevant subject matter via restructuring the current curriculum around a career development orientation.
2. To provide all individuals prior to leaving school the opportunity to develop marketable skills.
3. To provide all individuals who complete secondary school the knowledge and skills necessary to secure gainful employment.
4. To provide all individuals appropriate guidance and counseling to develop self-awareness, to enlarge career awareness, and to develop appropriate attitudes toward work.
5. To provide placement services for individuals for either employment or further education purposes.
6. To promote greater involvement of the educational system to use all possible community resources.   (Brolin, 1976)

For special educators, the purpose of career education is to heighten the student's awareness of vocational options. The primary objective at the elementary school level is exposure to various occupational clusters. At the secondary level the objective is to refine this awareness into preparation for an occupation.

Thus far in this discussion on special education programs we have described what has occurred historically. The recent legislation (PL 94-142) to provide for all handicapped children is having considerable impact and resulting in greater integration of special education, regular education, students, and teachers, particularly at the elementary school level. The integration of handicapped youth into an integrated career education curriculum containing four essential aspects has proceeded slowly at the high school level.

A career education program for secondary school mentally retarded youth has been developed by Brolin (1976) and serves as a model for high incidence handicapped youth. The curriculum, which Brolin outlines as a competency based model, focuses on building independent life skills. The program is divided into three curriculum areas and within each curriculum are specific competencies. The three curriculum areas are: (1) daily living skills; (2) occupational guidance and preparation; and (3) personal-social skills. The focus of the daily living skills curriculum is on enhancing the opportunity for independent living. Occupational guidance and preparation affords the student the opportunity for career awareness, occupational skill development, simulated work experience, and job placement. Personal and social skills stresses the need to build appropriate intra- and inter-personal skills for adjustment into community and employment settings.

The philosophy of career education offers a vast number of implications to the education of high incidence handicapped youth. Complete implementation of the concept has not as yet materialized; thus, the purported values are only hypothesized. Career education has garnered many advocates in special education which should lead to the further development of model programs. Interestingly, some authorities have preceded the initiation of these programs with voices of caution. Williamson (1975) has outlined issues which must be addressed if career education is to be successfully implemented:

1. Career education must emphasize development of the basic literacy skills.
2. Career education must provide numerous career choice options to students, including the alternative of college attendance.
3. Career education must offer insightful guidance in career options rather than be limited to vocational training.
4. Career education needs to be researched as a viable alternative to present educational programs for secondary school learning disabled youth.

VOCATIONAL EDUCATION

Vocational education and vocational educators would all agree that special education in some combination of academic experiences with vocational preparation are a very necessary "mix" for handicapped students. One objective for vocational programming with high incidence handicapped youth is to prepare adolescents for gainful employment. Each vocational program assists the handicapped individual by assessing his vocational skills and competencies. After the evaluation, each student is trained to develop vocational skills for employment in the competitive marketplace. A second objective of vocational programs is to place each handicapped individual in a job where the likelihood for successful adjustment is maximized. To attain these objectives, vocational programs provide educational and rehabilitation services including evaluation, vocational training, counseling, placement, and follow-up. The inclusion of these services demands the development of a multi-disciplinary model encompassing such professionals as physicians, counselors, psychologists, teachers, special educators, and employers. Program success is dependent on the capacity of these professionals to form a team. The efforts of vocational programs, while commendable, have been blemished by internal conflicts. The necessary communication and participation between disciplines unfortunately has not been forthcoming and many vocational programs have stagnated. The following review outlines many of the unresolved issues.

Vocational education has had to fight to maintain its place in educational institutions and has in the past faced not only a poor image, but also apathy (Wells, 1973). The unfavorable image of vocational education has had a major impact on the vocational training of handicapped youth. As Dunn noted, "vocational and technical schools have tended to bar low IQ pupils because of their alleged tarnishing effects on the status of these facilities" (p. 1975). Amendments to the Vocational Act of 1963 stated that 10 percent of federal funds allocated for vocational programs must be used to serve the handicapped and their vocational needs. Nonetheless, Wolfe reported that during the 1970–1971 fiscal year only a minute percentage of these funds were used. Wrobel and Colella indicated that special education has reinforced its own feeling of autonomy and consequently isolated itself from the mainstream of education (Lake, 1973). Colella acknowledged that vocational education demands a bringing together of services but noted that professionals from occupational and special education have not communicated mutual concerns and planned cooperative endeavors beneficial to all pupils. Moreover, vocational educators, according to Klinkhamer, have not wanted handicapped students in their programs (Lake, 1973). It is apparent that a lack of harmony between various educational groups has not fostered the *esprit de corps* needed to undertake the massive job of vocational education. Vocational programs exist in order to provide handicapped youths with job survival skills. The facilities and services provided represent the foundation on which to develop a dynamic program. They key to success, however, is the extent to which the various participating disciplines can constructively function together as a team. Until now these disciplines have fostered internal conflicts which have fractured the rehabilitation process. Vocational programs, therefore, will become more productive as teamwork increases.

THE PROBLEM

Scranton and Downs (1975) surveyed state directors of special education on the availability of elementary and secondary school programs for learning disabled individuals. Although Scranton and Downs restricted their survey to learning disabled youth, their data are germane to programming for all high incidence handicapped youth. A questionnaire was forwarded to each state director requesting information on the number of school districts offering elementary and secondary school programs. Of the 37 states that report on a per district basis, elementary school programs were listed in 40% of the districts; whereas only 9% had secondary school programs. Furthermore, the differences between states ranged from no programs at the secondary level (e.g., Indiana, Louisiana, Nebraska, North Dakota, and South Carolina), to 100% in Hawaii. The authors acknowledged that predicting a discrepancy in program availability was easy, but the magnitude of difference between elementary and secondary programs was not anticipated. Reasons for the discrepancy were solicited from the directors and the more relevant opinions are described.

1. A shortage of trained personnel is predominant. Teacher training institutions have focused solely on the preparation of primary and intermediate teachers to the exclusion of the secondary school level. Therefore, for school districts contemplating development of such programs, the task of staffing is demanding.

2. The field of special education has been guided by the philosophy of the earlier the intervention the greater the likelihood for successful remediation. The logic of this philosophy is appealing but the aftermath unfortunately has halted concerted efforts with adolescents. Also, federal and state agencies by placing highest priority on early intervention programs have reinforced the overriding philosophy.

3. Information and knowledge on how to implement secondary programs is limited.

4. Secondary school personnel are reluctant to identify and recognize handicapped children. Educators at this level are more "content" oriented than child centered. Teachers at the secondary level view themselves as subject specialists, and the concept of special education is foreign to their perception of job responsibilities and training.

5. Administrators are reluctant to explore the use of alternative school structures to meet the unique needs of these children. The curriculum, methods, and school structures developed for the average child are not appropriate for the adolescent child experiencing learning and behavior problems.

6. The vocal support of parents which led to the proliferation of elementary school programs has been absent. Parents of secondary school high incidence handicapped children, either because of the child's past failure, acceptance of the child's academic retardation, or lack of belief in the school's capabili-

ties, have not vociferously advocated for program development. If present activities follow past events, programs at this school may be neglected until parental advocacy is forthcoming.

 7. The belief that many exceptional children outgrew their problems with puberty.

In perspective, we suggest the following recommendations:

 1. Researchers must initiate activities to explore relevant diagnosis and remediation models for secondary school high incidence handicapped youth.

 2. States which do afford services for adolescent handicapped youth should serve as models for other states. A consortium of states could facilitate sharing of information and providing guidance to states which are not so well developed.

 3. Every effort should be made to evaluate the efficacy of curriculum, materials, methods, and alternative teaching models for secondary school handicapped youth.

 4. College and universities must now turn their attention and resources to the training of individuals who are competent to work with adolescent handicapped persons.

 5. Federal and state agencies must start to fund model secondary programs. Dissemination of information from these centers should also be encouraged.

SUMMARY

This chapter reviewed programs for truants, dropouts, vandals, chronic aggressive, and the traditional, so-called handicapped secondary school age youth. There are three generalizations which can be drawn from these discussions. First, individual teachers and counselors exist as an effective first line of defense. However, they are not capable of impacting the necessary changes in curriculum which provide for a continuum of programs and services to assist adolescents with educational handicaps.

Second, many of the programs are currently alternative schools, based on our public school settings. However, if alternative programs are not articulated to regular teachers and administrators, their acceptance and efficacy will be questionable. Furthermore, the integration of these programs, or at least their desirable features, will not take place. Regular secondary teachers are genuinely interested in high school students, but they have been conditioned to believe they are employed to teach subjects and not students. They only want to hear differently.

In searching for programs, the professional literature was exhaustively reviewed. Simply stated, there are not many viable programs. The current literature is depleat of any organized means of examining the high school curriculum to account for chronic disruptive youth. Why are there more than 100 percent fewer high school than elementary school special programs? Why are high school special education structures exactly like elementary programs? More important, education is a discipline (or applied art) that must communicate its best practice procedures to its members. Where is that communication? Is the state of the art as dismal as the review shows, or have secondary special educators failed to report their years of work with exceptional student groups? It appears that universities must focus on training and demonstrating school building programs, and teachers voicing an interest for an expanded frontal attack on the means by which secondary school age youth can be educated efficiently and effectively.

REFERENCES

Adams, G. R. "Classroom Aggression: Determinants, Controlling Mechanisms, and Guidelines for the Implementation of a Behavior Modification Program." *Psychology in the Schools* 10 (April 1973): 155–167.

Anderson, H. H.; Brewer, J. E.; and Reed, M. F. "Studies of Teachers' Classroom Personalities III: Follow-up Studies of the Effects of Dominative and Integrative Contacts on Children's Behavior." *Applied Psychology Monographs* 11 (1946).

Aronfreed, J. "Punishment Learning and Internalization: Some Parameters of Reinforcement and Cognition." Paper presented at The Biennial Meeting of the Society for Research in Child Development, March 1965, at Minneapolis.

Azrin, N. H. "Sequential Effects of Punishment." *Science* 131 (1960): 605–606.

Berman, A. "Incidence of Learning Disabilities in Juvenile Delinquents and Nondelinquents: Implications for Etiology and Treatment." Paper presented at International Federation of Learning Disabilities, Brussels, Belguim, January 1975.

Besant, L. "The Rodman Experience with Drop-Outs." *Today's Education* 58 (February 1969): 52–54.

Bingham, J. In Joseph Grealy's "Criminal Activity in Schools: What's Being Done About it?" *NASSP Bulletin* 58 (May 1974).

Brolin, D. E. *Vocational Preparation of Retarded Citizens.* Ohio: Charles E. Merrill Publishing Co., 1976.

Brooks, B. D. "Contingency Management as a Means of Reducing School Truancy." *Personnel and Guidance Education* 95 (Spring 1975): 206–211.

Buchner, R. J. "Ways of Fighting Vandalism." *Today's Education* 57 (Dec. 1968): 32.

Cumming, E. *Systems of Social Regulation.* New York: Atherton, 1968.

Dauw, E. G. "Individual Instruction for Potential Dropouts." *NASSP Bulletin* 54 (September 1970): 9–21.

DeGracie, J. S. *"The Picture of a Dropout."* Phoenix, Arizona: Arizona State Department of Education, Phoenix. Division of Vocational Education, 1974 (ERIC Document Reproduction Service No. ED 110 777).

Douglass, H. R. "An Effective Junior High School Program for Reducing the Number of Dropouts." *Contemporary Education* 41 (October 1969): 34–37.

Dreikurs, R., and Grey, L. *Logical Consequences: A Handbook of Discipline.* New York: Meredith Press, 1968.

Dreikurs, R., and Soltz, V. *Children: The Challenge.* New York: Ducee, Sloan, and Pearce, 1964.

Dunn, L. M. "Children with Mild General Learning Disabilities." *Exceptional Children in the Schools: Special Education in Transition* 2nd ed. New York: Holt, Rinehart, and Winston, 1973.

Dysinger, D. W. *Title VIII Student Support Program: Minneapolis Public Schools.* Final Evaluation Report 75 Minneapolis, Minnesota: Dept. of Education, 1975 (Eric Document Reproduction Service No. ED 117 852).

Fink, A. H. "Teacher-Pupil Interaction in Classes for the Emotionally Handicapped." *Exceptional Children* 38 (February 1972).

Furno, O. F., and Wallace, L. B. "Vandalism, Recovery, and Prevention." *American School and University* 44 (July 1972): 19–22.

Gallagher, P. A. "A Synthesis of Classroom Scheduling Techniques for Emotionally Disturbed Children." In. E. Meyer, G. Vergason, R. Whelan (Eds.) *Strategies for Teaching Exceptional Children.* Denver: Love Publ. Co., 1972.

Grala, C., and McCauley, A. "Counseling Truants Back to School: Motivation Combined with a Program for Action." *Journal of Counseling Psychology* 23 (March 1976): 166–169.

Grealy, J. I. "Criminal Activity in Schools: What's Being Done about it?" *NASSP Bulletin* 58 (May 1974): 73–78.

Hanks, G. A. "Dependency Among Alaskan Native School Dropouts: A Synthesis of some Alaskan School Dropout Studies during the Academic Year 1972." Salt Lake City, Utah: Univ. of Utah, 1972 (ERIC Document Reproduction Service No. ED 119 920).

Hartocollis, P. "Aggressive Behavior and the Fear of Violence." *Adolescence* (Winter 1972): 479–490.

Hewett, F.; Taylor, F.; and Artuso, A. The Santa Monica Project: Demonstration and Evaluation of an Engineered Classroom Design for Emotionally Disturbed Children in the Public School, Phase 1: Elementary Level, Final Report. Project 62839, Demonstration Grant DEG-4-7-062893-0377, Office of Education, Bureau of Research, U.S. Dept of HEW, 1967.

Hoffman, M. L., and Saltzstein, H. D. "Parent Discipline and the Child's Normal Development." *Journal of Personality and Social Psychology* 5 (1967): 45–57.

Holland, J. G., and Skinner, B. F. *The Analysis of Behavior*. New York: McGraw-Hill, 1961.

Hollenberg, E., and Sperry, M. "Some Antecedents of Aggression and Effects of Frustration in Doll Play." *Personality* 1 (1951): 32–43.

Kohler, L. T. "The Student Absentee." Paper presented at the Annual Convention of the American Association of School Administrators (108th), February 1976, at Atlantic City, New Jersey (ERIC Document Reproduction Service No. ED 117 852).

Lake, T. P. "Career Education as a Philosophy and a Practice: An Interview with George Kinkhamer." *Teaching Exceptional Children* 5 (1973): 124–127.

Larsen, D. N., ed. *Violence and the Mass Media*. New York: Harper and Row, 1968.

Lloyd, R. "Ways of Fighting Vandalism." *Today's Education* 57 (December 1968).

Macoby, E. E. "Effects of the Mass Media." *Violence and the Mass Media*. Edited by D. N. Larsen. New York: Harper and Row, 1968.

Marland, S. P., Jr. "Career Education." *Today's Education* 60 (1971): 22–25.

Mertens, W. J. "Review of Some Dropout Research and Literature." Washington, D.C.: Office of Education (DHEW), July 1972 (ERIC Document Reproduction Service No. ED 116 103).

Metz, A. S. "Number of Pupils with Handicaps in Local Public Schools" (Bureau of Education for Handicapped, Report No. DHEW-OE-73-11107). Washington, D.C.: U.S. Government Printing Office, 1973.

Nation's Schools, "How Schools Combat Vandalism." 81 (April 1968): 58–65.

Newman, R. *Psychological Consultation in the Schools*. New York: Basic Books, Inc., 1967, pp. 111–114.

Pablant, P., and Baxter, J. C. "Environmental Correlates of School Vandalism." *American Institute of Planners Journal* 41 (July 1975): 270–279.

Redl, F. "Aggression in the Classroom." *Today's Education* 58 (Sept. 1968): 30–32.

Reese, E. P. *The Analysis of Human Operant Behavior*. Dubuque: Wm. C. Brown, 1966.

Reynolds, M. C. "A Framework for Considering Some Issues in Special Education." *Exceptional Children* 28 (1962): 369–370.

Schooling, E.; Miller, H; and Woock, R. *Social Foundations of Urban Education*. Hinsdale, Ill.: The Dryden Press, 1970, p. 26.

Scott, M. "Some Parameters of Teacher Effectiveness as Assessed by an Ecological Approach." *Darcee Papers* 3 (1969): Darcee, George Peabody College for Teachers, Nashville, Tennessee.

Scranton, T. R., and Downs, M. L. "Elementary and Secondary LD Programs in the U.S.: A Survey." *Journal of Learning Disabilities* (June/July 1975): 394–399.

Severino, M. "Who Pays or Should Pay when Young Vandals Smash Things up in your Schools?" *American School Board Journal* 159 (June 1972).

Splaine, J. "Compulsory Schooling: The Legal Issue." Washington, D. C.: U.S. Dept. of Health, Education and Welfare, 1975. ERIC Document Reproduction Service No. ED 117 801.

Underwood, E. W. "Ways of Vandalism." *Today's Education* 57 (December 1968).

Walters, R. H.; Park, R. D.; and Cane, V. A. "Timing of Punishment and the Observation of Consequences to Others as Determinants of Response Inhibition." *Journal of Experimental Child Psychology* (1965): 10-30.

Washington, R. "A Survey-Analysis of Problems Faced by Inner-City High School Students who have been Classified as Truants." *High School Journal* 56 (February 1973): 248-257.

Wells, C. E. "Will Vocational Education Survive?" *Phi Delta Kappan* 54 (1973): 369-380.

Williamson, A. P. "Career Education: Implications for Secondary LD Students." *Academic Therapy* 10 (Winter 1974-75): 193-200.

Wright, H. F. "Observational Child Study." *Handbook of Research Methods in Child Development*, by P. H. Hussen. New York: John Wiley, 1960, pp. 7-139.

Wrightsman, L. S. *Social Psychology in the Seventies: Brief Edition.* Monterey, Calif.: Brooks/Cole, 1973.

Zeisal, J. "Architect says Schools Issue an Invitation to Damage in 'Vandalism: Special Report ' " *Nations Schools* 92 (December 1973): 32.

2

Career and vocational education: the necessity for a planned future

SIDNEY R. MILLER

New realities are compelling society and the individuals who manage the educational networks to acknowledge that everyone does not have to practice law, medicine, or become the chairman-of-the-board for the culture to survive. The 1960s and 1970s produced an abundance of university educated persons and created a shortage of highly trained craftsmen, who are generally less enamored with spinning sophistries and are more interested in keeping the world functioning and aesthetic. The movement which has sought to operationalize the migration from the university campus to the craftsman's bench is career education.

Since its birth in the late 1960s, career education has become the depository for new laws that guarantee the rights of individuals, and for trends which recognize the need for the unity of educational experiences. The overview of career education is education from birth to death, but its prime advocates have emphasized its importance from adolescence to adulthood. The movement has subsumed vocational education, which during the 1940s, 1950s, and early 1960s became blemished through its association with non-collegebound individuals who were often norm-violating and disruptive. Like its newer and more glittering brother, vocational education is now an acceptable concept when unified with academic preparation.

For the chronic disruptive, career education offers the opportunity to identify professional paths that will result in acquired work competencies and improved employment opportunities. During the 1960s dash to the college campuses, most educators developed a single-minded goal—to provide all students with college level competencies in reading, language, and mathematics, irrespective of their interests, aptitudes, and motivations. This approach victimized the student and the society.

The disruptive youth has been traditionally provided with experiences which have failed to meet their needs and interests. Until the turn of the twentieth century, disruptive youths were generally dealt with as troublemakers or criminals, with incarceration or exclusion from society by direct or indirect methods as the primary societal treatment. Through the evangelistic efforts of Jane Addams and William James, public attitudes began to modify in the early 1900s and norm-violating youths were treated less as problems of society and more as societies' problems. This change in attitude was reflected in new programs for such youth. Communities, the courts, and institutions began to employ habilitation and rehabilitative efforts as a substitute for punishment.

The efforts at habilitation and rehabilitation were sporadic until the 1950s and 1960s when local, state, and federal agencies supported and funded the development of career/vocational training for these youths. The difficulty in habilitation and rehabilitation has been that most chronic disruptive youth receive training at the end of their education preparation (McCandless, 1970; Rice, 1975) rather than at the onset of adolescence. The latitude of career choices given to youth has been regulated by their standing on five factors: (1) socioeconomic background; (2) parental attitudes; (3) school achievement; (4) peer values; and (5) intelligence (Rice, 1975; Shaw & McKay, 1972). Of these five factors, the chronic disruptive youth, regularly seen in conflict with community values, has tended to be rated low on three or more (Heggen & Irvine, 1967).

Those youths currently being provided career/vocational training by private and public institutions are generally in the lower range of normal intelligence, as measured primarily with verbal language instruments. The tendency has been to place low achieving youths in routine, repetitively simple, and low-paying occupations (Kokaska, 1971; Oswald, 1968); even though they have demonstrated vocational sophistication far greater than their conventional academic competency. The author's survey found only two programs in all of vocational education that sought to develop the appropriate social and vocational skills among individuals with average or above-average intelligence (Klapper & Neff, 1966; Scurlock, West, Keith, & Viaille, 1964). Supporting this position, Goldstein (1969) believes that too much emphasis is placed on academic instruction and too little on the development of socio-occupation competence.

Interest in career/vocational programs has increased since the court decisions of the early 1970s (Mills vs. Board of Education, 1972; and Diana vs. State Board of Education, 1970) and subsequent education legislation in such states as Pennsylvania, Maine, California, and Illinois. These court decisions and legislative acts have resulted in broadened public school responsibilities toward all students, from birth to twenty-one years of age.

LEARNING CHARACTERISTICS

In studying adolescent youth with learning problems, Walter and Krenzler (1970) noted that school dropouts tended to exhibit several common characteristics associated with school performance. These factors were: age, low intelligence, grade lag, reading and arithmetic achievement retardation, socioeconomic level, high absenteeism, undistinguished school participation, and poor grade point average. McCandless (1970) reports that 14% of all dropouts were at or above the 64th percentile in intelligence test scores. In other words, many students viewed as being disruptive were in the top 36% of the national population intellectually. This finding agrees with others (Glueck & Glueck, 1950; Roman, 1957; Quay, 1965) who note that around 75% of dropouts and norm-violating youth have reading disabilities and are not necessarily intellectually retarded. This data only illuminates the failure of vocational programs to reach a critical population which could benefit from such training.

Pursuing this, Sabatino (1974) indicated that many of the neglected adolescents in our schools with average or above average intelligence, who are failing in the traditional educational setting, should be considered learning disabled. If secondary schools were to adopt this definition, a significant break with the past would occur. Until now, public education has dealt with the troubled adolescent as either retarded, lazy, or turned off, and have placed them into *maintenance* programs where the primary thrust was to keep them out of the mainstream of intellectual, academic, social, and vocational development. As a result, many of the secondary school disruptive students have either an aversion to or lack the skills and information necessary to deal with testing situations (Clarke & Waters, 1972).

McCandless (1970), Jenson and Rohwer (1968), Glueck and Glueck (1950), Scrofani, Suziedelis and Shore (1973) sought to determine whether low socioeconomic students also tended to have lower intelligence tests because of genetics or because of training. They found that when the lower socioeconomic group was given conceptual training their scores rose to a comparable level with middle socioeconomic student scores. These authors concluded that lower socioeconomic students—who often become troubled—suffer not from intellectual capacity, but from lack of sufficient training in the information and skill areas measured by intelligence tests. These findings are compatible with the earlier findings reported by Clarke and Waters (1972) and Wade and Shertzer (1970).

Further studies have been completed on the relationship between reading and adolescent problems. Alsop (1973), and Staats and Butterfield (1965) showed the validity of diminishing reinforcement techniques in the teaching of reading to a 14-year-old norm-violating male with a second grade reading level. The subject was able to increase his reading level 2.8 grades. His behavior in school also improved. Earlier, Dorney (1967) demonstrated the modification of attitudes of adolescents through the use of reading instruction, and Raygor's (1970) study suggests that results on the Cooperative English Test enhance the prediction of potentially troubled adolescents. Fendrick and Bond (1936) discussed adolescence and reading as did other early studies (Glueck & Glueck, 1934, 1950, 1953; Kvaraceus, 1964). The Illinois Curriculum Program, Counteracting School Dropouts (1967), shows that a number of Illinois schools use special education programs geared to diminish the soaring dropout rates. Developmental and/or remedial reading courses, vocational classes, and work-study programs were among those receiving the highest ratings in effectiveness and use.

The United States Department of Health, Education and Welfare publication, Positive Approaches to Dropout Prevention (1973) discusses many projects around the country using various means to decrease dropouts. Among these projects are expanded career education programs, teacher awareness and training programs, and changes in counseling services. A counseling Learning Center was established in St. Louis (Project Stay) whose purpose was to work with pupils referred to as potential dropouts and provide technical and preventative assistance to teachers in the regular classroom. Other programs relating norm violation to specific learning disabilities have seemingly illuminated an otherwise dark area (Closson, 1971; Dinitz et al., 1957; Frease, 1972; Graubard, 1967; Kelgord, 1968; Schlichter & Ratliff, 1971; and Walle, 1972). The value of these programs has not yet been determined.

The lack of clear definitions and well enunciated programs and instructional strategies has resulted in efforts at delineating behavioral data so that the educator can gain insights when interacting with the disruptive adolescent. The most common approaches in working with the youths have been either counseling or behavior modification, both of which have some demonstrable short-term effects, but have not generated long-term value. Jersild (1957), in defining parameters affecting deviant adolescent behavior, contended that a majority of adolescent behavior disorders are merely exaggerated manifestations of emotional instability. Since then, Erickson (1968), Mussen, Conger, and Kagan (1969), and Piaget (1969) have all noted that adolescence is an inherent crisis in each individual's development. It is a period in which an individual is beginning to experiment with such abstract notions as democracy, freedom, identify, and equality.

In looking at alternative approaches, Anandam and Williams (1971) found in working with adolescents that teacher-student consultative models of classroom management were more effective than the more traditional teacher-curriculum model. Wagner (1972) concluded that many disaffected students feel alienated and believe that the curriculum is irrelevant and fails to appeal to their individual interests and needs. Ariel (1971) allowed adolescents to monitor their own behavior, and demonstrated increased learning through the use of a student established and maintained goals and objectives record inventory. McCandless (1970) noted that the sharing of goals with the class is essential, particularly where the student-teacher values differ and where the student is male and the teacher demands conformity and obedience. He further states that the peer group is a more compelling force than any school official. Kurtz and Neisworth (1976) believe that the shared management efforts will ultimately produce an improved self-control approach where the locus of control will move from the teachers to the student. They also contend that this strategy will change the management effort from control of specific behavior to training individuals in general problem solving that can be used to deal with future difficulties.

Inappropriate behavior of secondary students is a universal problem (Eichorn, 1967), and the deviant student presents additionally confounding problems since he is troubled not only with his developmental cycle, but is also frustrated by his inability to adequately achieve and interact with peers and society. The need to establish a personal identity, and the requirement of society that an individual between ages 13 and 18 begins to establish career goals, results in a need of the adolescent to participate in professional-life decisions. Thus, both personal and societal demands require the student to become an integral part of the educational system decision making process.

The traditional psychiatric-psychological therapeutic model has failed to meet the needs of such youths (Sabatino, 1974). Furthermore, there is evidence that such correctional techniques may be harmful in an adolescent's emotional and educational maturation. It is for this reason that efforts to expand behavior management has occurred so rapidly in just a few short years. Several studies have been conducted with adolescents (Atthowe & Krasner, 1965; Meichenbaum, Bowers, & Ross, 1968; Slack & Schwitzgebel, 1960; Steffy, 1966). Many of these programs have resulted in behavioral changes. Slack and Schwitzgebel (1960), using food and money, were able to reduce the chronic disruptive behavior of ghetto area boys, who historically have been in conflict with school and society. Cohen, et al. (1966), has demonstrated the effectiveness of food and money in positively altering behavior among adolescents in academic environments. Wilkinson, Saunders, and Reppucci (1971) developed a three level program for institutionalized chronic disruptive youth. The three levels progressively sought increased exemplary behavior from the students. The levels have various scales which could be adopted for learning disability programs for adolescents. Two studies (Smith & Riebock, 1971; Pendrak, 1974) demonstrated the effectiveness of performance contracting with adolescent students in reading. Both studies reported that overt behavior and reading performance improved through the use of contracting. Wagner (1972) noted the disadvantaged often feel disenfranchised by the educational setting. He recommends behavioral changes in the schools. Among these modifications are: (1) making the curriculum relevant; (2) teaching to the students' strengths; (3) having teacher-parent conferences near the student's home; and (4) providing the student with close and continual behavioral and educational monitoring.

The issue of what motivates an adolescent has been an ongoing debate among investigators. Senborn and Niemiec (1974) claimed material accomplishment, recognition, social involvement, and personal development were the four factors rated highest by high school students. The investigators concluded that none of the four trends were preeminent over the others. It has been noted that some troubled youths know right from wrong in social and personal encounters, but are unable to act on this knowledge. It is further reported that these adolescents are unable to maintain an overriding abstract personal or social ideal. When they attempt to hold an idea, new conditions often arise which frustrate them. One cause of this frustration is the inability to adapt when new parameters are introduced. This phenomenon was noted by Strauss and Lehtinen (1947), and Clements and Peters (1967) in primary brain-damaged learning disability children.

PROBLEMS

In the review of the literature, three distinct difficulties loom for the educators seeking program and instructional guidance. The first difficulty deals with the inadequacy of information related to program efficacy. The literature searches end with the finding that numerous programs have been proposed and few have been formally evaluated to search out strengths and weaknesses. Those programs now being assessed are being judged on interview and site observation data. The second difficulty is the physiological, biological, and cognitive development of the adolescent; the most often cited is the chronic disruptive school-age offender. As has been noted by numerous researchers (Erickson, 1968; Bruner, 1966; Ausubel, 1957; Piaget, 1969), adolescent youth experience significant physical, biological, and cognitive changes, beginning around 11 years of age. These changes continue until the adolescent is approximately 17. The disruptive adolescent's problems are multiplied by the fact that resulting school performance difficulties make the transition from childhood to adulthood additionally trying.

The third difficulty is that only an estimated one-fourth to one-third of all special education programs in the United States were directed at the adolescent student (Martin, 1972), and fewer than 10% were specifically designed for disruptive youth. It was further observed by Martin that only 20% of the youth leaving schools in the next few years will be fully employed, or seek higher education. Of the remaining students, 40% will be underemployed, and 20% will be unemployed. Martin recommended the development of an integrated curriculum in which related skills be taught. Since Martin conducted this survey, the number of programs has increased, but the money, time, and personnel directed to serving the problem adolescent is still far less than that provided for children in the pre-primary and primary grades.

Hudson (1971), supporting Martin's position, reported that success in leaving a controlled public setting and integrating back into society was dependent on job training and subsequent employment. Miller (1975) and Sabatino (1974) held that this training depends on a properly integrated academic and vocational curriculum. Yet a review of the 40 vocational programs found only five (National Education Association, 1967; Bail & Hamilton, 1967; Crump, et al., 1966; Cowles, Condon, Falkner & Jackson 1967; Deno, Henye, Krantz & Barklind, 1965) which provided specific educational instruction along with the vocational curriculum for the participating youth. Of the same 40 programs, only three (Deno, Henye, Krantz & Barklind, 1965; Cowles, et al., 1967; Eddy, Windle, de la Cruz & Wolford, 1966) delineated responsibilities for educators in such vocational training programs.

Gadlin (1966), surveying the personnel working in a program for emotionally disturbed and socially maladjusted individuals, found that two-thirds of all those personnel employed in these vocational programs were psychiatrists, physicians, psychologists and vocational counselors. Personnel such as teachers, prevocational work coordinators, or curriculum directors were generally not included, or were under-represented on the professional staffs.

The evaluation instrumentation used by the 40 programs was predominantly intellectual, vocational, and psychoanalytical. Among the instruments used to measure intelligence were the Wechsler Intelligence Scale for Children; the Wechsler Adult Intelligence Scale, and the Stanford-Binet. The vocational measures were the Minnesota Paper Form Board, the Purdue Pegboard Test, and the Kuder Interest Test. The psychoanalytical instruments used were the test of Anxiety for Children, the Child Complaint Questionnaire, and SRA Survey of Interpersonal Values. Academic assessment instruments were used in only four of the 40 programs (Neff & Koltuv, 1967; Eddy, et al., 1966; Deno, et al., 1965; Plue, 1972). The two academic areas assessed by the instruments were reading and mathematics. There were no learner aptitude measures of perception, sensory-motor, language, conceptual abilities, social competency, or language arts.

Disruptive youth often have trouble comprehending and coping with community and societal demands, and Bail and Hamilton (1967) stated that the success of any secondary program is dependent on seven essential ingredients:

1. Use of community leaders with competencies in vocational training.
2. Use of community facilities when appropriate and relevant.
3. Counseling from various state agencies concerned with vocational training.
4. Concern for practical application of the academic and vocational training.
5. Indepth preplanning of programs and facilities.
6. Adequate equipment and facilities to facilitate continuity between the program and career goals.
7. Teachers trained to recognize the needs of the youth and the community.

In spite of this, only five programs (New, 1972; Gruelle, 1967; Scurlock, et al., 1964; Deno, et al., 1965; Cowles, et al., 1967) had direct liaison with outside agencies related to employment, vocational development, welfare, and judicial. Among the organizations with whom these programs established contact and from whom they sought assistance were the Department of Employment, Bureau of Vocational Rehabilitation, Departments of Education, the Welfare Department, and the courts. The large number of programs performing without outside agency assistance is perplexing considering the demonstrated need to have a coordinated and integrated program with community groups (Scurlock, et al., 1964).

Work experience has been incorporated into the secondary school curriculum, often with the cooperation of the state rehabilitation agency, employment service, and sheltered workshops. These work study programs have had the benefit of involving agencies in the vocational habilitation of disruptive students prior to graduation, but as yet, have not been as effective as they were designed to be.

Communication problems, in many cases, have existed between the secondary school and the rehabilitation agency, resulting in sporadic services and inadequate continuity of service (Hammerlynck & Espeseth, 1969). State employment services generally do not have a working relationship with secondary special education programs and many do not feel it is their responsibility to find employment for these high school low achieving or disruptive youth.

PROGRAM STUDIES

Neff and Koltuv (1967) found in a five year study that youths introduced to vocational training at an early age tended to accommodate to the training more readily than did youths who entered into the programs at a later age. James (1966) reported, however, that older youths tended to be more realistic in career outlook. It was also found that students from higher socioeconomic backgrounds foresaw a greater number of job possibilities. Conversely, youths from lower socioeconomic neighborhoods tended to underestimate themselves and their career opportunities, and thus, limit their potential in obtaining positions that might be closely allied with their training and interests. James noted that those who had outside experience tended to do better than those who remained in restricted environments. Gorelick (1966), in contrast, found that youths with realistic expectations were not more successful in obtaining jobs than those with unrealistic vocational expectations.

Cegelka (1976) found fewer females in career/vocational programs, and that those in such programs were trained for low paying jobs not covered by federal wage regulations. These findings were previously cited by Gillespie and Fink (1974), noting that females received training in housekeeping while males received preparation in carpentry, construction, and auto repairs. Parnicky and Kahn (1963), reporting on 437 youths, said the most accurate criteria for measuring the future success of youth was the youth's performance in the field. Deno, Henye, Krantz, and Barklind (1965) reported that out of 483 youths involved in a vocational program, those with high intelligence quotients remained in school and were the most successful in obtaining appropriate employment. Those who had trouble in retaining a position were more often nonwhite, left school early, tended to be in conflict with societal codes, and had multiple handicaps.

From this synopsis it is evident that the data provided to vocational counselors, educators, and correctional officers is scant. The designing of programs with integrated curricula dealing with educational and vocational needs must turn again to theoretical postulates to generate a data base upon which future programs can be built.

TRAINING AND INSTRUCTIONAL PREPARATION

While the demand for improved and increased integrated programs grows, and the thirst of administrators for more appropriately trained teachers mushrooms, there has been a documented lack of direction from state governments in improving the level of preparation among educators and counselors needed to work with the disruptive individuals. Simultaneously, there is a need to upgrade the quality of programs for these youths. A study by Miller (1976) of program needs indicates that the public schools are requiring more people with specialized training in behavior management, curriculum instruction, and diagnosis for secondary youth. In another study, Clark and Oliverson (1973) found that only 9 states out of 47 had any secondary certification requirements for work-study coordinators. This same study found that only 8 colleges or universities out of 207 surveyed had a differentiated elementary-secondary special education program, also demonstrating the lack of directions from training institutions.

Despite the documented inappropriateness of university programs to train professional personnel and inadequate certification standards by various states, disruptive youth still require unique social, educational and personal responses from the teacher (McCandless, 1970; Ausubel, 1957). The disruptive youth who is entering the period of role experimentation (Erickson, 1968) has the inability to think abstractly (Piaget, 1969; Flavell, 1963) without the assistance of sensory data. During this period, the adolescent begins defining his or her role in society (Erickson, 1968; Evans & Potter, 1970; McCandless, 1970) and seeks to determine the career path he or she wants to explore and eventually trod. It is not a period in human development where instructors can be casually selected and instructional and management procedures can whimsically be determined.

The need for highly qualified personnel in secondary education becomes more acute when the student is the disruptive youth with a history of social conflict and school failure; and whose crisis of identity, self-worth, and identifying potential self as a contributing member of society is being questioned by adult authority, peers, and self.

PROGRAM DIRECTIONS

The dichotomies between and among programs, services, personnel, and goals in career/vocational education has produced doubts among public officials over the efficacy of the concept and the educability of the chronic disruptive youth. Too frequently career/vocational programs have featured a separation of the academic from the vocational program, though operationally they are dependent and ultimately rise or fall, based each on the efficacy of the other. The imperative, then, is to build an integrated career/vocational education program which includes the components of academic and vocational assessment; career exploration, programming, and instruction, job coaching, and program evaluation.

Integrated curriculum

The belief has been perpetuated among educators that there are stark differences between the interest and efforts of those who teach the basic academic areas and those who teach in the vocational/craft areas. Yet, the United States Congress, in passing the Cooperative Vocational Education Programs, noted that meaningful work experience, and training should be combined with formal education, enabling students to acquire knowledge skills and appropriate attitudes. Sloan (1975) broadens the concept from simply academic and vocational preparation to include basic life management, personal-social development, and career/vocational placement, producing a prototype of the integrated curriculum. An analysis of any configuration of career-education demonstrates that a student's success is dependent on not only academic and vocational competency, but also the ability to manage finances, attend to health needs, and successfully interact with others. It is also evident that these components of life cannot be instructionally separated from the others, and a student whose career goal is carpentry cannot ignore measure, blueprint interpretation, and colleague interaction.

Herr (1972), noting the broad mandate of the integrated career education concept, called for a systems approach to the treatment of chronic disruptive and norm-violating youth. It is necessary, then, to look at the total program and the total student need. The program, as expressed in Figure 2.1, should first consider the students' interests, needs, levels of performance, and motivation through a process of formal testing and informal interviewing.

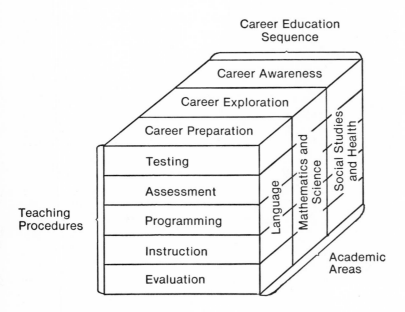

Figure 2.1 Career Education Matrix

Teaching procedures

Testing. The formal testing of chronic disruptive and norm-violating youth should involve measurements of academic, career/vocational and social behavior. The academic tests must include the measurement of reading, writing, social studies, and mathematic skills. These basic academic skills can be measured through the use of such instruments as the Wide Range Achievement Test, the Peabody Individual Achievement Test, the Gates-MacGinite Reading Test, the California Achievement Test, and/or Informal Evaluation of Thinking Ability. They are but a few of the instruments that could be used to measure individual performance of youth in the academic areas. In addition, career/vocational measures should be used. These measures often assess not only career preparation aptitude, but also self-concept and intellectual level. Among some of the tests that can be used are the California Life Goal Evaluation Schedule, the Vocational Interest and Aptitudinal Test, and the Flanagan Industrial Tests. The use of these tests, along with formal interviews for assessing the student's ability to orally communicate and interact with other individuals, should provide the career education personnel with adequate information related to the educational process.

In some programs for chronic disruptive and norm-violating youths, a psychologist is called on to use projective tests which are designed to expose the underlying psychological factors that are believed contributing to the youths' deviant behavior. As the literature demonstrates, the efficacy of the projective measures and their appropriateness to education have not only been questioned, but some investigators have suggested that treatment related to the projective tests is detrimental to the individual's growth and development.

Assessment. The interpretation of test results and observational data has tended to focus on the overt, provocative performance of the youth. Resulting recommended treatment of the student laid heavy emphasis on conduct management, with a secondary emphasis on the basic academic skills. When the reverse was the case—heavy emphasis on academics and a lesser emphasis on management—the results were essentially unsatisfactory. This lack of payoff, in either management or academic programming, along with the well-cited dubious efficacy of most purely vocational programs, clearly demonstrates that the overall look at youth has been inadequate. The disruptive youth, like the society, cannot be viewed in component parts to the exclusion of other parts. The assessment must be based on the student's needs, interests, and how the test and observational data interface. The assessment cannot be based solely on vocational and psychological projective information. It must encompass the total of the youth's interests, academic and career/vocational skills, and social aptitude. These competencies must be assessed in a manner that provides a wide number of personnel with operational information. Too frequently the results of testing are couched in language not easily understood by a wide variety of personnel. The resulting data reports must communicate clearly the youth's educational needs.

Programming. Unlike testing and assessment, which takes into consideration the individual's needs, interests, and goals, the programming efforts must interface the student's competencies in a variety of areas. To effectively achieve this interface, the instructors must possess or have at his or her disposal a wide variety of instructional materials and aids. The program configurations include:

1. Self Contained Classroom (full-time): the student spends the entire day in the classroom receiving the prescribed instruction.

2. Resource Room (part-time): the student spends a minimal amount of time in the resource room, receiving assistance and support at a level which enables him to function successfully in the regular classroom.

3. Peer Tutoring and Support: the peer provides assistance to student in areas of skill development, socialization, and career direction while the youth participates in an ongoing program.

4. Academic/Vocational Preparation: the student spends one-half the time in academic areas and one-half the time in shop and industrial arts training.

5. Work Study: the student attends regular classes for a short period in the morning and then works during the afternoon at a monitored site for a regulated amount of time.

6. Vocational Study: the student receives instruction in academic areas, while also attending a vocational training center where preparation in specific career/vocational preparation is emphasized.

The above program configuration should be carefully interfaced with the student's identified needs, interests, and competencies.

Instruction. The demand for increased and improved programs for chronic disruptive and norm-violating youth has also resulted in more and improved instructional materials and procedures. While there has been an over-reliance on materials for the elementary schools in the past, there is now emerging a core of instructional materials, tactics, curriculum guides, and program outlines that appear to meet the needs and interests of adolescents. It is essential that these materials be used in providing instructional assistance for the adolescents who require programs and materials which deviate from the traditional formats and performance levels. The glaring weaknesses of instruction has been the dichotomy between the programs and materials for college-bound students, and the materials and programs for those individuals whose interests and skills deviate from the normative efforts of the public schools. Among the types of materials now surfacing are:

1. Programmed instruction for low achievers.
2. High interest, low vocabulary needs.
3. Career oriented materials for adolescents concerned with craftsmanship in vocational areas.
4. Reading material emphasizing retention of basic information.
5. Material requiring only short term memory.
6. Material geared to conceptual understanding and response.

This list includes just a few of the many factors that must be taken into consideration in selecting and using materials. One of the variables found by many secondary school teachers to be a reliable motivator with the chronic disruptive and norm-violating youth is multiple material selection and use. A second concept is that the material should interface with the student's interests and goals, and be written at the student's competency level. When necessary material is not available in the classroom or school, it can often be obtained through regional media and materials centers.

Evaluation. Educators are guilty of establishing programs in the fall and then waiting until spring to scrutinize the efficacy. The gap between the program initiation and evaluation is too great. By the time the educator knows the effectiveness of the program, it is often too late to redirect or organize it to better meet the student's needs. Evaluation, thus, must be part of the ongoing educational experience, and should occur every two to three weeks. The evaluation does not have to feature the use of formal, standardized tests (i.e., the Minnesota Multiphasic Test, N-GATB, and the Wide Range Achievement Test). The student's and program's efficacy can be viewed by measuring the performance of the students against delineated objectives formulated for the evaluation period. If the student's progress is in concert with the objectives, then learning is occurring. Should there be a lag, then the educator must either reassess, reprogram, and/or develop new instructional goals, objectives, materials, and strategies for the student(s).

Career education sequence

Career awareness. Many students are not aware of the large number of career/vocational opportunities that can be identified and pursued. Some chronic disruptive norm-violating youth have a restricted view of their career/vocational opportunities, and thus foredoom their ultimate success. Most of these same students are unfamiliar with the thousands of listings of career opportunities found in the major Sunday newspapers, or in the Department of Employment listings. Such students need to be informed about these opportunities through reading various types of materials published by governmental and private agencies, by discussing their career/vocational interests with a counselor, by talking with recruitment officers, and by viewing films designed to inform youth about such opportunities. These same individuals also are unable to perceive the overlapping knowledge and skills that a wide variety of career/vocational opportunities require, such as radio and television repairs with computer maintenance, or automobile and truck mechanics with small aircraft repair. Only through a well-designed career awareness program will the students begin to recognize the wide variety of opportunities available to them, and the overlapping nature of the opportunities.

Career exploration.   Once the student has identified fields of interest, a program can then be established which enables this same individual to explore the skills and competencies demanded by the potential careers. This exploration can occur at a job station within the school, at a local business or agency which employs individuals with similar training, or through discussions with professional individuals with training and practice in the selected career areas. Too frequently individuals select a career goal without exploring the essential skills required for its successful performance, and without knowing the advantages and disadvantages of the potential career. As a result, a high number of trained individuals become disenchanted with their chosen career either prior to formal entrance into the field or shortly after gaining employment. To minimize this phenomenon, individuals must be exposed to the advantages and vulgarities of the careers they have chosen prior to training.

Career preparation.   Once a decision has been made as to which of the careers explored is most preferable, and the counselor has determined that the selection is appropriate to the student's interests and skills or potential skills, training begins. This preparation includes not only the technical competency specifically associated with the career, but the underlying academic and informational levels associated with effective career performance which must be provided through directed instruction. In the past, the lack of joint academic and career/vocation preparation has led to the failure of participating youth. Counselors and teachers should use the career choice as the guideline for academic and work oriented competencies. The primary aim of career preparation is to prepare youth to assume a responsible career position in the community, and it is not to legislate them into undesired conditions. Thus, classical scholarship must give way to pragmatic instruction and skill attainment, whether it be more psychomotor than cognitive, or the converse.

Academic areas

Career analysis has demonstrated the interrelation of language, mathematics, science, social studies, and health to successful career attainment and maintenance. The successful shipping clerk, like a successful lawyer, must be able to use language in a variety of ways, even though society and the professions have differing levels of achievement expectation. It is essential that preparatory personnel recognize the necessity of the interface of the academic with the other areas.

Language. Communication, whether sent via words, pictures, audio media, or some combination of the three, has been demonstrated to be essential for career success and growth. A shipping clerk must be able to read and interpret invoices, a mechanic must be able to read parts and repair manuals, and the construction worker must be able to read blueprints. But reading is only one portion of language competency which is essential for success and growth. Writing and oral speech whether terse and to the point, or long and detailed, are prerequisites to success for the lawyer, philosopher, physician, or fast food cooks and waiters. Programs for the chronic disruptive youth must take these variables into consideration in charting an educational program. Educators can no longer assume that because students are not seeking a college degree they do not need basic language competencies.

Mathematics and science. Whether one be an aerospace engineer or automotive mechanic, he or she must have an understanding of mathematics and science. The mechanic needs mathematics to measure and compute the size of a gasket, and science to comprehend the function of the combustion engine; just as the engineer needs these two skills and competencies to design an electrical system or appreciate a new development into electromagnetic energy production. Mathematics and science are essential to the man or woman determined to contribute to their own and the community's growth and welfare.

Social studies and health. Without the recognition of how a chosen career interfaces with society's needs and directions, and how good health contributes to improved job attendance and effectiveness, the individual is at a severe disadvantage. One of the major difficulties contributing to a youth's inability to maintain prolonged employment is the lack of position-stability awareness in an ever changing economic market. Often, youths will select a career that within a short time is no longer considered critical by the community and is soon phased-out. Such experiences often provoke frustration and anger in the youth, and contribute to renewed conflicts with society. A recognition of the job market's ebb and flow can assist the youth to read the changes and adjust his or her career direction. Health, whether mental or physical, has a less tangible, though equally significant influence on career retention and growth. Whether appropriate, the youth's appearance, attendance, and rapidity of performance often determine the duration of employment in a particular position. Poor attendance and work effectiveness can be as important a factor as knowledge. If the chronic disruptive norm-violating youth is to succeed, he or she must recognize such influences and learn how to deal with them on the job.

Career direction

To develop effective career/vocational education programs, counselors, teachers, and youths should first consult reference material which outlines the nature of the career and its prerequisite skills. These career reference outlines are found in the Dictionary of Occupational Titles (1965), the Dictionary of Occupational Titles Supplement (1968), and the Supplement of the Occupational Outlook Handbook (1974–1975). Such material generally describes the career but does not specifically describe vocations as they exist in the local community where the disruptive youth resides. Information concerning local opportunities are generally best found in the local newspaper's job classified section, the state's department of employment, private job placement agencies, and school placement services.

Beyond traditional schooling

Another failure of most career educational programs is the lack of concern in preparing the youth to deal with the world beyond school. Another preparation program must ready the youth for the world beyond the formal education milieu. This orientation must be supervised and structured so the youth is readied to move beyond the full range of opportunities, which will better prepare him or her for the adult world.

The following range of experiences are recommended:

1. *Appraising.* Appraising provides an experiental awareness of academic needs and career availability in the community. This can be achieved through a wide variety of films, field trips, reading material, recordings, and slide presentations.

2. *Witnessing.* The youth spends time at specified commercial establishments developing improved awareness concerning the skills and competencies required in identified career paths.

3. *Work Experience.* At this level actual experience at a learning center in work situations or simulated work situations is provided. Similar experiences can be made available to the youth at training stations in the community, such as retail stores, industries, or special workshops. The academics are generally directly related to the work experiences, but when appropriate, may have a global direction.

4. *Work Study.* This phase has a general vocational curriculum which is related to the employment or career planning program the youth is developing outside the educational setting. The youth will learn skills on the job and relate his academic and vocational work in the community to his classes.

5. *Career Cooperative Education.* This phase is intended to provide youth with a sequence of academic and experiental opportunities in school, which prepare them for a specific career or career class that will be pursued upon completing school. While working in the community, the youth is supervised on the job by his employer and by a job coach assigned as a coordinator.

6. *Community Work.* This is the terminal stage in the career/vocational program for the student. Upon completing formal schooling, the youth will work independently in the community.

To successfully carry out such experiences, teachers, psychologists, psychometrists, counselors, work coordinators, shop instructors, and administrative personnel must be harmoniously bonded. Programs for the disruptive youth have been fragmented and have concentrated on the psychological, and not the educational aspects of the career/vocational preparation process (Gadlin, 1966; Sabatino, 1974). Only through the fusing of essential and appropriate personnel can a total integrated program be designed and successfully accomplished. There is a growing recognition of this as demonstrated by the new programs now being designed by universities, state departments of education, and local school districts (Cooperative Occupational Education, 1974; Work Experience Career Exploration Guide, 1974; Handbook for Career Guidance Counselors, 1975).

Facilities and agencies

Besides the community or regional high school, other facilities and agencies must be utilized to service the disruptive youth. These facilities and agencies must work in cooperation rather than at odds with each other. Should the high school be a large facility with a comprehensive program, the need for outside support is reduced, but not eliminated. Among the services the high school can be expected to provide are:

1. Diagnostic services
2. Counseling
3. Programs
4. Academic Instruction
5. Career/Vocation Awareness, Exploration, and Preparation
6. Off-Campus Experience
7. Program Evaluation and Reprogramming

This wide range of services requires not only regular classrooms and teachers, but also psychologists, psychometrists, career counselors, work-school coordinators, shop teachers, and administrators working in specialized environments designed to provide essential experiences and skills required in career skill attainment and competency. When such high schools are not available, services from the state vocational/technical educational agency, regional career/vocational centers, cooperative program agreements among high schools for sharing facilities, and special agreements with either state institutions or private organizations can be achieved to obtain necessary services and facilities. Among the state and private agencies that can be used are the state employment agency, state department of commerce and industry, the chamber of commerce, the state department of education, the Salvation Army, Goodwill Industries, and the Jewish, Catholic and independent vocational skills training centers.

Curriculum

Sabatino (1974) recommended a vocational curriculum which de-emphasizes the use of standard textbooks and emphasizes an instructional approach with preprogrammed high interest, low vocabulary material. This material would be specifically geared to the reading and interest level of the students and would interface with the students' vocational direction. While there has been some attempt at developing this material, the review of the literature reveals significant gaps in its availability. Extensive use of audio-visual equipment and guest lecturers heightens the interest of disruptive youth. In selecting materials, the personnel should remain aware of the types of material and the variety of skills and motivational factors which should be represented by the curriculum materials. Whether the subject be language, mathematics, or science, the material should reflect the interests of adolescence—cars, sex, jobs, personal identity, career directions, and other subjects demanding the attention of youth. As was noted in the discussion of instruction, the material must reflect the global and discrete competencies of the student.

Management tactics

A program of instructional approaches and materials without appropriate behavioral management tactics is ultimately doomed when working with the youth who has experienced years of school frustration. An effective teacher should be acquainted with the theories of Skinner (1968), Bandura (1969), and Lazarus (1971). The application of these theories are contained in programs of Hewett (1968), Peter (1965), Kunzelman, et al. (1970), and Smith (1970).

Each of the theories and programs acknowledges the necessity of moving from the concrete reinforcement to more abstract social reinforcers. The literature also supports the thesis that reinforcement procedures must consider not only the production phase of learning but also time factors. Too frequently educators have reinforced the completion of a task —referred to as a ratio measure. They have not supported the length of time the student will work at a task (interval measure), nor have they measured the intensity of the student's involvement in an activity.

In working with an adolescent, baseline behavior (the point at which the student is operating in a specified area) must be pinpointed so teacher and student know where they are and where they are going. Once this has been determined, the teacher and student can develop meaningful and realistic goals and objectives as they relate to reading, mathematics, social studies, science, and vocational development. This type of behavioral management can be best implemented through the use of performance contracting.

Performance contracting is the form of an agreement between a teacher and a student. In the agreement, the student acknowledges that for a specified quantity of performance he will receive a reward (either money, tokens, food, or free time). Before the performance contract is initiated the diagnostic-assessment process must be completed. From this data the teacher can establish baseline expectations (the level of performance) for the student. Among the types of instruments used in the diagnostic-assessment process are intelligence, aptitude, achievement, and criterion measurement tests. Each of these instruments enables the instructor to more aptly identify the student's skills and interests.

Once the baseline data has been determined, the teacher, in conjunction with the student, establishes realistic goals and objectives. If the student is unable, or not ready to work in consultation with the teacher, the teacher alone must establish the goals and objectives. In addition, once realistic objectives are established, contingencies for completion of the specific quantity at a specified level of quality are determined.

When the student has reached the point of being able to work in concert with the teacher, the teacher must consult the student about objectives and contingencies. It is a designated purpose of performance contracting that the agreement be a joint and not a unilateral decision.

Once every two to three weeks an evaluation of the goals, objectives, methods and materials is necessary to determine whether the program is on track and on time. Often student and teacher, once the goals and objectives have been pinpointed, neglect to determine whether the original conclusions were appropriate, relevant, and effective. If they fail to meet the test of appropriateness, relevancy, and effectiveness, then they must be redrawn. Evaluation and re-evaluation is an essential component of any program.

Reinforcers during the remainder of the program must be continuously evaluated to measure student effectiveness. The re-evaluation process must again include the use of criterion tests which measure academic development, performance charts which measure overt behavior, and student-teacher conferences which pinpoint personal attitudes as they relate to achievement, general behavior, and self-image.

Job coaching

As noted, the tendency in career education has been to ignore or minimize the implementation facet of the program. The primary emphasis has been on preparation within the school. As a result, little consideration has been given to the development of career coaches, whose responsibilities include identifying job markets, contacting potential placement sites, making the student placement, and insuring the relationship between the student and the on-site supervisor is appropriate and results in learning. Contemporary texts and work manuals (Work Experience and Career Exploration Guide, 1975; and Work Experience Career Exploration Guide, 1974) have ignored the career coach and his responsibilities, though they imply the need for such individuals and recognize the necessity of outside implementation practices. Traditionally, vocational personnel have sought to work with disruptive youth in the institution and/or school, providing career counseling, job stations, skill teaming, and instilling in the youth the prevalent social and philosophical values of the community.

To increase the effectiveness of career programs, state and local legislative bodies provide funds for the development of career coaches and the support of youth once placed out on the job market. The need for career coaches is particularly imperative when the youth has a history of chronic disruptive behavior. Among such youth the recidivism is high and the potential for new societal conflicts is high (Sabatino, 1974). While the reasons for the recidivism are multiple, major contributions are poor follow-up once the youth is placed out beyond the school environment, and the lack of close cooperation with business, industry, and other agencies in the community.

Cooperative efforts among various community and business agencies are essential for career education programs to succeed (Burt and Lessinger, 1970). Such cooperative efforts (1) produce programs of instruction more effective than those provided solely in training centers; (2) enable both training and business officials to measure instructional and training appropriateness; (3) provide an ongoing quality control process; and (4) insure relevance of career training for youth. The necessity for cooperation and the integration of training and on-site experiences was cited by Clark and Sloan (1960). They report a general attitude among school officials that training ends with the conclusion of schooling, and they contend that this position is not in keeping with contemporary findings. Borow (1973) noted that the interfacing of training and practical experience generally benefits the youth's performance in training and in school. He cited studies which indicated that youth in work programs generally showed gains in schooling. Educators and counselors have known for some time that theory and practice without practical experience tended to make the latter less relevant to the trainee. Williamson (1965), in reviewing the responsibilities of the counselor, noted that there must be a connection between the theory and the practice, the thought and the performance. Similarly, Rhodes (1970) advocated that all segments of the community must become involved in the implementations of career planning and experience. He noted that parks, school boards, industry, business, labor leaders, and state and federal government officials must participate in guaranteeing effective progress. Hayes, Hopson, and Daws (1971) supported Rhodes, noting:

> . . . work experience, organized either by the counselor as part of the career program or by the student himself has an important influence on [the student's] development. (p. 26)

It was further suggested that practical experience can contribute to the individual's assessment of self as well as the world of work. Such experience can be provided either on a full-time or part-time basis. The management of this experience involves the student arriving at the work station at the starting time and following all the regulations applicable to other employees. Hayes, Hopson, and Daws took a different position:

1. Treat the work experience as an educational experience, and not a final answer to their career goals and needs.

2. Students ideally should be given a variety of work experiences so they can become acquainted with alternative career directions.

3. Safeguard any experiences against violation of various legal restraints.

4. Cooperation of business, industry, community agencies, and other interested groups is essential. It was recommended that the employer: (a) provide experiences of the least and most attractive features of the position; (b) offer varieties of experiences during a single day; (c) insure the youth against injury; and (d) designate an experienced, understanding adult to assist the youth.

5. Follow-up of the experiences should be made, so the usefulness of the placement can be assessed.

6. Parents should be a part of the placement and assessment process.

Ginzberg (1971) feels that the public must be made part of the career experience. Ultimately, without the support of the public, funds to implement career programs will not be forthcoming.

Coaching requirements

The career coach needs to have familiarity with all the components of the preparation and program design. Many of the chronic disruptive youths who are serviced by this program do not accept the contemporary middle-class values of our society. Thus, a career coach unwilling to acknowledge these differences will ultimately fail in seeking to assist the youths and the community. The criteria for hiring such coaches should not be a college education. Rather, the coach should be expected to possess the following skills:

1. *Adaptability.* He or she must be an individual conversant with the background of the youth being served and the teacher and/or employer who works with the chronic disruptive youth.

2. *Job Market Information.* The coach must know the job market and be able to identify potential employment and training areas, and the individuals who are able to facilitate participation in the chosen area.

3. *Counselor.* The coach must be capable of understanding the youth's and the teacher's and/or employer's needs and resolve any differences that may exist between the two.

4. *Competency Awareness.* The coach must be able to identify the skills necessary for success in various settings and be certain the youth referred has the competencies.

5. *Public Relations.* The individual, working as a coach, must recognize that success in his or her position is measured by one's ability to familiarize potential employers, the youth, the community,

and the school with strategies that result in positive adjustment for all parties.

6. *Alternatives.* The coach must recognize that all youth will not benefit from one single program. Alternatives must be available to meet each youth's individual needs, interests, and competencies.

The coach who identifies various alternative positions should also make the placements and maintain contact with all parties during the familiarization-placement-integration period. This program strategy maintains program continuity of placement and integration, and prevents channels of communications from being clogged. Too often division of efforts creates programmatic and personal difficulties, resulting in distrust and suspicion.

Curriculum

Any instruction provided by the career coaches is expected to supplement the career education curriculum provided by the schools. This curriculum will include language skills, science and health, mathematics, and social studies. The responsibility of the personnel prior to placement are:

1. Insuring the youth does possess the primary skills for obtaining a job.
2. Identifying settings and professional areas where the youth can be placed.
3. Providing orientation to the youths so they can make appropriate social and career adjustments.
4. Conducting follow-through field surveys and counseling to determine effectiveness of placement and make necessary placement adjustments.

Alternative programs

Wide varieties of alternatives exist for placement of chronic disruptive youth. As was noted in the literature, such youth require wide ranges of experiences so they can measure themselves and the potential career choice. It is imperative that the youth recognize the flexibility he has in selecting careers so that he is not trapped by the first choice. The coach, in making placements and establishing alternatives, ought to weigh a number of variables. They are:

1. Career choice
2. Age
3. Aptitude skills

4. Social skills
5. Academic level of achievement
6. Reliability
7. Honesty
8. Leadership ability
9. Commitment to goals
10. Health

Once these factors have been assessed, the job coach must decide which of the following best matches the youth's needs, interests, and abilities.

1. Full-time school
2. Part-time school, part-time work
3. Part-time school, part-time vocational training
4. Full-time vocational training
5. Part-time vocational training, part-time work
6. Full-time work

Whether the placement be full-time schooling or full-time work experience, the job coach can best service the youth by insuring that the client's skills are being constantly upgraded. It is the essence of career education that levels of competencies are regularly assessed and developmental career goals are revised to meet societal, personal, and economic realities. Without such continual review and program alteration, the youth may tire or become frustrated with career placement.

Career placement criteria

Numerous considerations require assessment prior to career placement. These considerations range from working conditions to the personal and professional ability of the potential placement station to assist the youth. They are: (1) convenience of location; (2) health and safety conditions; (3) hours which must be worked; (4) adequacy of facilities and equipment; and (5) the potential agencies compliance of applicable laws.

The purpose of such cooperative career education is learning. Both the job coach and the work station supervisor must have the skills to instruct youth so that they can develop new skills and performance competencies. In identifying personnel that will work with the disruptive youth, the job coach must be certain the individual can: (1) manage the youth's general behavior; (2) provide professional technical assistance; (3) exhibit exemplary behavior for the youth to model; (4) organize the work experiences; (5) communicate with the youth; (6) understand the career education program and the youth; and (7) recommend alternatives in the career program for the youth.

Besides the responsibilities to the youth, the job coach must recognize his responsibilities to the employer and/or placement site supervisor. The youth needs to be acquainted with the requirements of those he will be interacting with during a particular placement. If it is a business employer, the youth must be informed about the nature of the business, the fact that the business is operating for profit, that it is seeking to promote either its services or products, and, that when the youth works for an employer he tacitly accepts responsibility for promoting the business's efforts. If it is a training or school site, the youth needs to be informed about the school's needs and problems, and how he might succeed in such an environment. Should the youth refuse to cooperate with the placement site officials, he should be told of the consequences of his activity, which may be interpreted as disruptive. Termination should only follow after the youth understands both the positive and negative consequences of his actions, and has demonstrated an unwillingness or inability to interact effectively.

Delivery of services

Any program developed by a public school must establish clear operational procedures for assessment of the students' skills, delineate how a program will be provided, and the types of experiences the youth will be provided. In addition, the personnel who will participate in the vocation program must be identified. Personnel considered to be most effective with the disruptive youth are special education teachers, prevocational counselors, a psychometrician or school psychologist, and a work experience and/or a job coach. One individual, possibly a vocational coordinator, ought to be given overall program management responsibilities.

Once the disruptive youth has entered the program, it is recommended that the program proceed through five steps.

1. Diagnosis-Assessment. At this level the student is given a selected test battery (N-GATB, Durrell Reading Test and a Selected Interest Inventory) to evaluate his basic aptitude. Also, the prevocational counselor interviews the individual to identify personality (variables which may effect success or failure on the job) and determines the general career orientation of the youth.

2. Staffing. A conference is held at this point with all involved, or soon to be involved personnel. Past school and institutional records, in addition to new diagnosis-assessment data, are used to determine the youth's recommended direction in schooling, training, and job experience.

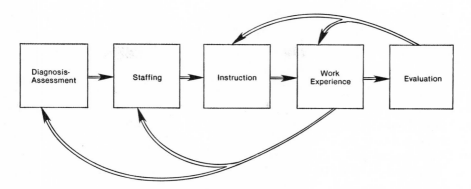

Figure 2.2 Programming Procedures

3. *Instruction.* Here the youth begins the specified program outlined in the staffing. The program may involve regular schooling, jobstudy, technical training-study, and/or prevocational orientation. The intent of this level is to provide the disruptive youth with controlled experiences, such as a specific job preparation or training in specific skills, which will enable him to develop a career profession.

4. *Work experience.* This level functions as an integral part of *instruction*. This is the point when the job coach assists the youth in adjusting to the world of work. The coach also acts as an intermediate between the youth and the employer in the event of a misunderstanding.

5. *Evaluation.* The staff reassembles to assess the progress of the student and determine what new skills and experiences ought to be provided the youth.

In the event that a difficulty with the program at either level 3 or 4 occurs, the youth can be reassessed and programmed so that his needs and levels of competencies can be accounted for in the revised curriculum.

SUMMARY

Chronic disruptive and norm-violating youth have been treated by public school, court, and correctional personnel as societal burdens. They have been provided programs that have been ineffective, watered down, and often irrelevant. The predominant skills of the personnel working with such youth are in psychology, not education. Thus, the treatment has failed to meet the educational and social needs of the student.

The literature demonstrates that many of these youths are not necessarily retarded or emotionally disturbed. They are, in fact, largely turned off and tuned out. What they need is not more therapy and advice. Rather, they need vocational direction. Given these personal directions, the disruptive youth can begin to perceive purpose to the educational experience.

Currently, disruptive youth view many programs as irrelevant and non-productive, and the efforts in developing and redeveloping meaningful programs for such youth have not proven to be successful. The reason is that they have failed to incorporate the academic, vocational, and personal needs of each student. If society is going to provide these youths with a meaningful educational experience which will enable them to contribute to society, then it is essential that a well integrated program be developed.

This requires that the schools, the courts, and counseling agencies join with the various state and community agencies, such as the Department of Employment, the Rehabilitation Services, and the United Way, so that the transition from training to employment is smoother and more successful.

The chronic disruptive norm-violating youth require a more structured and life oriented program that offers positive alternatives to social conflict. Whatever the program configuration and the personnel employed, the efficacy of the program and the youth's short and long term behavior must be assessed. Assessment neglect of vocational and career education programs has cast a shadow over these educational configurations, and has led many administrators to question whether funding should be provided. Efficacy of programs, student progress, personnel performance, delivery of services, on- and off-campus components must all come under the careful scrutiny of administrators and outside evaluators. The issue is not whether career education works, but what makes it work and how those essential changes can be made. Like democracy, freedom of speech, and human dignity, career education can become something more than an educational fad whose time has come and will soon pass.

REFERENCES

Alsop, M. "Programming for Reading Disabilities in Juvenile Delinquents." Paper presented at the Convention for the Association for Children with Learning Disabilities, March 1973.

Anandam, K., and Williams, R. "A Model for Consultation with the Classroom Teacher and Behavior Management." *The School Counselor* 18 (1971): 253–259.

Ariel, A. "Behavior Therapy for Self-Direction." Doctoral dissertation, University of Southern California, 1971. *Dissertation Abstract International* 32 (1971): 4408-A.

Atthowe, J., and Krasner, L. "The Systematic Application of Contingent Reinforcement Procedures (Token Economy) in a Large Social Setting: A Psychiatric Ward." Paper read at the American Psychiatric Association Meeting, 1965, at Chicago, Illinois.

Ausubel, D. P. *Theory and Problems of Child Development.* New York: Grune and Stratton, 1957.

Bail, J. P., and Hamilton, W. H. "A Study of the Innovative Aspects of Emerging Off-Farm Agricultural Programs at the Secondary Level and the Articulation of Such Programs with Technical College Curriculm in Agriculture." Ithaca, New York: State University of New York, 1967 (ERIC Document Reproduction Service No. ED 012 792).

Bandura, A. *Principles of Behavior Modification.* New York: Holt, Rinehart and Winston, Inc., 1969.

Borow, H. et al. *Career Guidance for a New Age.* Boston, Massachusetts: Houghton Mifflin Company, 1973.

Bruner, J. S. *Toward a Theory of Instruction.* Cambridge, Massachusetts: Belknap Press of Harvard University, 1966.

Burt, S. M., and Lessinger, L. M. *Volunteer Industry Involvement in Public Education.* Lexington, Massachusetts: Heath Lexington Books, 1970.

Cegelka, P. T. "Sex Role Stereotyping in Special Education—A Look at Secondary Work Study Programs." *Exceptional Children* 42 (1976): 323-328.

Clark, G. M., and Oliverson, B. S. "Education of Secondary Personnel: Assumptions and Preliminary Data." *Exceptional Children* 39 (1973): 541-546.

Clark, H. F., and Sloan, H. S. *Classrooms in the Factories.* New York: Fairleigh Dickinson University, 1960.

Clarke, J., and Waters, H. "Counseling the Culturally Deprived." *The School Counselor* 19 (1972): 201-209.

Clements, S. D., and Peters, J. E. "Minimal Brain Dysfunction in the School Age Child." *Educating Children with Learning Disabilities: Selected Readings.* New York: Appleton-Century-Crofts, 1967.

Closson, F. I. "Delinquency: Its Prevention Rests upon the Academic Community." *Clearing House* 45 (1971): 290-293.

Cohen, H. L.; Filipczak, J. A.; Bis, J. S.; and Cohen, J. E. "Contingencies Applicable to Special Education of Delinquents." Publication of the Institute for Behavioral Research, Inc., Silver Springs, Maryland, 1966.

Cooperative Occupational Education. Springfield, Ill: Board of Vocational Education & Rehabilitation, Division of Vocational & Technical Education, 1974.

Cowles, A.; Condon, R. W.; Falkner, J. F.; and Jackson, S. "Pre-Vocational Preparation of Exceptional Children and Youth in the City of Everett, Washington." Everett, Washington: Everett School District, 1967 (ERIC Document Reproduction Service No. ED 012 526).

Crump, W., et al. "Vocational Rehabilitation for Mentally Retarded Pupil-Clients—Final Report." Georgia State Office of Vocational Rehabilitation, 1966 (ERIC Document Reproduction Service No. ED 011 729).

Deno, E.; Henye, R.; Krantz, G.; and Barklind, K. "Retarded Youth—Their School Rehabilitation Needs—Final Report." Minneapolis, Minnesota: Minneapolis Public Schools, 1965 (ERIC Document Reproduction Service No. ED 010 926).

Dinitz, S. et al. "Delinquency Proneness and School Achievement." *Educational Research Bulletin* 36 (1957): 131–136.

Dorney, W. P. "Effectiveness of Reading Instruction in the Modification of Attitude of Adolescent Delinquent Boys." *Journal of Educational Research* 60 (1967): 438–443.

Eddy, M.; Windle, J. L.; de la Cruz, Z.; and Wolford, J. "A Cooperative Job Training Program for Retarded Youth. Part 1. The Establishment and Operation of Cooperative Work-Study Program." Lafayette, Indiana: Purdue University, 1966 (ERIC Document Reproduction Services No. 014 538).

Eichorn, D. H. "Rational for Emergence—A Look at the Middle School." Pittsburgh, Pennsylvania: University of Pittsburgh, 1967 (ERIC Document Reproduction Service No. ED 017 977).

Erickson, E. H. *Identity: Youth and Crisis.* New York: W. W. Norton, 1968.

Evans, E. D., and Potter, T. H. "Identity Crisis: A Brief Perspective." *Adolescents-Readings in Behavior and Development.* Edited by E. D. Evans. Hinsdale: The Dryden Press, Inc., 1970.

Fendrick, P., and Bond, G. "Delinquency and Reading." *Pedagogical Seminary and Journal of Genetic Psychology* 48 (1936): 236–243.

Flavell, J. H. *The Developmental Psychology of Jean Piaget.* New York: Van Nostrand Reinhold Company, 1963.

Frease, D. E. "The Schools, Self-Concept and Juvenile Delinquency." *British Journal of Criminology* 12 (1972): 133–146.

Gadlin, W., ed. "Directory of Sheltered Workshops Serving the Emotionally Disturbed." Altro, New York: Altro Health and Rehabilitation Services, 1966 (ERIC Document Reproduction Service No. ED 011 164).

Gillispie, P. H., and Fink, A. H. "The Influence of Sexism on the Education of Handicapped Children." *Exceptional Children* 41 (1974): 155–162.

Ginzberg, E. *Career Guidance.* New York: McGraw-Hill Book Company, 1971.

Glueck, E., and Glueck, S. *One Thousand Juvenile Delinquents—Their Treatment by Court and Clinic.* Cambridge: Harvard University Press, 1934.

Glueck, E., and Glueck, S. *Unraveling Juvenile Delinquency.* Cambridge, Massachusettes: Harvard University Press, 1950.

Glueck, S. S. "Home, the School and Delinquency." *Harvard Educational Review* 23 (1953): 17–32.

Goldstein, H. "Construction of a Social Learning Curriculum." *Focus on Exceptional Children* 1 (1969): 1–10.

Gorelick, M. C. "An Assessment of Vocational Realism of High School and Post-High School Educable Mentally Retarded Adolescents." Los Angeles, California: Exceptional Children's Foundation, 1966 (ERIC Document Reproduction Service No. ED 011 163).

Graubard, P. S. "Psycholinguistic Correlates of Reading Disabilities in Disturbed Children." *Journal of Special Education* 1 (1967): 363–368.

Gruelle, M. C. "A Pilot Project in Curriculum Development for 'Work Experience and Occupations' Courses for Educable Mentally Retarded Students." Oakland, California: Oakland Unified School District, 1967 (ERIC Document Reproduction Service No. ED 023 207).

Hammerlynck, L. A., and Espeseth, V. K. "Dual Specialist: Vocational Rehabilitation Counselor and Teacher of the Mentally Retarded." *Mental Retardation* 7 (1969): 49–50.

Handbook for Career Guidance Counselors. Urbana, Illinois: University of Illinois, 1975.

Hayes, J.; Hopson, B.; and Daws, P. P. *Career Guidance: The Role of the School in Vocational Development.* London, England: Heinemann Education Books, 1971.

Heggen, J. R., and Irvine, F. "A Study of the Factors that may Influence the Implementation of a Vocational Education Curriculum at the Utah State Industrial School." Utah: Utah State University, 1967 (ERIC Document Reproduction Service No. ED 016 786).

Herr, E. L. "Review and Synthesis of Foundations for Career Education." Washington, D. C.: Office of Education, 1972.

Hewett, F. M. *The Emotionally Disturbed Child in the Classroom.* Boston: Allyn and Bacon, Inc., 1968.

Hudson, J. B. "An Evaluation of the Training Provided in Correctional Institutions under the Manpower Development and Training Act, Section 251, Volume 1: Perspectives on Offender Rehabilitation—Final Report." Springfield, Virginia: National Technical Information Service, 1971.

James, P. R. "The Relationship of Vocational Outlook and Special Educational Programs for Adolescent Educable Mentally Handicapped." Urbana, Illinois: University of Illinois, 1966 (ERIC Document Reproduction Service No. ED 018 883).

Jenson, A. R., and Rohwer, W. D. "Mental Retardation, Mental Age, and Learning Rate." *Journal of Educational Psychology* 59 (1968): 402–403.

Jersild, A. T. *The Psychology of Adolescence.* New York: The MacMillan Company, 1957.

Kelgord, R. "Brain Damage and Delinquency: A Question and a Challenge." *Academic Therapy* 4 (1968–69): 93–99.

Klapper, M., and Neff, W. S. "Vocational Readiness for Young Disabled Students in New York City. A 3-Year Interim Report of a 5-Year Collaborative Study." Albany, New York: New York State Education Department, 1966 (ERIC Document Reproduction Service No. ED 015 314).

Kokaska, C. "The Need for Economic Security for the Mentally Retarded." *Preparing Teachers of Secondary Level Educable Mentally Retarded: Proposal for a New Model*. Edited by D. Brolin and B. Theruas. Menomenia, Wisconsin: Stout State University, 1971.

Kunzelman, H. P. et al. *Precision Teaching: An Initial Learning Sequence*. Seattle: Special Child Publications, 1970.

Kurtz, P. D., and Neisworth, J. T. "Self Control Possibilities for Exceptional Children." *Exceptional Children* 42 (1976): 213–217.

Kvaraceus, W. C. *Juvenile Delinquency: A Problem for the Modern World*. UNESCO, Paris, 1964.

Lazarus, A. A. *Behavior Therapy and Beyond*. New York: McGraw-Hill, 1971.

Martin, E. W. "Individualism and Behaviorism as Future Trends in Educating Handicapped Children." *Exceptional Children* 38 (1972): 517–525.

McCandless, B. R. *Adolescents—Behavior and Development*. Hinsdale: The Dryden Press, Inc. 1970.

Meichenbaum, D. H.; Bowers, K. S.; and Ross, R. R. "Modification of Classroom Behavior of Institutionalized Female Adolescent Offenders." Research report from the Ontario Reception and Diagnostic Center, Gault, Ontario, 1968.

Miller, S. R. "Secondary Assessment and Programming." Unpublished paper, 1975.

Miller, S. R.; Lotsof, A. B.; and Miller, T. "Survey of Secondary Program Needs and Directions." Unpublished report, 1976.

Mussen, P. H.; Conger, J. J.; and Kagan, J. *Child Development and Personality*. New York: Harper and Row Publishers, 1969.

National Education Association. "Regional Educational Service Agency Prototypes, Optional Statutory Arrangements and Suggestions for Implementation." Washington, D.C.: Department of Rural Education, National Education Association, 1967 (ERIC Document Reproduction Service No. 017 381).

Neff, W. S., and Koltuv, M. "Work and Mental Disorders—A Study of Factors Involved in the Rehabilitation of the Vocationally Disadvantaged Former Mental Patient—Final Report." New York: Institute for the Crippled and Disabled, 1967 (ERIC Document Reproduction Service No. ED 016 100).

New, F. E. "Guidelines, Work-Study Phase of EMR Programs." Columbus, Ohio: Ohio State Department of Education, 1972 (ERIC Document Reproduction Service No. ED 073 605).

Office of the Superintendent of Public Instruction. "Counteracting School Dropouts." *Illinois Curriculum Program,* 1967.

Oswald, H. "A National Follow-Up Study of Mental Retardates Employed by the Federal Government." Grant RD-2425-6, Washington, D.C.: Department of Vocational Rehabilitation, 1968.

Parnicky, J. J., and Kahn, H., eds. "Evaluating and Developing Vocational Potential of Institutionalized Retarded Adolescents." Bordentown, New Jersey:

Edward R. Johnstone Training and Research Center, 1963 (ERIC Document Reproduction Service No. 022 268).

Pendrak, M. "Performance Contracting and the Secondary Reading Lab." *Journal of Reading,* 17 (1974): 453–454.

Peter, L. J. *Prescriptive Teaching.* New York: McGraw-Hill Book Company, 1965.

Piaget, J. *The Mechanisms of Perception.* Translated by G. N. Sedgrim. New York: Basic Books, 1969.

Plue, W. V. "Vocational Education for the Educable Mentally Retarded. Research Monograph #11, Volume 1." Hattiesburg, Mississippi: University of South Mississippi, Bureau of Research, 1972 (ERIC Document Reproduction Service No. ED 070 900).

Positive Approaches to Dropout Prevention. U.S. Department of Health, Education and Welfare publication. #DE 73/12300, 1973.

Quay, H. C. *Juvenile Delinquency.* Princeton, New Jersey: D. Van Nostrand Company, Inc., 1965.

Raygor, B. R. "Mental Ability, School Achievement and Language Arts Achievement in the Prediction of Delinquency." *Journal of Education Research* 64 (1970): 68–72.

Rhodes, J. A. *Vocational Education and Guidance.* Columbus, Ohio: Charles E. Merrill, 1970.

Rice, F. P. *The Adolescent-Development Relationships and Culture.* Boston: Allyn and Bacon, Inc., 1975.

Roman, M. *Reaching Delinquents through Reading.* Springfield, Illinois: Thesuas, 1957.

Sabatino, D. A. "Neglect and Delinquent Children." EDC Report, Wilkes-Barre, Pennsylvania: Wilkes College, 1974.

Schlicter, K. J., and Ratliff, R. G. "Discrimination Learning in Juvenile Delinquents." *Journal of Abnormal Psychology* 77 (1971): 46–48.

Scrofani, P. J.; Suziedelis, A.; and Shore, M. F. "Conceptual Ability in Black and White Children of Different Social Classes: An Experimental Test of Jensen's Hypothesis." *American Journal of Orthopsychiatry* 43 (1973): 541–553.

Scurlock, V. C.; West, J. A.; Keith, D. L.; and Viaille, H. "Vocational Rehabilitation in Juvenile Delinquency. A Hanning Grant to Determine the Rolvof Vocational Rehabilitation in Juvenile Delinquency—Final Report." Stillwater, Oklahoma: Oklahoma State Board for Vocational Education, 1964 (ERIC Document Reproduction Service No. 052 334).

Senborn, M. P., and Niemiec, C. J. "Identifying Values of Superior High School Students." *The School Counselor* 18 (1974): 237–245.

Shaw, C. R., and McKay, H. D. *Juvenile Delinquency and Urban Areas.* Chicago: The University of Chicago Press, 1972.

Skinner, B. F. *The Technology of Teaching.* New York: Appleton-Century-Crofts, 1968.

Slack, C. W., and Schwitzgebel, R. "A Handbook: Reducing Adolescent Crime in Your Community." Privately printed, 1960. In D. A. Sabatino, *Neglected and Delinquent Children*. EDC Report, Wilkes-Barre, Pennsylvania: Wilkes College, 1974.

Sloan, C. A. "Curriculum Integration and its Implementation for Chronic-Disruptive Youth." *Integrated Career Education Handbook*. Edited by E. Sloan, S. Miller, and D. A. Sabatino. State of Illinois Department of Corrections, 1975.

Smith, G. "The Mentally Retarded: Is the Public Employment Service Prepared to Serve Them?" *Mental Retardation* 8 (1970): 26–29.

Smith, L. L., and Riebock, J. "A Middle School Tries Contractual Reading." *The Clearing House* 45 (1971): 404–406.

Staats, A. W., and Butterfield, W. H. "Treatment of Non-Reading in a Culturally Deprived Juvenile Delinquent: An Application of Reinforcement Principles." Child Development, 1965. In A. Bandura, *Principles of Behavior Modification*. New York: Holt, Rinehart, and Winston, Inc., 1969.

Steffy, R. "A Treatment of Schizophrenic Patients by Operant Conditioning." Personal Communication, 1966. In D. A. Sabatino, *Neglected and Delinquent Children*, EDC Report, Wilkes-Barre, Pennsylvania: Wilkes College, 1974.

Strauss, Alfred A., and Lehtinen, L. E. *Psychopathology and Education of the Brain-Injured Child*. New York: Grune and Stratton, 1947, p. 55.

U.S. Department of Labor. "Dictionary of Occupational Titles, Volumes I and II, 1965." Washington, D.C.: U.S. Government Printing Office, 1965.

U.S. Department of Labor. "Supplement to the Dictionary of Occupational Titles, 1968." Washington, D.C.: U.S. Government Printing Office, 1968.

U.S. Department of Labor. "Supplement of the Occupational Outlook Handbook, 1974–75." Washington, D.C.: U.S. Government Printing Office, 1974.

Wade, A., and Shertzer, B. "Anxiety Reduction through Vocational Counseling." *Vocational Guidance Quarterly* 19 (1970): 46–49.

Wagner, H. "Attitudes of and toward Disadvantaged Students." *Adolescence* 7 (1972): 435–446.

Walle, E. "Learning Disabilities and Juvenile Delinquency." Paper presented at the International Conference of the Association for Children with Learning Disabilities, 1972, at Atlantic City, New Jersey.

Walter, H. E., and Krenzler, G. D. "Early Identification of the School Dropout." *The School Counselor* 18 (1970): 97–104.

Wilkinson, L.; Saunders, J. T.; and Reppucci, N. D. "The Development of a Behavioral System for an Established Institution: A Preliminary Statement." Project report presented at the Fifth Annual Meeting of the Association for the Advancement of Behavioral Therapies, September 1971, at Washington, D.C.

Williamson, E. G. *Vocational Counseling: Some Historical, Philosophical and Theoretical Perspectives*. New York: McGraw-Hill Book Company, 1965.

Work Experience and Career Exploration Guide. Springfield, Illinois: Board of Vocational Education and Rehabilitation, Division of Vocational and Technical Education, 1974.

Work Experience and Career Exploration Guide. Springfield, Illinois: Board of Vocational Education and Rehabilitation, Division of Vocational and Technical Education, 1975.

3

behavior modification with adolescent problems

DOUGLAS CULLINAN

Widespread interest and controversy has lately grown around programs for dealing with adolescent learning, conduct, and adjustment by means of *behavior modification*. Behavior modification treatments, and those purporting to be so, have been applied to many maladaptive behavior patterns in a wide range of educational, correctional, and related settings involving adolescents and youth. This chapter presents a behavioral conceptualization of the acquisition and performance of maladjusted behavior, basic assumptions underlying behavior modification intervention, a brief description of intervention techniques, and three composite behavioral treatments for adolescent adjustment problems.

The efforts of most teachers, caseworkers, counselors, therapists, and other helping professionals are guided to some extent by the intervention philosophies subscribed to. Readers are no doubt aware of many theories about the causes of adolescent maladjustment and norm-violation. The causal variables emphasized in favored theories affect both how a professional perceives an adolescent's deviance and which interventions are selected for use. Therefore, practitioners must recognize and critically examine assumptions which guide their intervention activities.

In the following section, a behavioral viewpoint on adolescent deviance is described and contrasted to the personality model of deviance. Although there is no single behavioral theory, the behavioral viewpoint does give more emphasis to certain factors in the development and maintenance misconduct. These factors will later be translated into procedures for behavior modification intervention.

DEVIANT PERSONALITY

Many accounts of adolescent deviance are based on personality theories which assume that behavior is merely outward evidence of inner personality tendencies; that is, stable predispositions or motivations to act and think consistently, even when circumstances vary widely. According to personality theories, deviant behaviors are impelled by mental forces (often abnormal ones) of which the individual may be partially or totally unaware. The exact nature of these forces depends on the particular level of analysis chosen.

Deviant personality has been traced, for instance, to biological factors, such as evolved tendencies to aggress (Lorenz, 1966; Storr, 1970), unusual characteristics of nervous system functioning (Eysenck, 1964; Hare, 1970), or chromosomal irregularities (Court Brown, 1969; Polani, 1967). Other analyses point to mental structures or states, proposing that intrapsychic tensions (Slavson, 1961), impoverished self-image (Vorrath, 1972; Reckless, 1961), defective ego or superego functioning (Reiss, 1952), underdeveloped conscience (Weiner, 1970), or other unfortunate mental conditions are implicated in personalities which generate or cannot inhibit performance of disruptive, or otherwise deviant behavior.

Captivating and imaginative as they are, interpretations of adolescent behavior problems as signs of either inborn disabilities to acquire cultural norms or inner personality forces warped by unfortunate earlier experiences, carry certain practical drawbacks. For example, deviant personality tendencies typically are both inferred from current deviant behavior and used to explain subsequent deviant behavior. Explanations based on the circular logic can cause practitioners to overlook important situational determinants of deviant behavior while they search for medical or mental evidence which supports a personality explanation. An additional shortcoming of many personality models of disturbance is that causal factors are seldom stated in terms specific enough to permit an objective evaluation of those factors. Thus, the model can indefinitely remain immune from scientific scrutiny and continue to generate treatment applications of unknown worth. In fact, there is little evidence for the effectiveness of personality-based treatments for adolescent maladjustment (Levitt, 1971; Guttman, 1963).

Behavioral view of deviance

A distinctly different conceptualization of adolescent deviancy arises from the psychological technology of *behavior analysis*. In behavior analysis, the existence of covert mental events, personal feelings, remote childhood experiences, or biological conditions is not necessarily denied, but the importance of these factors is de-emphasized in planning for meaningful changes in deviant behavior patterns. Instead, an adolescent's behavior, deviant or otherwise, is viewed in terms of current environmental circumstances, including events produced by the behavior of others and by the adolescent's own behavior, as well as impersonal events. It is convenient to consider separately the ways in which deviant behavior is *acquired* and the factors which *maintain* it.

Acquisition. Children are often directly trained to behave in disruptive or otherwise deviant ways. For example, disputes between a child and an adult or another child are often resolved on the basis of whoever can coerce the other more effectively. Coercive child behavior such as demanding, crying, screaming, pushing, or hitting often produces compliance by the other party in the dispute; this compliance encourages the coercer to employ similar disruptive behavior in subsequent disputes (Patterson, Cobb, & Ray, 1973). Further, if mild coercion is initially unsuccessful, the child learns to use more intense forms.

In addition adults often unintentionally train deviance by allocating most of their attention to disturbing behavior patterns rather than prosocial and adaptive ones. When youngsters behave deviantly, parents and teachers frequently attempt correction through appeals for proper behavior, criticism, shouted commands, or discussion of the problem. It has repeatedly been shown that these tactics are often only temporarily effective, and that adult attention (even unfavorable attention) can encourage deviant child behavior in the long run (Becker, Madsen, Arnold, & Thomas, 1967).

Children also learn deviant behavior by observing family, peer, or community persons model disruptive and norm-violating modes of behavior. If, as is the case in some subcultures or communities, there are many persons who exhibit deviant behavior, the children are repeatedly exposed to disruptive behavior. Films, television, reading matter, and verbal accounts of aggression or lawbreaking are also rich sources of information on how to act deviantly.

The above descriptions of some of the ways in which disruptive behavior is learned do not exhaust the possibilities. They are merely intended to show that personality assumptions such as biological predispositions, warped mental forces, or mysterious inner impulses are not required to account for the acquisition of norm-violating behavior. Almost all children are exposed to models and unintentional training of deviate behavior. Only a fraction engages in patterns of behavior which eventually are likely to bring them to the attention of the helping professions.

Maintenance. The performance of deviant behavior can be strengthened and sustained by the direct consequences it produces. Some of the consequences of disruptive, norm-violating, or other deviant behavior are obvious: possession of tangible items which otherwise would be unavailable, income to support everyday nondisruptive activities; escape from distasteful requirements such as employment or education; acclaim from deviant peers and increased status in their eyes; or access to prohibited privileges. Since these desirable consequences are often more immediate and predictable than adverse consequences such as retaliation from victims, criticism and censure, or apprehension by the police, it is understandable how the consequences of some deviant behavior serve to support this behavior.

Deviant behavior is also influenced vicariously because people judge the success of others' actions and regulate their behavior accordingly. When a child's peers violate rules, rarely get punished, and enjoy the benefits of their deviant activities, the child may be motivated to behave similarly. Aside from direct consequences and vicarious influences, self-control is also an important factor governing deviant behavior. For instance, through instructions, direct training, and example, adolescents learn to set standards for their own social behavior and to reward (or punish) their own behavior if it meets (or falls short of) those standards. By aiming for antisocial goals and self-rewarding for achievement of these, norm-violating adolescents could maintain deviant behavior patterns despite repeated penalties and intensive contact with rehabilitation programs.

To recapitulate, the abundance of opportunities for acquiring deviant behavior suggests that almost any adolescent is capable of aggressive, disruptive, norm-violating, or other deviant behavior. More important are the factors which govern whether these types of activities are likely to be performed. Direct behavioral consequences, vicarious effects, and self-control systems are three main ways in which performance of behavior is regulated; virtually any deviant behavior pattern could be accounted for in terms of these situational influences. By analyzing these factors and manipulating ones which can control behavioral problems, rehabilitative personnel may employ behavior modification to catalyze important improvements in the life patterns of deviant youth.

BEHAVIOR MODIFICATION ASSUMPTIONS

Behavior modification is not a unitary technology of intervention. For many reasons—incomplete or conflicting evidence on certain issues, differences in training and personal philosophies, etc.—there is a good deal of variability among adherents as to which techniques of analysis and modification receive greater emphasis. However, certain points of agreement exist among the various versions of the behavioral approach. The most important of these are discussed in the following section, which includes one way in which behavior modification interventions can be categorized. Important details beyond the scope of this brief discussion, such as origins and development of behavior modification, research considerations, evidence for various aspects of the behavioral approach, mistaken and valid conceptions of or objections to behavior modification, ethical considerations, and other important areas are available in many sources (Bandura, 1969; Kanfer & Phillips, 1970; Kazdin, 1975; O'Leary & Wilson, 1975).

Observable phenomena

One major thrust of the behavioral approach is its focus on observable phenomena. For a variety of reasons, behavior modification is concerned with changing the behavior of the person in need of intervention rather than his supposedly defective personality traits, maladjusted mental states, or other presumptive conditions. To do this, the actual behavior to be changed (target behavior) must be stated in such unambiguous terms that a minimum of inference is required in judgments as to whether the target behavior has occurred or not. Alternatively, easily measurable products of behavior can be used as the data in a behavior modification intervention. That is, if an adolescent is to be taught to accurately fill out a job application blank, it makes little difference whether the actual behavior of writing in the pertinent information is observed directly or the completed application is checked; in this case, measurement of the product (the completed application) is tantamount to observing the behavior (unless someone else could have completed it for him).

There are other observable phenomena besides the target behavior which must be specified. Environmental conditions associated with the target behavior require some attention. Behavior always happens in some situational context, including those things which happen before the behavior occurs and those which happen afterward. Many behaviors are selected for change because they occur under the wrong circumstances.

For instance, cursing per se is unlikely to be seen as adolescent deviancy, but cursing in the presence of teachers or following parental requests might be considered part of an adolescent's maladjustment, because his cursing behavior is performed without proper regard to the situation. On the other hand, some problems may stem from target behavior which is too discriminating, that is, which occurs in a maladaptively limited number of circumstances. The fact that many interventions, behavior modification and otherwise, can produce target behavior changes in certain circumstances—classroom, group home, detention center, caseworker's office, etc.—but the improved behaviors do not necessarily generalize to untrained situations. Behavior modification interventions explicitly recognize that behavior is often situation-specific; therefore, the situations in which behavior change is to occur must be specified. In the process of specifying the circumstances in which target behavior is to occur, information about these circumstances may come to light which can aid decisions about intervention practices.

Additionally, observing the events which typically follow target behavior is very important. If a target behavior is not being performed enough, the environment may be devoid of a consequence which could strengthen and support that behavior. If a target behavior occurs too often, there may be some consequence which is supporting the deviant behavior. In either of these cases, careful scrutiny of the consequential environment of a behavior may suggest an intervention strategy.

In addition to careful specification of the target behavior and the environment (antecedent and consequent) in which the behavior occurs, the focus on observable phenomena issue requires that intervention practices be specified in such a way that they could be exactly duplicated by other helping professionals. This point is somewhat redundant with the foregoing requirements, because intervention practices are activities carried out with a specific target behavior, before and after occurrence of that behavior.

When helping professionals come into contact with adolescent deviancy, the problems of maladjustment are generally stated in the form of a complaint which is not amenable to behavioral intervention. Keeping in mind behavior modification's focus on observable phenomena, the complaint must be restated in directly measurable terms. For instance, *aggression* may be restated in terms of certain types of physical contact between the adolescent and other persons; statements which threaten harm to others; damage to or disruption of the property of others, etc. *Poor self-image* might be restated in terms of compliance with unwarranted demands of peers; statements of one's own incompetence, unworthiness, or unattractiveness; failure to engage in a task a second time following a first unsuccessful attempt at the task; etc. Although complaints such as aggression or poor self-image may refer to more phenomena than can be specified and observed, correction of only those which can be specified and observed will very likely go a long way toward remediation of the complaint. If necessary, subsequent interventions can focus on uncorrected aspects of the problem.

Depending on how the complaint or problem is stated, intervention may attempt to reduce some target behavior and increase others. In many intervention programs, it is necessary to work on various behaviors simultaneously, reducing some, increasing others.

Target assessment

After the problems of an adolescent are stated so that observable phenomena are focused on, regular, repetitive measurement of target behaviors or other observables is undertaken. The most obvious rationale for this is that relatively objective information as to the effectiveness of an intervention is required. Reliance upon informal judgment, intuitive impression, or clinical estimate of improvement may reflect changes in judgmental standards as often as actual changes in target behavior.

Of course, changes in measurement standards may take place even when target behavior has been carefully specified, possibly misrepresenting the extent of behavior change. This danger is reduced in behavior analysis by a requirement that a second observer independently measure target behavior concurrently with the main observer on several occasions throughout the behavior modification project. If the two observers are not substantially in agreement, adjustments in the operational definition of target behavior must be made. On the other hand, if agreement is obtained there is reason to believe that recording will accurately represent the status of the target behavior. Interobserver agreement considerations are described in many texts on behavior modification (Hall, 1971; Kazdin, 1975).

Another rationale for ongoing assessment of target behavior is that the extent of the target behavior prior to intervention provides valuable information for treatment decisions. Adults who make complaints about adolescent deviancy often hold different standards for deviancy; varieties, intensities, and frequencies of behavior which are intolerable to some may not be noticed by others. In fact, measurement of pre-intervention levels of target behavior may occasionally show that the complaint about the adolescent was inaccurate because the extent of his target deviant behavior was about the same as that of peers who were not complained about. In this case, assuming that the adult had a legitimate complaint, it would then be necessary to reconsider exactly which behavior was actually the source of disturbance and therefore the target of intervention.

Ideally, certain characteristics of the target behavior (how often it occurs, whether it has definite beginning and ending points, whether it results in a tangible product, etc.) indicate preferred methods of assessment. Different strategies for carrying out the regular, repetitive measurement necessary in behavior modification are described in detail elsewhere (Cooper, 1974; Hall, 1971). Practical limitations usually dictate the strategies used and the situations selected for recording, however.

Effectiveness verification

Given that the target behavior and other important observable phenomena involved have been clearly described, and that an appropriate assessment procedure has been provided, the helping professional is in a position to evaluate the effect of his intervention on the target behavior. A built-in capability for skeptical self-scrutiny is an important contribution of the behavioral viewpoint to the helping professions. Through the use of appropriate verification evaluation designs, the effects of behavioral or other intervention practices on target behavior can be determined, not only after intervention (as in group research designs) but in detail, during intervention. Interventions which are ineffective for particular problems or individuals can be put aside, the relative effectiveness of different treatments for particular problems can be compared, the most powerful components of a generally effective intervention can be identified, and other information can be gathered. These verification designs can be used in combination with group research designs where sufficient subjects are involved.

Two of the verification designs for scrutiny of treatment effectiveness are described below. Helping professionals who, whenever possible, employ these to evaluate their interventions with deviant adolescents are joining in an effort to move treatment beyond its present standing as little more than a craft.

Multiple-baseline design. Suppose that a detention center caseworker counsels three boys, Al, Bob, and Charles, 30 minutes each day on an individual basis. The goal of counseling is meaningful discussion of the problems which could lead to later parole violations, but most of counseling time is usually wasted because each boy constantly gripes about petty institutional grievances. The caseworker decides to note the duration of this griping on a daily basis by unobtrusively starting a stopwatch when griping begins, stopping it when griping ceases, restarting the watch when griping is renewed. The caseworker also carefully considers what griping is, and writes this down so as to reduce the risk of day-to-day shifts in his criteria for recording griping.

During the initial phases of this project, whenever Al, Bob, or Charles griped, the caseworker sympathetically assured the boy that he understood how annoying the grievances were, then firmly attempted to redirect the conversation toward more relevant areas of discussion (post-release adjustment). This Sympathy and Redirection treatment had also characterized his counseling technique with these boys prior to data collection.

Beginning on day 7, the caseworker used a different strategy during Al's counseling sessions. Recording of gripes proceeded as usual but each time Al griped, the caseworker intentionally ignored the boy by either looking away, attending to paperwork, giving the appearance of being bored, or in some other way showing disinterest in his client. When there was a pause in the griping, the caseworker directed conversation toward the relevant topics. Also, if Al made statements pertaining to post-release adjustment, the caseworker gave the boy his total attention by looking at him, nodding, and entering into dialogues. This new strategy took place only with Al during days 7 to 13; with Bob and Charles, the Sympathy and Redirection technique remained in effect.

The caseworker's subjective impression was that the new procedure was having no effect on Al's griping, but when the graphic record of gripes (see Figure 3.1) was considered, a small but consistent decline in wasteful griping was noted. This encouraged the caseworker, but he realized that many institutional happenings besides his new counseling tactics could have been responsible for the decline. Beginning on the 14th day he decided to use these tactics in Bob's counseling session as well as Al's, maintaining the original tactics with Charles. The graphic record showed clearly that the level of griping during counseling dropped for Al, then for Bob, and for each boy only after the Ignore Griping procedure was put into effect. Yet Charles' griping continued at a high level under the original counseling conditions. The caseworker was becoming convinced that his changed counseling tactics, rather than other factors, were responsible for the desired effects on behavior, because it would be an unlikely coincidence that the other factors affected Al, then Bob, only after the caseworker began his new procedures. To assure himself beyond reasonable doubt, the caseworker extended the ignoring treatment to Charles' counseling sessions beginning on day 23. The results of the entire project are graphed in Figure 3.1.

After 30 days, the caseworker discontinued recording minutes of griping. He had not only provided desired change in the boys' behavior but, perhaps more important, was able to state with confidence how he

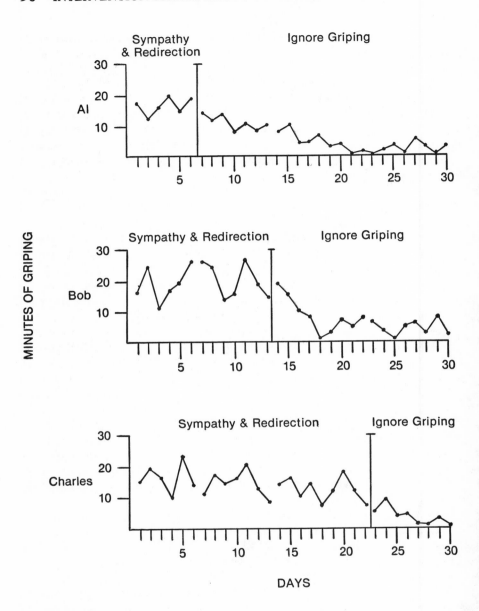

Figure 3.1 Multiple-Baseline Design

had done this. In other words, he had located environmental events (in this case, his own social attention) which potentially could modify Al's, Bob's and Charles' behavior, and had verified that these events, not unknown influences, were responsible for the behavior change.

The above case involved evaluating a treatment designed to reduce griping by the use of a *multiple baseline* verification procedure. In this strategy, several behaviors (the same behavior of several people, different behaviors of the same person, or a single behavior of one person in different settings) are measured simultaneously. A specific treatment is implemented for one of the behaviors; if the behavior changes in the desired direction, the same treatment is extended to the next behavior being measured. If this behavior also is modified, the treatment is extended to the third behavior, and so on. If, after implementation of the treatment sequentially on several behaviors, each behavior is predictably changed, the most reasonable conclusion is that the treatment produced the changes.

Reversal Design. Besides the multiple baseline design, another procedure for determining treatment effectiveness is the *reversal* design. As in the multiple baseline design, behavior (or the product of behavior) is regularly measured throughout a project. The different conditions to be contrasted (often intervention vs. nonintervention) are repeatedly instituted and withdrawn. If during intervention periods desired behavior changes occur, but are not present during nonintervention periods, a cause-effect relationship between treatment and changed behavior becomes believable.

For example, the teacher of a junior high remedial reading class was disturbed by the fact that many pupils came to class late. The late pupils not only missed instruction themselves but their tardy arrival disrupted the flow of teaching for others. In order to quantify her idea about the extent of the problem, the teacher defined a pupil as tardy if he was not seated when the class bell began to ring. Each day the number of tardies to this class was tallied with the use of a small button-operated golf score counter. More than 10 pupils were tardy on each of the first three days; this period served as a nonintervention baseline against which subsequent changes in tardiness could be contrasted.

Toward the end of the third day, the teacher divided the class into three teams of seven pupils. A poster for each team displayed the names of team members. She announced that the class learning center, which contained comic books, paperbacks, language training games, and other activities very popular with the pupils, would be reserved each day for the team which had the fewest tardies that day. The winning team could enter the learning center during the last 15 minutes of the period; in case of ties, the 15 minutes was to be split equally among tied teams. This *promptness contest* was in effect for the next four days.

Both by subjective judgment and by consulting her graphic record (see Figure 3.2), the teacher knew that tardies were much less frequent during the promptness contest (averaging 5 per day) than before (more than 11 per day on the average). Was this reduction due to the contest? Between

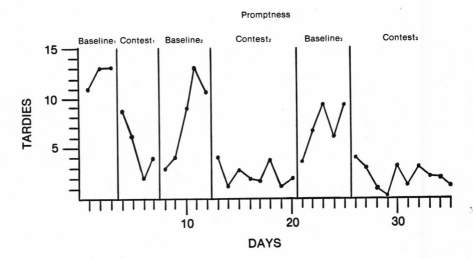

Figure 3.2 Reversal Design

days 3 and 4 many things happened which could conceivably have produced less tardiness. The teacher reasoned that if her promptness contest was the important factor, discontinuing the contest would probably produce a reversal of the improved level of tardiness.

The contest was discontinued on days 8 to 12; during these days, access to the learning center area was available to anyone who finished regular class assignments early. The increased level of tardiness during this time suggested that the teacher's reasoning was correct. During the next several weeks (days 13 to 35), repeated implementation and withdrawal of the promptness contest resulted in a convincing demonstration that other influences were not involved, since it was unreasonable that these would have come into play only during contest periods. The entire promptness contest project is represented by Figure 3.2.

This method of alternately applying and withdrawing treatment conditions in order to confirm or disconfirm the ability of a treatment to produce desired changes is called a *reversal verification* procedure. The number of required alternations between treatment application and withdrawal depends on the magnitude and stability of the changes produced, and on how convincing the demonstration must be. As with the multiple baseline verification design, the reversal design is well suited for testing the effectiveness of many types of intervention, not merely behavior modification treatments. There are other designs, but these two are well suited for application to one or a few children.

Verifying that a specific treatment technique is responsible for improved functioning is not an idle research exercise. Counselors, educators, therapists, and other professionals know that there are myriads of treatments available, each recommended by its own set of authorities. The professional who works with deviant adolescents wants these children to improve, but wants also to know with some confidence whether or not the treatment used was responsible for the improvement. Analysis of an intervention technique by use of the multiple baseline or reversal design leads to more confident decisions about the role of an intervention in a particular improvement. By verifying the effectiveness of a treatment (or demonstrating its lack of effectiveness), the professional is more able to intelligently select appropriate treatments for subsequent problems and to recommend demonstrably effective treatments to fellow workers.

BEHAVIOR MODIFICATION PROCEDURES

In general, any intervention which focuses on observable phenomena, involves regular, repetitive measurement of these phenomena, and evaluates the course of measured phenomena by means of a verification design, satisfies the requirements of behavior analysis. In other words, interventions based on psychoanalytic theory, self theories, or any philosophical basis could undergo these verification procedures, and nonbehavioral treatments should be evaluated in this way. However, there are a number of treatment procedures which are more commonly associated with behavior modification. These interventions have satisfied the foregoing criteria with such a wide range of clients, situations, and problems that they are considered "good bets" by behavior modifiers.

Many behavioral techniques are concerned with regulating the performance of behavior which is already familiar; other techniques promote behavioral competence by facilitating the acquisition of information about how to behave. The performance regulation techniques are discussed first; they can be subdivided into techniques for strengthening or increasing behavior, and those for weakening or decreasing behavior.

Regulating performance

Strengthening behavior. Behavior may be strengthened through direct reinforcement techniques, which capitalize on the fact that a behavior which currently produces favorable environmental changes is more likely to be performed in a similar future situation. By intentionally arranging environmental events which follow behavior, behavior modifiers have changed a wide range of simple and complex human behavior, ranging from thumb twitches (Sasmor, 1966), smiling (Brackbill, 1958), and heartbeats (Weiss & Engle, 1971) to conflict negotiation (Kifer, Lewis, Green & Phillips, 1974), improved reading (Staats & Butterfield, 1965), and creative activity (Glover, 1974).

Reinforcement is the process in which a behavior becomes stronger (more likely to occur) as a result of its producing environmental consequences. All rewards do not necessarily reinforce behavior, and an event which reinforces behavior is not necessarily perceived by the individual as subjectively pleasant. An increase in the frequency or other strength of the target behavior is what indicates the operation of reinforcement.

Some forms of direct reinforcement are termed *positive reinforcement*. In positive reinforcement, something is added to the environment (a positive reinforcer) following a behavior, and the behavior is strengthened. Typical positive reinforcers include interpersonal attention (praise, recognition, sometimes even criticism); consumable, symbolic, or other tangible items (cigarettes or gum, money or other tokens, gifts); and access to desirable activities (opportunity to be alone, time spent in a recreation area, opportunity to talk with a counselor). Positive reinforcement was used to increase membership in an urban recreation room program for children and teenagers (Pierce & Risley, 1974). In order to encourage recreation within the structured program (rather than in the neighborhood at large), recreation program membership drives were conducted in which children who brought in new members received one extra hour of recreation time and had their names posted. Not only was membership increased dramatically, but a reversal design showed that the positive reinforcement procedures were responsible for this beneficial effect.

Another kind of direct reinforcement is called *negative reinforcement*. Negative reinforcement is a process in which something is subtracted from the environment (a negative reinforcer) following behavior, and the behavior is strengthened. Suppose that all the residents of an institution for chronic disruptive youths are required to get a short haircut every two weeks. This requirement can be avoided, however, by any boy who completes and turns in all remedial reading exercises assigned for the two-week period preceding a haircut. Boys who fulfill this requirement are excused from the haircut; and if they repeatedly fulfill the requirement and avoid haircuts, it is a negative reinforcement procedure.

In addition to direct reinforcement, behavior can be strengthened through *vicarious reinforcement* procedures. Vicarious reinforcement is in operation when an observer witnesses the behavior of a model, and as a result, some behavior of the observer is strengthened. There are several variations of vicarious reinforcement (Bandura, 1969). Often the model is seen to receive favorable consequences for his action, and the observer behaves similarly in order to receive those benefits. On the other hand, if the model is prestigious in the eyes of the observer (is known to be very competent, possesses desirable resources or status, etc.), the model's behavior may be imitated even though no favorable consequences are observed. Additionally, if the model's behavior violates known rules or conventions but no unfavorable consequences are forthcoming, similar behavior in the observer may be vicariously reinforced.

In one demonstration of vicarious reinforcement, young delinquents learned to give up immediate benefits in order to obtain even greater delayed rewards by watching other delinquents (whom they respected) engage in delay of gratification (Stumphauzer, 1972). Vicarious reinforcement procedures are more difficult to implement than direct reinforcement techniques; but since vicarious reinforcement is occurring unintentionally and in unstructured ways all the time, it is a potentially powerful method of behavior modification which should be more widely used.

Another means of strengthening behavior is through *self-reinforcement* procedures. Self-reinforcement is similar to direct reinforcement except that the individual is also the manager of his own environment. Adolescents can be taught several strategies which can lead to self-reinforcement: careful observation and recording of one's own target behavior, setting standards for behavior or giving directions to oneself, and applying positive or negative reinforcement to one's own behavior. Self-reinforcement was the intervention procedure in a project to improve various task-oriented behaviors of pupils in a junior high school class (Broden, Hall, & Mitts, 1971). A girl who did not consistently perform assigned classwork was taught to mark herself as on-task when she was performing assignments appropriately. Evaluation with a reversal design showed that not only was the self-recording procedure an effective way of strengthening on-task behavior, but it was also as effective as a direct reinforcement intervention used by the teacher (praise for on-task behavior). Self-recording has also been used to increase work performance and other adaptive behaviors of institutionalized juvenile offenders (Seymour & Stokes, 1976).

Weakening behavior. Other performance regulation techniques are designed to weaken or decrease behavior. Behavior modification techniques for weakening behavior are more or less the reverse of ones for increasing behavior.

Behavior which is repeatedly ineffective in achieving any change in the environment will less frequently be performed in the future; this is the *extinction* process. Procedures using extinction involve identifying the events which reinforce a particular behavior so that they can be prevented from occurring after that behavior, rendering the behavior futile. Many disruptive verbal or motoric behaviors in classroom, home, institution, or other setting function to focus social attention on the behavior. In many of these instances, the behavior will weaken and eventually cease if other persons will carefully ignore the unwanted response.

Human behavior is, fortunately, responsive to the unfavorable effects it produces. The process of punishment is in effect when behavior is followed by unfavorable additions to or subtractions from the environment, and the behavior is weakened. Penalties, admonitions, and chastisements do not necessarily function as punishment; conversely, punishment often occurs without pain or physical coercion. In other words, in the behavior modification context, punishment is said to take place when target behavior produces consequences and becomes less likely to recur.

Depending on the nature of the unfavorable event which follows the target behavior, punishment may be of two types. *Aversive punishment* is indicated when behavior is weakened due to the addition of something to the environment which follows the behavior. For instance, the teacher of low-track high school english classes reduced disruptive actions of pupils talking and turning around by consistently using a reprimand as the consequence for instances of these behaviors (McAllister, Stachowiak, Baer, & Conderman, 1969). Although in this particular case a verification design was used to show that the systematic use of reprimands was effective in punishing disruptive talking and turning around, adult reprimands are frequently ineffective in reducing adolescents' deviance.

Another direct punishment procedure is called *cost punishment*. The cost punishment procedure is in effect when target behavior produces subtraction of something from the environment which follows the behavior, and the behavior is weakened. One common cost punishment strategy with adolescent deviant behavior is the use of fines in a token economy: inappropriate behaviors cost the adolescent some of the tokens previously earned through appropriate behavior.

A cost punishment intervention was applied to disruptively high noise levels in public school home economics classrooms of behaviorally disordered and other girls (Wilson & Hopkins, 1973). Popular music was played over a radio for the girls to listen to while they carried out assigned tasks; during intervention, the music was interrupted briefly when talking and other noise exceeded a certain level. A verification design demonstrated that this intervention effectively punished noisy behavior and produced a tolerably quiet classroom.

A variation of cost punishment is termed *time out from reinforcement*. If any situation contains many sources of social and other positive reinforcement for behavior, a brief period of deprivation from these desirable events can serve to punish whatever behavior it follows. A time-out punishment procedure was used to reduce rule violations, other disruptions, and threats to peers by the leader of a group of institutionalized delinquent adolescents (Brown & Tyler, 1968). Time-out is particularly subject to faulty application and abuse, and requires special caution and planning when it is employed.

Another way in which behavior is weakened is through vicarious punishment. In vicarious punishment, the behavior of an observer is discouraged as a result of his witnessing the behavior of a model. The model's behavior may have produced unfavorable consequences; the model may have followed rules or otherwise acted appropriately, but was not seen to receive rewards; or the behavior witnessed may have been performed by an incompetent, despicable, or otherwise disrespected model. In each of these cases, the observer is less likely to perform the behavior which was modeled.

Behavior can also be weakened through *self-punishment* procedures. Self-punishment is closely analogous to self-reinforcement in that target behavior may be weakened through close self-observation and/or recording, the self-setting of criteria or standards, and self-dispensed penalties.

Promoting acquisition

In addition to behavior modification procedures for regulating the performance of familiar behavior, behavioral interventions often promote the acquisition of competence to behave. Although it may be true that "there is nothing new under the sun," behavior which an individual has never performed before is novel to him. Novel behavior includes new combinations or sequences of smaller, familiar behavioral components; performance of familiar behavior under circumstances in which the behavior has not been performed before; and behavior which was not previously possible due to organismic limitations.

Persons who are to acquire a new ability often possess skills which vaguely resemble the one to be learned. The new ability may arise from present behavior through a series of gradual behavior steps, each of which is a closer approximation to the terminal skill to be learned. Each of the successive approximations to the terminal skill may be reinforced directly by the environment (if increasing skill produces increasing payoff) or they may be self-reinforced (as the learner sees that he is becoming more proficient).

Shaping is an intervention in which the progressively closer behavioral approximations to a final behavior goal are intentionally reinforced. Shaping was used by Schwitzgebel and Kolb (1964) to induce deviant youths in a community to promptly attend counseling sessions and to perform in desirable ways during couseling. Shaping was also used by Tharp and Wetzel (1969) to increase verbal responses to requests. In this application, deviant children and adolescents were asked to supply information about their own activity, and item preferences and dislikes. This information is then used in selecting potentially powerful consequences for target behavior and persons who could dispense them. Children who initially gave no or few responses to the questionnaire items were reinforced with consumables and praise for providing progressively more detailed responses. Shaping can be a powerful technique for inducing desired responses; however, it is often tedious, laborious, and time consuming.

Alternatively, novel responses can be transmitted through observational learning, a process in which attentive observers acquire competence to perform novel behavior from a skillful model. If intricate or highly unfamiliar behavior is to be demonstrated, observational learning can be enhanced by carefully sequencing the behaviors to be learned; demonstrating the behavior repeatedly using one or several models; drawing the observer's attention to particular aspects of the demonstration; and encouraging the observer to use strategies for remembering what he observed (such as verbal labels, mental imagery, overt or mental rehearsal of the behavior, etc.).

It should be clear from the preceding discussion that behavior modification involves few mind-blowing new psychological principles. In fact, many of the techniques correspond to common sense. Translating these treatment principles into successful practice is not always a simple matter, however, especially with deviant adolescents. Some of the basic requirements involve time and effort which many practitioners are unwilling to expend (for example, the regular assessment requirement).

It is reiterated that almost any intervention technique could be considered a behavior modification treatment if it satisfies certain prerequisites, that is, focus on observable phenomena, repetitive assessment of these phenomena, and evaluation within some type of verification research design. Conversely, teachers, counselors, rehabilitation workers, therapists, and other helping professionals often claim to employ behavior modification merely because they pass out trinkets, generously praise, use threats or seclusion, or ignore complaints; but obviously these practices are not necessarily behavior modification.

It is often helpful to conceptualize adolescent's problems and potential interventions in terms of the above behavior modification techniques. However, in actual practice single techniques are rarely used.

Important and complex problems of adjustment are not likely to be solved in simple ways, and many of the successful programs have been based on concurrent and successive use of various simple techniques in a composite intervention. The possibilities for combining the behavioral techniques are very large and many have, perhaps, yet to be explored. Three successful composite behavior modification interventions are presented below.

COMPOSITE BEHAVIOR MODIFICATION TECHNIQUES

Behavioral contracting

One widely used composite behavior modification strategy is called behavior contracting. A behavioral contract is a document which specifies relationships between behaviors and consequences. The contract specifies in some detail the desired consequences (privileges) and the behavior required of the adolescent before these privileges will become available (responsibilities). Responsibilities and privileges are arrived at by negotiation between the adolescent and his parents, his teachers, or other authorities who wish behavior change. Often, these negotiations are referred by a counseling behavior modifier.

There are several important elements which help insure effective behavioral contracting. Responsibilities and privileges must be stated in some detail to avoid later grief due to loopholes, misinterpretations, and so on. The responsibilities to be performed by the adolescent must be easily measurable. Responsibilities which require arbitrary judgments on the part of the observer, which are a lot of trouble to observe and record, or which are performed at times or places which are not monitorable, are not suitable for inclusion into a behavioral contract. The relationship between responsibilities and privileges goes both ways; that is, when responsibilities are not performed, privileges are not dispensed, but when responsibilities are discharged, the privilege must be forthcoming.

In addition to arrangements in which completed responsibilities yield privileges while neglected ones do not produce the privileges, other incentives are often written into a behavioral contract. For example, performance of responsibilities which is highly consistent or otherwise above and beyond what was expected may receive an extra bonus. The criterion for receiving a bonus is written into the contract. Likewise, penalty clauses which describe unfavorable consequences for unusually poor performance of responsibilities can strengthen the behavioral contract as well.

Other contract clauses should cover the ways in which responsibilities are monitored and recorded. Record keeping can help insure consistent adherence to the contract by all parties, reducing questions or arguments about performance of responsibilities, and indicate how well the contract is working. Further information about behavioral contracting with specific cases of adolescent behavior problems is available elsewhere (DeRisi & Butz, 1974; Dinoff & Rickard, 1969; Dinoff, Serum, & Rickard, 1972; Jesness & DeRisi, 1973; MacDonald, Gallimore & MacDonald, 1970; Stuart, 1971; Stuart & Lott, 1972; Tharp & Wetzel, 1969).

The steps in writing a behavioral contract are illustrated in the case of Jim D., a 14-year-old in the eighth grade at a junior high school. Even since the second semester of the seventh grade, he performed near-failing work in his classes. There were numerous home and school conduct problems, but the one which brought Jim and his parents to the school counselor was his repeated truancy. Jim was frequently absent from school either all day or part of the day, although his parents did not let him stay home unless he was physically ill. The school was considering initiating a juvenile court complaint about his failure to attend school. The parents indicated willingness to try to work with the school counselor on this problem, although their lack of control over Jim in the home and community was not encouraging.

In order to arrive at Jim's responsibilities, it was only necessary to think in terms of behavior incompatible with missing school: attending each class in school. A listing of privileges for which Jim might work was obtained by questioning teachers, parents, friends, and others as to Jim's preferred activities, and by asking Jim himself about preferred people and activities. (An interview form, the Mediator-Reinforcer Incomplete Blank [Tharp & Wetzel, 1969] can be helpful in obtaining this information from the adolescent.) In Jim's case, most of the potential privileges seemed to involve passing time with his father in some way, such as throwing ball, playing cards, practicing driving, doing homework jointly, walking the dog, or other activities.

Once Jim's responsibilities and privileges had been specified, the next step was to decide how the responsibilities were to be monitored. This was achieved by use of an *attendance signatures* card, a simple 3 × 5 card with spaces for 14 teacher signatures on it. Jim was instructed that in order to receive a teacher's signature on his card, he had to approach the teacher and ask for the signature. The homeroom teacher would sign his card before 8:45 a.m. and during a 15-minute period immediately after school was over. Teachers in each of his other six class periods would sign the card if approached before the class bell rang and at the very end of the period. It was Jim's responsibility to request the signatures, and the teachers were not to sign at any other time. Each day upon Jim's arrival at home, Mrs. D. was to check and record the number of attendance signatures gathered that day, entering this onto a weekly chart. Later, when Mr. D. arrived at home from work, he was obligated to spend two minutes with Jim in the boy's choice of activity for each attendance signature collected that day.

Although there was a total of 70 possible attendance signatures to be collected in a week, Jim's attendance had been so spotty that perfect attendance at all classes was not immediately expected. However, to discourage extremely poor attendance, a penalty clause was added to the contract. If Mrs. D.'s record of attendance signatures indicated that Jim collected less than 40 in a week, he would not be permitted to leave his room on Saturday until noon. As a bonus for relatively good attendance, if Jim collected 55 or more attendance signatures during the week, his parents agreed to take him and one of his friends to the Friday night car races.

Several characteristics of this contract are worth noting. First, although even if school attendance successfully improved, there would still remain other significant problems. The selection of school attendance as a contracting target was wise because it was the immediate source of concern of the community authorities, and the monitoring of Jim's responsibilities was easy for his parents to do. Second, responsibilities and privileges were both broken down into small chunks so that the relationship between behavior and consequences was clarified. Further, both the bonus and penalty clauses involved consequences that were totally separate from the daily privileges so that if Jim realized late in the week that he was not going to achieve his bonus (or was sure to receive a penalty), he could still carry out his daily responsibilities in order to receive the daily privileges. Finally, the school counselor checked with Jim's parents through occasional phone calls to encourage them to carry out their duties of monitoring and providing consequences.

Jim collected only 22 attendance signatures the first week of the contract, and received his penalty that week. Each of the next two weeks he collected more than 60 signatures and received the bonus along with his daily privileges. The school counselor's graph of Mrs. D.'s record of daily attendance signatures collected for this three-week period is shown in Figure 3.3 (note that this is not a verification design). At the end of the third week, this attendance behavior contract was renegotiated with higher criteria for the bonus and penalty clauses. A separate behavioral contract on homework assignment completion was also negotiated at this time between Jim and one of his teachers. With the school counselor's help, Mr. and Mrs. D. began to negotiate other behavioral contracts aimed at reversing some of the other areas of disturbance. The original school attendance behavioral contract, excluding the clauses specifying details of responsibilities, privileges, and monitoring, is shown in Figure 3.4.

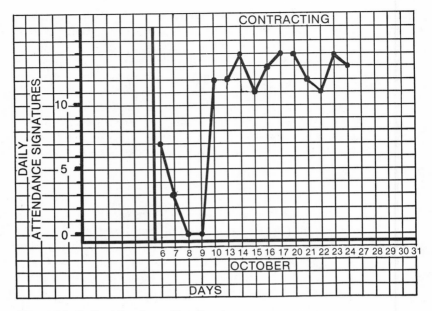

Figure 3.3 Daily Attendance Signatures

Behavioral contracting was one of the major intervention strategies in the Youth Center Research Project, a large-scale, long-term correctional experiment carried out in two California institutions for juvenile delinquent boys (Jesness, 1975). In this project, institutional caseworkers and the detained youths assigned to them negotiated behavioral contracts aimed at improving academic and other educational performance, behavior required for orderly functioning of the institution and everyday getting along, and critical patterns of behavior which could influence parole success or failure following release. Recidivism rates for youths released from this program were significantly less than those for youths released from appropriate comparison institutions. Behavioral contracting has been useful in community, public school, and home-based interventions in adolescent deviant behavior, as well as with institutionalized delinquents.

Token economies

A widely used (and misused) behavior modification strategy for altering the behavior of groups of deviant adolescents has been the token economy. Particulars of implementing and operating token economy are available from many sources (Ayllon & Azrin, 1968; Drabman & Tucker,

__*Jim D.'s*__ PRIVILEGES AND RESPONSIBILITIES DEAL

Effective from __*Oct. 6*__ to __*Oct. 24*__

RESPONSIBILITIES	PRIVILEGES
☐1 *School Attendance*	
a) *For each "Attendance Signature" Jim collects*	a) *Mr. D. will spend 2 minutes with Jim in Jim's choice of activity.*
b)	b)

Bonus

- *If Jim collects 55 or more "Attendance Signatures" from Monday – Friday*
- *Mr. and Mrs. D. will take Jim and one friend to the Friday night car races*

Penalty

- *If Jim collects less than 40 "Attendance Signatures" from Monday – Friday*
- *Mr. and Mrs. D. will not permit Jim to leave his room on Saturday until 12 Noon.*

☐2 _____

| a) | a) |
| b) | b) |

Bonus

Penalty

This deal is scheduled to be renegotiated on __*Oct. 24*__ __*at 3:45 pm. at the D. home*__
Details of responsibilities and privileges are spelled out on the attached sheet. This deal suits me and I agree to take part in it.

_____ _____

_____ , counselor

Figure 3.4 School Attendance Behavioral Contract

1974; Kazdin & Bootzin, 1972; O'Leary & Drabman, 1971; Stainback, Payne, Stainback & Payne, 1973), and its effectiveness on a large scale with institutionalized juvenile delinquents has been verified (Hobbs & Holt, 1976). Basically, a simulated economic system is implemented within a limited environment, and various aspects of this system are manipulated to produce desired changes in the behavior of participants. The main elements of a token economy are: (1) consideration of what behavior changes are required and clear specification of target behaviors; (2) establishment of back-up reinforcers—items or activities for which the participants are willing to work; (3) selection of appropriate tokens (symbolic rewards which function like money) on the basis of portability, durability, resistance to forgery, ease of dispensing, low cost, and other characteristics; (4) specification of rules governing acquisition of tokens and subsequent exchange for the back-up reinforcers; and (5) identification of persons who will dispense the tokens, based on proximity to participants, ability to dispense tokens according to rules, and other factors related to token economy functioning.

Token economies have been used with deviant adolescents in their natural homes, foster or community group homes, detention centers and institutions, public school and institutional classrooms, and other settings. Behavior changes have included academic and other educational responses, conduct and other interpersonal behavior hygiene and other self-care behavior, and additional kinds of activities.

There are several major advantages to the use of token reinforcement, and token economies in general. For instance, consequences can be delivered immediately, without interruption of the target behavior. This means that token reinforcement can maintain performance by bridging the delay between a correct response and the later back-up reinforcer. Since tokens, like money, are redeemable for a wide range of desirable back-up rewards, deviant adolescents are not likely to tire of receiving them, as is the case with many reinforcers. Tokens can be accumulated in order to achieve larger back-up rewards, thereby motivating stable performance over long periods of time. Token systems can be arranged to simulate many features of real economic systems, including wages, prices, inflation, supply-and-demand, and other capitalistic phenomena; savings, loans, interest, and other banking processes; profits, losses, sales, lay-aways, and other marketing techniques. For this reason, tokens are useful in teaching mathematical, consumer, and various other skills in addition to motivating desirable conduct. One of the major advantages of token economies is that the behaviors of many participants in a token economy can be managed relatively easily because they are all reinforced with the same token, even though there are divergent preferences for the back-up rewards.

There are also some important disadvantages to the use of token economies. These disadvantages are not necessarily inherent in the use of token reinforcement, but primarily arise from unskilled, careless, or unscrupulous use of tokens by those who designed the token economy or those who actually dispense tokens to the participants. For instance, token economies can easily encourage the participants to be overly dependent of the person dispensing tokens or on the system in general. Although adolescents in a token economy usually carry out legitimate instructions given to them, it is more important that they be able to act competently without requiring direction from others. Much foresight and careful planning is required in this sensitive area, which is certainly not unique to the use of token economies or behavior modification in general.

This issue of over-dependency of participants is a specific case of a more general potential disadvantage of token economies. Assuming that powerful back-up reinforcers are available and adequate rules of exchange are .in effect, dramatic changes in a wide range of target behaviors can be achieved for participants in the token system. But most token economies are quite different from the real world in which the adolescent's deviancy was identified: tokens are obviously not money, the consequences of correct and incorrect behaviors are not as immediately or consistently forthcoming in the real world, and so on. The beneficial changes brought about within a token economy may abruptly vanish when the token economy is no longer in effect. If adaptive changes in behavior produced by a token economy are to continue after release from the treatment setting, programs for therepeutic generalization must be planned and carried out.

The Achievement Place Project illustrates effective use of token reinforcement procedures with deviant adolescents. This is a Teaching-Family group home model, intended to serve as a community-based and directed alternative to detention center placement for adolescents who are in trouble. One of its most important components is a token economy. The Teaching-Family model is described in detail elsewhere (Bailey, Wolf, & Phillips, 1970; Bailey, Timbers, Phillips, & Wolf, 1972; Fixsen, Phillips, & Wolf, 1972, 1973a, 1973b; Phillips, 1968; Phillips, Phillips, Fixsen, & Wolf, 1971, 1972; Phillips, Wolf, & Fixen, 1973; Wolf, Phillips, & Fixsen, 1972).

Briefly, the Teaching-Family model includes the following components. The community, school, home, and legal problems of adolescents are seen to stem from inappropriate and incompetent behavior with respect to several areas of adjustment. Therefore, a large number of structured teaching interactions between the adolescent and the Achievement Place Teaching-Parents are carried out in order to instruct and encourage appropriate behavior in a number of areas, including social, self-care, prevocational, family living, and self-control within the group home setting. Training is also geared to encouraging behavior required for appropriate adjustment in the community, the school, and the adolescent's natural family to which he will return. The Teaching-Parents are highly trained to carry out these structured teaching interactions, as well as other activities required for successful implementation of the Teaching-Family model. Intensive evaluation through verification designs and group research designs is a major concern of the Teaching-Family model. Not only is this group home model evaluated in an overall sense in many ways, but the structured teaching interactions and other treatment procedures are also closely analyzed. Within this framework, the learning and performance of boys and girls assigned to Achievement Place group homes are motivated through the use of a token economy.

The Achievement Place token economy is a series of progressively less structured token exchange arrangements, differing in the amount of delay between the token transaction and the time when accumulated tokens are exchanged for back-up reinforcers. Early in his stay at Achievement Place, the adolescent may be on the hourly point system, in which points are accumulated over an interval of several hours and are then used to buy various privileges for the following interval of several hours. On the daily point system, points are accumulated over a 24-hour period, then used to purchase privileges for the following 24-hour period. On the weekly point system, the same procedure holds except points are accumulated and privileges bought for a seven-day period. Also on the weekly point system, daily minimum of points must be earned or the right to use the privileges previously bought is temporarily suspended.

The next higher system is called the merit system. Participation in the merit system is earned by youths on the weekly point system who consistently accumulate more points than they need to buy their privileges for the following week. The excess tokens are used to purchase supertokens (bonds). When enough bonds are earned, the youth can enter the merit system, in which privileges are freely available and no points are earned or lost. However, regular ratings of merit system participants take place, in order to make sure that behavioral gains are being maintained. There are also special arrangements for youths who temporarily show maladjustment or who chronically fail to make necessary improvements in a particular area.

The general sequence of progression through these systems is from more immediate to more remote point redemption and finally access to privileges without the need for points to be exchanged. However, inadequate performance in any system leads to a return to the next lower system. During progression through the systems, the youth is also spending progressively more time in his natural home, and home behavior is tied into the point system as well. As the youth shows that he can maintain appropriate behavior in the home, and as parents demonstrate their ability to deal with everyday management of the youth and crisis situations, the Teaching-Parents' guidance is phased out gradually.

In the various token systems, points can be earned for a variety of desirable behaviors, including participation in the regular decision-making family conference, volunteering for unpopular tasks, taking part in meal preparation, housekeeping tasks, yard work, good school grades, completion of homework, helping fellow residents complete their tasks, practicing adaptive behavior recently learned from a structured teaching interaction, and in other ways. A wide range of misbehavior also costs the youth points. For instance, fighting, temper tantrums, rowdiness, arguing, other aggressiveness, moodiness, poor table manners, dishonest behavior, misuse or damage to property, disobedience to Teaching-Parents, not reporting a peer's infraction, poor personal appearance, problems with teachers or other school officials, poor school grades, and other misbehaviors are fined specific numbers of points. The Achievement Place token economies are constructed so that a youth who loses even a large number of points may, through extra effort and work, make up his losses. This means that only if a youth misbehaves excessively, and stubbornly refuses to work to make up his losses will he fail to earn at least some of the privileges potentially available to him.

The back-up reinforcers for which points are exchanged include items and activities that are available around most homes, one-of-a-kind opportunities, and other special events. The privilege which must be bought first is called *basics*; this includes access to the telephone, radio, recreation room, use of tools, and going outdoors. The privilege which must be bought next is snacks. Next, access to TV at certain times of the day must be bought. Next, the right to go home from Friday evening to Sunday evening must be purchased. After these four privileges are bought, if the youth has accumulated additional points, he is free to select any of a number of additional privileges including allowance, the right to work for money, other special or occasional privileges, and the bonds required to earn his way onto the merit system.

Points earned or lost are recorded on a point card which each adolescent carries with him throughout the day. Points earned are kept separately from points lost, and for each point transaction the youth writes the amount of the transaction and the reason that points were earned or lost. The Teaching-Parent or a person designated by the Teaching-Parent then initials the point card. Regardless of which token system the youth is operating under, his point accumulation is the difference between those made and those lost; it is possible (but unusual) that this difference will be negative.

Special earning arrangements are available for those who fail to accumulate required point totals.

Many of the Achievement Place token economy procedures, as well as other components of the Teaching-Family model, have been evaluated through verification designs. (Some of the evaluation reports are cited at the beginning of this section.) These reports confirm the effectiveness of the token motivational system as implemented in the context of the overall Teaching-Family model. Many of the advantages of token economies in general are also characteristic of the Achievement Place token economy, and it is doubtful that the large number of structured teaching interactions and other re-educational activities could be successfully carried out in the absence of the point systems.

The overall efficacy of the Teaching-Family treatment model is encouraging. Phillips, et al. (1972) reported a follow-up comparison between a group of youths admitted to Achievement Place and two other groups of similar youths sent to either a state juvenile detention center or placed on probation. The status of boys in these three groups was identified two years after release from their respective placements. Over half of both the institution boys and the probation boys had been readjudicated and institutionalized, whereas this had occurred with less than one-fifth of the Achievement Place youths. Additionally, three semesters after release only 9% of the institution youths and 37% of the probation youths were still attending school, while 90% of Achievement Place youths remained in school. Of all youths who attended school, the institution youths and probation youths passed less than half of their classes, while Achievement Place youths passed more than 90% of theirs. In the same report, it was pointed out that the per client initial costs for an Achievement Place home were less than one-third that of a state institution, and operating costs about half that of an institution. These comparisons are not specifically evaluations of the token economy, but the token economy was a crucial component of the Teaching-Family model.

Reinforced modeling

It is frequently reported that deviant adolescents consistently show certain patterns of maladjustment, such as inability to accept criticism appropriately or failure to delay immediate gratification in order to receive later benefits. Both instances bring adolescents to the attention of the helping professions originally, and complicate or undermine successful adjustment after intervention. Many of these deviant behavior patterns have been successfully treated through a composite behavior modification strategy that features reinforced modeling (Alexander & Parsons, 1973; Bandura, 1973;

Gittelman, 1965; Mahoney, 1971; Prazak, 1969; Sarason, 1968; Sarason & Ganzer, 1969, 1973).

Besides criticism and immediate gratification problems, reinforced modeling has been employed with other patterns of maladjustment. These include (1) rejection of the authority of parents, teachers, policemen, and others; (2) inability to resist peer pressure to deviate; unwillingness to accept responsibility or blame for mistakes; (3) inability to back down from an argument or a fight; (4) failure to complete necessary tasks such as school work, job requirements, and so on; (5) unwise use of leisure time, leading to deviant behavior; (6) lack of ways to express assertion except through anger, aggression, argumentativeness, or other troublesome responses; (7) frequent showing-off by deviant behavior in order to get attention of others; (8) habitual failure to make preparations or plans for upcoming situations; (9) inability to approach caseworkers, counselors, or other potentially helpful adults to ask for assistance; and (10) poor performance in formal interview situations, such as interviewing for a job or reporting to a probation or other court caseworker.

The reinforced modeling treatment assumes that the above and other related problems are evidence of a lack of required skills for dealing with that particular situation. Whereas nondeviant adolescents are more likely to perform competently in these types of situations, the deviant adolescent may never have acquired the needed skills or is uninformed as to which skills should be performed in the various situations.

There are four separate components of the reinforced modeling technique. First, the specific behavioral skills required for successful performance in the particular situation to be trained must be decided on. This step may call for a good deal of cleverness on the part of the trainer. Some of the most important behaviors required for success in any given situation are not immediately obvious, so the trainer must reflect on what exactly is done by a person who is successful in the situation. Physical appearance, facial expressions, verbal behavior, and other subtleties must be considered. When the important skills have been decided on, they must be stated in such a way that the adolescent knows what is expected of him and the trainer knows when each skill has been correctly performed.

The second component involves repeated demonstration of each of the required skills. These demonstrations may be performed by live, videotaped, or filmed models, and demonstration by several models is probably preferable. For each skill that is modeled, a rationale in terms of its importance to the complex skill to be learned should be given. A discussion of the fine points in performing this skill may also be helpful. Finally, typical mistakes in performing each skill are pointed out, and may also be modeled and critiqued by the trainee (or group of trainees).

The next component of reinforced modeling is guided practice by the trainee under "safe" training conditions. Adolescents who are reluctant to perform an unfamiliar skill or one which would ordinarily be criticized by their peers may be more likely to practice the skill if it is presented as a role-playing job. Practice, correction, and repractice is continued until performance is skillful and spontaneous in the training situation. At each step of the way, approval for correct performance and other kinds of positive reinforcement should be provided by the trainer or the other members of the training group. If practice is videotaped, the trainee can monitor and critique his own performance. For complex skills, imperfect approximations to the terminal skill are temporarily accepted as correct, with successively more perfect approximations required (shaping). Note that this component of reinforced modeling is not an unstructured roletaking situation, but planful, guided practice in appropriate skills.

After component skills are quite familiar and the entire adaptive behavior pattern can be performed with ease, further practice takes place in more realistic situations. Guidance by the trainer is gradually withdrawn as the trainee continues to remain proficient at performing the skills in successively more difficult realistic situations.

As with almost any intervention, the reinforced modeling technique can be applied to adolescents who are not motivated to participate. External motivations of various kinds may be required to induce recalcitrant clients to take part in treatment. However, once the target behavioral skills have been acquired, trainees may recognize that their new abilities can provide them with previously unavailable benefits in the natural environment. Performance of the skills would then be maintained or regulated like other behavior.

The reinforced modeling treatment can be illustrated for problems of arguing and other unproductive responses of conflict between predelinquent adolescents and their parents. (This example is loosely based on Kifer, Lewis, Green, & Phillips, 1974.) In this case, communication between the adolescents and their parents often led to arguments, stand-offs, and ill feeling which continued beyond the specific conflict, detrimentally influencing other areas of family living.

Adolescent and parent were trained together in a simulation situation. Both parties typically approached a conflict situation by making demands on one another, refusing to compromise, diverting attention from the particular issue by bringing up past faults or offenses of the other party, or chronically behaving in other ways which not only produced little resolution of the particular issue but also resulted in counterproductive relationships in many areas. The trainers decided that skills required for successful negotiation might include: (1) complete communication—a statement that clearly put forward one's position, exactly what one thinks or wants out of this situation, plus a request to the other person to state his thoughts or wishes about the situation or about the original position expressed by the first party; (2) issue identification—a statement that unambiguously identifies the point of conflict by contrasting the two opposing positions, attempting to clarify or get more information about the other person's position or relating the specific conflict to another overriding issue; and (3) suggestion of options—statements that offer a course of action which might resolve the conflict, but which are not simple restatements of an original position. Statement of many options was encouraged to increase the chance that there would be grounds for agreement.

The next component in this reinforced modeling approach would be to repeatedly model to the trainees how to make a statement of complete communication, one which identifies the issues, and one which suggests numerous possible options. These behaviors were considered important in increasing the likelihood that negotiation would take place. Mistakes which might commonly be made were pointed out, along with why these were mistakes.

Next, practice of the skills was carried out under guidance from the trainers. Trainees were told which skills to use at each point, were praised for correct use, and were reminded which negotiation skill was appropriate at what time. The trainees could look at videotapes of a session whenever they wished.

Finally, the adolescent and his parent had to use the three negotiation skills in a simulated conflict situation. The trainers used progressively less guidance until the three negotiation behaviors (complete communication, identification of issues, and suggestion of options) were skillfully and spontaneously used to arrive at a negotiated settlement.

This reinforced modeling intervention continued for several sessions with each pair of trainees. Data from both the training simulations and from home observation carried out with each family pair indicated that the trainees began using the three negotiation behaviors more frequently and that agreements were more likely to be reached, following the training procedure.

The use of reinforced modeling or other procedures to enhance negotiation skills between deviant adolescents and other persons has much potential in school and community counseling, rehabilitation programs for chronic disruptive youth, and other settings. In the particular example of reinforced modeling discussed above, instruction and discussion played a large role along with modeling. In other examples, however, the skills to be learned may be so complex that verbal instruction is less useful than the modeling. Just as a picture is worth a thousand words, a clear modeling demonstration may be worth a thousand instructions for some intricate behavior patterns. Therefore, other applications of reinforced modeling have more heavily relied on the modeling component. The general rationale and principles, however, are the same.

SUMMARY

Although behavior modification procedures alone can bring about beneficial changes in adolescent deviance, intervention programs or projects may often use behavior modification techniques in combination with other treatments. There are few treatments with which behavioral procedures cannot be made compatible, especially if the basic requirements—focus on observable phenomena, repetitive assessment, and treatment verification —are met.

All treatment approaches must be responsive to scientific evidence about new methods of changing deviant behavior. Since this responsiveness is largely built into behavior analysis, frequent revisions of the assumptions and practice of behavior modification are to be expected. Those who wish to keep abreast of changes and adaptations are advised to consult behavior modification journals, including *Behavior Modification: A Quarterly Journal, Behavior Research and Therapy, Behavior Therapy, Journal of Applied Behavior Analysis,* and *Journal of Behavior Therapy and Experimental Psychiatry.*

REFERENCES

Alexander, J. F., and Parsons, B. V. "Short-Term Behavioral Intervention with Delinquent Families: Impact on Family Process and Recidivism." *Journal of Abnormal Psychology* 81 (1973): 219–226.

Ayllon, T., and Azrin, N. H. *The Token Economy: A Motivational System for Therapy and Rehabilitation.* New York: Appleton, 1968.

Bailey, J. S.; Timbers, G. D.; Phillips, E. L.; and Wolf, M. M. "Modification of Articulation Errors of Pre-Delinquents by their Peers." *Journal of Applied Behavior Analysis* 5 (1972): 19–30.

Baily, J. S.; Wolf, M. M.; and Phillips, E. L. "Home-Based Reinforcement and the Modification of Pre-Delinquents' Classroom Behavior." *Journal of Applied Behavior Analysis* 3 (1970): 223–233.

Bandura, A. *Aggression: A Social Learning Analysis.* Englewood Cliffs, New Jersey: Prentice-Hall, 1973.

Bandura, A. *Principles of Behavior Modification.* New York: Holt, Rinehart, and Winston, 1969.

Becker, W. C.; Madsen, C. H.; Arnold, C. R.; and Thomas, D. R. "The Contingent Use of Teacher Attention and Praise in Reducing Classroom Behavior Problems." *Journal of Special Education* 1 (1967): 287–307.

Brackbill, Y. "Extinction of the Smiling Response in Infants as a Function of Reinforcement Schedule." *Child Development* 29 (1958): 115–124.

Broden, M.; Hall, R. V.; and Mitts, B. "The Effects of Self-Recording on the

Classroom Behavior of Two Eighth Grade Students." *Journal of Applied Behavior Analysis* 4 (1971): 191-199.

Brown, G. D., and Tyler, V. O. "Time Out from Reinforcement: A Technique for Dethroning the 'Duke' of an Institutionalized Delinquent Group." *Journal of Child Psychology and Experimental Psychiatry* 9 (1968): 203-211.

Cooper, J. O. *Measurement and Analysis of Behavioral Techniques.* Columbus, Ohio: Merrill, 1974.

Court Brown, W. M. "Sex Chromosome Aneuploidy in Man and its Frequency, with Special Reference to Mental Subnormality and Criminal Behavior." *International Review of Experimental Pathology* 7 (1969): 31-97.

DeRisi, W. J., and Butz, G. *Writing Behavioral Contracts.* Champaign, Illinois: Research, 1974.

Dinoff, M., and Rickard, H. C. "Learning that Privileges Entail Responsibilities." *Behavioral Counseling.* Edited by J. D. Krumboltz and C. E. Thoresen. New York: Holt, Rinehart, and Winston, 1969.

Dinoff, M.; Serum, C.; and Rickard, H. C. "Controlling Rebellious Behavior through Successive Contracts." *Child Care Quarterly* 1 (1972): 205-211.

Drabman, R. S., and Tucker, R. D. "Why Classroom Token Economies Fail." *Journal of School Psychology* 12 (1974): 178-188.

Eysenck, H. J. *Crime and Personality.* Boston: Houghton-Mifflin, 1964.

Fixsen, D. L.; Phillips, E. L.; and Wolf, M. M. "Achievement Place: Experiments in Self-Government with Pre-Delinquents." *Journal of Applied Behavior Analysis* 6 (1973): 31-47. (a)

Fixsen, D. L.; Phillips, E. L.; and Wolf, M. M. "Achievement Place: The Reliability of Self-Reporting and Peer-Reporting and their Effects on Behavior." *Journal of Applied Behavior Analysis* 5 (1972): 19-30.

Fixsen, D. L.; Phillips, E. L.; and Wolf, M. M. "The Teaching-Family Model of Group Home Treatment." *The Closing Down of Institutions: New Strategies for Youth Services.* Edited by Y. Bakal. New York: D. C. Heath and Co., 1973. (b)

Gittleman, M. "Behavior Rehearsal as a Technique in Child Treatment." *Journal of Child Psychology and Psychiatry* 6 (1965): 251-255.

Glover, J. A. "Creative Responding and Contingency Management." Middle Tennessee Symposium on Behavior Therapy. Nashville: Tennessee State University Press, 1974.

Guttman, E. S. *Effects of Short-Term Psychiatric Treatment* (Research Report No. 36). Sacramento: California Youth Authority, 1963.

Hall, R. V. *Managing Behavior: Behavior Modification: The Measurement of Behavior.* Lawrence, Kansas: H and H Enterprise, 1971.

Hare, R. D. *Psychopathy: Theory and Research.* New York: Wiley, 1970.

Hobbs, T. R., and Holt, M. M. "The Effects of Token Reinforcement on the Behavior of Delinquents in Cottage Settings." *Journal of Applied Behavior Analysis* 9 (1976): 189-198.

Jesness, C. F. "An Overview of the Youth Center Project: Transactional Analysis and Behavior Modification Programs for Delinquents." *Behavioral Disorders* 1 (1975).

Jesness, C. F., and DeRisi, W. J. "Some Variations in Techniques of Contingency Management in a School for Delinquents." *Behavior Therapy with Delinquents.* Edited by J. S. Stumphauzer. Springfield, Illinois: Thomas, 1973.

Kanfer, F. H., and Phillips, J. S. *Learning Foundations of Behavior Therapy.* New York: Wiley, 1970.

Kazdin, A. E. *Behavior Modification in Applied Settings.* Homewood, Illinois: Dorsey, 1975.

Kazdin, A. E., and Bootzin, R. R. "The Token Economy: An Evaluative Review." *Journal of Applied Behavior Analysis* 5 (1972): 343–372.

Kifer, R. E.; Lewis, M. A.; Green, D. R.; and Phillips, E. L. "Training Pre-Delinquent Youths and their Parents to Negotiate Conflict Situations." *Journal of Applied Behavior Analysis* 7 (1974): 357–364.

Levitt, E. E. "Research on Psychotherapy with Children." *Handbook of Psychotherapy and Behavior Change.* Edited by A. E. Bergin and S. L. Garfield. New York: Wiley, 1971.

Lorenz, K. *On Aggression.* New York: Harcourt-Brace-Jovanovich, 1966.

MacDonald, W. S.; Gallimore, R.; and MacDonald, G. "Contingency Contracting by School Personnel: An Economical Model of Intervention." *Journal of Applied Behavior Analysis* 3 (1970): 175–182.

Mahoney, M. J. "A Residential Program in Behavior Modification." Paper presented at the Fifth Annual Meeting of the Association for the Advancement of Behavior Therapy, September 1971, at Washington, D.C.

McAllister, L. W.; Stachowiak, J. G.; Baer, D. M.; and Conderman, L. "The Application of Operant Conditioning Techniques in a Secondary School Classroom." *Journal of Applied Behavior Analysis* 2 (1969): 277–285.

O'Leary, K. D., and Drabman, R. "Token Reinforcement Programs in the Classroom: A Review." *Psychological Bulletin* 75 (1971): 379–398.

O'Leary, K. D., and Wilson, G. T. *Behavior Therapy: Application and Outcome.* Englewood Cliffs, New Jersey: Prentice-Hall, 1975.

Patterson, G. R.; Cobb, J. A.; and Ray, R. S. "A Social Engineering Technology for Retraining the Families of Aggressive Boys." *Issues and Trends in Behavior Therapy.* Edited by H. E. Adams and I. P. Unikel. Springfield, Illinois: Thomas, 1973.

Phillips, E. L. "Achievement Place: Token Reinforcement Procedures in a Home-Style Rehabilitation Setting for 'Pre-Delinquent' Boys." *Journal of Applied Behavior Analysis* 1 (1968): 213–223.

Phillips, E. L.; Phillips, E. A.; Fixsen, D. L.; and Wolf, M. M. "Achievement Place: Modification of the Behaviors of Pre-Delinquent Boys within a Token Economy." *Journal of Applied Behavior Analysis* 4 (1971): 45–59.

Phillips, E. L.; Phillips, E. A.; Fixsen, D. L.; and Wolf, M. M. *The Teaching-Family Handbook.* Lawrence, Kansas: University Printing Service, 1972.

Phillips, E. L.; Wolf, M. M.; and Fixsen, D. L. "Achievement Place: Development of the Elected Manager System." *Journal of Applied Behavior Analysis* 6 (1973): 541–561.

Pierce, C. H., and Risley, T. R. "Recreation as a Reinforcer: Increasing Membership and Decreasing Disruptions in an Urban Recreation Center." *Journal of Applied Behavior Analysis* 7 (1974): 403–411.

Polani, P. E. "Occurrence and Effect of Human Chromosome Abnormalities." *Society Symposium: Social and Genetic Influences on Life and Death.* Edited by R. Platt and A. S. Parkes. New York: Plenum, 1967.

Prazak, J. A. "Learning Job-Seeking Interview Skills." *Behavioral Counseling.* Edited by J. D. Krumboltz and C. E. Thoresen. New York: Holt, Rinehart, and Winston, 1969.

Reckless, W. C. *The Crime Problem.* New York: Appleton-Century-Crofts, 1961.

Reiss, A. J. "Social Correlates of Psychological Types of Delinquency." *American Sociological Review* 17 (1952): 710–718.

Sarason, I. G. "Verbal Learning, Modeling, and Juvenile Delinquency." *American Psychologist* 23 (1968): 254–266.

Sarason, I. G., and Ganzer, V. J. "Developing Appropriate Social Behaviors of Juvenile Delinquents." *Behavioral Counseling.* Edited by J. D. Krumboltz and C. E. Thoresen. New York: Holt, Rinehart, and Winston, 1969.

Sarason, I. G., and Ganzer, V. J. "Modeling and Group Discussion in the Rehabilitation of Juvenile Delinquents." *Journal of Counseling Psychology* 20 (1973): 442–449.

Sasmor, R. M. "Operant Conditioning of a Small-Scale Muscle Response." *Journal of the Experimental Analysis of Behavior* 9 (1966): 69–85.

Schwitzgebel, R., and Kolb, D. A. "Inducing Behavior Change in Adolescent Delinquents." *Behavior Research and Therapy* 1 (1964): 297–304.

Seymour, F. W., and Stokes, T. F. "Self-Recording in Training Girls to Increase Work and Evoke Staff Praise in an Institution for Offenders. *Journal of Applied Behavior Analysis* 9 (1976): 41–54.

Slavson, S. R. *Re-educating the Delinquent.* New York: Colier, 1961.

Staats, A. W., and Butterfield, W. "Treatment of Nonreading in a Culturally Deprived Juvenile Delinquent: An Application of Reinforcement Principles." *Child Development* 36 (1965): 925–942.

Stainback, W. C.; Payne, J. S.; Stainback, S. B.; and Payne, R. A. *Establishing a Token Economy in the Classroom.* Columbus, Ohio: Merrill, 1973.

Storr, A. *Human Aggression.* New York: Bantam, 1970.

Stuart, R. B. "Behavioral Contracting within Families of Delinquents." *Journal of Behavior Therapy and Experimental Psychiatry* 2 (1971): 1–11.

Stuart, R. B., and Lott, L. A. "Behavioral Contracting with Delinquents: A Cautionary Note." *Journal of Behavior Therapy and Experimental Psychiatry* 3 (1972): 161–169.

Stumphauzer, J. S. "Increased Delay of Gratification in Young Prison Inmates through Imitation of High-Delay Peer Models." *Journal of Personality and Social Psychology* 21 (1972): 10–17.

Tharp, R. G., and Wetzel, R. J. *Behavior Modification in the Natural Environment.* New York: Academic, 1969.

Vorrath, H. H. *Positive Peer Culture: Content, Structure, Process.* Lansing, Michigan: Michigan Center for Group Studies, 1972.

Weiner, I. B. *Psychological Disturbance in Adolescence.* New York: Wiley, 1970.

Weiss, T., and Engel, B. T. "Operant Conditioning of Heart Rate in Patients with Premature Ventricular Contractions." *Psychosomatic Medicine* 33 (1971): 301–321.

Wilson, C. W., and Hopkins, B. L. "The Effects of Contingent Music on the Intensity of Noise in a Junior High Home Economics Class." *Journal of Applied Behavior Analysis* 6 (1973): 269–275.

Wolf, M. M.; Phillips, E. L.; and Fixsen, D. L. "The Teaching-Family: A New Model for the Treatment of Deviant Child Behavior in the Community." *Behavior Modification.* Edited by S. W. Bijou and E. L. Ribes-Inesta. New York: Academic Press, 1972, 51–62.

psychoeducational management of disruptive youths

RAYMOND J. DEMBINSKI

The psychological and educational needs and demands of chronically disruptive youths have been a major concern of educators, correctional officers, and mental health workers for decades. Essentially, *chronically disruptive* refers to youths who have been labeled emotionally disturbed, behavior disordered, juvenile delinquent, educationally handicapped, or socially maladjusted. These youths present a variety of problems—academic, social, psychological, affective, economic, and physical. Approximately 20% of chronically disruptive youth are considered to be mentally ill. Implicit in this statement are two factors: (1) 20% of chronically disruptive youth need intensive, long-term treatment which yields a rather poor prognosis; and (2) 80% of chronically disruptive youth are assumed to be responsive to some sort of intensive treatment.

The challenge is to develop treatment strategies to help the majority of chronically disruptive youths become constructive rather than remain destructive human beings. The responsibility for this task has traditionally resided with the physician, the educator, the psychologist, the social worker, and the corrections worker.

The purpose of this chapter is to review representative psychodynamic and/or psychoeducational treatment approaches designed for chronically disruptive youth. The treatment approaches will be discussed under three broad categories: client-oriented, group-oriented, and educationally-oriented interventions.

117

Table 4.1. A COMPARISON AMONG THE PROPONENTS OF THE MAJOR THERAPEUTIC APPROACHES ON SELECTED DIMENSIONS

Dimension	Solomon	Levy	Klein	A. Freud	Allen	Axline	Slavson	Behavior Therapists
Therapeutic Relationship	H	H	H	H	H	H	H	L
Expression of Feeling	H	H	H	H	H	H	H	L
Pointing Out Feeling—Recognition of Feeling	M	L	H	H	H	H	L	L
Interpretation	M	L	H	H	M	L	L	L
Transference	L	H	H	M	L	L	L	L
Past History of Individual	H	L	L	H	L	L	L	L
Parental Involvement	H	H	L	M	H	L	L	M
Age Range	L	H	L	N	N	H	H	L
Control of Child's Activity	H	H	L	L	L	L	L	H
Type of Disorder	L	H	H	H	L	L	M	L

H = Heavy emphasis; M = Moderate emphasis; L = Little emphasis; N = No specific discussion.

Clarizio, H. F. & McCoy, G. F., 1970, p. 373

CLIENT-ORIENTED INTERVENTIONS

Client-oriented therapists emphasize individual treatment on various psychosocial dimensions. Clarizio and McCoy (1970) developed a summary comparison of the various dimensions emphasized by traditional psychodynamic theorists (see Table 4.1).

Therapeutic relationship and *expression of feeling* are regarded as essential ingredients by all except the behavior therapists. Variable importance is attached to *pointing out feelings.* For example, the client-oriented therapists stress *recognition of feeling,* the psychoanalytically-oriented therapists stress *interpretation,* and the behavior therapists de-emphasize this total dimension. Use of the *transference relationship* is restricted primarily to the psychoanalytic group. The psychoanalytic theorists, together with the structured play therapists, Solomon and Levy, emphasize the *past history of the individual,* whereas the other theorists focus on the client's present situation. Considerable variation is observed with respect to *parental involvement.* Levy, Slavson, and Axline limit their treatment to a specific age range. Other theorists have not been as specific. The theorists are fairly well dichotomized with respect to *control of child's activity.* Viewed on a continuum, the structured approaches (Levy, Solomon, and the behaviorists) would be at one end of the continuum, and the "free" play therapists at the other. On the final dimension, *type of disorder,* Levy, Klein, and Freud view their treatment approaches as appropriate for specific types of behavioral deviations. Other theorists are more willing to treat a greater variety of disorders.

Efficacy studies (Levitt, 1957, 1963) on the psychotherapeutic outcomes of these approaches indicate limited effectiveness of the dynamic treatment procedures. For example, Achenbach (1974) reviewed psychiatric treatment programs in California training schools for boys. His findings suggest that psychotherapy may be beneficial in training school programs for some boys but harmful to others. Redl (1966) emphasized that alternative strategies were necessary to meet the needs of contemporary youth. Perhaps in reaction to Redl, client needs, or the results of the efficacy studies, new treatment strategies for disruptive youth began to evolve.

Reality therapy

Glasser (1965), in a break with traditional analytically based psychotherapy, developed *reality therapy.* Reality therapy differs from conventional therapy primarily on the basis of involvement between patient and therapist.

1. Reality therapists do not accept the concept of mental illness. The patient becomes involved with the therapist as a person responsible for his/her own behavior.
2. Reality therapists work in the present and toward the future. The past is considered beyond control.
3. They relate to patients as involved human beings, not as transference figures.
4. They do not accept the concept of unconscious conflicts as a cause or excuse for the patient's behavior.
5. They emphasize the morality of behavior, that is, direct the patient in distinguishing between right and wrong.
6. Reality therapists teach the patient more satisfactory patterns of behavior.

Glasser believes there are two basic human needs: (1) the need to love and be loved, and (2) the need to feel worthwhile to ourselves and to others. In order for youths to feel worthwhile, they must maintain satisfactory or appropriate behavior by learning to correct themselves when they are wrong and to approve or reward themselves when they exhibit appropriate behavior. Youths act responsibly when they can fulfill their needs in a manner that does not deprive others of the ability to fulfill their needs.

A teacher's task is to teach students to become more responsible. To do so, the teacher must: (1) achieve some level of involvement with the student; (2) reject the inappropriate or maladaptive behavior; and (3) teach the student more appropriate or responsible ways to fulfill his needs. Reality therapy is included in the discussion on psychoeducational interventions primarily because it concerns itself with attitudes as well as behavior. In addition, it is concerned with what Reinert (1976) refers to as psychic surface behavior.

Implementation of reality therapy in the classroom relies on two techniques: (1) developing plans or contracts aimed at achieving some desired behavioral goal; and (2) the use of class meetings to solve behavioral and educational problems. The contract or behavioral plan is developed by the teacher and the student. Care must be taken to insure the plan is realistic and attainable by the student. In fact, the student signs two contracts—a behavior change contract and a commitment to change contract. The youth is thus required to make a conscious decision regarding his behavior. Failure to realize the goals of the contract leads to renegotiation of a new contract.

In order to provide a youth with a feeling of involvement and success, Glasser advocates the use of class meetings. There are three types of meetings:

1. *Open-ended meetings.* Students discuss questions related to their lives or to the curriculum. The teacher attempts to stimulate the students to think. The open-ended meetings are the easiest ones to conduct and are held daily if possible.

2. *Social-problem solving meetings.* The purpose of this meeting is to solve the social problems of the school itself. The goal is to help students learn more effective ways of coping with problems. These meetings are not held as frequently as open-ended meetings, and are generally more difficult to organize and operate effectively.

3. *Educational diagnostic meetings.* The purpose of these meetings is to help teachers achieve an evaluation of whether or not they have reached their educational objectives. These meetings are related to topics that the class is currently studying.

The major purpose of the three meetings is to aid the student in the transaction between school and everyday life. The students begin to believe that they can shape their own destinies and that they are a vital part of their world. They develop confidence as a result of stating opinions without fear before others.

A major attraction of reality therapy is that it utilizes logic rather than insight to deal with a student's real, not past, problems. The approach has its limitations, however. It is appropriate only for those students willing to make a commitment to change. The uncommitted will continue to experience the consequences of their behavior. Conducting class meetings requires skill and a comfortable nonthreatened teacher. Training and encouragement in group skills is a critical need.

Glasser (1965) applied the reality therapy concepts to the treatment of norm-violating adolescent girls at the Ventura School. The goal of the treatment program was to take every girl, regardless of the severity of her problem, and within six to eight months, rehabilitate her to the extent that she would not become a serious problem in the community to which she returned. The treatment program consisted of a three-faceted, integrated intervention—custody, treatment, and school. The custody program was administered by counselors who indicated to the girl that she must take the responsibility for her behavior in an environment where responsibility is continually stressed. The treatment program was administered by a group of psychologists, social workers, and a consulting psychiatrist. Individual treatment with the girls was conducted as well as consulting supportive work with the custody staff to insure a unified, consistent treatment plan. The school program was academically and vocationally oriented. Glasser reported that the goal of successful community participation was attained in 80% of the girls treated.

Comprehensive vocationally-oriented psychotherapy (CVOP)

This technique was designed for male adolescents whose antisocial behavior caused them to be suspended from school or who had decided to withdraw from school. The underlying philosophy of CVOP (Massimo & Shore, 1967; Shore & Massimo, 1969) was based on an understanding of the maturational aspects of adolescents as well as the psychodynamic needs of chronic disruptive youth of the lower socioeconomic class. Initial contact was made with the boys within 24 hours of severing their relationship with school. Assistance in seeking employment or in coping with any problem they had or might encounter was offered. The vocational interests of the boys were used as vehicles for introducing remedial education and psychotherapy. The importance of the early contact was determined on the basis of studies on the concepts of alienation and crisis intervention. The treatment period lasted 10 months. Three stages were identified: (1) the contact or initial phase—"the big hurdle;" (2) the middle phase—"working together;" and (3) termination or "commencement." Traditional service or treatment models were felt to be inadequate in meeting the needs of these youths. Consequently, interagency and interdisciplinary involvement was specifically eliminated from this program. A single therapist was assigned to provide the vocational, educational, and therapeutic services needed.

Twenty subjects were included in this study. The selection criteria were as follows: male, school dropout, 15–17 years of age, IQ between 85–110, not psychotic or brain-damaged, and not enrolled in another treatment program. The subjects were randomly assigned to treatment and control groups. Pre- and post-test data were collected on the following variables: overt behavior, academic functioning, and three aspects of personality functioning (self-image, control of aggression, and attitude toward authority). Although no data were reported, the investigators indicated significant improvement in all areas tested. In overt behavior the treatment group showed a significant drop in contact with the police, and a better employment record than the control group. Significant improvement in reading, arithmetic, and vocabulary was reported for the treatment group. Personality functioning was assessed by means of response changes in thematic stories measuring self-image, control of aggression, and attitude toward authority. The greatest changes occurred in self-image and control of aggression. All the subjects were retested on the same measures three years after leaving the project. Continued improvement, but at a slower rate, was reported for the treatment group. The control group scores deteriorated in all areas. Caution must be exercised in accepting the conclusions of the investigators, as results, not data, were reported.

Adlerian approach

Krasnow (1971) describes the Adlerian approach as psychoeducational in nature, that is, it is designed to instruct rather than treat. In this respect, it is similar to reality theory. Adlerian psychology is based on a holistic model. This theory assumes that each youth has its own motivational attitudes, purposes, and goals in every life situation. All actions will reflect the youth's individual goal. The unconscious goal that the youth pursues is determined partly by hereditary endowments and partly by the interpretations and evaluations of his total life experiences. The assumption is that no one part of the youth can be dealt with separately without affecting the personality of the whole youth. The major purpose of an Adlerian-oriented program includes the youth's psychological or academic adjustment as well as total rehabilitation for constructive social integration (Krasnow, 1971).

Youths are viewed as social beings, seeking to belong, to be accepted, and to be fulfilled within a group setting. Disturbing or deficient behavior is the result of discouragement or insecurity. The youth assumes that the inappropriate behavior will gain him or her a place within a group. The four goals relating to disturbed and deficient behavior are: (1) to attract attention; (2) to demonstrate power in order to defeat the power of authority figures; (3) to get even or punish; and (4) to display real or assumed deficiency in order to be left alone and avoid any possible failure. Dreikurs and Cassel (1972) point out that the four goals refer to the purpose of a child's misbehavior. Table 4.2 refers to the techniques of modifying the motivation rather than the behavior itself.

The therapists's task is to secure the cooperation of the youth through influence rather than by force or pressure. Mutual respect for each person's ideas is stressed within a democratic environment. Natural and logical consequences are utilized to exert pressure and motivate. A natural consequence is one which takes place without adult interference; for example, a youth tilts a chair to the point that it slips out from under him and he falls on the floor and hurts himself. A logical consequence is structured and arranged by an adult and is experienced by a student as logical in nature; for example, the teacher removes the chair so that the student cannot use it. Logical consequences are the appropriate corrective procedures for Goal 1 behavior. Natural consequences are used on Goal 2 and Goal 3 behavior. Neither type of consequence is appropriate for Goal 4 behavior. The use of consequences instead of punishment allows reality to replace the authority of the adult. Consequences permit the

Table 4.2. HOW TO CORRECT CHILDRENS MISBEHAVIOR

By Interpretation of the Four Mistaken Goals

Up to 10 Years Old

Childs Action and Attitude	*Teachers Reaction	†Ask These Specific Questions to Diagnose...	Corrective Procedure
		GOAL 1	NEVER GIVE ATTENTION WHEN CHILD DEMANDS IT
NUISANCE SHOW OFF CLOWN LAZY Puts others in his service, keeps teacher busy. Thinks "He occupies too much of my time." "I wish he would not bother me."	FEELS ANNOYED GIVES SERVICE IS KEPT BUSY REMINDS OFTEN COAXES Thinks "He occupies too much of my time." "I wish he would not bother me."	ATTENTION A "Could it be that you want me to notice you?" OR B "Could it be that you want me to do something special for you?"	Ignore the misbehaving child who is bidding for attention. (Punishing, nagging, giving service, advising, is attention) Do not show annoyance. Be firm. Give lots of attention at any other time.
		GOAL 2	DON'T FIGHT— DON'T GIVE IN
STUBBORN ARGUES WANTS TO BE THE BOSS TEMPER TANTRUMS TELLS LIES DISOBEDIENT DOES OPPOSITE TO INSTRUCTIONS DOES LITTLE OR NO WORK Says "If you don't let me do what I want you don't love me." Thinks "I only count if you do what I want."	FEELS DEFEATED TEACHERS LEADERSHIP IS THREATENED "Thinks "He can't do this to me." "Who is running the class? He or I?" "He can't get away with this."	POWER A "Could it be that you want to show me that you can do what you want and no one can stop you?" OR B "Could it be that you want to be boss?"	Recognize and admit that the child has power. Give power in situations where child can use power productively. Avoid power struggle. Extricate yourself from the conflict. Take your sails out of his wind. Ask for his aid. Respect child. Make agreement.

Childs Action and Attitude	*Teachers Reaction	†Ask These Specific Questions to Diagnose...	Corrective Procedure
VICIOUS STEALS SULLEN DEFIANT Will hurt animals, peers and adults. Tries to hurt as he feels hurt by others. Kicks, bites, scratches. Sore loser. Potential delinquent. Thinks "My only hope is to get even with them."	FEELS DEEPLY HURT OUTRAGED DISLIKES CHILD RETALIATES (CONTINUAL CONFLICT) Thinks "How mean can he be?" "How can I get even with him?"	GOAL 3 REVENGE A "Could it be that you want to hurt me and the pupils in the class? OR B "Could it be that you want to get even?"	NEVER SAY YOU ARE HURT Don't behave as though you are. Apply natural consequences. (Punishment produces more rebellion) Do the unexpected. Persuade child that he is liked. Use group encouragement. Enlist one buddy. Try to convince him that he is liked.
FEELS HOPELESS 'STUPID' ACTIONS INFERIORITY COMPLEX GIVES UP TRIES TO BE LEFT ALONE RARELY PARTICIPATES Says "You can't do anything with me." Thinks "I don't want anyone to know how inadequate I am."	FEELS HELPLESS THROWS UP HANDS DOESN'T KNOW WHAT TO DO Thinks "I don't know what to do with him." "I give up." "I can't do anything with him."	GOAL 4 DISPLAY OF INADEQUACY A "Could it be that you want to be left alone?" OR B "Could it be that you feel stupid and don't want people to know?"	ENCOURAGE WHEN HE MAKES MISTAKES Make him feel worthwhile. Praise him when he tries. Say "I do not give up with you." Avoid support of inferior feelings. Constructive approach. Get class co-operation with pupil helpers. Avoid discouragement yourself.

*Teachers reaction must not be expressed since the 'natural' reaction in these circumstances will only reinforce the childs mistaken goal. Except in Goal 2

†All four questions must be asked of the child in this order. Even though the goal may be suspected do not change wording.

youth to decide what he can and wants to do about a situation. The skill ful use of encouragement is seen as an effective method for facilitating behavior change.

Practitioners utilizing the Adlerian approach rely on case study and anecdotal accounts to report their successes. Consequently, com parisons between pre- and post-treatment behavior, as well as alternative treatment, are difficult to make.

GROUP-ORIENTED INTERVENTIONS

Group-oriented therapies refer to intervention systems which attempt to achieve attitudinal and behavioral change as a function of group forces to which a client is exposed. The programs selected for review represen either significant intervention philosophies and/or developments in the field within the last decade. A major feature of these group interventions is that they emphasize community adjustment, that is, the successfu adjustment of a disruptive adolescent to community living as a result of either institutional or community-based group treatment programs.

Differences on the causes and treatment of disruptive youth abound. At one end of the continuum is the assumption that the source of maladjustment lies primarily with the individual, that is, in his affective deficits. At the other extreme is the notion that if youths are failing, it is the social-educational system itself which is in need of funda mental rehabilitation. Two intervention systems which represent both ends of this philosophical continuum are the Fricot Ranch Study and the Provo Experiment. Both of these approaches have been described exten sively elsewhere (Empey & Rabow, 1966; Grant, 1965; Jesness, 1970). A brief description of each, however, will serve to exemplify the major differences in treatment orientation.

Fricot ranch study

The Fricot approach was an attempt to develop an institutional therapeutic culture for 8- to 14-year-old chronic disruptive youths. Approximately 220 youths were experimentally assigned to 20- and 50-boy living units. Differences in the intervention process were studied as a function of the differing group sizes of the living units. The first process difference explored was control-punishment versus permissiveness-reward. Primarily because of size, the 50-boy unit was considered conducive to the utilization of stricter limitations on behavior, greater use of punishment, and less time for coping with problems on an individual basis. The smaller 20-unit setting was envisioned as a vehicle for de-emphasizing group punishment, focusing on individual problems, and emphasizing greater autonomy for each individual. The second process difference was authoritarianism-equalitarianism. The dynamics of the larger living unit forced supervisory personnel to act in an authoritarian fashion, thus curtailing the amount and quality of corrective interaction between youth and staff. In addition, the demands of a 50-member unit led to the discouragement of youth dependency on staff for the resolution of problems or clarification of relevant personal issues. Initial observations of the smaller unit situation indicated that the boys received 4 times as much individual attention than the boys who resided in the 50-person units. Boys in the large living units were described as more aggressive and superficially self-sufficient than the boys in the smaller units. The smaller units fostered greater informality, trust, respect, and expression of feelings. Jesness (1970) describes the Fricot orientation as still very regimented with little obvious variation in routine between units. He indicates that control rather than counseling is still emphasized. He points out that the following attitudes characterize the Fricot approach: (1) there is a feeling that a boy should be tough and self-sufficient and should not show dependency on an adult; (2) there is a belief that the ideal boy is one who does not hesitate to be aggressive as long as he fights fair; (3) the learning-through-lecture theme pervades the counseling relationships as well as most verbal interactions between staff and boys; (4) rehabilitation is rated primarily on whether or not a boy has respect for authority and if he is sincere; and (5) alliances with boys who have significant peer influence are sought by supervisors.

In addition, Jesness indicates the rigid structure of the Fricot setting de-emphasizes the need for decision making or initiative on the part of boys. Grant's (1965) analysis of preliminary data on the parole records of the graduates of the two living units indicates that the smaller living units may be achieving the desired goal of successful community adjustment. The 20-boy unit's graduates had a lower (18% to 39%) parole revocation record than did the 50-unit graduates.

Provo experiment

The Provo Experiment is a sociologically-oriented intervention system. The focus is on peer group phenomenon to treat behavior. Empey and Rabow (1966) delineate the theoretical assumptions on which the project rests. Provo is a community-based program. Other than spending part of the day at the program center, the boys are free in the community. Habitual offenders, 15 to 17 years of age, are assigned to the program. The group is limited to 20 boys. Each group of 20 is subdivided into independent discussion groups. Release from the program is contingent upon a youth's own behavior and the maturation processes occurring in his group. This process is usually accomplished within four to seven months.

The program is divided into two phases. Phase I is an intensive group program, emphasizing work and the norm-violating peer group as the principal instruments for change. There is little formal structure in the program. Other than requiring boys to appear each day and to work hard on their jobs, there are no formal demands. Daily group discussions are optional. These discussions are patterned after the technique of Guided Group Interaction or Positive Peer Culture (Vorrath, 1972). The group is the vehicle through which a boy can resolve his problems. The treatment system places responsibility on a youth and his peers for changing behavior, not on adults. Adult authorities intervene only in those cases where a youth does not become involved in a group, or where the group is unwilling or unable to take action against the uncooperative youth. Several options may be exercized: (1) the youth may be assigned to work without pay; (2) he may be placed in jail; or (3) he may be assigned to a situation in which he has no role, that is, allowing him to wander around the center without engaging in work and conversation with others.

Phase II, community adjustment, involves an effort to maintain reference group support and employment for a boy after intensive treatment in Phase I. After his release from Phase I, he continues to meet periodically for discussions with his old group. The goal is to utilize this group to accomplish three things: (1) act as a check on a youth's current behavior; (2) serve as a law-abiding reference group; and (3) aid in the solution of new problems.

Comparisons regarding the efficacy of the Fricot and Provo philosophies must be made with caution. First, the programs are designed for two different settings, one institutional and the other community. Second, each deals with a different age group. Fricot is designed for 8- to 14-year-olds, most of whom are probably first-time offenders. Provo focuses on 15- to 17-year-old habitual offenders. It is interesting to note that the element of control, considered as essential for habitual offenders, is minimal in the Provo Experiment. On the other hand, it seems to form the basis for the Fricot Ranch Study which deals with young, supposedly more easily managed children.

Adolescent self-concept group

One of the few reported projects for norm-violating girls is the Adolescent Self-Concept Group (James, Osborn, & Oetting, 1967). Adolescent girls in therapy, or wanting treatment at the Southeast Wyoming Mental Health Center, were invited to join this program. These were mostly acting-out girls, runaways, court cases, and school dropouts. Fourteen girls, 13 to 17 years of age, entered the program. A 10-week program, held every Wednesday from 1 to 5 p.m., was planned based on what the girls said they wanted to know and on what the staff felt they needed to learn. The program schedule is shown in the accompanying table (see Table 4.3).

Table 4.3.   SCHEDULE OF CLASSES

Week	Content
1	Testing. Make-up. Complete skin analysis by beauty counselor representatives.
2	Make-up. Beauty counseling. Skin care. Diet.
3	Hair grooming and care.
4	Posture, carriage, poise, sitting, etc.
5	Dancing.
6	Figure analysis. Exercises.
7	Clothing: How to make use of accessories, when hat and gloves are appropriate, how to make basic clothes work for different occasions, etc.
8	Dating etiquette: How to conduct themselves on a date, etc.
9	Review on make-up. Discussion. Summary session. Rolled hair, make-up, etc.
10	Dining out.
11	Final discussion. Testing.

The content of the course was not threatening, as group therapy might have been. The group leader was able to carry discussion into areas that would not have been considered in group therapy. Both the content and the discussions were reported to be valuable to the girls. In addition to the group leaders, two college students and a full-time student assistant met with the group. There was considerable identification with these youths. At least nine girls attended each session. The girls indicated a desire to continue as a group through some sort of activity. They were allowed to continue, through a sewing and knitting group, in a biweekly group therapy session.

Analysis of pre- and post-test data on several personality measures indicated a reduction in general anxiety in the group situation over a period of time. Half the girls improved in their identification with feminine roles. Although greater acceptance and tolerance for authority and school were observed, there was little evidence of changes in attitudes toward parents.

EDUCATIONALLY-ORIENTED INTERVENTIONS

The educational development of school aged youth is a major area of concern. The ability to arrest and remediate learning deficiencies in disruptive or problem youths is viewed as a significant preventative weapon against delinquency. For economical as well as political reasons, community and institutional programs for juvenile offenders assess their impact in terms of reduction in arrest rates, rates of recidivism, and reduction in parole violations. Educational programs, for the same reasons, report their successes in the form of increases in achievement scores, improvement in intelligence quotients, reductions in truancy and dropout figures, and numbers of secondary school graduates. A number of different approaches have been developed to meet the educational needs of disruptive youth. These approaches, though varied in their theoretical orientations, are categorized as educationally oriented inventions.

The psychoeducational model

The psychoeducational model utilizes data from the areas of human development, school learning, mental health, and group dynamics. This model applies these data directly and indirectly to educational problems and activities. The following major assumptions underlie the psychoeducational model:

1. An educational milieu must be developed in which attention is given to everything that affects pupil interaction with school, staff, peers, and curriculum.
2. It is important to understand the teacher-pupil relationship.
3. Learning must be invested with feelings to give it interest, meaning, and purpose.
4. Conflict can be used productively to teach new ways of understanding and coping with stress.
5. Collaborative skills are essential for teachers using the curriculum.
6. Creative arts are vital forms for learning and for the program.
7. Each pupil is different in style and functional level.
8. The same behavior can have many causes, while the same cause can be expressed through many behaviors.

(Fagen, Long, & Stevens, 1975)

The principal concepts of this intervention approach have also been formulated by Fagen, Long and Stevens (1975).

. . . the *psychoeducational approach postulates a circular, interacting relationship between thoughts and feelings such that cognitive experience affects emotional experience, etc.* Thus, the child who cannot learn to read might develop intensely adverse emotional reactions to failure, while the child with severe anxiety over performance might experience great difficulty learning to read.

In essence, the following conceptual attributes identify a psychoeducational approach:

1. Cognitive and affective processes are in continuous interaction at all times.
2. Behavior comprises verbal and nonverbal expressions of a total functioning person, and it is that person, not the expression, that is most important.
3. Behavior is a source of concern when it promotes or perpetuates personal unhappiness, conflict, and self-depreciation; or when it creates serious disturbance with existing social norms, thereby resulting in feelings of rejection and alienation.
4. Understanding behavior means understanding phenomenally relevant aspects of a child's life space. For the teacher, this means appreciating transactions between the child and the teacher, the curriculum, the peer group, and the educational system.
5. Understanding behavior requires an awareness of cognitive, affective, and motivational processes in self and others.
6. Understanding behavior is achieved through assessment of and communication with and about the learner and significant others in his life space.
7. Changing or modifying self-defeating behavior involves a process of establishing identifiable objectives which are set in relation to total personal functioning.
8. Understanding behavior facilitates creating conditions for optimal behavior change.
9. The ultimate criterion for personal growth is the extent to which positive behavior derives from *self-control* rather than external control.
10. Emotions are critical personal events that must become understood, accepted, and valued.
11. The scope of learning involves increasing understanding and satisfactions in relationship to things, symbols, the self, and others.

(Fagen, Long, & Stevens, 1975, pp. 52, 53, 54)

Two of the major proponents of the psychoeducational model are Long (1976) and Morse (1976). Both have been influenced by Redl (1957, 1959, 1966) and Caplan (1961, 1963). Long developed the Conflict Cycle (see Figure 4.1) as a means of understanding and coping with youth's

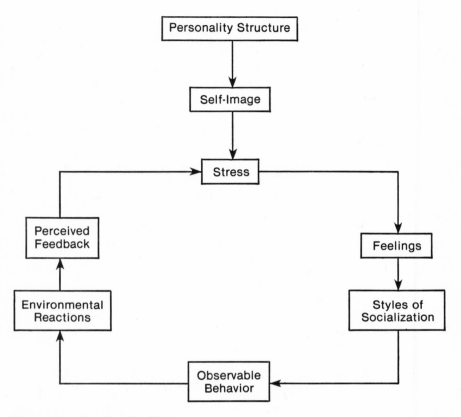

Figure 4.1   The Conflict Cycle

maladaptive behavior. Morse (1976) developed the concept of a crisis teacher. Long began the integration of both of these concepts with those of Redl on Life Space Interviewing, discipline, punishment, and the management of children's behavior at Hillcrest Children's Center in Washington, D.C. He later refined his approach at Rose School, also located in Washington, D.C.

Long believes that teachers can become more comfortable and confident in dealing with disruptive behavior once they understand the cyclical nature of behavior and the degree to which environment perpetuates a problem. The operational concepts provided by the conflict cycle are:

1. A child in conflict views the classroom through the eyes of his life history.
2. A child in conflict has learned to be vulnerable to specify school tasks (i.e., competition, separation, etc.).

3. Acceptance of positive and negative feelings within and between children is normal, healthy and necessary to a fulfilling life.

4. Each child has been socialized to process feelings by direct expression, defense mechanisms, or coping techniques.

5. Under severe stress, a child in conflict will regress from coping techniques, to defensive techniques, and to primitive expressions of feelings.

6. The problem behavior of a child in conflict represents his present solution to stress, although it may cause difficulties with adults, peers, learning, rules, and self.

7. A child in conflict creates feelings and behaviors in others (peers and adults) which almost always perpetuate his problem.

8. The child's awareness and skills in perpetuating negative environmental reaction to his behavior justifies his conviction that it is not safe to change his view of the world or himself. In other words, he has been successful in maintaining his self-fulfillment prophecy of himself and his world.

(Long, 1974, p. 182)

Teachers are provided skills in helping youth cope with feelings and in Life Space Interviewing. Coping with a child's affective behavior requires training in the concepts of decoding, labeling, and redirecting behaviors (Long, Alpher, Butt, & Cully, 1976). Simply, decoding is a process by which teachers become aware of a youth's verbal and nonverbal forms of communication in order to obtain clues to his or her inner life. Labeling and accepting feelings is a two phase process, not so much for the youth as for the teacher. The first step requires a teacher to put in words (label) what he thinks the youth is seeing and feeling, such as, "You look angry, sad, excited, etc." The second phase is critical. The teacher must accept the youth's feelings but not his behavior. This is an important but subtle distinction and one that often leads to a charge of permissiveness for the psychoeducational model. This is a misconception. One can sanction feelings but not behavior. Youth who act inappropriately experience the consequences of their behavior. Redirection is simply finding appropriate ways of expressing a feeling in behavior. Either the youth or the teacher can suggest an alternative means of expressing a feeling.

Teachers must handle spontaneous behavior in addition to understanding a youth's affective dynamics. Long offers a series of twelve influence techniques for interfering with behavior (Long & Newman, 1976). Clarizio and McCoy (1976) categorize these influence techniques on three dimensions: (1) support of self-control; (2) situational assistance; and (3) reality and value appraisal.

Support of self-control. This group of techniques is most effective when used with youths whose controls, though generally adequate, need strengthening at times. These youths generally do what is expected of them, but they have momentary lapses because of overexcitement, forgetfulness, and so forth. The following teacher interference techniques usually help these youths re-engage in on-task behavior:

1. *Signal Interference.* These are simply cues from the teacher, such as staring, snapping a finger, tapping the chalk, or clearing one's throat.

2. *Planned Ignoring.* The teacher intentionally ignores a behavior with the belief that it will decrease in frequency if not rewarded.

3. *Interest Boosting.* The teacher rekindles a pupil's wandering attention back to the work at hand by conveying interest in the student's work. The assumption is that the student has the skills necessary to successfully complete the task.

4. *Humor.* The use of humor shows a student that the teacher is human and that he is secure enough in his role to be able to joke.

5. *Proximity Control.* Often times the mere close physical presence of a teacher is sufficient to enable a student to regain control or to keep from losing control.

These supportive techniques require minimal interference from the teacher. Consequently, students are less likely to react aggressively or hostilely to them. Supportive techniques are preventative in nature, that is, they have the potential of preventing small incidents from developing into more difficult situations. The low level methods are of limited value with students who have a difficult time regaining control on their own, and when the misbehavior has become contagious.

Situational assistance. Teacher assistance is necessary when misbehavior occurs as a result of frustration. When social and/or academic demands strain the coping skills of a student, the teacher may attempt to direct the student to the task by means of the following techniques:

1. *Hurdle Help.* Sometimes misbehavior occurs because a student cannot understand or execute the required assignment. In choosing not to ask for help, his frustration and anxiety increase, particularly when he sees that his classmates are working diligently on the task. He is prone to pester others. At this point, the teacher offers the student the help needed to grasp the concept or skills involved rather than focusing on misbehavior. It is important to note that the teacher's assistance is appropriate for learning social skills as well as academic skills.

2. *Restructuring the Class Setting.* Students become bored or overly excited on occasions. Sometimes, it may be more profitable to alter the teaching environment than to call attention to the restlessness. For example, instead of conducting spelling bees in the traditional manner, tension could be relieved by having the students compete as teams following a game show format. The key to restructuring classroom activities is whether the change will facilitate the learning process. Change for change's sake is not encouraged. The reasons are explained in the following technique.

3. *Routines.* Students exhibiting maladaptive behavior need and benefit from structure. The predictability stemming from routine offers students guidelines for their actions and a sense of security. Established routines, such as the start of the school day, recess periods, subject sequence, free time periods, and so forth, should help to minimize classroom behavior problems.

4. *Removing Seductive Objects.* Some objects hold an irresistible appeal to pupils, especially to those with inadequate behavioral controls. Leaving food, athletic gear, and valuables about only invites trouble. It is unfair to expose students with inadequate personal controls to temptations they cannot resist.

5. *Antiseptic Bouncing.* This technique simply calls for a teacher to send a student out of the room to cool off and regain self-control before returning to class. Sending the student on an errand or to another teacher or principal with a note explaining the situation enables the student to save face with his classmates and spares his teacher the problem of having to cope with temper flareups.

6. *Physical Restraint.* Sometimes a student erupts aggressively and physical restraint is the only course of action open to the teacher. Restraint exercised by an adult on a student must be protective and not counteraggressive. The youth must be reassured that he is not going to be hurt, but simply that he is going to be restrained until he regains his control. Policies and techniques regarding restraint vary. Teachers should be aware of local policies for their own and their student's protection.

Reality and value appraisal. In order to use appeals the teacher must be aware of a student's value system. Teachers may appeal to a student's conscience, to group codes, to pride in personal improvement, to the student's sense of fairness, or to the personal relationship between teacher and student. Task appeals such as, "We won't get done if you're going to make noise," appear to be more effective in eliciting task behavior than personal appeals, for instance, "I don't like kids that yell a lot." (Kounin, Gump, & Ryan, 1961).

Another major skill used in conjunction with the influence techniques discussed previously is Life Space Interviewing (LSI). The technique is rooted in crisis theory. It is based on the assumption that people are better motivated to seek and use the help afforded them when they are engaged in a crisis situation. Critical incidents in the classroom thus offer teachers excellent opportunities to teach students appropriate adaptive behavior.

The two goals of LSI are (1) emotional first aid; and (2) clinical exploitation of life events (Redl, 1959). Redl indicates that it is not the nature of the event which defines the need for a LSI but the teacher's decision as to what she chooses to do with the event. Consequently, it is difficult to know in advance which of the two broad objectives one will pursue in an interview. There are occasions when both objectives are combined in a single interview. The key is to make use of a momentary life experience in order to draw out of it something that might help the teacher achieve her goal of behavior change with the student involved.

Morse (1976) suggests that there is a process inherent in the LSI. In conducting a LSI, the teacher should:

1. *Explore instigating conditions.* Explore the student's perception of what occurred without interjecting higher opinions.

2. *Test for depth and spread.* Explore the significance of meaning the student ascribes to incident, i.e., is the problem an isolated event or is it of real concern to the student?

3. *Clarify the content.* Help the student reconstruct what happened based on his perceptions.

4. *Enhance a feeling of acceptance.* Convey empathic understanding of student feelings.

5. *Avoid early imposition of value judgments.* Refrain from implying *wrongness* while encouraging thinking about other viewpoints and feelings.

6. *Explore the internal mechanics for "change" possibilities.* Select a strategy for "clinical exploitation."

7. *The two resolution phases.* Develop and state a plan for constructive future action with student. This plan may be based on mutual working or on needed adult view.

The objective of LSI is to assist students with momentary crisis situations, that is, provide emotional first aid to the student in order to:

1. Drain off hostilities or frustrations to prevent an intolerable accumulation which may lead to further emotional upheaval.

2. Provide emotional support when students are overwhelmed by feelings of panic, guilt, or fury.

3. Maintain a relationship with the student so that he does not withdraw into his own world as a consequence of emotional upheaval.

4. Govern social traffic, i.e., remind wayward pupils of house policies and regulations.

5. Umpire disputes, fights, and other loaded transactions.

These are basically short-term goals. Longer term goals are achieved through clinical exploitation of life events. The teacher emphasizing this aspect of the LSI would be engaged at one time or another in:

1. *Reality rub-in.* Help the student see it like it is. The goal is to increase the student's acceptance of reality and his role in a chain or sequence of events.

2. *Symptom estrangement.* Reduce value of self-defeating symptoms or problem behaviors. The goal is to increase the student's discomfort about his present maladaptive behavior.

3. *Massaging numb value-areas.* Help reinforce or identify potential values within the student for more constructive behavior. The goal is to increase the student's commitment to positive behavior values.

4. *New tool salesmanship.* Help the student to identify and appreciate alternative ways of behaving. The goal is to strengthen the possibilities for utilizing new behaviors.

5. *Manipulating the boundaries of self.* Help strengthen the student's resistance to group contagion. The goal is to help the student become constructively independent.

The major features of LSI are: (1) it is insight producing; (2) it focuses on behavior or attitude change; (3) it has promise of long-term behavior gain; (4) it yields a plan for constructive future action; and (5) it helps the student become responsible for his behavior without focusing the blame on the student. LSI is an extensive clinical technique requiring extensive training. Implementation in the classroom is facilitated by the adoption of a crisis teacher concept (Morse, 1976) and the cooperation of all members of the school staff.

Several public school programs have been developed based on the presumption that sound, systematic, and sensitive teaching can overcome a student's feelings of inadequacy and academic failure. Two examples of the application of the psychoeducational approach are the programs offered at Rose Demonstration School in Washington, D.C., and the Mark Twain School in Montgomery County, Maryland. Data regarding the impact of these two programs are just now becoming available. The results should be of considerable interest because of the age range encompassed in the two programs. The Rose School program is designed primarily for pre-adolescents. The Mark Twain program focuses on secondary level students.

Catch-Up Program

Popenoe (1971) described a very successful Catch-Up Program in Montgomery County, Maryland. All those in the program were between the ages of 8 and 14 years, and had exhibited a severe learning disability, usually in reading. All had at least average intelligence and possessed no apparent organic or pathological problems. The catch-up classes developed out of a need to find a program for underachieving emotionally disturbed students who were referred for help. In the program, individualized instruction was given to a small ungraded group of students with similar learning problems. Emphasis was placed on giving the youths successful learning experiences in order to build up their self-concepts. Much praise was given to each student. The student was also given only work with which he was sure to succeed. A 12-year-old may have been in the first grade reader and the third grade arithmetic book. Instruction was given according to need.

To assist the students in feeling more secure, the program was structured so that they knew exactly what was to be done each hour of the day every day. After the students began to develop confidence in their ability and feel at ease in their environment, they were able to work in groups. By joining the group, the teacher was able to help the student develop a sense of belonging. The student became aware that others liked him, and he in turn began to like others. As a result, the youth no longer felt it necessary to defend himself against loss of esteem by aggressive or withdrawal behavior. His energies were vented toward learning.

The results of the Catch-Up Program are very impressive. In 1964–1965, the average gain in reading was two years and one month. Similar gains were found in three other academic areas tested. Of the 206 students who have been enrolled in Catch-Up Programs, approximately one-third have been able to return to regular classes after the first year and the others after the second year. Follow-up studies indicate that the academic gains not only were maintained but continued to improve as the students progressed through school.

Project Re-Ed

The theoretical basis for Project Re-Ed resides in the social competence model. The social competence model repudiates psychiatric treatment of emotionally disturbed youths; the total commitment to individual and group psychotherapy; the preoccupation with the youth's psychic life; and the theories of transference, regression, and resistance. It suggests instead a

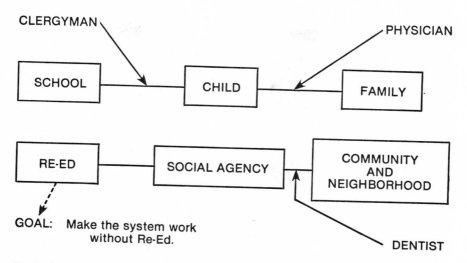

Hobbs, N., 1966. Reprinted with permission of American Psychological Association.

Figure 4.2 Social Competence Model

systems or ecological model of helping emotionally disturbed youth. The social competence model assumes that the youth is an inseparable component of an ecological unit which consists of his family, neighborhood, school, and community. The teacher is not concerned with adjusting the youth to the reality of his or her system, but rather to simultaneously modifying the youth and the various parts of his or her system until a balance is obtained between environmental demands and needed social skills. For example, in residential care one must change both the youth's behavior and classroom environment to fit the pupil. In order to teach new job skills and social habits, one must also prepare the community to accept these skills and habits (Lee, 1971).

The Children's Re-Education Program is designed for mildly to moderately disturbed youths who have average or above-average intelligence but who are often retarded academically. Re-Ed encompasses the youth's entire ecological system by contact with the youth and his family, school, neighborhood, and community. The purpose of Re-Ed is to promote behavioral change and increase skill competencies on the part of the youth and his ecological system so that he can successfully function within the system. The philosophy of Re-Ed contends that the entrance of the program into the youth's life should be as brief as possible, granting time only for readjustments that would allow successful re-entry into an attuned environment. Figure 4.2 (Hobbs, 1966) schematically illustrates the ecological system of a youth.

The Re-Ed Program is used within the open setting of a 5-day week residential school and also within established small group living situations (8 to 12 youths per group) in which the youth must interact with his peers. A three-member team of teacher counselors (day, night, and liaison) with the help of specialized teacher counselors, a diagnostician, and supervisors, carries out a coordinated 24-hour day curriculum plan with a given group of youths. The day teacher counselor is responsible for the execution of the morning classroom, placing emphasis on remediation and enhancement of specific academic competencies. The night teacher counselor extends daily activities by arranging evening experiences so that learning takes place in every informal learning situation. The liaison teacher counselor links the Re-Ed school with the youth's ecological system.

The diagnostician gives an educational diagnosis and evaluation for each youth. Assistance in program planning is also provided by psychiatric, pediatric, psychological, and educational consultants. Growth and developmental changes in the youth and in his environment are the positive goals of the Re-Ed Program. These goals permit various philosophical and theoretical practices while maintaining some basic educational assumptions. Some assumptions are that emotionally disturbed youths do learn; and that most emotional, social, and cognitive behaviors are learned. Educationally, these assumptions are operationalized when the *treatment plan* is curriculum based. The following steps are involved in the curriculum design: gathering information, integrating data, developing specific goals, implementation, coordination, and evaluation. Teaching methods, materials, and techniques vary according to each student's learning style. Some skills learned in the classroom include the student raising his hand for assistance, contributing appropriately to a group discussion, researching a topic of interest, or left-to-right ocular control which is necessary for reading. A short attention span may interfere with a student's performance; therefore, all tasks presented were designed for a specific duration of time, allowing for successful completion and reward. The time structure is gradually lengthened.

The purpose of the clinical physical education program is for the remediation and development acquisition of basic sensory-motor skills. It is also conducive to peer cooperation and group participation. Arts and crafts are designed primarily for creative expression and development of fine motor coordination.

Weinstein (1969), in a study on the home and school adjustment of youth enrolled in two Re-Ed schools, reported that:

1.   Parents indicated their children displayed fewer symptoms, were more socially competent, and were less discrepant from parental standards than before Re-Ed.

2. Teachers viewed the children as being less disruptive in class, working harder, being more able to face new or difficult situations, and having better relationships with their classmates.

3. Improvement in academic adequacy was significant for children from one of the two schools; that is, they showed a substantial increase in rate of acquisition of academic skills after Re-Ed, but they were not up to age or grade norms.

The important aspect of this study is that it demonstrates, at least with Re-Ed, that significant psychoeducationally-oriented variables can be identified, measured, and, in this case, maintained a year after the termination of the treatment program.

The Bryant Youth Educational Support Center (YES)

The YES program was designed for 50 students, ages 12 to 16, who had withdrawn or who had been withdrawn from Minneapolis schools because of social or emotional maladjustment (Boedeker, 1972). The students were equally proportioned between blacks and whites, males and females. The faculty-student ratio was 5:1. An old factory building served as the school. The goals of the social studies program were to:

1. Provide an environment in which caring for self and others was not only acceptable but also actively nurtured.

2. Teach students to perceive their own and teacher behavior as related to the roles they enact within the school.

3. Develop an experimental attitude toward the application of problem-solving skills to social situations related to personal or school problems.

The social studies program developed the following strategy to achieve its objectives: (1) the use of guided group interaction; (2) the use of community resources; and (3) the use of role reversal, psychodrama, and other role-playing techniques. Basically, the group situation followed the Provo model, that is, the peer group had to assume the responsibility for disciplining and coping with individual problems. The community resource people were used to broaden the students' knowledge of social, economic, and political issues they identified as personally important. Exposure to a number of points of view, for example, on the use of drugs, was determined an effective method in challenging stereotyped thinking. Role playing and role reversal were utilized to teach the students how to perceive themselves. Although no definitive data were reported, the investigator concluded that the social studies program was effective in: (1) fostering an increase in communication between teachers and students; and (2) decreasing the number and frequency of disruptive situations.

The Dupage Study

Unlike YES, the DuPage Study evaluated the impact of Positive Peer Culture (PPC) on the educational program within a correctional institution (Sutliff, 1974). Although described previously under the group-oriented interventions, PPC is presented here primarily because the technique was utilized and evaluated within an educational environment. The study provides a comparative data on the reading achievement of 9- to 14-year-old boys experiencing two different institutional treatment programs. The traditional program consisted of each teacher's specializing in a subject area, for example, math, reading, language arts, etc. Students were grouped according to grade level. Classes changed on the hour. The academic program was supplemented by a traditional counseling program. High recidivism rates under this model led to the adoption of PPC as a major program emphasis. Simultaneously, the academic program was restructured. A core curriculum was adopted in which each teacher was responsible for language arts, social studies, and science. Laboratory specialists in the areas of math and reading were integrated into the school program. Grouping was accomplished on the basis of a boy's delinquency sophistication and not on the basis of reading level. The immediate impact on the academic program was the emphasis of programmed instructional materials. The students ranged in age from 9 to 16 years. They were primarily black and considered academic underachievers. Comparisons of the pre-PPC population with the PPC population on several variables indicated:

1. PPC parolees had a significantly shorter incarceration period than did pre-PPC parolees.
2. PPC parolees had a lower rate of parole violations than the pre-PPC parolees.
3. The average month-per-month change in reading score rates was significantly higher for PPC students than for pre-PPC students.

Preliminary data indicated that PPC students were achieving at the rate of one month per month of instruction. Pre-PPC students averaged 0.36 month change per month. The results are similar to Re-Ed's in that the students are not acquiring skills at an expected rate, but their levels of achievement are still below their age or grade norms.

Off-Campus Learning Center (OCLC)

The Off-Campus Learning Center (Schack, 1975) was established as an *alternate school* for pupils unable to make constructive use of a standard school program. A storefront facility houses this suburban Chicago program. The program is designed for approximately 75 adolescents with behavior problems. The staff consists of seven instructors, two full-time social workers, a psychiatric consultant, a secretary/aide, and a full-time director.

This program is a team effort in which parents, students, and home high school staff join together with the OCLC staff in designing individual social and academic affective and cognitive objectives for each student and in assisting students achieve these objectives. The overall goal of the OCLC program is total reintegration of the student into the standard high school setting. In order to achieve this purpose, several educational goals were established:

1. Improve self-concept and self-respect.
2. Proceed more smoothly in the passage from the child to adult status.
3. Deal with frustrations with less anxiety, depression, hostility, and rejection.
4. Modify specific antisocial performance within high school and community.
5. Improve academic achievement so that it approximates potentials and measured abilities.
6. Develop academic skills in order to cope in a standard high school.
7. Develop ethical attitudes about learning.
8. Make decisions regarding academic and vocational goals.
9. Form and maintain meaningful relationships with adults and peers.
10. Be able to improve communication and rapport with the members of his family, peers, school, community, and society in general.

Generalized student profile

Pupils found eligible for the Off-Campus Learning Center tended to be aggressive or withdrawn in addition to experiencing multiple academic failures. Symptomatic expressions of aggressive behavior included physical or verbal abuse or destruction of property. Symptoms of withdrawn behavior included poor study skills, truancy, tardiness, and general apathy. Case study or psychiatric diagnosis generally supported the view that the behavior of these pupils reflected serious personality disorders requiring therapy and sometimes prolonged treatment.

In addition to the generalized profile, specific characteristics of OCLC students included:

1. An average or above-average IQ was indicated by the WISC.
2. The majority (60%) of the students referred to the program were sophomores.
3. Of the students 80% were the youngest or second to the youngest sibling in the family.
4. Of all students 42% referred had previously been placed in either residential schools, psychiatric wards, or institutions.
5. Approximately 40% of the students had only one parent in the home.

The referral and placement process begins in the standard high school with identification by counselor, teacher, social worker, or other professional who refers the youngster to a division referral review board in order to determine whether or not it would be appropriate to develop a case study. The case study contains a psychological evaluation, complete social history workup, academic evaluation, and medical reports. When the case study is complete, a special education staffing is held by the referring school pupil personnel services in conjunction with the OCLC staff.

If eligibility is determined, an educational prescriptive plan is designed for the student. Thereafter, the student and his family meet for two initial interviews with the Learning Center staff. At this juncture the placement plan is solidified with the student, his or her family, and the standard school. This placement procedure is followed up until the first six weeks of the semester have been completed. Pupils staffed after that time are placed at the beginning of the following semester. Student enrollment is maintained at approximately 75.

The Off-Campus Learning Center provides small classes (not to exceed eight) where students are directed toward individual academic and social-skill building activities as determined by the individual performance objectives. Students have one teacher instructing them in three academic areas. Subjects include Math (both basic and algebra), English, Social Studies (including United States History), and Communication Skills; plus a daily Physical Education class, including team and individual sports as well as crafts and adaptive games.

All students are encouraged to participate in group counseling with the social worker, teacher, and his fellow classmates on a weekly basis.

These group sessions are a regularly scheduled part of the week for each classroom. Psychiatric social workers are also available to students for individual counseling. Regular weekly parent group meetings are available to all parents who have students in the program.

The instructor's role.   The instructor is primarily a communication expert. He is skilled in both verbal and nonverbal communication with others. He is able to monitor his own feelings to avoid being misperceived and viewed as inconsistent and thus dishonest. Only through clear communication can the instructor perform his two major duties. One, he seeks to foster positive relationships with students and parents and between students and parents. Two, he assists skill-building by attending to each student's unique mode of learning, interest, and abilities.

Successful communication includes evaluation. The instructor has the obligation to give the student feedback as to his performance, both social and academic. Such evaluation includes data on how well the student has performed in comparison to his past behavior, but also data on how the student's present performance compares with those behaviors expected in the standard educational program and in the larger competitive society. The instructor may or may not be an expert in one or more areas of content. However, content is significant only as it enhances the development of social and academic skills. Further, he does not function as a psychologist or social worker. The instructor does not interpret intra-psychic processes to the student or to his parents. Two other functions of the OCLC teacher are to be available to other teachers during their free time for crisis intervention and to communicate with parents through phone calls and conferences when necessary and at six regularly scheduled parent/teacher meetings throughout the school year.

Teachers work individually with students to establish performance objectives. The initial planning stage begins with a weekly evaluation sheet formulated between teacher and student which lists specific behavior and academic objectives. In almost all cases when a student is first placed in the program, his school day is self-contained for the first semester. The second semester and thereafter, students are gradually fed back into the division and scheduled for specifically recommended courses. Schedules are usually a combined effort of the student, OCLC teacher, and division counselor. It is possible to choose division teachers who are best able to deal effectively with the learning center student. Total reintegration of the student back into the standard high school is the ultimate goal. This goal is accomplished within two academic years.

Objectives.   The following represent general course objectives for English, Social Studies, Mathematics, Communication Skills, and Physical Education:

English

English Skills 1, 2, 3, and 4 (Reading; writing, language, and vocabulary skills in four areas of English study)

Course Titles

A.   Skills 1—Man as Individual (to increase awareness of self)

B.   Skills 2—Man in the Family (to increase awareness of roles in the family)

C.   Skills 3— Man in Society (to increase awareness of roles in society)

D.   Skills 4—Man in the Future (to increase awareness of the future)

General Behavior Student will Exhibit in These Courses

A.   Cognitive

    1.   To improve reading skills;

    2.   To gain a knowledge of literary techniques;

    3.   To gain a knowledge of specific authors and techniques.

B.   Affective

    1.   Insight into the multiple varieties and pleasures of reading;

    2.   Insight into the relationship of literature to their lives.

Mathematics

Math Skills 1 and 2 (Basic Math)

Consumer Related Math: The student will demonstrate the ability to use Math concepts so that he achieves economic success.

Math Skills 3 and 4 (Algebra)

The student will demonstrate an ability to advance in self-fulfillment by an increase in his knowledge and in his ability to communicate.

Social Studies

Social Studies Skills 1, 2, 3, and 4

A.   Skills 1—Anthropology. The student will be provided with an understanding of the unique nature of man and his culture.

B.   Skills 2—Geography. The student will be provided with an understanding of how the area in which man lives on this earth is known as his spatial environment with physical, cultural, political, and economic characteristics.

C.   Skills 3—Sociology. The student will be shown how man lives and interacts in societies. Societies determine the norms and values that organize man's behavior.

D.   Skills 4—Government. The student will be provided with an analysis of the decision-making process in any society or group. This decision-making is defined as those political activities from which choices are made between alternate courses of action within a political system.

History

History Skills 1 and 2

A. Skills 1—This course will demonstrate to the student how history is the selection, recording, and interpretation of man's total experience.
B. Skills 2—This course is designed to develop student understanding of United States foreign policy today; it analyzes the historical intricacies that played a role in shaping that policy.

Communication Skills

Communication Skills 1 and 2

The student will be provided with the skills to fulfill his needs to know how and what he is and to relate and contribute to his environment.

Physical Education

Physical Education Skills 1, 2, 3, and 4

The student will be provided with physical activities that correlate fair play; group cooperation; physical and mental well being; and activities that assist the academic pursuits by providing an outlet of channel frustration.

This combination of a small class situation plus supportive therapeutic services provides a milieu geared to assist the individual in attaining academic and social skills, and in building and fostering positive relationships with adults and peers. The criteria for success are determined by the achievement of the individual's performance goals and objectives.

There are fundamental rules and regulations regarding attendance, behavior, and social and academic expectations. Students are made aware that they will be evaluated on their social and academic behavior. The most common means of effecting this understanding is at the initial conference with the student and his parents. With infraction of rules, parent conferences are again called with further communication between the home and OCLC staff.

Consequences for inappropriate behavior include extra assignments, cleanup chores, loss of privileges, and occasional suspensions. Continuous and blatant failure to adhere to rules is interpreted as the student's inability to adjust to the structure of the program, thereby indicating that he is not benefiting from the services provided. Termination staffing is then the probable recommendation and procedure.

Evaluation. Documented evaluation is done at OCLC on a weekly basis, six-week basis, and yearly basis. The final report is the principal component for determining a continued placement and educational plan. The report is decided on at an annual review staffing held at each of the three standard high school buildings. Each student's prescriptive plan is discussed in terms of the student's progress, current status, and projected needs. A final recommendation is arrived at after careful consideration by OCLC and Pupil Personnel Division staff.

After three years, observation indicates that students who were in the program for a year or two for the most part are either succeeding in the standard high school (meaning that they are attending on a regular basis, passing course work, and coping with the rules and regulations of the school); or they have graduated from high school, are in the armed services, are working regularly, or have gone on to higher education.

General Studies Program (GSP)

The General Studies Program (GSP) is a suburban Chicago program designed for disruptive high school students (Verdonck, 1975). The program is an attempt not only to constructively recognize the deficits of a group of students with whom the prevailing mode of education has not been too successful, but also to provide an adjusted program, curriculum, and approach designed to be ameliorative.

GSP is designed to meet the needs of students who are categorized as *educationally handicapped,* that is, students who are unable to make maximum use of their school experience due to such factors as cultural deprivation, educational retardation (functioning two or more years below expected grade level in basic academic areas of reading and math), population mobility (reflecting frequent interruptions in previous school attendance), socioeconomic considerations, and inadequate school opportunities. As a result of these and other factors, these students are not able or willing to function constructively in school in spite of the fact that they are not significantly handicapped by intellectual limitations, neurological impairment or dysfunction, perceptual handicaps or significant emotional problems.

While there is no one characteristic typical of all these students, one or more of the following criteria is diagnostically selective:

1. The student is over age for his grade placement.
2. The student has low achievement in reading and mathematics. Basic skills in math and reading are two or more years below a level which would be commensurate with the student's overall level of intellectual functioning. In other words, basic academic skills are very much below that which could be reasonably expected of the student.
3. The student's school attendance record shows a pattern of absences.

4. The student has a high rate of failure or near failure in academic courses, has been previously retained or shows a pattern of frequent social promotions.

5. The student is considered to be a potential dropout because of additional lack of interest and motivation.

6. The student does not participate in extracurricular activities and generally exhibits little, if any, commitment to the total school environment.

These are students who have experienced either years of failure in the regular school setting or, at best, only marginal success. By the time they enter the secondary school, they are indifferent, generally alienated, and unable to compete academically. Selection for placement is based on an evaluation of the student's past record of achievement, social history, high school placement test scores, health information, and other pertinent data. Recommendations for placement are formulated by professional staff including classroom teachers, social worker, psychologist, and guidance staff.

All basic academic requirements for graduation, both state and district, are met through credits earned in the General Studies Program. Special classes are provided in academic areas. Students are integrated into regular classes in nonacademic subjects according to interest and aptitude. Class sizes are sufficiently limited to allow for individualized instruction.

The program adopts a positive teaching approach in which various techniques are utilized to build appropriate social behavior and a positive attitude toward learning. Although not clearly described, discipline is managed within the classroom. Recurring disciplinary problems are referred to a staff meeting. The specific scope and sequence of the General Studies Program curriculum is as follows:

Freshmen

	Units
English I — Social Studies	2
Math (Applied) — Science	2
Industrial Arts — Home Economics	1
Physical Education	1/2

Sophomores

	Units
English II — Social Studies	2
Elective or a Work-Study Program	1–2
Math — Science	2
Physical Education	1/2

Juniors

	Units
English III	1
United States History	1
In-School Work: e.g. Cooperative Work Training	2
Physical Education	1/2

Seniors

	Units
English — Social Science Survey	2
Community Work Experience	1
Elective	1
Physical Education	1/2

Diagnostic achievement batteries are administered periodically to provide additional evaluative material relating to student needs, to assess student progress and program effectiveness. Students in the program are not given regular study hall assignments. Study periods are considered to be more productive if provided through the general studies classrooms. There are opportunities for typing, art and music appreciation activities, as well as a required course in consumer education and units designed to prepare the student for successful completion of the drivers' education course.

Program Design

1. The structure of the freshman curriculum involves two major areas of emphasis:

   a. intensive work in communication skills utilizing the concept of the learning center classroom, and

   b. vocational survey.

As an example, a freshman student is assigned a one and one-half hour block of time for English—Social Studies. Math and science subject matter is structured toward an applied approach. A practical arts emphasis replaces the more traditional industrial arts program.

All teachers working in the learning center are given extensive support by a curriculum director. When subject matter is interrelated, as is often the case in math and science areas, teachers may adopt a team-teaching approach. Much attention is given to molding subject matter to the student's interests, needs, and achievement levels. In addition, whenever possible, subject matter is related to the vocational survey portion of the program.

Remedial reading assignments are provided for all students in groups and on an individual basis. Consultation service is provided by Learning Disabilities and Learning Resource Programs special education teachers.

During the freshman year, certain periods are devoted to work with a career counselor. The students are exposed to major vocational areas such as health occupations, food service, distributive and marketing occupations, business and office occupations, and technical occupations. Vocational areas are presented to enable the student to make a more realistic vocational choice as he progresses into more specific vocational course work in the sophomore, junior, and senior years.

2. In the sophomore year, the 1½ hour block of time in the English and Social Studies area is maintained. Communication skills, including intensive remedial reading, continue to be emphasized. Work assignments are carefully graduated to the ability level of the students. The most severely disabled in reading continue to receive intensive work in reading.

In the vocational area, most boys receive a basic mechanics course. This course covers training from the use of tools through basic power mechanics. Mechanical training is considered basic to all vocational-technical areas.

Sophomore students also select an elective course from the total school offering. Care here is taken to see that this elective course is in line with the student's abilities, interests, and emotional-educational level of maturity. This choice affords some of the higher ability students in the program an opportunity to take part in some of the more academically-oriented course work in the regular school program.

Students who, for one reason or another, are unemployed due to an inability to find or hold a job may be involved in an in-school work experience. Work experiences include such areas as library assistants; custodial, maintenance, cafeteria services; grounds keeping; school office; secretarial, clerical; and possibly assisting on building projects necessary for providing shelving and other materials to other school buildings in the district.

Other professional staff are assigned to the program to provide both consultative and direct mental health services. A school social worker and psychologist provide consultative services for all students in the program. In some cases, intensive counseling is provided for those with more serious adjustment problems. Group counseling is offered. The goals of the group program are to assist the students in developing a better understanding of their feelings, the attitudes of their peers, and to improve their capacity to more effectively communicate with others. Group counseling with parents is occasionally utilized to help parents better understand both the problems of their youngsters and the problems of the school.

Both GSP and the Off-Campus Learning Center report similar results. Definitive data regarding academic achievement, truancy rates, job success, and reintegration figures are now being compiled. Both programs are designed for similar populations but emphasize different treatment philosophies. GSP is a vocationally-oriented program; OCLC is more psychoeducationally-oriented.

SUMMARY

Treatment, as a concept, has to be viewed in its proper perspective. Basically, treatment, to be effective, has to consist of a range or continuum of services. Access to treatment should be initiated and terminated with a diagnostic or evaluative process which first verifies a problem, and then verifies the absence or control of the formerly identified problem. In addition, a treatment strategy must be able to specify the instructional or intervention rules which govern its use. When children or youth achieve and/or display adaptive behavior, the intervention is perceived as successful. But as Sabatino (1973) emphasizes, the reasons for their achievement or adjustment are largely unknown. In addition, when youths fail to respond to the intervention, the reasons for their failure remain hidden. Psychoeducational approaches still must address the need for developing an ordered, sequenced set of intervention tasks which others can replicate and evaluate.

There have been several responses to this challenge. Texas (Mintz & Skipper, 1974) and Massachusetts (Ohlin, Coates, & Miller, 1974) have deemphasized traditional institutionalization and have moved toward developing a continuum of services for disruptive youth. A number of supportive psychoeducational approaches have been incorporated into the reorganization. Data collection has recently been initiated.

Educators are also responding to the challenge. Fagen, Long, and Stevens (1975) have designed a Self-Control Curriculum (see Table 4.4) to provide pupils with skills for coping with life situations.

The curriculum units contain educational goals which can be translated into student-centered behavior objectives. A series of tasks utilizing games, role playing, and lessons or discussions are used in teaching the self-control curriculum. The authors emphasized the rationale and model on which their curriculum was based in their initial publication (1975). Few teaching strategies are described in the book. The development and field testing of a number of teaching activities based on the Self Control Curriculum at the primary, intermediate, and secondary school levels is underway (Dembinski, Fagen, Long, and Mauser, 1976). Although designed as a preventative intervention, the curriculum may have some promise as an intervention or treatment tool.

The challenge is clear. There is a critical need to test treatment strategies and curricula against youth behaviors and learning aptitudes. This *interaction design* model provides a vehicle to obtain data upon which sound decisions can be made for using or rejecting treatment and curricula models.

Table 4.4. THE SELF-CONTROL CURRICULUM:
OVERVIEW OF CURRICULUM AREAS AND UNITS

Curriculum Area	Curriculum Unit
Selection	1. Focusing and concentration 2. Mastering figure-ground discrimination 3. Mastering distractions and interference 4. Processing complex patterns
Storage	1. Developing visual memory 2. Developing auditory memory
Sequencing and Ordering	1. Developing time orientation 2. Developing auditory-visual sequencing 3. Developing sequential planning
Anticipating Consequences	1. Developing alternatives 2. Evaluating consequences
Appreciating Feelings	1. Identifying feelings 2. Developing positive feelings 3. Managing feelings 4. Reinterpreting feeling events
Managing Frustration	1. Accepting feelings of frustration 2. Building coping resources 3. Tolerating frustration
Inhibition and Delay	1. Controlling action 2. Developing part-goals
Relaxation	1. Developing body relaxation 2. Developing thought relaxation 3. Developing movement relaxation

REFERENCES

Achenbach, T. M. *Development Psychopathology*. New York: The Ronald Press Company, 1974.

Boedeker, L. "Teaching, Learning: Strategies for Coping." *NASSP Bulletin* 363 (1972): 82–90.

Caplan, G. "Opportunities for School Psychologists in the Primary Prevention." *Mental Hygiene* 47 (October 1963): 525–539.

Caplan, G. *Prevention of Mental Disorders in Children*. New York: Basic Books, 1961.

Clarizio, H. F., and McCoy, G. F. *Behavior Disorders in Children*. 2nd ed. New York: T. Y. Crowell Co., 1976.

Clarizio, H. F., and McCoy, G. F. *Behavior Disorders in School-Aged Children*. Scranton, Pa.: Chandler Publishing Co., 1970.

Dembinski, R. J.; Fagen, S. A.; Long, N. J.; and Mauser, A. J. *The Self-Control Curriculum: Experimental Copy*. Dekalb, Illinois: Northern Illinois University, 1976.

Dreikurs, R., and Cassel, P. *Discipline Without Tears*. New York: Hawthorne Books, Inc., 1972.

Empey, L. T. and Rabow, J. "The Provo Experiment in Delinquency Rehabilitation." *Juvenile Delinquency—A Book of Readings*. Edited by R. Giallombardo. New York: John Wiley and Sons, Inc., 1966.

Fagen, S. A.; Long, N. J.; and Stevens, D. J. *Teaching Children Self Control—Preventing Emotional and Learning Problems in the Elementary School*. Columbus, Ohio: Charles E. Merrill Publishing Co., 1975.

Glasser, W. *Reality Therapy—A New Approach to Psychiatry*. New York: Harper and Row, 1965.

Grant, J. D. "Delinquency Treatment in an Institutional Setting." *Juvenile Delinquency, Research, and Theory*. Edited by C. Quay. Princeton, New Jersey: D. Van Nostrand Co., Inc., 1965, pp. 263–297.

Hobbs, N. "Helping Disturbed Children: Psychological and Ecological Strategies." *American Psychologist* 21 (1966): 1105–1111.

James S. L.; Osborn, F.; and Oetting, E. R. "Treatment for Delinquent Girls, and Adolescent Self-Concept Group." *Community Mental Health Journal* 3 (1967): 377–381.

Jesness, C. C. *The Fricot Ranch Study. Becoming Delinquent: Young Offenders and the Correctional Process*. Edited by Peter Garabedian and Don Gibbons. Chicago: Aldini Publishing Co., 1970, pp. 226–237.

Kounin, J.; Gump, P.; and Ryan, J. "Explorations in Classroom Management." *Journal of Teacher Education* 12 (1961): 235–246.

Krasnow, A. "An Adlerian Approach to the Problem of School Maladjustment." *Academic Therapy Quarterly* 7 (1971–72): 171–183.

Lee, B. "Curriculum Design: The Re-education Approach." *Conflict in the Classroom: The Education of Children with Problems*. 2nd ed. Edited by N. J. Long, W. C. Morse, and R. G. Newman. Belmont, California: Wadsworth Publishing Co., Inc., 1971, pp. 383–394.

Levitt, E. "Psychotherapy with Children: A Further Review." *Behavior Research and Therapy* 1 (1963): 45–51.

Levitt, E. "Results of Psychotherapy with Children: An Evaluation." *Journal of Consulting Psychology* 21 (1957): 189–196.

Long, A. J.; Alpher, R.; Butt, F.; and Cully, M. "Helping Children Cope with Feelings." *Conflict in the Classroom*. 3rd ed. Edited by N. Long, W. Morse, and R. Newman. Belmont, California: Wadsworth, 1976, pp. 297–301.

Long, N.; Morse, W.; and Newman, R., eds. *Conflict in the Classroom*. 3rd ed. Belmont, California: Wadsworth, 1976, pp. 337–342.

Long, N. J. "Nicholas J. Long." *Teaching Children with Behavior Disorders: Personal Perspectives*. Edited by J. M. Kauffman and C. D. Lewis. Columbus: C. E. Merrill, 1974.

Long, N. J., and Newman, R. G. "Managing Surface Behavior of Children in School." *Conflict in the Classroom*. 3rd ed. Edited by N. J. Long, W. C. Morse, and R. G. Newman. Belmont, California: Wadsworth, 1976, pp. 308–317.

Massimo, J. L., and Shore, M. F. "Comprehensive Vocationally Oriented Psychotherapy." *Psychiatry* 30 (1967): 229–236.

Mintz, J. A., and Skipper, K. C. "Proceedings of the Annual Fall Conference: Teacher Educators for Children with Behavioral Disorders, November, 1974." Gainesville, Florida, pp. 81–85.

Morse, W. "The Crisis or Helping Teacher." *Conflict in the Classroom*. 3rd ed. Edited by N. Long, W. Morse, and R. Newman. Belmont, California: Wadsworth, 1976, pp. 207–213.

Morse, W. "Worksheet on Life Space Interviewing for Teachers." Conflict in the *Classroom*. 3rd ed. Edited by N. Long, W. Morse, and R. Newman. Belmont, California: Wadsworth, 1976, pp. 337–342.

Ohlin, L. E.; Coates, R. B.; and Miller, A. D. "Radical Correctional Reform: A Case Study of the Massachusetts Youth Correctional System." *Harvard Educational Review* 44 (February 1974): 74–111.

Popenoe, E. P. "Breakthrough for Underachievers." *Conflict in the Classroom: The Education of Children with Problems*. Edited by N. Long, W. C. Morse, and R. G. Newman. Belmont, California: Wadsworth Publishing Co., Inc., 1971.

Redl, F. "The Concept of the Life Space Interview." *American Journal of Orthopsychiatry* 29 (1959): 1–18.

Redl, F. *When We Deal with Children*. New York: The Free Press, 1966.

Redl, F., and Wineman, D. *The Aggressive Child*. Glencoe, Illinois: The Free Press, 1957.

Reinert, H. R. *Children in Conflict*. St. Louis: C. V. Mosby, 1976.

Sabatino, D. A. *Neglected and Delinquent Children*. Wilkes-Barre, Pennsylvania: Educational Development Center, Pennsylvania Department of Education, Wilkes College, 1973.

Schack, M. "Off-Campus Learning Center." Paper presented to Illinois Conference on Behavior Disorders at Northern Illinois University, June 30, 1975, at DeKalb, Illinois.

Shore, M. F., and Massimo, J. L. "The Alienated Adolescent: A Challenge to the Mental Health Profession." *Adolescence* 4 (1969): 19–34.

Sutliff, C. A. *The DuPage Study*. Springfield, Illinois: Illinois Department of Corrections, 1974.

Verdonck, D. H. "General Studies Program." Paper presented to Illinois Conference on Behavior Disorders at Northern Illinois University, June 30, 1975, at Dekalb, Illinois.

Vorrath, H. H. *Positive Peer Culture: Content, Structure, Process*. Michigan: Michigan Center for Group Studies. 1972.

Weinstein, L. "Project Re-Ed School for Emotionally Disturbed Children: Effectiveness as Viewed by Referring Agencies, Parents, and Teachers." *Exceptional Children* (May 1969): 703–711.

5

behavior related to suicides, runaways, alcoholism, and drug abuse

ANTOINETTE B. LOTSOF

In the past two decades public attention has been focused on troubled youth. The public media has deluged the American people with dramatic stories concerning the drug problem, juvenile alcoholism, and runaways. Such publicity tends to emphasize the more lurid aspects, often distorting fact. It behooves the modern day educator to have accurate information upon which to plan effective programs for selectively differentiated norm-violating youth.

Today, more than ever, American culture is youth oriented. The vast amount of human potential wasted when adolescents reject society is disturbing to adult society. Young people feel powerless to deal with increased pressures, sensing a futility in altering adult attitudes. Adolescents who cannot reduce anxieties, conflicts, nor develop coping mechanisms necessary to deal effectively with frustrating situations frequently see no alternative but to extricate themselves. Some of the escapes selected are physically running away, committing suicide, or removing the pain by seeking refuge in drugs and alcohol.

Today's society fosters rapid change resulting in stresses. Toffler (1970) states in *Future Shock:* "Much that now strikes us as incomprehensible would be far less so if we took a fresh look at the racing rate of change that makes reality seem, sometimes, like a kaleidoscope run wild" (p. 10).

Young people are victims of this rapid change, and according to McLeod, "there is every reason to believe that many of the newer features of contemporary American culture make growing up more, rather than less, difficult" (McLeod, 1973, p. 1). A 1970 White House Conference on Children Forum states its concern: "Millions of our children are turning to drugs. Venereal disease ratios are soaring. The teen suicide rate is shocking. FBI reports show the juvenile crime rate hitting the record highs . . . great numbers of young people are alienated from their parents."

The number of youths who run away each year may be indicative of the unhappiness felt by young people. This number is estimated as high as one million. Youcha states: "There is no typical runaway: they come from all social and economic backgrounds, from suburbs and inner cities, from intact and from seriously disorganized families" (1973, p. 48).

During the late 1960s and early 1970s, the accelerated increase in drug usage by young people became a frightening yet fascinating phenomenon to the general populace, particularly parents. Although drug abuse had been with us for many years, it had not reached the conscience of the public until the use of illicit drugs became evident among the middle-class youth. Prior to this time, the use of illegal drugs had been fairly confined to the ghettos. But when middle-class youngsters became entranced with the use of drugs, the whole nation took notice. Puzzled and bewildered parents asked the question, "How could this happen?" The times were affluent. Children had many more advantages than their parents, many of whom experienced the austere days of the depression. Why were the young people not happier, more satisfied, more capable of taking advantage of the abundant opportunities available to them? McLeod in *Growing Up in America: A Background to Contemporary Drug Abuse,* noted:

> Drug abuse by the young seems a violent repudiation of this familiar dream. The use of drugs for sensation or escape would seem to signal a deep dissatisfaction with life as it is, yet so many adults, the life of at least the middle-class youngster of the 1970's looks far more comfortable and more privileged than was their own in the teen years. (1973, p. 1)

Teenage alcoholism is rapidly becoming the number one drug problem in the United States. Although alcohol is not considered a drug by many, a realization is fast developing that the consumption of beer, wine, and hard liquor by adolescents is just as serious (or more so) as the consumption of illegal drugs.

Traditionally, much of the amelioration for the problems faced by adolescents fell outside the jurisdiction of the schools. That situation is damaging. All educators have a responsibility in educating troubled youth; the practicing special educator a major mission, the regular educator the first line of defense. To be forewarned is to be forearmed, and the ammunition necessary is information that permits an accurate assessment of the amount and degree of problem, and the resources needed to help.

The school provides an excellent place to instigate preventative programs; it is the place to explore with adolescents the alternatives to suicides, running away, or use of alcohol and drugs.

SUICIDES

Suicide and suicidal attempts are not uncommon among adolescents. Although all suicide attempts may not reflect a true desire to end one's life, an alarming number of adolescents do kill themselves. Toolan (1975) indicated the fourth leading cause of death among adolescents in the United States is suicide. It outranks death by tuberculosis, leukemia, rhumatic fever, appendicitis and all contagious diseases. Although self-destructive behavior does occur earlier in childhood, the number of young people who kill themselves between the ages of 15 and 19 is about 8 times greater than the number of children under 14 years of age. Suicidal behavior is on the rise but the increase in self-destructive behavior has been greater among adolescents than among any other group.

There are a variety of reasons for the lack of accurate statistics in this field of completed suicides and suicidal attempts. (1) Many suicide deaths are reported as accidents in order to protect the immediate family from the emotional agony of public admission. (2) There is no way of accurately assessing how many accidents are deliberate attempts to end one's life. A car in the hands of an adolescent determined to end his life could become a lethal weapon. (3) Drug overdoses may or may not be deliberate acts of self-destruction. (4) Not all cases of attempted suicide are reported. Needless to say, the number of such deaths is unknown. There seems to be some evidence, however, that adolescents threaten or attempt suicide more often than adults. It is estimated that in the range of 15- to 19-year-olds, the ratio of suicide gestures or attempts at actual suicide is from 50:1 to 150:1 (McIntire & Angle, 1971; Toolan, 1975). Girls far outnumber boys in attempted suicide, whereas more boys than girls actually take their own life.

Suicidal gestures are not necessarily bona fide attempts to do away with one's life. A gesture not uncommon among teenagers is making several slight cuts on the arms from the wrists to the elbows, or similar cuts across the chest. It is not infrequent for young people to make several attempts at suicide. If their life situation does not improve, the attempts become more and more serious with the chance of success increasing each time. Toolan (1975) suggests that such attempts are a signal of distress. Teenagers often feel a need to make a dramatic gesture to draw parents' or other authority figures' attention to their dilemma. Anger at a parent, boyfriend, girfriend, or other significant person in an adolescent's life may promote manipulation in the guise of a suicide threat or attempt. After the death of a teenager has occurred, many guilt-laden adults have bemoaned the fact that they did not respond when such threats were first expressed. History of difficulties in coping with life stresses is an integral part of the causal factors. The precipitating event may seem trivial if taken by itself. McIntire & Angle note, "Precipitating stress (often) revolved around the five P's, parents, peers, privation, punctured romance, and pregnancy" (1971, p. 920). An argument between parent and child may constitute the crisis situation. A stable, mentally healthy youth can take such argument in his stride whereas a potential suicidal young person may react to the crisis as if it were the final straw. A youth who has experienced years of disharmony in the home, feelings of rejection, worthlessness, and who perceives no way out, may attempt to end it all by killing himself.

The events in a young person's life history which have been contributing factors to suicidal behavior have included loss of a parent, marital discord, and social-psychological isolation. Toolan (1975) found in the teenagers he studied that less than one-third lived with both parents. The fathers were often missing from the family. Stanley and Barter (1970) found the loss of a parent before the child was 12 years of age to be a significant variable in predicting suicide attempts. If the loss of a parent occurred later in the young person's life, it was not predictive. He also found that the kind and extent of marital disharmony was more important than whether or not disharmony existed. Arguments centering around separation or divorce occurred much more frequently in families of potential suicidal youth than nonsuicidal youth. Early parent loss or the threat of parent loss through divorce seems to be a significant factor contributing to self-destructive behavior in teenagers.

Sabbath (1972) concurs with the parent role as a powerful contributing factor. He suggests that parents who reject their children pass this message on to the child either consciously or unconsciously by word and deed. Rejection may be manifested by hypercritical discipline or by absence of mothering. The struggle and conflict results in a cycle of misbehavior: anger on the part of the parent or parents to recorded misbehavior by the child, to more anger by the parent. The battle increases in intensity as time goes on. Then at adolescence, if a girl, for example, is rejected by a boyfriend, it is perceived as a reenactment of the rejection of the parent, and the teenager may resort to suicide to terminate her frustration.

Renshaw (1974) suggests that depression is not uncommon among teenagers. Such young people, when they feel trapped in an insoluble conflict, can be considered potential candidates for self-destructive behavior. Depression is often seen as aggression turned inward against oneself resulting in feelings of poor self-esteem and helplessness. This feeling of helplessness appears to be a major factor in precipitating suicide. Self-destructive behavior has been linked to diminishing problem solving behavior among adolescents more frequently than with adults, primarily because adolescents have had fewer life experiences to draw on in order to seek alternative behaviors. Levenson (1971) found suicidal young people, when compared with psychiatric patients and normal adolescents, were significantly less able to activate successful problem solving techniques. The results of this study indicate that a potential suicidal teenager is generally unable to concentrate and cognitively assess the situation, evaluate realistically, and select alternative ways of satisfying school and social responsibilities.

School and societal responsibility: suicides

Drug and crisis hot lines have been established throughout the United States in an attempt to provide the potential suicider with on-the-spot crisis intervention. Over 200 suicide prevention centers now exist within the boundaries of the United States. It is one technique to increase the problem solving potential of an endangered teenager. The school can also respond to this lethal phenomenon in several ways. (1) School personnel should be cognizant of the enormity of the problem and begin to identify those students who seem particularly unhappy or depressed. Humanistic education may provide adults who will listen and can refer the student to helpful resources. (2) The schools should make a concerted effort to work with parents on the problems of youth. Parents are often at a loss as how to deal with the behavior their off-springs are exhibiting. The cooperative efforts between school and home provide an arena whereby each can contribute to the understanding of the present problem. Working together they can search for solutions. (3) Although the need for affective education was brought to the attention of educators by Bloom several years ago, our secondary educational system still concentrates almost exclusively on acquisition of cognitive skills. The schools should provide some opportunity for students to explore developmental problems, to examine life goals, and to procure training in decision making and problem solving techniques. Helping students discover alternatives to suicide should be a major goal.

RUNAWAYS

Runaways have become a concern to Congress, law enforcement agencies, courts, and most of all, parents. The actual number of adolescents who leave their homes is difficult to determine. In 1973, a total of 178,432 young people were arrested in the United States for running away. This number can be considered only the tip of the iceberg as the estimated number ranges anywhere from 6,000,000 (*U.S. News and World Report, 1972*) to one million (Youcha, 1973) a year. Accurate information is difficult to obtain and numerical estimates are imprecise. The Runaway Youth Act (U.S. Congressional Record) states: "the number of juveniles who leave and remain away from home without parental permission has increased in alarming proportions, creating a substantial law enforcement problem for the communities inundated, significantly endangering the young people who are without resources and live on the streets" (p. 3566).

During the 1960s and early 1970s the romantic myth of running away was perpetuated by the publicity generated around the "flower-children" in the Haight-Ashbury section of San Francisco. The dream of "doing one's own thing" surrounded by other misunderstood young people had little in common with the realities of street life and its involvement with drugs, sexual abuse, poverty and violence. Some young people bitterly regretted their decision to run away once they experienced the reality of the road, but were hesitant to contact their parents because of fear of retribution.

Although some research has been generated around this concern, we still do not have a clear understanding of the runaway phenomenon. The reasons range from the search for excitement to the desire for experience; however, a preponderence of people run to avoid a wide variety of personal or situational problems (Ambrosino, 1972; Robey, Rosenwald, & Rosenwald, 1964; Youth Crisis Services, 1972; Canadian Welfare Council, 1972). A great majority of adolescent runaways perceive themselves as being in conflict with their parents. Bayer, Nolt, Reid, and Quinlan (1973) found that many of the adolescents who run away come from broken homes and their pre-adolescent years were disrupted by parental separation and remarriage. However, other studies do not substantiate these findings. The Canadian Welfare Council (1971) found, in a study including 119 transients ranging from 16 to 24 years of age, that 70.6% of these young people came from homes where both parents were living. However, they did find that 44.7% of the girls who were on the road did come from one-parent households. A study done at The Bridges, a youth services house in Minneapolis, whose clientele was young people aged 14 and 15, found that 77% were young people from two-parent homes. It is interesting to note that more girls than boys make up the runaway population of those 16 years of age or younger, while those 17 or older are more frequently male than female.

The reasons for leaving home vary, according to the investigator, from trival conflicts over eating with the family, church attendance, associating with certain boys and girls, to parental complaints concerning mode of dress, sufficient privacy, and interference with dating practices. Severe punishment and/or child abuse occurs more often in families of runaways than in other adolescent families (Allen & Sandhu, 1967).

Underlying the present problem is the availability of need satisfaction within the home environment. Conflict can occur in homes which basically provide for adolescent needs without it being so disruptive that the only alternative the young person perceives is to leave. The need for love is strong and one of the major factors influencing runaways is the lack of expressed parental affection (Robey, et al., 1964; Allen & Sandhu, 1967; Youth Crisis Service, 1972). Blood and D'Angelo (1974) found that lack of demonstrative love-giving was interpreted by teenagers as signifying that there was no love. The higher the intensity of conflict with parents, the less likely any positive reinforcers were present to indicate to the teenager the presence of affection.

Closely associated with the concept of love is that of acceptance. Youths who have a high level of self-esteem tend to have parents who respect their ideas and judgment. Runaways tend to have less self-esteem, show inadequate self-confidence, and see themselves in negative ways (Blood & D'Angelo, 1974; Cull, 1976). If the student feels a lack of acceptance by the family as well as peers, and if he does not have some manner of achieving recognition either through academics, athletics, or other means, the potential for leaving the immediate environment increases.

The common complaint of runaways is the lack of communication between adults and themselves. Comments as "They don't know what I feel or what I do," "They don't understand me," or "I can't talk to them" are constantly reiterated by transient youth. Blood and D'Angelo (1974) suggest that love or attention is manifested in communication. If adults are willing to listen to the adolescent, the implication is that the youth is a worthwhile individual. The beginning of communication is listening. Adults who promote the teenager's rights for self-expression are demonstrating acceptance of that individual.

School and societal responsibilities: runaways

A need for a system of crisis intervention to assist young people who leave home or are drug-involved manifested itself in the growth of hot lines throughout the nation. In 1970, 73 hot lines, switchboards, and other kinds of telephone crisis centers were identified. By April 1971, this number had increased to 378, and by 1972 the number of hot lines had increased to 656. By 1972, 62 runaway programs were established which included crisis intervention for young people and their families. In 1974, the Department of Health, Education, and Welfare (HEW) earmarked $2.3 million to be spent by the end of the fiscal year of 1974 to work on the runaway problem. By July 1974, a total of 32 projects were awarded monies from the runaway funds by HEW; 18 projects were awarded for demonstration, 10 for training, and 6 for evaluation. By November 1974, the Office of Youth Development (OYD), Department of Health, Education, and Welfare had established a Runaway Youth Task Force. The purpose of the task force included redefining the definition of *runaway* and to develop a model runaway program.

In August 1974, a demonstration project was established called the National Runaway Switchboard, which was an outgrowth of Metro-Help in Chicago. It has a national toll-free number (800-621-4000). This demonstration project, according to Covert, was designed to fulfill three objectives:

1. Provide a service in which young people can anonymously obtain information and help concerning runaway-related topics.
2. Provide a system for relaying messages between runaways and their parents.
3. Document the incoming calls. (Covert, 1975, p. 7)

By the end of 1974, Title III of the Juvenile Justice and Prevention Act, better known as "The Runaway Youth Act," was passed. This act provided grants and technical assistance to localities to deal primarily with needs of runaway youth. The act allocated $10 million for fiscal years 1975–1977. By August of 1976, 132 runaway programs received money under this grant.

The number of agencies dealing with the needs of runaway youth has mushroomed from a modest beginning to over 200 programs in 1976. These programs offer places for runaways to stay, counsel, crisis intervene, and work with parents and runaway youths. Many of the programs offer assistance in related areas such as drugs, venereal diseases, and problem pregnancies.

Generally speaking, schools have not been involved with these programs, but they should be aware of the possibilities and be familiar with the progress, information available, and resources in their immediate neighborhood. The schools should address the problem of identification of the potential runaway. Cooperation between runaway services and secondary schools for potential runaways would attack the issue before it manifests itself. Programs developed to deal with problems of youth would hopefully alleviate the need to runawy.

ALCOHOL USE AND ABUSE

Ethel alcohol or ethanol is the active ingredient in alcohol beverages which cause intoxication. This toxic liquid has become one of the most widely used drugs among young people today. Although the use of alcohol among teenagers has been a phenomenon for many years, recent surveys have indicated that alcohol use is on the increase. In the early 1960s, Maddox (1964) found that 92% of 11th and 12th graders had at least tasted alcohol, but only about 6 percent reported frequent consumption. More recent surveys have indicated approximately the same number of teenager experimenters, but a sharp increase in those who drink regularly. In San Mateo County, California, a drug survey has been taken every year since 1968. This survey reported a rise from 27% in 1970 to 44.8% in 1974 of senior boys who had consumed some type of alcoholic beverage at least 50 times in the preceding year. The same study reports that regular use by girls jumped from 13.5% in 1970 to 30.6% in 1974.

The use of alcohol is not confined to secondary aged youth. A recent survey conducted by the National Institute on Alcohol Abuse and Alcoholism (1975) showed that over half the 7th graders they polled had at least tried an alcoholic beverage once in the last year. The fact that most young children can identify the smell of alcohol and that alcohol is completely familiar to most of the population is no surprise. The amount of exposure to alcoholic beverages in advertising, in televised dramatic stories, in use by adults, and in the number of establishments which serve liquor indicates our social acceptance of this drug.

Teenagers drink for a variety of reasons. During the late 1960s and early 1970s the nation experienced an era of adolescent rebellion against the status quo, with much of this negative attitude being expressed in the widespread use of drugs. That era has passed and the drinking behavior of adolescents can now be considered an attempt to join the adult world. Although the first drink is usually taken out of curiosity, continual drinking is the thing to do when modeling after parents and other significant individuals. Many parents condone this behavior preferring their children's use of alcoholic beverages over that of marijuana or other drugs. In fact, most adolescents are first introduced to liquor in their own homes (Maddox, 1970).

Peer pressure exerts tremendous influence on the older adolescent and adult's drinking behavior (Maddox, 1964; Bosma, 1975; Fox, 1973). Carrying around a glass of ginger ale is a common practice among nondrinkers at a party where alcohol is served. No one can tell whether or not liquor is in the glass, and it wards off the insistent host or hostess who feels somehow that the party is not perfect if even one guest is not imbibing. Drinking is a social act and many teenage drinkers tend to have friends who also drink.

Many reasons are cited for this increase in both the number of teenagers participating and in the amount consumed. Alcohol is readily available and is inexpensive. Now that many states have reduced the legal drinking age to 18, it is not as difficult to procure alcohol as it is other drugs. Those who never had access to illicit drugs do have access to liquor. Cheap wines which mask the alcohol taste have flooded the market. Sweet tasting beverages enhance the probability for the beginning drinker to continue. Being able to drink represents a sign of maturity to some teenagers (Bosma, 1975). The social acceptability of drinking at a legal age makes teenagers feel grown up. Bars that cater to the young adult abound, and fake identification cards are easily come by for those under the legal age.

The vast majority of adolescents are abstainers or occasional drinkers. However, it is estimated that from 2–6% of the teenage population are problem drinkers (Braucht, Brakarsh, Follingstad & Berry, 1973). These are the young people who use alcohol alone or in combination with other drugs to help alleviate psychological problems (Bosma, 1975). About 5% of teenagers use alcohol to reduce tension and nervousness (Stach, 1975). The potential alcoholics are adolescents who drink to provide courage to participate in some aggressive act or to participate in pre-marital sex. When alcohol is used for more than sociability or for the fun derived from it, and is used as a crutch on which an individual relies to get him through the day, it becomes a potential danger. In a review of psychological correlates of teenage drug abusers, Braucht, et al. (1973) report various studies which identify depression as a major personality variable among problem drinkers. Jessor, Carman and Grossman (1968) found among college students a high correlation between low expectation for attainment and social recognition, and alcohol consumption. Other studies (Williams, 1970; Mackay, 1961; Jones, 1968, 1971) indicate that juveniles who drink excessively are often impulsive, aggressive, anxious, and depressed.

As Jacobson states,

> Ethenol is, without question, the number one psychoactive drug problem in the United States in all drug using groups. In terms of mortality, morbidity, economic and social disability it far overshadows the much more publicized heroin problem. The marijuana problems fade to insignificance when the above factors are considered. (p. 52)

The potential hazard of alcohol is not being recognized simply because alcoholism in part has been around too long. Irwin (1974) ranked many of the recreational drugs according to their potential hazard to the individual when there was maximum chronic abuse. Seven physicians or scientists ranked and assigned weights to such hazards as potential death, tissue damage, psychomotor impairment, physical deterioration, social deterioration, overdose hazard, physical dependence hazard, rapid loss of control, and psychological dependence. The same type of ranking was performed on hazards to society with violence, impaired judgment, impaired coordination, impaired vigilance, social deterioration, passivity, and rapid loss of control as the variables. He then assigned adjusted weights to each of the several drugs on these variables. When converting these scores to percent of total possible score, distilled spirits headed the list, both for hazards to the individual and hazards to society. The ratings were 81% for individual hazards and 79% for social hazards. Next came wine with 77% and 79%, respectively, Secobarbitol ranked next with 65% and 83%, while herion ranked 48% and 47%. Marijuana was considered more dangerous than only caffeine, cigars, and coffee, with a percentage of hazardness of 25% for individual and 29% for social.

As with all drugs, the deteriorating effect of alcohol is related to the dosage as well as the frequency of use. Three ounces of 90-proof whiskey may produce relaxation, slight reduction in reflexes, and increased talkativeness. Six ounces of 90-proof whiskey may cause gross intoxication, disturbed judgment, impaired gait, and aggressiveness. Approximately 18 to 30 ounces of 90-proof whiskey can cause coma and/or respiratory cessation with resulting death. The amount of alcohol necessary to keep one drunk varies from individual to individual. Also, the effects on personality vary from one occasion to another, as well. At any cocktail party, one drunk may be quarrelsome and unpleasant while another may be affectionate and playful.

School and societal responsibilities: alcoholism

Until very recently, alcoholism was a legal problem rather than a medical one. Those who were drunk were put in jail. However, the attitude toward alcoholism is changing and various states are beginning to recognize the need to treat alcoholics as ill rather than as criminals. Detoxification centers located in hospitals and treatment centers with psychological medical help are becoming more prevalent. Alcoholics Anonymous, a self-help group, is organizing AA groups specifically for teenagers. The realization that alcoholism affects teenagers not only as consumers, but also when living with a problem-drinking parent, has been influential in the establishment of Alateen, a division of Alcoholics Anonymous. Alateen's purpose is to provide understanding and direction to those teenagers whose lives have been disturbed by alcoholic parents or other relatives.

Therapeutic communities have been established to provide help for the teenage drug and alcohol abusers. A major goal is to change the values and life style of the residents. Heavy reliance is placed on group therapy techniques accompanied by education and vocational training to help the individual confront the real world. Other adolescent treatment programs use indepth family therapy under the rationale that disharmony is a large contributor to the adolescent's problems.

Some public schools in Oregon provide group therapy programs through the Department of Mental Health, Alcohol Studies and Rehabilitation Section. The emphasis is on the adolescents' recognition of what part their actions play in what happens to them. Only if individuals recognize this fact can remediation be effective.

The increase of alcohol use among teenagers has so concerned communities as to cause a reevaluation of the attack on preventative programs. There has been an increased push to get information concerning alcohol abuse to the potential teenage user. Programs are now being developed which place emphasis on causes rather than effects of alcoholism. Recognizing the ineffectiveness of expounding on the dire consequences of alcoholism, schools are presenting programs designed to help young people cope with life's problems and stresses. Developing alternative means to need satisfaction is seen as a way to prevent young people from using alcohol or other drugs as a false escape.

DRUG USE AND ABUSE

The subject of illegal drug use is fraught with emotionality and irrationality as the knowledge held by many teachers and parents is a mixture of fact and fantasy. The fear generated when discussing drugs is almost pathological. These ineffectual social attitudes must be dispelled before any rational approach to the problem can be taken.

Many adults do not differentiate between the effects of the use of different kinds of drugs. The assumption is made that all drugs are dangerous, addictive, and cause lack of control on the part of the user. Marijuana and heroin have been considered equally dangerous. It is often thought that once marijuana has been used the user will eventually become a heroin addict.

The application of legal procedures has not differentiated between experimenters, users, abusers, addicts, or dealers. This approach is ineffective because of the need for different approaches for each group. If educators are to be effective in helping youth in trouble, it is necessary for them to familiarize themselves with the basic facts in the area of drug use and abuse.

The tremendous increase in the use of illegal, as well as legal, drugs is indicative of a social phenomenon which we are hard pressed to explain. To rationalize the misuse of drugs as a reaction to the stresses and strains of modern life does not go far enough and oversimplifies a very complex problem. It must be understood that drug-taking is a behavior. It follows all the laws and rules of any other type of behavior. It will persist if it provides pleasure or reduces pain. Drugs, in and of themselves, are neither good nor bad. It is the behavior of the individual with which we should be concerned.

Drug-taking adolescents come from many walks of life, from the tiniest of villages to the largest of cities. The attractiveness of chemicals to make one feel good draws to it the richest of suburban youth to the poorest of slum dwellers. It has no respect for ethnic lines or religious differences. The motivations for the use of an external recreational chemical are as varied as are the users. Although isolating these motivational factors provides some understanding of the complexity of the problem, it does not provide us with a tool to instigate prevention.

Dohner (1972), in his article entitled, "Motives for Drug Use: Adult and Adolescent," suggests that curiosity; imitation; peer pressure; the search for feelings of well-being, instant achievement, instant happiness, relaxation, recreation, psychological support, insight into himself and personal identification; and rebellion and rejection of parental values are the major motivational factors. Girdano and Girdano (1973) add to this such factors as feelings of alienation, expressions of belonging to a sub-culture group, boredom, and withdrawal. Availability must certainly be added; whether one considers the availability of drugs as a motivating factor or not, it certainly contributes to the use of particular drugs. Cornacchia, Bentel, and Smith (1973) go further by suggesting:

> Personal factors involved in drug abuse may center around overwhelming psychic conflict, present especially during adolescence, and center around adult sexuality, hostility, dependency-interdependency issues, and identity confusion. These conflicts are the results of demands for conforming placed on the individual by society. (p. 45)

The normal agonies of adolescents such as the fear of competition and failure, the fear and reality of homosexuality, or the anxieties and confusion concerning the whole dating and sexual area can be alleviated at least temporarily by the consumption of mood-altering chemicals.

Thomas Crowley (1972), in his article, "The Reinforcers for Drug Abuse: Why People Take Drugs," discussess drug-taking behavior from a learning theory point of view. In operant conditioning terms, when a particular behavior is regularly reinforced, the individual will exhibit that behavior with increasing frequency. Certain illicit drugs act as primary reinforcers, that is, they are reinforcing in and of themselves, they cause a pleasurable feeling. Methamphetamines ("speed"), when injected intravenously, produce an immediate intense physical pleasure often described as "a whole body orgasm." Intravenous injection of heroin produces a similar reaction. This immediate reaction is followed by a sense of well-being and euphoria.

Animal studies have confirmed this contention that certain drugs act as primary reinforcers while others do not. Confined, isolated monkeys will press levers to obtain injections of morphine, codeine, cocaine, amphetamines, phenobarbital, ethanol, and caffeine (Deneau, Yanagita, and Seevers, 1969). Monkeys do not press the lever for injections of certain other slower-acting drugs. Even some drugs taken orally can act as primary reinforcers. The fast acting barbiturates will increase drug-taking behavior more than slow-acting barbiturates.

According to social learning theory (Rotter, 1971), individuals need some satisfactions (positive reinforcements) in their lives. If other areas of their lives do not produce them, then they are more vulnerable to the temptations of the pleasures of experiences in drugs. Recognizing the human animal as a social being, one of life's most needed satisfactions is social interaction. Students who have developed no warm relationships with peers or parents have a real lack in their lives. If, at the same time, they receive no recognition for some type of accomplishment, have difficulty with authority figures, or live in a drab poverty-stricken environment, the potential for turning to the pleasures of chemical agents increases alarmingly. They have no positive reinforcers available to them in their environments. Drugs, at least, provide a feeling of pleasure.

A negative reinforcement, as differentiated from punishment, is a stimulus which, when stopped, continues to reinforce behavior. The sudden, complete discontinuation of drugs or physical addiction (alcohol, barbiturates, and opiates) causes withdrawal symptoms. These symptoms are aversive in nature, that is to say, they are extremely unpleasant to the person experiencing withdrawal reactions. Therefore, they are negatively reinforcing. The drug addict will go to great effort to obtain the drug of addiction and ingest or inject it to avoid the aversiveness of withdrawal. The withdrawal symptoms of heroin cause chills, cramps, nausea, and other symptoms quite similar to an extreme case of the flu.

A drug addict will do almost anything to get a "fix" in order to avoid the aversive effect of withdrawal illness. As one addict states: "I take heroin to feel normal." The termination of the withdrawal state negatively reinforces drug administration.

Many adults have felt the glow after alcohol intake. Unpleasant environmental factors become less unpleasant. The heroin user can reduce the pain of environmental unpleasantness by escaping into the euphoric sensation that heroin use produces. Barbiturates provide the same sort of insulation against aversive environmental factors.

The way drugs are used

Drugs are used by almost everyone in many ways, but most users do not become abusers. Users can be classified as episodic, religious, experimental, recreational, or compulsive. Yet any type of user can become another, as these categories are not mutually exclusive.

Some individuals use drugs only when under stress. They turn to alcohol or other drugs as solace when under particular strain. They may consume a quantity of drugs during certain episodes in their lives and not at other times. Thus, they are considered episodic users.

When the use of LSD became fashionable, many young people considered it a medium through which they sought a spiritual awakening. The LSD experience was considered a religious happening, a way of finding the truth of being closer to the ultimate in life. Hallucinogens of all types have been used by individuals interested in mystical religious experiences.

There are those who have heard of the effects of mood-altering drugs and are eager to try them. Experimental drug use evolves from curiosity and peer pressure. Adolescents who experiment with psychoactive or recreational chemicals are people who are acting out the same basic actions as the average person. Curiosity is a part of normal healthy personality and the desire to experience new sensations is not pathological. As one high school student said after he and all the rest of the school's students were required to attend an all-day workshop on drugs with the cessation of all other academic work, "There must be something there worth trying."

Mood-altering drugs are often used for social facilitation. Recreational chemicals are served at social gatherings to help the guests become more relaxed and congenial. The pot party and the cocktail party are part of our culture, and the substances used help facilitate social interaction. The chemicals are used to heighten the enjoyment of an already pleasureable occasion. With some teenagers, the use of drugs gives them an entry into a social group. Many of these youngsters have been on the outside looking in when it comes to peer interaction. The use of drugs, then, not only provides socialization but also furnishes youths with a peer group identification which they do not have without drugs.

A certain percent of episodic religious, experimental, or social users may become compulsive abusers. These people are persons with definite personal and emotional problems. Dohner (1972) says:

> Mood-altering drugs may serve as psychological support (escape, release) in a large number of stressful situations. They can be used in attempts to blunt or alleviate pain and discomfort, real or imagined, due to physical, psy-

chological, social, or vocational conditions. The abusers may be attempting to diminish frustration, depression, tension, or anxiety related to job, school, home, family, or self-image.   (p. 329)

The chronic drug abuser is unable or unwilling to solve his own problems. With the use of chemicals, his problems appear less painful, and the realities of his life less harsh.

Drug addictions

The term *drug addiction* is usually reserved for those chemicals producing physical dependency. However, concern has been expressed in referring to drugs as addictive simply because of the misconceptions surrounding the whole are of physical addiction. These misconceptions include the belief that one shot of heroin causes physical addiction or that all users of opiates or their derivatives become addicted.

These misconceptions have led to prejudice and punitive attitudes by society expressed by the courts and law enforcement agencies. In reality, it is well known that the vast number of polydrug users include opiates in their repertoire of drugs. These individuals do not necessarily become addicted. More and more individuals have been identified as spasmodic users of heroin with the ability to use it or leave it alone. Heroin users are differentiated form heroin addicts.

A committee of recognized authority from the World Health Organization (1964) preferred the use of the word *dependency* when referring to the desire for any drug. Drug dependency then could be qualified by the specific drug in question, such as "drug dependency of the barbiturate type." This recommendation to discontinue the use of the word *addiction* has not had popular support, nor has it been accepted by the United Nations Commission on Narcotic Drugs. Physical addiction is characterized by three conditions:

1. Withdrawal symptoms occur upon immediate, complete cessation of the drug taking. Withdrawal illness is noxious in nature and in some cases, depending on the drug being used, can be fatal.

2. The drug user requires larger and larger doses to produce the desired effect, as a tolerance to that drug is developed.

3. A craving develops to continue using the drug even after months or years have passed since the last intake occurred.*

---

*It is thought that the term *cold turkey,* used when a person is withdrawing from heroin without medical help, originates from the appearance of the individual undergoing withdrawal. The body is often covered with goose pimples reminiscent of the appearance of a plucked turkey. The term *kick the habit* probably originated from the kicking movements of the extremities caused by muscle spasms characteristic of heroin withdrawal.

Brecher, of *The Consumers' Union Report* (1972), defines an addicting drug as:

> . . . one that most users continue to take even though they want to stop, decide to stop, try to stop, and actually succeed in stopping for days, weeks, months, or even years. It is a drug for which men and women will prostitute themselves. It is a drug to which more users return after treatment . . . . It is a drug which most users continue despite the threat of long-term imprisonment for its use—and to which they promptly return after experiencing long-term imprisonment. (p. 84)

Not all drugs are capable of producing physical addiction; only barbiturates, alcohol, anti-anxiety drugs, opiates, and their derivatives, all of which are depressants. Although some drug experts suggest that amphetamines can become physically addictive, the potentiality is much less than with depressants. It is known, however, that drug users can develop a very strong psychological dependency on amphetamines.

The pleasure sought by the intake of mood-altering chemicals is basically one of two different varieties. The intensifiers, as the term implies, increase the awareness and change the perceptions of the environment in a way that makes the whole world seem enriched. The intensity of this apparent change depends on the drug used and the amount ingested. Marijuana, hallucinogens, and stimulants have these properties. The desensitizers, on the other hand, help the individual to withdraw from the world, and have a calming effect. They provide the user with a euphoric state in which the real world is forgotten. Alcohol, depressants, and opiates produce these effects.

Societal conditions which encourage drug consumption

The common practice when confronting the drug problem is to refer to illegal drugs only. Little or no concern is exhibited with the intake of legal drugs. Drugs purchased by prescription or across the counter are overlooked as a potential hazard. Yet the statistics showing the vast quantities of legal drugs consumed each year would indicate that America is a drug-oriented society. It is estimated that half the sedatives and tranquilizers prescribed by physicians are given unnecessarily. As Cornacchia, Bental, and Smith state, "In 1970, 202 million legal prescriptions for psychoactive drugs—stimulants, sedatives, tranquilizers, and anti-depressants—were filled in pharmacies for patients or physicians" (p. 9). Sleeping aids, aspirin compounds, vitamins, cough syrups and drops, laxatives, and pain killers fill the shelves of drugstores. In 1970, it was estimated that about 15 billion aspirin tablets were consumed by the population of this country each year (Bureau of Narcotics and Dangerous Drugs, 1970). This amounted to about

750 pills for every person per year, approximately two a day per person, in the United States. There is no evidence that the American public is less prone today in relying on aspirin for relief of headaches, nervous tension, or many other human ailments.

The American public is urged by the mass media to solve their problems through chemicals. Television alone has tremendous impact. "Everyone has a sleepless night once in a while, so take a Sominex," "Got a headache? Take an aspirin." Even the dramatic stories coming to use through this media stress the use of chemicals. Whenever a crisis arises, the hero either lights up a cigarette or takes an alcoholic drink. Inevitably, the hero or heroine goes to the well-stocked bar, fills his or her glass from an ice bucket (which is always supplied with fresh ice), and pours a drink from an array of bottles. It is no wonder young people look to chemicals for relief from the slightest unpleasantness.

Our society provides more comforts, more gadgets, more free time, and fewer tedious tasks. Young people are taught to crave immediate gratification, which negates delayed gratification for long-term goals. They are questioning the *Protestant ethic* for the value of work. The cynicism exhibited toward their elders' materialistic values negates the postponing of pleasureable experiences. Having been reared in an affluent society, middle-class youths have little fear of poverty that many of their parents exhibit in their need to accumulate financial security. Some adolescents are disenchanted with the values of their elders and see the old myths as unrewarding and meaningless. Those who have been turned on by psychodelic drugs seem to be searching for new personal identities and new ideologies by which to live. There is a close relationship between the sociocultural attitudes of young persons and their abuse of drugs.

The use of drugs continues to increase in the United States. Although not all users are abusers, the number of young people dependent on drugs alarms and concerns the American people as drug abuse is a continuous threat to national health and welfare. Drug abuse potentiates the possibility for delinquency and disruptive behavior in both the effects on the individual and on society. The need for society to understand the many ramifications of this problem is paramount, for the abuse of drugs is a phenomenon which will be with us for many years to come.

Diagnosis of potential drug abusers

School personnel are greatly concerned with the ability to spot the drug user among their students and ask for the physical symptoms which will positively identify such students. Because many of the physical symptoms are similar to other common ailments, this means of identification has proved useless. In the early days of the drug scare any student with long hair and dirty jeans was suspect. The lack of differentiation in the type of drug usage made diagnosis difficult; experimenters or social users were considered as serious a problem as compulsive users.

The recognition of the variance in seriousness of amount, frequency, and kind of drug used has enabled both professionals and nonprofessionals to delineate the symptoms of when an individual has a drug problem. However, determining a definite delineation of the characteristics of a drug problem is a difficult matter. Subjective opinion often clouds the issue, and what might be considered a drug problem to one individual might not be considered one by another. The symptoms of a compulsive user should include some of the following criteria. However, these criteria used to determine a drug problem should be used with caution as they can also be the symptoms of other problems. These behaviors are often interactive clues to possible drug problems:

1. Does the individual appear not to obtain satisfactions from the usual, socially accepted means that other students use in the school setting?

   a. Does the student lack means of achieving recognition within the school confines (academic, athletic achievement, or any other means which are acceptable to school personnel)?

   b. Does the student exhibit poor peer relationships with students other than those who exhibit problem behavior?

   c. Does the student suddenly change the group of students he associates with to those who are known as drug users?

2. Is the student absent from school without legitimate excuse often enough to be considered truant?

3. Does the student lose interest in school?

4. Does the student often appear to be daydreaming, high, or "nodding off" in class?

If the answer is yes to several of the above questions, the school personnel may be assured that the student has problems, with the great possibility that drug abuse is one of them.

School personnel working with such troubled youth would be well advised to be somewhat familiar with the varying effects of the different chemicals. Although there is no need to be an expert, their credibility among drug users is enhanced if school personnel know the difference, for example, between "angel dust" and "junk."

The following classification provides a very brief categorization of the more common drugs. The reader must keep in mind the fact that drugs affect individuals in different ways depending on dosage and frequency of use.

CLASSIFICATION OF DRUGS

Intensifiers

Classification	*Examples*	*Examples of Slang Names*
1 Stimulants	Amphetamines	Speed
	Methadrine	Crystal, Meth
	Benzedrine	Bennies, Roses
	Dexedrine	Dexies, Hearts
	Cocaine	Snow, Coke
	Ritalin	
	Caffeine	

Effects. Stimulates respiration; reduces appetite; elevates mood; increases talkativeness, aggressiveness, initiativeness, wakefulness, and confidence; increases motor activity; may produce anxiety, excitement, and confusion; produces suspiciousness.

Possible Adverse Reactions. There is a high potential for psychological dependence but not usually considered physical dependence. Severe depression can occur in withdrawal. A "speed freak" may be in poor physical condition resulting from lack of proper food (because of the suppression of appetite) and lack of proper rest; it is possible to collapse from exhaustion. An overdose may be followed by chills, collapse, and loss of consciousness. Fatality from overdose is rare but has occurred.

2. Cannabis Sativa	Marijuana	Grass, Pot, Weed, Dope, Mary Jane, Joint, Reefer
	Hashish	Hash

Effects. Produces mild alcohol-like intoxication; tends to heighten sensory perception; causes gaiety, relaxation, excitation, talkativeness; increases awareness and involvement; produces pleasurable feeling of well-being; increases appetite for food (usually sweets); possible impairment of depth and time perception.

Possible Adverse Reactions. There is moderate potential for psychological dependence but no physical addiction. Extremely heavy use may contribute to reduced motivation.

3. Hallucinogens	LSD-25	Acid, Windowpane, Orange Sunshine Purple Wedges, Blue Dots, and others
	Mescaline (from peyote cactus)	
	STP (DOM)	

Psilocybin (from Mexican mushroom)		
PCP (animal tranquilizer)	Angel Dust, Peace Pills	
DMT	Businessman's Acid Trip	

Effects.   Exhibits extraordinary sensitivity to visual, auditory, or tactile stimuli; produces intense emotional activity; may produce either panic or tranquility; distorts perception of time; alters perceptions (hear colors, see sounds); produces distortion of visual perception, causing hallucinations.

Possible Adverse Reactions.   There may be panic reactions (bummers) and "flashbacks." There is a slight possibility for psychological dependency, but no potential for physiological dependency or fatality from overdose.

Desensitizers

Classification	*Examples*	*Examples of Slang Names*
1. Depressants	Barbiturates	Golf Balls, Downers, Barbs
	Nembutal Seconal	Yellow Jackets, Nemmies, Red Devils, Red Birds, Reds
	Amytal	Blue Devils, Blue Heavens
	Truinal	Rainbows, Tooies

Effects.   Produces drowsiness, difficulty in thinking, talkativeness, slurred speech, loss of inhibitions, faulty judgment, respiratory depression, sedation; causes poor memory; acts as a general depressant.

Possible Adverse Reactions.   It is physically addictive and can produce unconsciousness. An overdose can be lethal, particularly when mixed with alcoholic beverages. Withdrawal illness is more severe than heroin and can be fatal.

2. Narcotics	Opium	Op
	Opium Derivatives:	
	Morphine	M, White Stuff
	Heroin	H, Smack, Horse, Harry, Stuff, Junk
	Codeine	Schoolboy
3. Synthetic Narcotics	Methadone	
	Demoral	

Effects.   Produces euphoria, drowsiness, mental clouding, apathy; reduces aggressiveness and sex drive; depresses respiration and slows heart beat;

reduces hunger and ability to concentrate on activity; may cause constipation, nausea, and vomiting.

Possible Adverse Reactions. Narcotics are physically addictive. Withdrawal symptoms are similar to a bad case of the flu. An overdose can be lethal. Once a person is physically addicted, it is very difficult to "kick the habit."

4. Alcohol

	Wine	about 15% alcohol (Vol.)
	Beer	about 4.5% alcohol (Vol.)
	Whiskey	about 50% alcohol (Vol.)

Effects. There is a range of effects from slight reduction of reflexes to reduction of inhibitions, impaired judgment, uncoordination of movement, distorted judgment, aggressiveness, and gross impairment of thinking and memory.

Possible Adverse Reactions. Alcohol is physically addictive. Withdrawal symptoms are potentially fatal. High doses may be lethal due to respiratory paralysis.

5. Solvent Inhalants

	Airplane Glue	Toulene
	Rubber Cement	
	Paint Thinner	Hydrocarbons
	Lighter Fluid	

Effects. Produces dizziness, floating sensation, breakdown of inhibitions, loss of appetite, grandiose feelings, exhilaration, intense feelings of well being, euphoria, and giddiness; can also cause (depending on substance) blurred vision, drowsiness, stupor, and gross mental disorientation.

Possible Adverse Reactions. Depending on the solvent inhaled, toulene may cause damage to central nervous system, liver, and kidneys. Hydrocarbons can produce hallucinations, seizures, delirium, coma, and, in some cases, death.

School and societal responsibilities: drug abuse

Schools and communities should, and in some cases have, worked together to help students before they become victims of drug abuse. The recognition of the serious waste of human potential through the compulsive use of drugs is not just a school problem but is one which should concern the total community. Some citizens see it only as a school problem, probably because the school houses the young people for a substantial period of the day. These same young people however, live, play, and work within the community.

During the latter half of the 1960s and early 1970s many members of the drug culture offered their help to those who were experiencing panic reactions when on drugs. Drug hot lines were established throughout the United States; these hot lines provided crisis intervention, telephone counseling and information about drugs.

Many of the drug culture youths were extremely suspicious of the already established mental health facilities, viewing them as places that little understood the problems entailed in drug usage. Helping facilities which represented the establishment were scorned as potential resources for the drug user. Consequentially, the drug hot line facilities served unique clientele. As time passed, the hot lines expanded their services to include information dissemination, educational programs, drug analysis, and psychotherapy. Alternative ways to gain satisfaction had become the major aim for many of these drug centers.

A large percentage of all treatment procedures for drug addiction is concentrated on attempts to rehabilitate the opiate addict. There is a wide diversity of treatment methods used. None of these has demonstrated a high cure rate if *cure* is defined as total abstinence of all drugs. The lack of complete understanding of drug addiction adds to the confusion concerning treatment. Two of the more promising methods of treatment are methadone maintenance techniques and therapeutic communities.

Methadone maintenance is now the most widely used method for rehabilitation of the heroin addict. Methadone, a synthetic narcotic, is an addicting drug which creates a blockade to the euphoric effects of opiates. If an individual uses heroin while on maintenance doses of methadone, he will not experience the usual euphoria of heroin usage. Methadone maintenance clinics established primarily in cities not only provide the addicts with their daily dose of methadone, but also provide additional treatment such as group counseling, family therapy, and vocational training.

The critics of methadone treatment decry the use of one addictive drug to replace another. However, the use of methadone as a treatment has had considerable success. The advantages of being addicted to methadone in lieu of heroin are several. First, methadone can be administered orally. This eliminates the hazards accompanying "mainlining" (intervenous injection), with its diseases caused by use of unsterile needles. Second, methadone is very inexpensive and is administered either free or at a very minimal charge. The advantages of this are tremendous inasmuch as the crime rate actually drops in areas where methadone clinics are located. There is no longer a need to participate in antisocial behavior to obtain money to support a heroin habit. Third, it frees the addict to pursue a normal productive life.

Another approach to rehabilitation of the heroin addict is the therapeutic community. Therapeutic communities are residential treatment centers which provide a therapeutic milieu in an attempt to deal with the psychological factors underlying addiction. The emphasis is on the individual's need to change himself and his life style to prepare him to withstand the old influences upon his re-entry to the street.

Therapeutic communities screen out, in their intake procedures, all those individuals who are not highly motivated to really "kick the habit." The programs are extremely structured and difficult for the addict to go through. Even with their screening procedures, a large proportion of those who enter themselves drop out within the first month. Most of the therapeutic communities are run by ex-addicts who have been through the program. Encounter groups and other group therapy techniques are used to help the individual thoroughly understand his weaknesses and strengths in order to affect change.

Drug education

Although the use of illicit drugs had been a phenomenon in the ghettos for many years, it did not hit the American conscience until the white, clean cut, middle-class youth discovered the pleasures of being stoned, high, strung out, or otherwise under the influence of chemicals. When this happened in the 1960s, the nation panicked. "We were not too upset if our sons and daughters stole a drink or two from the family liquor cabinet but we were horrified if we discovered a 'joint' hidden in their bedrooms" (Lotsof and Floyd, 1976, p. 2). Parents, educators, and to some extent, law enforcement officers were faced with a very complicated problem they little understood. The problem was complicated by a variety of philosophies based on beliefs, attitudes, values, and life styles. Fact was mixed with fiction, with little recognition of the complex interaction between drugs and living organisms. This is not to say that there were not some experts in the field that had long worked in the area of drug abuse who understood many of the problems and were using their influence to establish prevention programs. But they were few in number.

Drug education was viewed as the greatest potential force toward prevention. Consequently, many federal dollars and much effort was placed in encouraging states to develop drug education curriculum or guidelines for local educational agencies to follow. Many of the early attempts were doomed to failure both on the basis of erroneous assumptions and ineffective methodology. Many of the programs reflected the hysteria and confusion felt by the originators of the drug education present at that time. School personnel, knowing very little or nothing about drug problems, about the drug culture, or motivation of young people experimenting in drugs, lumped all users in one category and considered them emotionally disturbed. The objectives of their drug education program was to eliminate all use of drugs despite the advice of experts who recognized the fallacy of this position. Common sense would indicate that as a nation we would have recognized the stupidity of this attempt by reflecting on the nation's use of alcohol. But in the early days of struggle with the drug problem, few lay people recognized alcoholic beverages as drugs.

Teachers were asked to teach a subject about which they had little knowledge. To complicate the problem, much of the material on which they relied was factually incorrect. In 1973, the National Coordinating Council on Drug Education systematically evaluated drug education, audio-visual aids for scientific accuracy, distortion, or unsound implication. Unfortunately, these films were the films most often shown in schools and communities across the country. Of the films 53% were considered useable only by skilled drug education professionals and required special care in public presentation. Only 16% were found to be scientifically and conceptually accurate. As an outgrowth of this report, in the spring of 1973, the federal government asked for a moritorium in the use of drug education films.

The first wide spread attempts at drug education reflected the fear, anxiety, and hysteria the older generation felt concerning illicit drugs. All the terrible things that might happen to a drug user were depicted in gory detail. Ex-addicts were paraded in front of classes to emphasize the horrors they had experienced during their life of degradation. This "scare tactic" approach coupled with the misinformation about drugs was not effective. Young people saw the discrepancies between what they were being told and what they were experiencing, and soon learned to disbelieve adults. In summary, the attempts at drug education using scare tactics were dismal failures.

Slowly, educators recognized the necessity for knowledge and sophistication concerning the complexity of the problem. Much of what was being taught in schools as drug education was ridiculed by adolescents familiar with recreational chemicals. To assume that young people "given the facts" will make the decision not to "mess with drugs" is fallacious. These assumptions neglect the values held by young people and the inability of some youths to make decisions and to act upon these decisions. Lotsof and Floyd state:

> The detrimental effects of alcohol both physically and socially have been known for a good many years. But the rate of alcoholism is ever increasing as evidenced by the fact that in recent years more and more teenagers are becoming alcoholics. (Lotsof & Floyd, 1976, p. 3.)

As early as 1973, Dr. Helen Nowles, head of the United States Office of Education's drug education division said, "I am more and more reinforced in my conviction that information alone is not the answer and at times may be counterproductive" (Attack on Narcotic Addiction and Drug Abuse, 1973, p. 2).

The emphasis on the subject of drugs has changed slowly to the emphasis on the potential user. There is truth in the cliche that drug abuse problems are, in reality, people problems. Drug taking is a behavior reflecting a decision by a person, in light of the reinforcement, personal needs, and situational pressures. As Floyd, Lang, and Lotsof state:

> When an individual experiences a problem, be it a drug problem or any other problem, it is not a phenomenon occurring in a vacuum. The problem is an integral part of the individual's past, present and expected future growth and development interaction patterns and decision making routines.
> (Floyd, Lang, Lotsof, 1974, p. 15)

The primary objective is to enhance the young person's assessment of himself, and to help him determine "How well can I do with what I've got?" mentally, physically and socially.

The focus of the program would be on the individual recognizing the human psychological needs and the various alternative methods of satisfying these needs. How does psychological need satisfaction influence the person's relation to others and the enhancement of his life? The more alternative ways a person has to satisfy his needs, the more freedom of movement he possesses in pursuing life's goals.

Which of the various alternative behaviors chosen is dictated by the expectancy held for positive reinforcement to be forthcoming and the value that reinforcement has for the individual (Rotter, 1971). Consequently, the values held by an individual can influence the choice of alternative behaviors. A major objective for any program which hopes to change or prevent problem behavior is to help the individual find more effective socially acceptable pathways to need satisfactions. Examination of one's present methods of satisfying needs, examination of value systems, and practice in decision making are integral parts of a program designed to deal with problems. Although this approach focuses on drug and alcohol prevention as the target problem, the same techniques could apply equally to other adolescent problems such as suicide behavior or running away.

Assumptions underlying a drug education program

1. The problem of drug abuse is similar to other personal or health problems inasmuch as it is a symptom of basic human needs unmet by other means.

2. Chemicals with the capacity to alter moods are always going to be available to people.

3. People like to feel good and the use of drugs is one sure way to feel good at least temporarily.

4. Drugs in and of themselves are neither good nor bad. It is the use to which human beings put these drugs which determines their effects.

5. When an individual experiences problems with drugs, it is not a phenomenon occurring in a vacuum. The problem is an intergral part of the individual's past, present, and expected future growth and development.

Goals for a drug education program

1. To promote respect for all drugs.

2. To indicate to the student that drugs differ and cannot categorically be labeled good or bad.

3. To inform the student about drugs from a holistic point of view—encompassing all drugs, legal and illegal, social and medical.

4. To indicate that introduction of any foreign chemical into the body system will have effects beyond the immediately ascribed effects.

5. To provide valid information about the short- and long-term consequences of use of various kinds of drugs and their interactions.

6. To elucidate the naturalness of human striving for pleasurable states of consciousness.

7. To encourage students to explore alternative behavior patterns that are non-self-destructing.

8. To provide the student with decision making skills that will enable him to make decisions regarding drug use and life goals that will lead toward long-term positive outcomes for the individual.

9. To provide opportunity for students to discover non-chemical alternative routes toward these pleasurable states.

(Randall & Wong, 1976, p. 21)

SUMMARY

Drug abuse is merely a system of life problems. To generate discussion solely around drugs misses the mark and can be of little help in changing drug taking behavior. Schools must recognize the tremendous need to provide an arena for discussion of life problems. Adolescent concerns such as sex, fear, self-doubt, love, loneliness, anxiety, and pain, are of extreme importance to young people; and nowhere in our schools today can troubled youth discuss these problems openly with teachers who respect them as individuals. Rather than drug education, ideally schools should provide education on how to deal with life problems. Any of these problems of adolescents could be addressed in the same manner after preliminary work in value clarification, priority setting, and decision making. The problems could be examined objectively while alternative methods of solving the problems and gaining need satisfaction could be explored. The ultimate goal of such a program is to help the student utilize alternative need satisfying behaviors. To develop skills to use the alternatives would be a major aspect of such a program. Schools have within their means the power to reduce alcohol and drug abuse, runaways, and suicides, providing they recognize their responsibility to address directly the problems of troubled youth.

FURTHER INFORMATION ON ILLICIT DRUGS

The recognition that drugs are here to stay emphasizes the necessity to provide accurate information concerning their use. The emotionality surrounding this topic based on misinformation and half-truths has led to confusion concerning the effects of many drugs. Although many chemical substances are abused, inquiry about drugs usually focus on LSD, marijuana, amphetamines, barbiturates and heroin. Further discussion of these five categories of abused drugs may dispel some misconceptions and myths surrounding their use.

LSD

LSD (Lysergic Acid Diethylamide) has been the most publicized chemical in the hallucinogen category. It was first synthesized by a Swiss chemist, Albert Hoffman, in 1937, but its hallucinogen properties were not discovered until 1943 when Dr. Hoffman accidentally ingested a small amount. Some experimentation occurred shortly thereafter with the hopes it could be helpful in the treatment of mental illness. Various attempts to use it as an adjunct to psychotherapy held some promise. Therapists felt that it reduced the patients' defensiveness and allowed repressive memories to be recalled. Controversy over the psychiatric use of LSD still exists with some researchers maintaining the efficacy of this use has not met rigorous scientific standards. LSD was not used for pleasure until about 1959. The popularity of this mood-altering drug increased tremendously during the 1960s when the illegal use of it became a major concern to society.

Since the beginning of the 1970s, most professionals who observed the drug scene believe there has been a marked decline in the use of LSD among young people. The evidence substantiating this hypothesis comes from various services. There are fewer calls to drug crisis centers requesting assistance with the adverse effects of LSD and there is less use reported among college students. The hippie movement, with its psychodelic subculture is slowly disappearing.

During the late 1960s, scientific investigation into the genetic effects of LSD reported chromosomal damage which tended to discourage widespread abuse of this substance. However, many of these reports were based on massive dosage levels in animals and therefore not applicable to the human population abusing this drug. Conflicting findings on recent investigations using human subjects have negated any conclusive evidence that such chromosomal damage does occur.

Research done on LSD sold on the street (street acid) is particularly difficult as this substance is often contaminated by other substances. To isolate the effect of the LSD content with its various dosage levels makes comparative studies suspect. The problem is complicated when the subjects studied are also using other substances.

Although LSD is classified as a hallucinogen, the use of it does not produce hallucinations in the true sense of the word. A true hallucination is seeing something that is really not there. The LSD user sees what is, but in a distorted or changing form. An LSD experience is referred to as a "trip," and can be a mystic wonderful experience making the environment seem intensely beautiful with brilliant colors and changing forms. But unlike the hallucinations produced by the intense use of alcohol with the visions of bugs or other frightening things during delirium tremors, the user is aware that the changing forms he sees are not real.

Synthetic LSD is a clear, odorless, tasteless liquid of great potency. Most drug doses are measured in milligrams. LSD doses are measured in micrograms—millionths of a gram. One hundred micrograms is usually a sufficient amount to send most people on a full-fledged LSD trip, with the intensity of the trip being dose-related. The hypersuggestibility produced by this drug accounts for the kind of trip experienced. Therefore, the emotional state of the user and the environment in which the drug taker finds himself, can trigger either a good trip or a panic reaction ("bummer"). LSD trips are not consistent. An individual may have many pleasurable LSD experiences and then, upon taking LSD again, have a panic reaction. An LSD trip may start slowly with a gradual change in perception or it may start with an explosive force. The major effect is the disruption of sensory input and processing.

A good trip is described in as many different ways as there are drug users. It lasts from six to nine hours or even longer and may include an intensification of color and sound. The senses flow into one another with the allusion of touching sound or hearing color. Commonplace objects such as doorknobs become fascinating, beautiful things. Solid objects may appear to undulate in rhythm to music. The passage of time seems to alter. With the rapid flow of sound, color, and changing forms experienced by the individual, his estimation of time is distorted. He may feel that hours have passed during a five-minute period.

A bum trip consists of extreme panic reaction. Some feel this panic reaction is triggered by the sensation of lack of control with the accompanying feeling that the body is not functioning. The individual may become supersensitive and exhibit feelings of persecution along with extreme fear and panic.

Talking a person down from a bum trip is a misnomer. No amount of talking will change the length of the trip or stop it in any way. What the helper attempts to do is reduce the panic through reassurance and, hopefully, change the bummer in quality to a good trip. Helping the bum tripper to concentrate on his breathing is reassuring to him that his body can and is able to function. It helps him hold onto reality.

There is no record of fatality in an overdose of LSD as there is in many other chemicals used for reaction. Scientifically, it is difficult to articulate adverse reactions to the street use of LSD because of the adulterants found in the substance ingested. As the use of LSD became widespread in the 1960s, reports indicated that the drug was hazardous. Users were being hospitalized or were reported to be jumping or falling out of windows, throwing themselves under trains, etc. Suicide rate of LSD users increased. Several reasons have been suggested as a cause for this increase in reported dangers. As the effects of the drug became better known, some who wished to try the drug approached the experience with apprehension. Because of the hypersuggestibility produced by the drug, those who were highly apprehensive of it would experience bum trips. The highly publicized ill effects only intensified this problem. The unknown dosage of street drugs plus contamination and adulteration with other substances produced toxic conditions which contributed to the problems experienced.

It is universally agreed that persons under the influence of LSD should not be left alone. When this substance hit the black market, many of the users were either unaware of this or ignored it completely with a resulting increase in accidents. A major cause of the increase in adverse effects was due to the more commonplace availability of the drug. Those individuals of questionable emotional stability are those most likely to experience adverse effects. As Brecher (1972) states: "Indeed there is some reason to believe that the young drug scene in general and LSD in particular had a special attraction to these troubled young people" (p. 379).

One of the most troubling hazards of LSD use is the occurrence of flashbacks—a sudden and unexpected re-experiencing of some portion of an earlier trip. These occur without apparent stimulus and are not within conscious control of the individual. The occurrence is startling and causes some of those experiencing this phenomenon to question their own sanity.

Marijuana

Marijuana is the popular name for the Cannabis Sativa plant whose psychoactive ingredient is mostly concentrated in the resin. The marijuana used as a drug is made from the dried leaves and flowering tops of the plant, and the quality of the marijuana depends on the genetic variation of the plant. The actual amount of the psychoactive ingredient varies with the conditions of growth, harvesting, and curing. Delat-9-tetra hydrocannobinol is usually believed to be the active ingredient which is responsible for the marijuana experience.

Great controversy has been waged over the legal appropriateness of the penalties imposed upon the use of Cannabis. It must be remembered that this substance has been used all over the world since ancient times. In the early history of the United States, records indicate the importance of Cannabis as a commercial product. Our founding fathers grew the marijuana plant for the hemp produced. Before the invention of the cotton gin, hemp was used not only in the production of rope but also in the making of cloth. George Washington grew hemp at Mount Vernon, and it is surmised that he cultivated it in a manner that was then believed to increase the intoxicating and medicinal potency of the active ingredient—THC. During the nineteenth century, the production of marijuana flourished. Large hemp plantations were located in Mississippi, Georgia, California, South Carolina, Nebraska, and other states, although the center of production was in Kentucky. Both the reduction in number of sailing vessels, with their need for rope, and the invention of the cotton gin were responsible for the decline in the commercial production of hemp. However, as late as 1937, the American commercial crop was estimated at 10,000 acres (Brecher, 1972). During World War II, the commercial production increased enormously to meet the demands made on the use of rope.

The ban on marijuana legally did not occur until 1933 when Harry J. Auslinger, the newly appointed Director of the Federal Bureau of Narcotics, introduced a Uniform Anti-Narcotics Act designated for adoption by state legislatures. By 1937, practically all states had laws against marijuana. Most of these laws included marijuana under the same rigorous penalties applicable to morphine, heroin, and cocaine. In 1937, the Marijuana Tax Law was passed. Although it did not actually ban the use of marijuana, it placed a tax on those who dispensed it, grew it, exported it, or imported it. From that time on, Congress passed more and more legislation against Cannabis.

Both state and federal laws placed heavy penalties on either the use, the selling, or the growing of this weed. By 1970, a mass of such oppressive state and federal laws was in operation. The penalties imposed by these laws varied from state to state. It was possible for a seller of this product to receive life imprisonment in Illinois. Other states had penalties equally as harsh.

Many thoughtful people were extremely concerned with what appeared to be irrational and oppressive legislation concerning a substance whose effects did not seem to warrant such actions. Young people invariably raised the question of the comparable deleterious effects of marijuana and alcohol. Parents and their offspring were frequently at the two extremes over this question. The proponents of marijuana found the hypocrisy of those who decry the use of marijuana but drink socially as intolerable. As one adolescent said, "It is *not* all right for me to smoke pot, but it is all right for you to have a cocktail. How stupid can you get?" Perhaps this declaration could have been more tactfully stated, but it still expresses the argument that the prejudice against marijuana is not supported by the evidence available.

The irony of the situation is well expressed in the book entitled *A Child's Garden of Grass* (Margolis & Clorfence, 1969). When turning to Chapter VIII entitled, "The Dangers of Grass," one finds the total chapter consists of two words—"getting busted." A favorite argument of the marijuana protagonists is the theory that if an individual starts smoking grass, he will eventually end up using heroin. This theory postulates that marijuana will lose its appeal because it lacks potency or that it does not provide enough of a thrill. Therefore, the user will progress from one drug to a more potent drug until he is hooked on heroin. This fallacious logic implies that if all heroin addicts started their drug experiences on marijuana, then all marijuana users become heroin addicts. The foolishness of this argument is illustrated if one postulates that all alcoholics started their drinking habits with beer, then all beer drinkers will become alcoholics.

A study done in a Philadelphia methadone clinic, reported in a June 1973 issue of *Addiction and Drug Abuse Report,* found that in 1969, 72.6% of its new patients stated marijuana as the drug they had first used. However, by 1971 this percentage had dropped to 46.5%, and in 1972 to 31.1%. This study also indicated that many of their new patients in 1972 started their drug usage with narcotics.

Both federal and state governments have recognized the discrepancy between the severity of the laws and the hazard of use. Reduction of severity of punishment has been accomplished in many states with the penalty of marijuana possession changed from a felony to a misdemeanor. By 1975, six states had substituted a civil fine, a noncriminal fine, thus removing the offender from criminal prosecution.

Much research has been done attempting to determine the effects of marijuana on health. Conflicting reports have been published. Allegations as to the harmful effects of pot have appeared in reputable scientific journals. However, the methodology of much of this research has been criticized as being inappropriate or inadequate. For example, Dr. Heath (1973) at Tulane University implanted electrodes into the brain of six rhesus monkeys in order to measure brainwaves. He then exposed the monkeys to heavy doses of marijuana smoke. After the monkeys had been exposed to large doses daily for months, he found persistent changes in the brainwaves. Two of the monkeys' brains, upon examination, were found to have structural alteration of the cells in the sepial region. However, the dosage of marijuana to which the monkeys were exposed would be equivalent to smoking 30 marijuana cigarettes three times a day for six months. The abuse of any substance to that extent would be detrimental if not lethal. To extrapolate this data to humans, one could cogitate on the effect of eating 30 candy bars three times a day for six months, or drinking that many martinis.

Spurious results of research of this kind are reported in newspapers, magazines, and other news media, and only perpetuate many of the misconceptions concerning marijuana. The general public is in no position to evaluate the efficacy of the research. Consequently, they continue to believe the results reported.

Research using human subjects has been conducted in various areas. The possibility of behavioral effects of chronic use of marijuana has been a concern among marijuana research investigators for a long period of time. Conflicting results have been reported in the literature. The difficulties encountered in such research as lack of adequate control groups, the concurrent use of narcotics of other drugs, differing life styles, and nutritional deficiencies make it difficult to isolate the effects of heavy use of marijuana.

Three field studies have been done in Jamaica, Greece, and Costa Rica. The results of these three studies found no evidence of prolonged psychopathological difficulties. Although the results of these studies are reassuring, definitive conclusions as to the lack of adverse effects of marijuana cannot be made. All of these studies used a small number of subjects. Also, these studies were carried out in cultures quite different than that of the United States, using psychological instruments which were not normalized on these differing cultures. Therefore, the results may be spurious. The controversy that rages over the dilatory effects of chronic use of marijuana will not abate until research produces conclusive evidence for or against. Meanwhile, young people will continue to smoke marijuana.

Amphetamines

Amphetamines are a class of synthetic drugs which stimulate the central nervous system. Although they are now a common illicit street drug, they have been used medically with considerable success. They were first synthesized in 1887, and it was not until the 1920s and 1930s that they were used to treat medical problems. Narcolepsy, a disease in which the patient falls asleep repeatedly, responds well to this medication. It was also discovered that hyperactive children, when given amphetamines, instead of making them more active as one would expect, helped them in concentrating on their school work. Thousands of youngsters in our classrooms today are maintained on one or another type of amphetamine. Many educators are greatly concerned over the excessive use of this type of drug with hyperactive children. The controversy over this type of treatment has not been resolved.

Amphetamines were prescribed as diet pills in the 1950s and 1960s as they have the capacity to suppress hunger. As a stimulant, amphetamines ward off drowsiness. Truck drivers with long distances to travel, find them helpful. Students studying for exams use them.

Young people having discovered the sense of well being they produce, began using amphetamines as recreational chemicals. Most doctors, concerned with what appeared to be a psychological dependency on amphetamines, stopped prescribing these drugs for weight reduction. The federal government, being concerned as vast quantities of amphetamines were being sold as street drugs, placed restrictions on their use with careful control on their production. Yet the number of speed freaks continued to rise.

The use of amphetamines can have unfortunate results. It must be emphasized that different individuals have different reactions to the same chemical; but, in general, amphetamine abuse may lead to insomnia, nervousness, talkativeness, agitation, and, in some cases, even violent behavior. The abuser may be unable to sleep, and may experience an increase in energy, elevation of moods, and a feeling of confidence. However, prolonged use of the drug is followed by mental depression and fatigue. Paranoid feelings and suspicion of other people may ensue, accompanied by other psychotic symptoms. Because amphetamines often reduce the desire for food, the prolonged heavy user may appear emaciated, not as an effect of the drug, but because of lack of proper diet, accompanied by vitamin deficiency.

Amphetamines are normally taken orally, but some heavy abusers prefer intravenous injection. Although some young people have tried injection of the drug once or twice and then discarded it, many continue. The reinforcement value of intravenous use is great. The effect of this means of use is different than that of "popping pills." The experience has been described as a "whole body orgasm;" it is ecstatic in nature. Usually the user will inject amphetamines once every few weeks. Gradually, the time interval shortens and the number of injections within a short period of time increases. Finally, the speed freak injects his drug several times a day and remains awake three to six days to be followed by a day or two of profound sleep. Upon waking, the speed freak starts another "run" for several days, after which he "crashes" for more profound sleep. The long-term intravenous use of amphetamines almost inevitably results in paranoid psychosis. However, for most individuals, the psychotic symptoms dissipate after six months to a year of abstinence. The sudden termination of use of this drug is very difficult because of the fatigue the abuser experiences. It is extreme at first, but gradually diminishes with time.

The compulsive speed user is generally middle class, usually white, and is totally lacking the skills used by the heroin addict to hustle the money necessary to support his habit. The typical speed freak sponges off others or deals in drugs. He cheats—usually other speed freaks who are paranoid like himself. They often live in a community where everyone is cheating or sponging off everyone else. The potential for violence is great and when it does erupt, it may include high-level violence such as homicide and rape.

Drug users are familiar with the phrase "speed kills." Actually, there have been very few cases of death attributed to amphetamine overdose. Confirmed drug users, knowing the effects of amphetamine abuse on the life style of the abuser, prefer not to get into that hassle. There has been a drop in the number of speed freaks in the last few years, partially due to this and partially due to the progression from amphetamine abuse to heroin abuse.

The intravenous use of amphetamines gives individuals an incredible sense of power. It is no wonder that this particular drug has appeal for individuals who lack self-confidence or have a low opinion of themselves. Whereas the use of barbiturates or heroin only tends to increase their sense of worthlessness, amphetamines make them feel extremely potent and good about themselves.

Barbiturates

Barbiturates, central nervous system depressants, have been a boon to the medical profession in dealing with insomnia, agitated states, and many disorders. The management of epilepsy with this drug has given such patients a chance to live a normal life. Phenobarbitol was introduced in 1912 and since that time many barbiturates have been synthesized. Unfortunately, with the wide use of this drug, abuse began among patients who used this drug to avoid the problems of life. It rapidly became apparent in the 1930s and 1940s that the misuse of this drug was potentially dangerous.

Barbiturates are physically addictive, and cause intoxication. Barbiturate addicts suffer much the same withdrawal symptoms as alcoholics, including delirium tremors. Abrupt withdrawal from either may result in death.

The amount of barbiturates needed to keep an addict "stoned" varies from individual to individual. However, sudden withdrawal from this substance progresses through definite stages. A barbiturate addict, suddenly deprived of his downers, will at first seem normal, then "the shakes" and anxiety set in, accompanied by vomiting. The next stage is more dangerous, as convulsions may develop, and finally a life-threatening condition occurs with accompanying hallucinations and delusions. Death can occur.

A cross tolerance between alcohol and barbiturates is built up in the human body by either of these drugs. A barbiturate addict, as he increases his dose, also increases his tolerance for alcohol and can drink enormous amounts. This also works in reverse. A hard-core alcoholic builds up a tolerance to barbiturates and could tolerate a large quantity of barbiturates the first time he tried them. The simultaneous consumption of these two substances is dangerous. The mixing of alcohol and "barbs" is not at all uncommon among polydrug users and undoubtedly causes many accidental deaths. One potentiates the other and there is no way to accurately predict the result. Unintentional death can also occur just because of the mind-clouding effect of the barbiturates. An individual concerned that he may not sleep takes one or two pills. Still being awake a little later, forgetting that he had already consumed some, takes more. This may continue until a lethal dose is ingested.

Barbiturates are abused by adolescents and adults alike, and the rate of misuse is second only to alcohol. In the slums and ghetto areas where life is harsh, the barbiturates offer a way out. Being stoned on "barbs" makes the ugliness and difficulty of life a little less intense. Its sedative action clouds the senses, preventing the reality of the environment to impinge upon the user's perceptions. Barbiturate use is commonplace in the inner cities. They are less expensive than heroin and readily available. The commonplace use of both barbiturates and alcohol intermixed only adds to the problem.

Generally, the adjustment of those individuals who have become dependent on barbiturates is not good. To avoid facing life with all its anxieties and strains, constant use of barbiturates prevents individuals from becoming constructive, productive citizens. Those who seek this way out usually have psychological problems which need attention.

In any rehabilitation program for the barbiturate addict, the psychodynamics of the drug dependency must be dealt with. Those groups of individuals who are subject to special tensions find barbiturates a way of escape. Being stoned on barbiturates is an adjustive mechanism used to deal with a style of life over which they have no control.

Heroin

Although all narcotics are abused, the one which the mass media, with its lurid stories, has helped make familiar to the general public is heroin. Heroin is a narcotic. Strictly speaking, narcotics refer to opium and its derivatives such as morphine and heroin. A group of drugs known as synthetic narcotics, of which methadone is an example, are not derived from opium. However, they resemble morphine and heroin in their effects.

The increase of the number of young people addicted to this drug, with all its ramifications, has become a blight upon the American scene. Heroin's potential for physical addiction with the tolerance effect has been instrumental in creating a large group of young people whose purpose in life is to get the next "fix." This craving for heroin has led to delinquent behavior or criminal acts on the part of young people. Few have the wherewithal to support a strong drug habit. It is necessary, then, to resort to illegal means to get the "bread" to buy a "fix." Girls often resort to prostitution to make the ready cash, while boys turn to robbery or mugging for their money. For a young person who is really hooked, the life style may change completely. Every waking minute is spent in obtaining enough money for the next "fix," making the "connection" to get the "stuff" and then enjoying the few hours while high. This whole cycle is repeated over and over again. The need to resort to antisocial behavior to obtain the funds contributes to the crime evident in the inner cities. Heroin addicts tend to congregate in cities, as the opportunities for obtaining the money to support such an expensive habit are greater there. Heroin is also one of the preferred drugs of those living in slums, as its capacity to help the addict psychologically withdraw from the surrounding environment alleviates the stresses and dismalness with which they are surrounded. The cost of a strong heroin habit can be high. Some heroin habits have been known to require $80 to $100 a day to support. Consequently, a brisk business in the illicit marketing of heroin has developed in this country with all it entails.

Opium is easily grown and is cultivated in China, Greece, Mexico, Thailand, Turkey, and other countries. Despite the attempts to control smuggling of this product, much comes into the United States. Morphine is extracted from opium and then converted into heroin. The equipment necessary is simple and relatively inexpensive with much less equipment than is needed for distillation of alcohol.

It has been recommended, time after time, in the recent history of the United States by various commissions, medical societies, and individual doctors, that heroin be sold to addicts by clinics on an experimental basis at the price that legally prescribed morphine is sold. The price is a fraction of what they pay on the black market for hazardous, adulterated, and contaminated heroin. Such a procedure would circumvent the illicit selling of this drug by eliminating the market. Controlled legal selling of heroin would also control the purity of the product.

The dangers connected with heroin addiction are not associated with the physiological effects of heroin on the body. Heroin death contributed to overdose is rarely caused by too much of the drug itself. In fact, various studies have shown that even enormous amounts of morphine or heroin do not kill addicts. The great number of addict deaths are considered to be due to various circumstances. It might be due to contaminations of the black market product or the injection of heroin with or just after other central nervous depressants have been consumed.

Because the favored way of using heroin is by injection ("mainlining"), and because the addict usually cares little about aseptic conditions, other physiological problems can arise. The continuous use of a hypodermic needle can collapse veins, leaving ugly, even ulcerated marks at the point of injection. A high incidence of hepatitis and other diseases are present among heroin addicts. VD among female drug addicts is a direct result of prostitution practices to obtain money.

Evidence for the actual dilatory effects of heroin on the body is nonexistent. Continuous of opiates seems not to have any adverse effects on the brain or any other body organs. Yet the cost to society concerning the use of this drug is tremendous. Deaths connected with the use of heroin are high; the methods used to obtain the funds to purchase heroin only add to our problems of the conflicts with the law, and contribute to the delinquency and disruptive behavior of our young people.

REFERENCES

"The Drug Scene is Changing." *Addiction and Drug Abuse Reports*. New York: Grafton Publications, June, 1973.

Alcohol and Health. Report from the Secretary of Health, Education and Welfare. New York: Charles Scribner's Sons (no date).

Allen, D. E., and Sandhu, H. S. "Alienation, Hedonism and Live Vision of Delinquents." *Journal of Criminal Law, Criminology and Police Science* 58 (1971): 325-329.

Ambrosino, L. *Runaways*. Boston: Beacon Press, 1971.

"Attack on Narcotic Addiction and Drug Abuse, Changing Scene for Drug Education." New York: New York State Narcotic Addiction Control Commission 6 (Spring, 1973): 2.

Bayer, M.; Holt, S. A.; Reid, T. A.; and Quinlan, D. M. "Runaway Youth: Family in Conflict." Paper presented at Eastern Psychological Association Meeting, May 1973, at Washington, D.C.

Blood, L., and D'Angelo, R. "A Progress Research Report on Value Issues in Conflict Between Runaways and Their Parents." *Journal of Marriage and the Family* (August, 1974).

Blackford, L. S. "Trends in Student Drug Use in San Maldo County." *California Health* 7 (1969).

Bosma, W. "Alcoholism and Teenagers." *Maryland State Medical Journal* 4 (1975): 62–88.

Braucht, G. N.; Brakarsh, D.; Follingstad, D; and Berry, K. L. "Deviant Drug Use in Adolescence: A Review of Psychological Correlates." *Psychological Bulletin* 79 (1973) 92–106.

Brecher, E. M., and Editors of Consumer Reports. *Licit and Illicit Drugs*. Mount Vernon, New York: Consumer's Union, 1972.

Brecher, E. M., and Editors of Consumer Reports. "Marijuana: The Health Questions. Is Marijuana as Damaging as Recent Reports Make it Appear?" *Consumer Reports* (1975): 143–149.

Bureau of Narcotics and Dangerous Drugs. *U.S. Department of Justice Guidelines for Drug Abuse Prevention Education*. Washington, D.C.: U.S. Government Printing Office, 1970.

"Changing Scene for Drug Education." *Attack on Drug Addiction and Drug Abuse*. New York: New York State Narcotics Addiction Control Commission 6 (1973).

Cornacchia, H. J.; Bentel, D. J.; and Smith, D. E. *Drugs in the Classroom: A Conceptual Model for School Programs*. St. Louis: C. V. Mosby, 1973.

Covert, J, ed. *Youth Alternatives*. Washington, D.C.: National Youth Alternative Project, Inc., 11 (1975).

Crowley, T. J. "The Reinforcers for Drug Abuse: Why People Take Drugs." *Comprehensive Psychiatry* 13 (1972).

Cull, J. G., and Hardy, R. E. *Problems of Runaway Youth*. Springfield, Ill.: Charles C. Thomas, 1976.

Deneau, G.; Yanagita, T.; and Seevers, M. H. "Self-Administration of Psychoactive Substances by the Monkey." *Psychopharmacologia* 16 (1969).

Dohner, A. V. "Alternatives to Drugs—A New Approach to Drug Education." *Journal of Drug Education* 2 (1972): 3–22.

Dohner, A. V. "Motives for Drug Use: Adult and Adolescent." *Psychosomatics* 13 (1972): 327–334.

Edwards, C. N. *Drug Dependence: Social Regulation and Treatment Alternatives*. New York: Jason Aronson, 1974.

Expert Committee on Addiction. "Producing Drugs Terminology in Regard to Drug Abuse." *World Health Organization Technical Report Series*, 1964, p. 273.

Farnsworth, D. L. "Drug Use for Pleasure: A Complex Social Problem." *The Journal of School Health* 43 (1973): 153–158.

Finch, S. M., and Pozanski, E. D. *Adolescent Suicide*. Springfield, Ill.: Charles C. Thomas, 1971.

Floyd, J.; Lang, R.; and Lotsof, A. "Drug Education: Suggested Guidelines for Conducting an Effective Course for Teachers." *Journal of American College Health Association* 24 (1975): 15–19.

Fox, U. "Alcoholism in Adolescence." *Journal of School Health* 27 (1973): 32–35.

Girdano, D. A., and Girdano, D. D. *Drug Education: Content and Methods*. Reading, Mass.: Addison-Wesley, 1972.

Goode, E. *Drugs in American Society*. New York: Alfred A. Knopf, Inc., 1972.

Goodstadt, M., ed. *Research on Methods and Programs of Drug Education*. Toronto, Canada: Addiction Research Foundation, 1974.

Grupenhoff, J. *Drug Abuse Films*. 3rd ed., The National Coordinating Council on Drug Education, 1973.

Hardy, R. E., and Cull, J. G. *Climbing Ghetto Walls*. Springfield, Ill.: Charles C. Thomas, 1973.

Heath, R. G. "Marijuana: Effects on Deep and Surface Electroencephalograms on Rhesus Monkeys." *Neuropharmacology* 12 (1973): 1–14.

Herndon, J. *How to Survive in Your Native Land*. New York: Simon and Schuster, 1971.

Hofen, B. Q. *Drug Abuse: Psychology, Sociology, Pharmacology*. Provo, Utah: Brigham Young University Press, 1973.

Irwin, S. "The Uses and Relative Hazard Potential of Psychoactive Drugs." *Bulletin of the Menninger Clinic* 38 (1974): 19–48.

Jacobson, L. D. "Ethanol Education Today." *Journal of School Health* 43 (1973).

Jessor, R.; Carman, R.; and Grossman, P. "Expectation of Need Satisfaction and Drinking Patterns of College Students." *Quarterly Journal of Studies on Alcohol* 29 (1968): 101–116.

Jones, M. C. "Personality Correlates and Antecedents of Drinking Patterns in Women." *Journal of Consulting and Clinical Psychology* 36 (1971): 61–69.

Jones, M. C. "Personality Correlates and Antecedents of Drinking Patterns in Adult Males." *Journal of Consulting and Clinical Psychology* 32 (1968): 2–12.

Levy, R. M., and Brown, A. R. "Untoward Effects of Drug Education." *American Journal of Public Health* 63 (1973): 1071–1073.

Lingeman, R. R. *Drugs from A to Z*. New York: McGraw-Hill, 1974.

Levenson, M., and Neuringer, C. "Problem-Solving Behavior in Suicidal Adolescents." *Journal of Consulting and Clinical Psychology* 37 (1971): 433–435.

Lotsof, A., and Floyd, J. "A Conceptual Model of Drug Abuse and its Implication for Special Educators." Workshop presented before International Council for Exceptional Children, Annual Convention. April 9, 1976.

Mackay, J. "Clinical Observations on Adolescent Problem Drinkers." *Quarterly Journal of Studies on Alcohol* 22 (1961): 124–134.

Maddox, G. L. "High-School Students' Drinking Behavior: Incidental Information from Two National Surveys." *Quarterly Journal of Studies on Alcohol* 25 (1964): 339–347.

Maddox, G. L., and McCall, B. C. "Drinking among Teenagers, a Sociological Interpretation of Alcohol Use by High School Students." *Rutgers Center of Alcohol Studies*. New Brunswick, New York, 1964.

"Marijuana and Health." Fifth Annual Report to the U.S. Congress from the Secretary of Health, Education, and Welfare. Washington, D.C.: U.S. Government Printing Office, 1975.

Margolis, J. S., and Clorfence, R. *A Child's Garden of Grass*. New York: Simon and Schuster, 1969.

McIntire, M. S., and Angle, C. R. " 'Suicide' as seen in Poison Control Centers." *Pediatrics* 48 (1971): 914–921.

McLeod, A. *Growing Up in America: A Background to Contemporary Drug Abuse*. Rockville, Md.: National Institute of Mental Health, 1973.

Moore, H. G. "My Name is Mr. Blank, A Retrospective Account of a Suicide Attempt by W. G." *Journal of Clinical Child Psychology* 4 (1975): 39–44.

National Clearinghouse for Drug Abuse Information. *Treatment of Drug Abuse: An Overview*. Rockville, Md.: Department of Health, Education, and Welfare 34 (1975).

Nowlis, H. H. *Contemporary Drug Problems*. New York: Federal Legal Publications 1 (1972).

"Positive Approaches to Dropout Prevention." Department of Health, Education and Welfare Publications, 1973.

Randall, D., and Wong, M. R. "Drug Education to Date: A Review." *Journal of Drug Education* 6 (Spring 1976): 1–21.

Ray, G. S. *Drugs, Society, and Human Behavior*. Saint Louis: C. V. Mosby, 1972.

Renshaw, D. "Suicide and Depression in Children." *The Journal of School Health* 44 (1974): 487–489.

Resnik, H. L. P., and Hathorne, B. C., eds. "Suicide Prevention in the 70's." *National Institute of Mental Health, Department of Health, Education, and Welfare*. Washington, 1973.

Robey, A.; Rosenwald, S.; and Rosenwald, L. "The Runaway Girl: A Reaction to Family Stress." *American Journal of Orthopsychiatry* 34 (1964): 762–767.

Rotter, J. B. *Clinical Psychology*. 2nd ed., Englewood Cliffs, New Jersy: Prentice-Hall, Inc., 1971.

"Runaway Children." *U.S. News and World Report*, April 24, 1972, 38–42.

Sabbath, Joseph C. "The Role of the Parent in Adolescent Suicidal Behavior." *Acta Paedopsychiatrica* 38 (1972): 211–220.

Schlicht, J. "Drug Addiction—Myth or Reality?" *Public Health* 87 (1973).

"Senate Hearings on the Runaway Youth Act." Senate Committee on Judiciary, 1972 (Report 92-1002).

Stanley, J. E., and Barter, J. T. "Adolescent Suicide Behavior."*American Journal of Orthopsychiatry* 46 (January 1970): 87–96.

"Stash. Adolescent Alcohol Use and Abuse." *Capsules, The Student Association for the Study of Hallucinogens, Inc.* (September–October 1975).

Taintor, Z. "The 'Why' of Youthful Drug Abuse." *Journal of School Health* 44 (1974): 26–29.

Toffler, A. *Future Shock*. New York: Random House, 1970.

Toolan, J. M. "Suicide in Children and Adolescents." *American Journal of Psychotherapy* 29 (1975): 339–344.

"Transient Youth." Report on an inquiry in the summer of 1969, Canadian Welfare Council, Ottawa, Canada, February, 1970.

U.S. Congressional Record, 93rd Congress, 2nd session, 1974.

Williams, A. "College Problem Drinkers: A Personality Profile." *The Domesticated Drug: Drinking Among Collegians*. Edited by G. Maddox. New Haven: Connecticut College and University Press, 1970.

Youcha, G. "Running Away—All the Way Home." *Parents' Magazine* 48 (May 1973): 82–85.

"Youth Crisis Sources." Hearings before the subcommittee on children and youth (Committee on Labor and Public Welfare—United States Senate 92nd Congress). Washington, D.C.: U.S. Government Printing Office, 1972.

6

developing reading strategies for youths with educational handicaps

AUGUST J. MAUSER

The purpose of this chapter is to assist the teacher of educationally handicapped adolescents and chronic disruptive youth in planning appropriate reading related activities. Specific approaches to the remediation of unique reading disabilities will be covered. Basic instructional materials related to teaching reading to secondary school-age youth with educational handicaps who display chronic disruptive behavior will also be discussed in a later section. Because of the diversity and heterogeneity of the population in question, an eclectic point of view will be proposed. A combination of many different reading interventions will be recommended. It is our contention and philosophy that in terms of pedagogical practices, educators can no longer stress the mechanical, isolated, teaching of reading to educationally handicapped adolescents and chronic disruptive youth. It is instructionally sound to delay the teaching of reading with functional readers until such a time that the student feels the importance of obtaining mastery of technical, vocational, and social reading vocabulary. Reading is not a subject that stands apart from school, job, career educational plan, life style, family, or friends. The teacher of adolescent youth is forced to be concerned with the attitudes, interests, and emotional reaction to reading and school work of the students. The "therapeutic teacher" is expected to be aware of group process and to use the group as a positive force to encourage academic success. To a certain degree, one might say that the modern secondary educator will, by necessity, employ a tremendous

199

repertoire of teaching skills in a therapeutic fashion. Traditional remedial and/or developmental programs in reading might be quite successful with achieving students, but the norm-violating and chronic disruptive youth present a unique learning experience. Approaching the problem adolescent and chronic disruptive youth with corrective or remedial measures, which in many ways might resemble his original traumatic experiences in reading, may actually inhibit the process of remediation unless his emotional reactions to the teacher and program are brought to the surface and handled therapeutically. Without a positive teacher-student relationship, the best remedial program will be of limited value to secondary school-age youth with educational handicaps and chronic disruptive youth.

Roman (1957) cites the superiority of "tutorial group" therapy over group remedial reading and straight group therapy with no remedial reading. The basic conclusions from this type of research is that straight remedial reading is not enough nor is psychotherapy in isolation appropriate. Rice (1970) is one of the many authors supporting "educo-therapy" which includes a balance of educational and therapeutic strategies.

Reasons why problem adolescents and chronic disruptive youth may dislike reading are:

1. Difference in language. Reading written words depends on the previously learned language skills that the student brings to the reading situation.

2. Inadequate reading readiness program. Beginning formal reading instruction before student is ready to read.

3. Lack of proper motivation for reading. The student may have no purpose for reading and see no relationship between reading and his other activities.

4. Physical handicaps, such as poor vision or hearing.

5. Reading materials that are too difficult. If the student's mental age is below the average of his grade, he is likely to find the regular reading requirements too difficult.

6. Poor visual memory, which makes it difficult for the student to remember the printed symbols of words and ideas.

7. Reading material is below the student's interest level.

8. Reading materials are too mature for student's interest level.

9. Reading materials in the schoolroom are inappropriate for the student's reading interests and abilities.

10. Over-use of one method or one approach to reading.

11. Inadequate mastery of the mechanics of reading.

12. Intense need for an immediate pay-off.

13. Interrupting the actual reading situation with too much word analysis, vocabulary study, or over-emphasis upon any one phase of the mechanics of reading.

14. Feelings of inferiority toward reading, resulting from student's inability to master reading, which may, in turn develop into a definite cause of reading failure.

15. Poor opinion of self, and low self-esteem.

16. Too much academic competition in the classroom, which creates tensions and sets goals far beyond the abilities and energies of the students.

17. Over-anxious teachers who push the student into a higher reading level before he has had sufficient practice with the easy materials.

18. Frequent school changes during the year.

19. Fatigue caused by too much close work, too heavy a schedule, too many outside activities, or excessive home or job responsibilities.

20. Student's home life not conducive to reward academic growth or promote academic achievement.

21. A lack of reading interests within the home.

22. Language other than English spoken within the home.

23. Too much required of the student by over-anxious parents who prod him to bring home high grades.

24. Serious social-emotional conflict.

READING: THE TOTAL CURRICULUM

A global or total curriculum scheme must be considered in planning reading programs for educationally handicapped adolescents. Reading, taught in isolation without significant relevance to the reader, will never work. A *life roles* curriculum model is strongly advocated. One such life roles model, proposed by Guerriero and Mauser (1974), includes the curriculum area of reading, and other curriculum areas such as mathematics and science. Specific activities revolve around a combination of four roles that the student will eventually take in adult life, namely the (1) consumer, (2) worker, (3) private person, and (4) citizen. The advantages of this life roles model is that it does make instruction relevant and useful for students, and it includes student-centered teaching strategies which will increase student participation and emphasize the use of real life situations rather than "canned" textbook data.

Fagan, Long & Stevens (1975) have recently introduced what they term a *Self Control Curriculum*. This approach has obvious utility for secondary school-age youth with educational handicaps and chronic disruptive youth in that it emphasizes the training of the most common and significant deficits possessed by them, namely, those behaviors characterized by lack of self-control. Four of the skill clusters in the self-control curriculum seem to depend heavily upon intellectual or cognitive development while the other four seem more related to emotional or affective development. According to Fagan, Long and Stevens (1975) the eight skill clusters include:

1. *Selection*—the ability to perceive incoming information accurately. This would include curriculum units related to focusing and concentration, mastering figure-ground discrimination, problems of distraction and interference, and processing complex patterns.

2. *Storage*—the ability to retain the information received. This includes curriculum units related to developing visual memory and auditory memory.

3. *Sequencing and ordering*—the ability to organize actions on the basis of a planned order. This includes specific units related to developing time orientation, auditory-visual sequencing, and developing sequential planning.

4. *Anticipating consequences*—the ability to relate actions to expected outcomes. This includes specific curriculum units related to developing alternatives and also evaluating consequences.

5. *Appreciating feelings*—the ability to identify and constructively use affective experience. This includes curriculum units related to identifying feelings, developing positive feelings, managing feelings and reinterpreting feeling events.

6. *Managing frustration*—the ability to cope with external obstacles that produce stress. This includes the acceptance of feelings of frustration, building coping resources, and tolerating frustration.

7. *Inhibition and delay*—this includes curriculum units for controlling action and also developing part-goals.

8. *Relaxation*—the ability to reduce internal tension. This includes activities and units related to developing body and movement relaxation.

The meshing and synthesizing of the life roles curriculum and self-control curriculum is strongly urged in the development of a curriculum, and specifically in the development of reading programs for educationally handicapped adolescents and chronic disruptive youth. The reader is urged to review thoroughly the chapters in this book that have been devoted to operant conditioning and precision teaching styles and strategies. From this point on we will talk about the basic content and concepts associated with the teaching of reading to secondary school-age youth with educational handicaps and chronic disruptive youth.

McDonald and Moorman (1974) have developed twelve objectives which comprise the basis of a Minimal Reading Proficiency Assessment (MRPA) related to functional reading. A functional reader will:

1. Identify stated main ideas.
2. Identify inferred main ideas.
3. Draw conclusions from a stated and/or inferred main idea.
4. Identify stated supportive details.
5. Draw conclusions from stated or inferred supportive details.
6. Identify stated and/or inferred sequences within selected contents.
7. Answer relationship questions, such as cause and effect, fact and opinion, and/or time and space.
8. Demonstrate the ability to follow written directions.
9. Demonstrate the ability to complete given tasks using an index and/or table of contents.
10. Demonstrate the ability to complete given tasks using a dictionary.
11. Demonstrate the ability to complete given tasks for extracting information from graphs, tables, maps, charts, diagrams, pictures, and/or cartoons.
12. Select an appropriate meaning, using context clues, for a given unfamiliar word.

These twelve objectives should serve as useful guidelines for the teacher of educationally handicapped adolescents and chronic disruptive youth in assuring that basic literacy in the area of reading is achieved.

The following section will describe the specific educational settings and personnel utilized in teaching reading to secondary school-age youth with educational handicaps and chronic disruptive youth.

THE REGULAR CLASSROOM AND MAINSTREAMING

The ability of the regular classroom to adequately meet educationally handicapped adolescents' and chronically disruptive youths' needs in reading will depend on the severity of the youth's behavior. The typical high school classroom is a busy, achievement-oriented environment that reinforces positively productive students, and negatively reinforces those who fail to achieve. The regular classroom is by far the most desirable setting for children to receive assistance; but, in most cases the chronically disruptive adolescent will not, at least at the onset, have the self-control to withstand a whole day in the regular classroom. The goals of special education for chronically disruptive youth and secondary school-age youths with educational handicaps is to offer the option of having the student remain with his peers. The regular classroom should definitely be regarded as the optimal focal point for the student's reading instruction if at all possible. Many regular classrooms will be unable to serve the needs of seriously educationally handicapped. What other options are there? In chapter 1, a review of special education program options was discussed. In the next section of this chapter, we will review them with an eye toward reading intervention.

The special class

Historically, the most popular alternative for dealing with students having severe behavioral problems has been the self-contained special class. Special classes have been under scrutiny because of research which reported that students placed in special classes achieve scholastically on the same level, or not as well as similar students who remain in the regular grades. Nonacademic variables such as social adjustment and self-concept levels have also been questioned in terms of the contribution special classes can make toward these variables. Dunn (1968) was among the first special educators to question the degree of utilization of the special class to handle handicapped children. Alternatives were suggested which have been a significant factor in the designing of less isolating and more prescriptive types of educational remediation. We must caution that much of the criticism and ultimate recommendations related to the special class as a delivery service model were made with the mildly handicapped in mind. It is our contention that secondary school-age youth with educational handicaps and chronically disruptive youth, by their nature, are not necessarily mildly handicapped in terms of categorical disability labels, but in a behavioral control reaction to school. A special class curriculum should provide: (1) specially trained teachers; (2) special materials; and (3) methods emphasizing individualized instruction with a workable teacher-pupil ratio.

Institutionalization—public and private

Placement of chronically disruptive youth and educationally handicapped adolescents in either private or public special schools generally follows the attempts to adjust to either the regular classroom or special class within a regular elementary or secondary school. In the special school, the chronically disruptive youth and secondary school-age youth with educational handicaps is not only segregated from norm-respective peers, but is also brought into direct contact with other antisocial role models. Special schools which are privately operated may be of either the residential or day-school variety. In analyzing the educational programs of residential facilities for adjudicated youth, Sabatino, Mauser and Skok (1975) have described the present status of these programs in correctional facilities, and have noted that relatively few teachers at the time of the study were specifically trained in special education. It is hoped that these residential facilities will increase in quality. Although public and private facilities serving chronically disruptive youth and educationally handicapped adolescents are quite expensive, the payoff in change of behavior may be quite high because of the great amount of control and milieu immersion into a total remedial program. Mandatory education of handicapped children has contributed to the success of the local districts who recommend the youth to the particular private facility. The correction institution, because of the segregation and stigma, oftentimes to both youth and family, should be considered and examined. But it should be regarded as an alternative placement after attempts to integrate the youth into the regular classroom or self-contained classes within a regular elementary or secondary school have been tried.

Diagnostic, curriculum, or learning centers

Larger and more affluent school districts have organized centers within their districts where adolescents having other types of educational problems are given temporary assignment. These students are generally assigned to the facility on an out-client basis for one or two hours a day for programs varying in duration from weeks to months. The adolescent who is placed in this setting usually receives a detailed diagnostic workup. An individual curriculum design and appropriate materials are developed by specialists for this youth, and upon termination of their evaluation, the teacher receives a complete curriculum guide to work with the individual. Available at this center are vast amounts of instructional materials and expert consultation to assist in the development of teaching strategies based on the adolescent's specific learning characteristics or career education plans.

The resource rooms

The resource room model is a delivery of services system that fits well into the educational needs of educationally handicapped adolescents, especially the mildly handicapped who can withstand longer periods of time in a regular class or special class. The resource room is an alternative to both self-contained and regular classes. Secondary school-age youth with educational handicaps and chronically disruptive youth, placed in a resource room setting, would be able to receive their instruction individually or in small groups. The resource room will generally include a collection of necessary instructional materials to focus on a specific academic deficiency. The resource room option could also be utilized for any other academic or therapeutic strategies that the adolescent might require. The youth is generally scheduled into a resource room on a regular basis having a home base in the regular, special, or vocational curricula. Reger (1973) discusses the philosophy and the administrative structure, including advantages and disadvantages of the resource room concept. Weiderholt (1974) offers additional information for the educator of mildly handicapped children who is interested in establishing resource rooms for his students. Hammill and Bartel (1975) have also cited some of the basic resource room types including categorical and non-categorical models.

Categorical resource room

The categorical resource room models are reserved for those children who fall within a community's particular disability labeling system. Separate resource rooms may be established for nonhandicapped academic underachievers. In the case of norm-violating, chronic disruptive youth, they would spend the majority of their school time in the regular classroom, but would also receive additional work in the designated resource room for children with behavioral disorders. Glavin, Quay, Annesley, and Werry (1971) have described resource room programs for the emotionally disturbed which may have implications for the programming of educationally handicapped adolescents and chronically disruptive youth. Sabatino (1971) gives similar comment as the categorical resource room approach may apply to learning disabled children.

Non-categorical resource room

The non-categorical resource room approach has received much support and acceptance. This type of delivery of service model is designed to meet the educational needs of all peoples in a given school, not just those who have been or are in the special education program. Non-categorical resource rooms have similarities in that specific areas of deficit in reading, spelling, and/or behavior are identified and consequently remedial programs are planned and implemented. The stigmatization associated with categorical resource rooms is removed in the non-categorical resource room approach as long as the scheduling includes a wide variety of students. Gifted and talented youngsters may also receive instruction in the non-categorical resource room. This maneuver alone does much in counteracting any stigma associated with special help given pupils in a resource room concept.

In some situations, the resource room teacher may, instead of having the specific student come to the resource room, actually go to the home classroom of the individual for certain periods of the day. This approach eliminates the "withdrawal from the classroom" technique which may attribute to stigmatization. Allowing the teacher to work with other students besides those identified as needing special help will also reduce stigmatization of such students. Such a *special education teacher consultant* model has been most effective in elementary programs. With some liaison with a supervisor or department head, it may be valid for use in the high school.

Other techniques

Many other modifications of standard procedures, and the standard delivery of service procedures, can be introduced to programs serving secondary school-age youth with educational handicaps and chronically disruptive youth. Paraprofessionals, according to Mauser (1970), can be a most valuable in-class or out-of-class support measure in working with handicapped children, especially in the area of reading. Ellson, Harris, and Barber (1968) have noted the effectiveness of trained paraprofessionals utilizing materials that are programmed not for the child but for the tutor administering the materials. Peer tutoring has also been receiving a great amount of attention recently and shows great promise as an alternative strategy in dealing with educationally handicapped adolescents and chronically disruptive youth with reading problems. Regardless of the delivery of service models initiated in a particular program for secondary school-age youth with educational handicaps and chronically disruptive youth, great attention must be given to flexibility in the grouping and scheduling of such students. Reading is certainly important in establishing any academic or vocational plan, and is a necessity in developing a career education plan for a student.

READING: ESTABLISHING A RATIONALE

Carroll (1970) and many others have specified the components of a reading program. A student must know the language that he is going to learn to read. This means that the student should be able to speak and understand the language at the level he is expected to read with comprehension. The reasoning behind language learning prior to traditional formal reading is to guarantee that the student receives the messages from print that are similar to the messages he can already understand in the language he speaks. Students who do not know the language, or who only understand but do not speak, will very likely require a mode of instruction specially adapted to them. McCullough (1968) cites the ingredients related to the acts of reading and emphasizes that these specific acts are actually interrelated and should not be taught in complete isolation. Consequently, in planning reading programs for educationally handicapped adolescents and chronic disruptive youth, we may wish to consider some, if not all, of her ideas.

1. *Word form.* The reader must be able to decode the symbols by sight methods, sound methods, or by contextual clues, to arrive at the English sound patterns.

2. *Sentence order and structure.* The reader must observe the role of the word in the order and structure in the sentence.

3. *Word meaning.* The reader must determine the meaning a given word should have, given its form, its role in the sentence, and the suggestions of its meaning from the larger environment: that is, previous sentences, physical setting, etc.

4. *Sentence meaning.* The reader must arrive at the meaning of the sentence in view of the sound, order, function, meaning of its parts, and the suggestions from the larger environment.

5. *Sentence function.* The reader must determine the kind of idea the sentence offers and its role in the pattern of thoughts around it.

6. *Evaluation and interpretation.* The reader must measure the author's style and views against his experience, filtering them through his cognitive and affective sieve. Interpretation includes the intonation which the readers possess and an understanding of the author's intention in vox. The reader must interpret beyond what the author has said, applying his own thought processes to the ideas, both as he meets them and after he has finished reading.

7. *Use.* The reader must use the ideas he gains and the ideas he generates from the reading. Some of these uses occur to him as he reads or even motivates him to read in the first place. Some of them appear later in dreams and old memories.

Although McCullough (1968) developed the previous axioms using the example of "one sentence," she cites that sentence to sentence relationships, paragraph to paragraph relationships, and chapter to chapter relationships are obviously aspects of the relativity principle, thus readily adaptable to the stated format.

Kerber (1975) offers some pertinent and timely teacher-oriented tasks that are applicable to any reading lesson that is taught, regardless of its length, specific material used, or specific skill involved. The teacher of secondary school-age youth with educational handicaps and chronic disruptive youth, should find great utility in the 13 tasks that require great amounts of teacher-pupil interaction and concern for the reading session. According to the author the following teacher-initiated tasks are given:

1. *Building your own substantive background knowledge.* The teacher must know and understand the specific reading skill or skills that will be presented to the students for them to learn in a day's lesson.

2. *Preparing materials.* The teacher must have everything available and ready that will need to be used in the lesson.

3. *Using resource persons, places or things.* The teacher must know how to operate or most effectively use the materials and resources that have been gathered together for the lesson.

4. *Showing evidence of planning.* The teacher should demonstrate or prove to students that as the teacher she knows what she intends to have them learn and has anticipated their needs.

5. *Introducing the lesson.* The teacher must make sure that the students are ready to learn and are as motivated as possible toward acquiring the reading skill that is the object of a day's lesson.

6. *Sticking to the original objective(s).* The teacher must help the students focus their attention and reach for a concept in a particular day's lesson.

7. *Managing the class.* As the lesson progresses, every strategy related to the students' guidance must be utilized in order to aid in the control of their actions.

8. *Involving readers actively.* The teacher must recognize the need of learners to be "doing something." The teacher must also engender new excitement and interest in the reading skill to be acquired.

9. *Soliciting responses.* The teacher must use all the skills of questioning in order to guarantee reactions from the students.

10. *Allowing for students' self correction.* The teacher must recognize the positive self-image for the reader is even more crucial than the reading skill being presented. (This is especially true with adolescents and chronic disruptive youth.)

11. *Checking out understandings.* The teacher must continuously observe and evaluate the progress of each student toward the acquisition of the reading skill being presented.

12. *Encouraging individual enrichment.* From constant evaluation the teacher must make individual recommendations for each reader's future action in relation to a day's reading skill.

13. *Ending the lesson.* The teacher must be able to judge or sense when it is time to change activities. Specifically, it is the knowledge of the teacher that it is time to end the reading lesson and move on to something else. (Kerber, 1975)

BASIC SKILLS FOR READING PROGRAMS

Considering that most secondary school-age youth will come to the educational setting with a wide variety of reading skill strengths and weaknesses, it is imperative to identify initial instructional strategies to teach (1) decoding or word recognition, and (2) comprehension skills.

Being able to quickly recognize known words is vital to becoming an efficient reader. The acquisition of rapid word perception skills enables the pupil to read more fluently and to derive more meaning from the print form presented. To become an able reader, though, the educationally handicapped adolescent and chronic disruptive youth must be adept in the use of various methods of identifying words. A singular approach to word identification in the secondary school-age youth with educational handicaps and chronic disruptive youth is hardly sufficient. Most often, as with the general population, educationally handicapped adolescents and chronic disruptive youth will simultaneously integrate several approaches that will function automatically on their behalf in securing independence in reading. The teacher of educationally handicapped adolescents' and chronic disruptive youths' first instructional task in reading is to assist her students in acquiring and maintaining essential vocabulary skills. The essential perceptuo-vocabulary skills most frequently utilized include: (1) sight vocabulary building; (2) expanding vocabulary and word meaning; (3) context clues; (4) picture clues; (5) language clues; (6) configuration clues; (7) phonic analysis; (8) structural analysis; and (9) dictionary usage. Each of these skills mentioned has many components which, if treated adequately, would involve an extensive statement. Specific attention, though, will be given to several methods of developing a sight vocabulary through various types of word analysis techniques, including sight vocabulary and word analysis techniques. Comprehension skills will also be discussed in this section.

ORGANIZATIONAL PLANS AND SYSTEMS IN TEACHING READING

The basic purpose of this section is to acquaint the reader with the major organizational plans and modifications which might be used in teaching reading to norm-violating chronic disruptive youth. Although certain biases on the part of the writer will surface during this section, it should be mentioned again that because of the diversity of the population in question, and also because we do not know exactly what specific types of materials they have had frustration with in the past, we will see some utility at one time or another in all of the approaches presented.

Four major plans evolve when one discusses basic organizational plans. Organizational plans should not be confused with the basic skills which each of the plans will attempt to develop. Organizational plans all have their specific strategies and degrees of emphasis given to specific word analysis techniques and comprehension skills. Organizational plans are basically related to the types of materials used and the manner in which they are presented. The four organizational plans that will be discussed include (1) individualized reading, (2) language experience approach, (3) basal series or group reading, and (4) programmed instruction. It is not the intent of the author to sell any one particular system or style of teaching reading, but only to get teachers to see the merits of each approach and how they can be best utilized in developing reading programs for problem adolescents and chronic disruptive youth. Since basal readers are used in at least 75% of regular elementary school classrooms, it is felt that if secondary school-age youth with educational handicaps and chronic disruptive youth have memories of failure experiences with reading that will be associated with those types of materials. Consequently, basal materials will be discussed but not in as much detail as the other approaches.

Individualized reading

Individualized Reading was developed on the basis of research conducted and described by Olson (1949). Seeking, self-selection, and pacing were behaviors considered to be exhibited by the healthy child, and are synonymous with individualized reading systems. It was felt that the child would naturally engage in active exploration of his environment (seeking behavior) and would extract from his environment those experiences and objects that are consistent with his needs and maturational level (self-selection). The teacher behavior that helps insure the provision of materials and instruction commensurate with his maturity is termed *pacing*. No single author can be primarily associated with the Individualized Reading approach as it does not represent a single method or technique. Barbe (1961) and Veatch (1959), because of their pioneer writing, have strongly influenced professionals in reading toward the merits of the Individualized Reading approach.

The Individualized Reading approach evolved from a basic discontent with traditional reading programs that were based too rigidly on grade level standards and graded basal texts. An additional discontent was that traditional methods (basal series) tended to become too rigid in a system of assigned reading and ability grouping which actually permitted the child to become subordinate to the system. Individualized Reading attempts to get the child back in on the action. The Individualized Reading approach will offer extensive recreational and self-selecting experiences in reading material which the child is able to master. It is assumed that the child or student will select materials not only of interest to himself, but which will develop his reading skills and capacities. The teacher does have control over the materials that the student will select by including only a certain range of materials. It is imperative for the teacher to thoroughly know the student's reading skill before this approach is initiated. A comprehensive evaluation in reading should be given to the student and there should also be information available related to the student's personal interests and emotional factors. The following statements characterize the Individualized Reading approach:

1. The teacher will provide numerous books on a variety of topics at many different levels of difficulty. These books covering a wide range of topics may include trade books, reference books, basal readers, comics, popular magazines, newspapers, etc.

2. The student will select his own reading materials from the options presented.

3. A regular period for free reading is established by the teacher. During this period the teacher will conduct individual conferences with the students or move about the room to assist as needed.

4. Individual pupil-teacher conferences are scheduled on a regular basis but are of a short duration.

5. Skill development sessions are provided to individuals or groups within the class on the basis of needs that are determined by the student-teacher conference. Group membership

in terms of skill development groups is flexible and the duration of the group's existence may be minimal. When the specific objective of the group has been met, the group is disbanded.

6. Careful records are kept by the teacher and the students of their progress. Skills checklists can be used and also records of the materials that the student has read are kept.

7. Small groups of students may be formed for instructional purposes as well as for social and creative activities related to reading. Opportunities for the students to share stories with classmates, giving puppet shows (for young children), and audience reading of material familiar to the child all are activities that might be conducted in connection with the student's favorite stories.

Fox and Fox (1964) cite three essential elements in individualized reading programs. These include (1) the use of pre-tests to determine each child's strengths and weaknesses; (2) developing the child's ability to select appropriate reading materials; and (3) continuous evaluation of each child's progress through the use of individual conferences and detailed record keeping. Individualized Reading, as an organizational plan for use with secondary school-age youth with educational handicaps and chronic disruptive youth, does have merit. Its effectiveness will probably be dependent upon factors such as the number of other students in the class or resource room and the availability of reading materials. Finally, an individualized approach requires a most unusual teacher who can guarantee that each child is adequately diagnosed and is presented with interesting and suitable materials.

Language experience approach

The Language Experience approach is an organizational plan that also has great promise for junior high and high school low achiever reading programs. It brings reading and other communication skills such as listening, oral language, and writing together in the instructional program. This method is a total language arts approach and there is no separation between the reading program and the development of listening, speaking, and writing skills. The Language Experience approach centers around the student's personal experiences and ideas. The student's speech patterns and language patterns for the reading materials and his experiences are the basis of the materials content in the Language Experience approach. This approach incorporates the idea that reading materials are more meaningful to the student if they are based on his experiences. With educationally handicapped adolescents and chronic disruptive youth we are certain that they will have a rich background of experiences to share. In this approach the learner is actively involved in the reading process as he creates and shares his reading with others. Inherent in the Language Experience is the relationship of spoken and written language. The teachers, as usual, are the most important variables, as they are responsible for providing the stimuli for language expression of the students which will be recorded and later used as reading material.

Allen (1964) offers extensive suggestions related to the utilization of the Language Experience approach. They are described as follows:

1. *Sharing experiences*—the ability to tell or illustrate something on a purely personal basis.

2. *Discussion experiences*—the ability to interact with what other people say and write.

3. *Listening to stories*—the ability to hear what others have to say and relate to their own experiences.

4. *Telling stories*—the ability to organize one's thinking so that it can be shared orally or through dictation in a clear and interesting manner.

5. *Dictating*—the ability to choose, from all that might be said, the most important part for someone else to write and read.

6. *Developing speaking, writing, and reading relationships*—the ability to conceptualize reading as speech that has been written.

7. *Making and reading books*—the ability to organize one's own ideas into a form that others can use, and the ability to use the ideas which others have shared through books.

8. *Developing awareness of common vocabulary*—the ability to recognize that our language contains many common words and patterns of expression.

9. *Expanding vocabulary*—the ability to expand one's vocabulary through listening and speaking, followed by writing and reading.

10. *Writing independently*—the ability to write one's ideas and present them in a form for others to read.

11. *Reading whole books*—the ability to read books for information, recreation, and improvement of reading skills on individualized and personalized basis.

12. *Improving style and form*—the ability to profit from listening to and reading well written material.

13. *Using a variety of resource materials*—the ability to recognize and use many resources in expanding vocabulary, improving oral and written expression, and sharing.

14. *Studying words*—the ability to find the correct pronunciation and meaning of words and to spell the words in writing activities.

15. *Improving comprehension*—the ability through oral and written activities, to gain skill in following directions, understanding words in the context of sentences and paragraphs, reproducing the thought in the passage, and reading for general significance.

16. *Outlining*—the ability of briefly stating ideas in the order in which they were written or spoken.

17. *Summarization*—the ability to express the main impression, outstanding ideas, or the details of what has been read or spoken.

18. *Integrating and assimilating ideas*—the ability to use reading and listening for specific purposes of a personal nature.

19. *Reading critically*—the ability to determine the validity and reliability of statements.

These previous statements were related to the various language experiences with which students learn to read. One will note a degree of developmental sequencing, as the items presented earlier in the list are much easier and will require less background experience than those near the end of the list.

The major components, though, in the construction of a language experience chart or story is that either the individual or the group will: (1) have a common experience as a basis for discussion; (2) have a discussion of this common experience; (3) record the individual or group's spoken language on the blackboard; and (4) edit the student's language on the blackboard then transfer the language recorded to chart paper. Specific word analysis techniques and comprehension techniques which will be discussed in detail later can all be incorporated into the Language Experience approach. By eventually transferring the written materials to "pocket charts" which utilize long strips of paper to record the students' work, the materials can then be analyzed and broken into various word analysis strategies.

Traditionally the Language Experience approach has been used most often with younger children. It is felt that there is a great amount of utility for this approach with older students falling into the category of educationally handicapped adolescents and chronic disruptive youth. Determining variables for interests in using the Language Experience approach for older students are the content of the stories and the manner in which they are presented. Instead of recording the stories in manuscript writing as one would do for younger children, it is recommended that cursive writing be utilized in dealing with older children as they discuss their more mature subjects and topics. The use of tape recorders and typewriters in the development of Language Experience stories are additional motivating techniques that can be used with educationally handicapped adolescents.

It should be mentioned, however, that language experience charts do have certain limitations.

1.   The vocabulary used in experience charts is generally not controlled. This may result in the beginning reader becoming confused by this bombardment of many different new words presented at one time.

2.   The Language Experience approach may foster memory reading rather than actual reading. Since the student has the opportunity to read and reread line by line with the group there is a tendency to purely memorize the material.

3.   The construction of language experience materials demands a great deal of the teacher's time. The recording of the materials on the blackboard, transferring them to the chart paper, and possibly transferring the materials to a pocket chart consume great amounts of time. Provisions should be made for this requisite.

4.   Language experience charts may, in some cases, become boring, dull, and uninteresting. Again, it is up to the teacher to be the motivator of the students. Additionally, students using the Language Experience approach may see other students using more "book type" approaches, thus wanting to be similar, may reject the language experience materials.

5.   The teacher using the Language Experience approach must be skillful in the development and recording of the child's language or they may be lacking in literary quality. It is important to record exactly the language that the student presents. Certain editorial changes must be made that are in agreement with both student and teacher.

Basal reader approach

In the elementary schools of the United States, the Basal Reader approach is still the most common organizational plan for teaching reading. The Basal Reader approach consists of a series of softbound and hardbound books which include stories with systematic vocabulary control and reading difficulty. Basal readers traditionally have included a variety of stories of which many revolve around a central core or theme. Basal readers today incorporate a variety of word analysis technique emphases based on the philosophies of the publishing company and authors of the materials. In some cases the emphasis is on phonics, in others, on linguistic principles, and still others have utilized special alphabets such as the Initial Teaching Alphabet (ITA). Certain basal readers are also including programmed styles of instruction.

Basal readers have changed drastically in terms of format and content within the last 20 years. Illustrations as well as language content have shifted from a standard white middle class emphasis to a variety of social-cultural backgrounds. The typical basal reading series begins with a readiness book, generally soft-covered and oftentimes in workbook form. Also included are relatively thin paper-covered preprimers. Following in sequence are the first hard-covered books, namely the primer and first reader, which so far is the standard reading material for individuals at the first grade level. Next are hardback readers for the remaining grades up through grade six. In addition to these materials, most basal series have accompanying workbooks. These workbooks are generally consumable and include activities related to various word analysis and comprehension techniques that are advocated by the publishing company. Although basal readers in their traditional form have been criticized by many, it has been because of misuse in many cases.

One of the most often stated advantages of the Basal Reader approach is the availability of a teacher's guide or manual. The teacher's manual, which is generally not available for those teachers using an Individualized approach or Language Experience approach, presents a general and detailed lesson plan for every selection. The teacher's manual will insure that the teacher is presenting an adequate amount of activities related to basic skill development.

Teachers of secondary school-age youth with educational handicaps and chronic disruptive youth should proceed very cautiously when considering the utilization of basal readers for such students. As indicated in an earlier section, many of the negative and frustrating experiences that these children have had in the school setting in terms of reading can be associated directly with many basal reader series and approaches. The teacher of secondary school-age youth with educational handicaps and chronic disruptive youth has the opportunity to utilize basal readers, being certain that the materials are those that the students have never had experience with in their previous school history. Additionally, if a basal series approach is being considered, it is strongly urged that multiple series and levels of materials be available for those students who reach frustration levels or plateaus with the present materials they are using. The teacher of educationally handicapped adolescents and chronic disruptive youth will generally find palatable the lesson plans provided within the basal series that will give direct suggestions applicable to the essential three steps of reading the materials: (1) preparation for reading the story; (2) actually reading the story silently and orally; and (3) enrichment or follow-up activities.

Programmed reading approach

Programmed reading materials have generally been associated with the Buchannon-Sullivan materials (1963). These programmed materials are being extensively used throughout the United States with both nonhandicapped and handicapped children. Included in the program are 14 paper-covered texts with accompanying manuals that emphasize a phonic-linguistic teaching strategy. The programming style for the materials is a linear one, based on self pacing. A level of 80% accuracy is required of the student before he is allowed to proceed to each stage. Accuracy percentages below 80% are more than cause for the teacher to provide individual tutoring. The teaching sequence initiated in the prereading level is a simple plan for introducing the student to reading by acquainting him with written symbols, then acquainting him with the relationship of the symbols to the sounds of words. Because of the nature of most programmed materials whereby the student progresses in very small steps, these types of materials are highly recommended for teachers working with secondary school-age youth with educational handicaps and chronic disruptive youth.

Additional programmed approaches emerging that have promise are those associated with the concept of computer-assisted reading instruction. Atkinson and Fletcher (1972) and Moore (1964) were early workers in the development of hardware and mechanical gadgetry designed to assist students in learning to read. Basically, the equipment and procedure involved material presented on a cathode-ray tube. The student utilizing this system makes his responses with a light pen with a computer determining the location of the touch and noting whether the location of the response was correct or incorrect. Atkinson and Fletcher (1972), in particular, used a branching type of program that allows for more rapid or slower progress by skipping or repeating items within the Computer Assisted Instruction (CAI) program. Moore (1964) developed the "talking typewriter" which is a computer based, multiple media, multi-sensory learning environment. Presently, the Borg Warner Company's *System 80* offers to the public a much refined automated prescriptive teaching approach that appears to have much promise. A reading program has been developed and the material may be a good self-programming addition to a Learning Center.

Ellson, Harris and Barber (1968) offer a unique kind of programmed approach. Programming the teacher rather than the materials is the basic premise of this system. Programmed tutoring as it is described utilizes the paraprofessional concept. The paraprofessionals or nontrained teachers are given step-by-step written directions on how to tutor a child who has had difficulty in acquiring the skill of reading. Program tutoring is a supplementary and complementary program to those students working with basal readers. The Ginn Company and Harper Row Company are examples of basal reader publishers who have offered the option of the tutorial component. Although the original materials were based on beginning reading materials, the concept has great merit and should be expanded to reading materials at the higher levels if it is to have a true impact on the teaching of reading skills to secondary school-age youth with educational handicaps and chronic disruptive youth.

Unique approaches—alphabets and symbols

Because of the irregular spelling to sound relationship in terms of conventional alphabet letters, Downing (1964) advocated the development of reading materials using an alphabet with regular sound-symbols correspondence. This approach, which was developed as a beginning reading and writing alphabet, was based on the work of Sir James Pitman who was the originator of the Initial Teaching Alphabet (ITA). The initial teaching alphabet consists of a 44 character alphabet that can be adapted to basal readers, language experience approaches, and individualized reading materials. This so-called 44 letter alphabet with consistent sight sound relationship is intended to replace the present 26 letter alphabet that is currently used but has so many phonetic or sound irregularities. Unique features of ITA include (1) capital letters that are written like lower case letters in shape except they are larger in size; (2) a single symbol for each 44 consonant and vowel sounds; and (3) many of the traditional letters of the alphabet which are said to aid in the making of the transition to traditional orthography (our standard alphabet).

The Peabody Rebus Reading Program developed by Woodcock and Clarke (1969) is a beginning reading program which uses Rebus pictures as a link between spoken language and reading. The rebuses, in many cases actual drawings of animals, parts of people, symbols standing for large or small, etc., create a linkage between spoken language and reading. The main contention is that a young nonreader can learn about 25 rebuses and then go on to read passages written with these rebuses. It must be emphasized that this approach is a beginning reading system in which a graduate transition to regularly spelled words is introduced to replace the rebuses. Secondary school-age youth with educational handicaps and chronic disruptive youth who have been exposed to other methods or systems of reading may well be able to benefit from the "rebus symbol system."

BEHAVIORAL OBJECTIVES AND READING INSTRUCTION

The utilization of objective-based approaches to reading instruction is based on goals stated in terms of pupil behavior. Currently, such goals are called *behavioral objectives.* Here, we will describe exactly what they are and how to go about writing them for educationally handicapped adolescents. Additionally, we will examine their benefits. The reader of this section is encouraged to read the writings of Cramer and Trent (1972) and Mager (1962) for further information on this topic.

What are they?

Educators have always had goals, but until fairly recently those goals have tended to be so broad and general in nature that they have been implicit rather than explicit. The testing and technological movements in education have, however, caused much more attention to be paid to the precise definition of objectives and the outcomes associated with them. Now, there is much agreement that precisely defined objectives are, of necessity, *behavioral* objectives. Such objectives focus on pupil behaviors—the observable outcomes of instruction.

Consider two frequently quoted definitions of behavioral objectives. A very concise definition is offered by Montague and Butts (1968): "A behavioral objective is a goal for, or a desired outcome of, learning which is expressed in terms of observable behavior (or performance, if you prefer) of the learner" (p. 33).

A definition stated in terms of three criteria to which the writer of behavioral objectives must comply is offered by Mager.

1. Identify the terminal behavior by name; you can specify the kind of behavior that will be accepted as evidence that the learner has achieved the objective.

2. Try to define the desired behavior further by describing the important conditions under which the behavior will be expected to occur.

3. Specify the criteria of acceptable performance by describing how well the learner must perform to be considered acceptable.

Each definition calls for a clear statement of what is expected; the latter gets even more specific by putting down where to look for the expected behavior and how to decide when it has been successfully demonstrated.

Similarly, Bloom, Hastings, and Madaus (1971) had this to say about Mager's definition of behavioral objectives:

Gagne (1965) summarizing the high degree of specificity described in the work of Mager. . . , breaks a statement of an objective into four basic components. The four are illustrated in this sentence taken from Gagne: "Given two numerals connected by the sign +, the student states orally the name of the number which is the sum of the two." First, the statement contains words denoting the stimulus situation which initiates the performance ("Given two numerals connected by the sign + "). Second, there is an action word or verb which denotes observable behavior ("states"). Third, there is a term denoting the object acted upon (which sometimes is simply implied). Finally, there is a phrase indicating the characteristics of the performance that determines its correctness ("the name of the number which is the sum of the two").

Lighthearted or scholarly, the consensus is that a good behavioral objective: (1) describes desired pupil performance, or behavior; (2) identifies competence level, or criterion or minimum level of acceptable performance; and (3) may specify the conditions of the performance. The last is not always needed, but when applicable, a statement of conditions helps to make the intent perfectly clear.

How to write them

First, remember that a behavioral objective is a goal stated in behavioral terms. In the examples that follow, the portion of each objective which describes the desired pupil behavior is italicized:

- The student is able *to locate* points *and describe* the location of points in relation to a simple street grid.
- The student is able *to tell* when the words in a pair have the same, opposite, or simply different meanings.
- The student is able *to alphabetize* words by attending to their first and second letters.

Note that in each objective the behavior is observable; that is, it can be observed, checked, and/or recorded. The behavior is, in effect, "point-at-able." Some verbs that denote point-at-able acts and pin down the *behavior* in a behavioral objective are:

to state	to write	to demonstrate
to recognize	to recite	to compare
to predict	to solve	to identify
to compute	to match	to discuss

Second, a behavioral objective identifies the expected competence level. The competence level is italicized in the examples that follow:

- Given a maximum one-second exposure per word in context, the child is able to recognize *all of the words* on the Dolch Basic Vocabulary List of 220 words.

- The child is able to identify the common—scr, shr, spl, spr, str, thr—three-letter consonant blends in *at least 80% of the real and nonsense words* containing such blends pronounced by the teacher.
- The child is able to focus *all previously mastered skills* in independent study and/or research.

Some writers refer to competency level as *optimum level, minimum level of acceptable performance,* or simply *criterion.* Competency level has to do with the measurement, evaluation, or description of the observable behavior specified in a behavioral objective. Adjectives and quantity words are used to identify competency levels. (Sometimes a single competency level is established for an entire set of objectives, e.g., 80% of the items correct on each objective-related test. Then, there is no need to identify the level in each objective.)

Third, a behavioral objective may specify the conditions of the performance. The statement of conditions is parenthesized in each of the examples that follow:

- (Given a brief written-oral selection in the active voice,) the child responds to questions about details found in the selection.
- (Given axis and coordinate referents,) the child is able to locate points and describe the location of points in relation to a simple picture grid.
- (Given two real or nonsense words pronounced by the teacher,) the child is able to tell when the words begin alike.

A statement of conditions should be included if it helps to clarify the objective by specifying whether certain data, tools, or materials are "given" or "withheld."

Now see if you can write a good behavioral objective. If you can honestly say that your objective has the following three (or four) qualities, you are on your way to focusing your own reading instruction!

1. Anyone who reads it can perceive its intent.
2. The expected pupil behavior is described in behavioral terms.
3. A competence level is clearly identified.
4. The materials, tools, or data that are given or withheld are specified. (This is optional, depending on the kind of performance required.)

If you feel you need some more practice, work through Mager's (1962) programmed book, *Preparing Instructional Objectives.* It has emerged as the classic how-to-do-it manual on writing behavioral objectives. Remember, though, that no matter how skilled one becomes at the technical aspects of writing them, the objectives produced will never be any better than the ideas they represent. Good objectives are no substitute for poorly conceived goals. Because they are tools that help us tackle certain jobs in education, they are intrinsically neither good nor bad. They become desirable or undesirable in their application. Consider some of the benefits and limitations of the use of behavioral objectives.

1. Behavioral objectives set clear purposes for both teachers and pupils. Objectives stated in observable terms specify expectations for both teachers and pupils. Thus, they facilitate planning and permit teachers and pupils to communicate about the pursuit and attainment of mutually understood objectives.

2. Specific objectives break broad content or curriculum areas into manageable bits. To say that functional literacy for all pupils is the goal in reading, is to say nothing that is useful to a teacher who is responsible for planning instruction. Certainly, the broad objective is a desirable one, but it offers no clues as to how it might appropriately be pursued. Specific, skill-related objectives can serve to outline a curriculum area like reading in terms that lend focus and direction to the instructional process that leads to functional literacy.

3. The sequence and/or hierarchical arrangement of content can be worked out in terms of objectives. In order to state behavioral objectives in the first place, their arrangement according to priorities and developmental sequences must be carefully considered. This means that task analyses must be done to identify the essential components of a given curriculum area; logical analyses must be made to fix priorities about what is retained and what is dropped from the curriculum; and developmental analyses must be made to determine what a pupil must know before he is able to tackle subsequent objectives. Once these initial analyses have been completed and the initial objectives have been described, the groundwork is laid for continuous analysis, justification, and improvement of the scope and sequence of objectives in a curriculum area. Teachers can begin to systematically decide which objectives are most important, which are most difficult, which must come first, which can be dropped, which must be modified, etc.

4. Behavioral objectives facilitate evaluation. An objective provides the basis for criterion-referenced assessment. That is, each objective describes the expected behavior in observable terms and sets a criterion level for performance. Evaluation, then, becomes self-evident in most cases, the pupil either can perform in the prescribed manner or he cannot.

5. Objectives aid in the organization and selection of instructional materials. Given behavioral objectives, it is possible to identify

materials and procedures that are in line with instructional goals in a much more systematic manner than is usually possible. Teachers of secondary school-age youth with educational handicaps would be encouraged to develop banks or resource files and materials appropriate for various types of objectives.

The following section based on the work of O'Reilly (1971) will offer a comprehensive sequence related to the teaching of reading. Major skill categories will be presented in addition to the various sub-categories

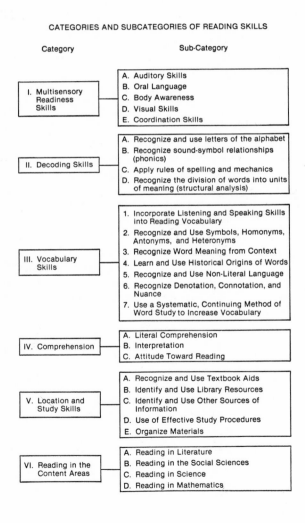

CATEGORIES AND SUBCATEGORIES OF READING SKILLS

Category	Sub-Category
I. Multisensory Readiness Skills	A. Auditory Skills B. Oral Language C. Body Awareness D. Visual Skills E. Coordination Skills
II. Decoding Skills	A. Recognize and use letters of the alphabet B. Recognize sound-symbol relationships (phonics) C. Apply rules of spelling and mechanics D. Recognize the division of words into units of meaning (structural analysis)
III. Vocabulary Skills	1. Incorporate Listening and Speaking Skills into Reading Vocabulary 2. Recognize and Use Symbols, Homonyms, Antonyms, and Heteronyms 3. Recognize Word Meaning from Context 4. Learn and Use Historical Origins of Words 5. Recognize and Use Non-Literal Language 6. Recognize Denotation, Connotation, and Nuance 7. Use a Systematic, Continuing Method of Word Study to Increase Vocabulary
IV. Comprehension	A. Literal Comprehension B. Interpretation C. Attitude Toward Reading
V. Location and Study Skills	A. Recognize and Use Textbook Aids B. Identify and Use Library Resources C. Identify and Use Other Sources of Information D. Use of Effective Study Procedures E. Organize Materials
VI. Reading in the Content Areas	A. Reading in Literature B. Reading in the Social Sciences C. Reading in Science D. Reading in Mathematics

of skills. Sample performance objectives will be presented as examples for the teacher of educationally handicapped adolescents to utilize in a reading program.

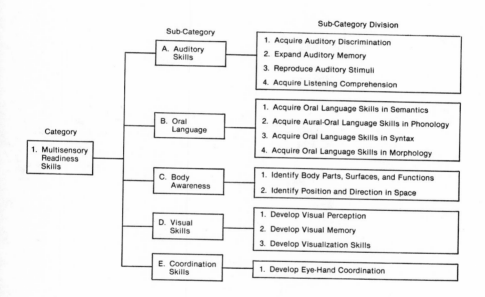

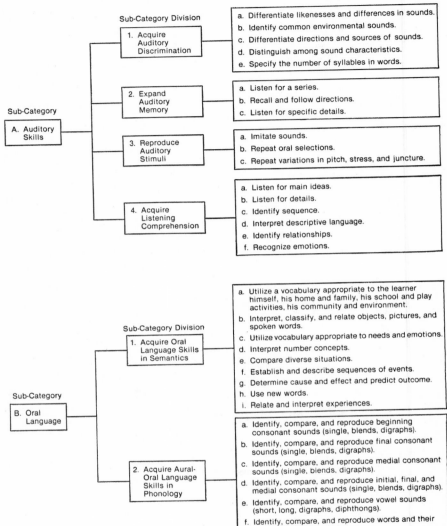

Proto-Objective

Sub-Category Division

1. Acquire Auditory Discrimination

a. Differentiate likenesses and differences in sounds.
b. Identify common environmental sounds.
c. Differentiate directions and sources of sounds.
d. Distinguish among sound characteristics.
e. Specify the number of syllables in words.

2. Expand Auditory Memory

a. Listen for a series.
b. Recall and follow directions.
c. Listen for specific details.

3. Reproduce Auditory Stimuli

a. Imitate sounds.
b. Repeat oral selections.
c. Repeat variations in pitch, stress, and juncture.

4. Acquire Listening Comprehension

a. Listen for main ideas.
b. Listen for details.
c. Identify sequence.
d. Interpret descriptive language.
e. Identify relationships.
f. Recognize emotions.

Sub-Category

A. Auditory Skills

Sub-Category Division

1. Acquire Oral Language Skills in Semantics

a. Utilize a vocabulary appropriate to the learner himself, his home and family, his school and play activities, his community and environment.
b. Interpret, classify, and relate objects, pictures, and spoken words.
c. Utilize vocabulary appropriate to needs and emotions.
d. Interpret number concepts.
e. Compare diverse situations.
f. Establish and describe sequences of events.
g. Determine cause and effect and predict outcome.
h. Use new words.
i. Relate and interpret experiences.

2. Acquire Aural-Oral Language Skills in Phonology

a. Identify, compare, and reproduce beginning consonant sounds (single, blends, digraphs).
b. Identify, compare, and reproduce final consonant sounds (single, blends, digraphs).
c. Identify, compare, and reproduce medial consonant sounds (single, blends, digraphs).
d. Identify, compare, and reproduce initial, final, and medial consonant sounds (single, blends, digraphs).
e. Identify, compare, and reproduce vowel sounds (short, long, digraphs, diphthongs).
f. Identify, compare, and reproduce words and their phonograms.

Sub-Category

B. Oral Language

(continued)

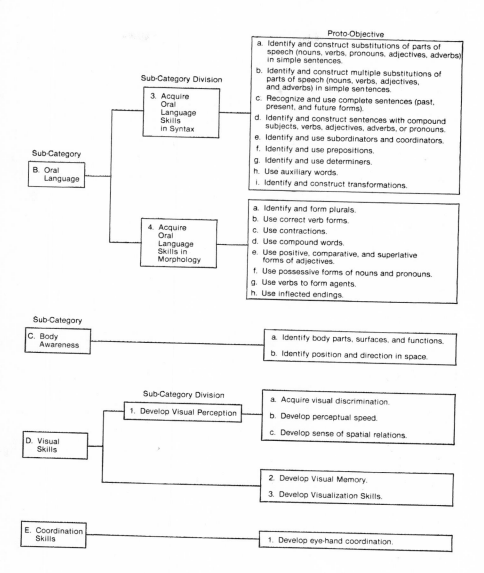

Proto-Objective

Sub-Category Division

3. Acquire Oral Language Skills in Syntax

a. Identify and construct substitutions of parts of speech (nouns, verbs, pronouns, adjectives, adverbs) in simple sentences.

b. Identify and construct multiple substitutions of parts of speech (nouns, verbs, adjectives, and adverbs) in simple sentences.

c. Recognize and use complete sentences (past, present, and future forms).

d. Identify and construct sentences with compound subjects, verbs, adjectives, adverbs, or pronouns.

e. Identify and use subordinators and coordinators.

f. Identify and use prepositions.

g. Identify and use determiners.

h. Use auxiliary words.

i. Identify and construct transformations.

Sub-Category

B. Oral Language

4. Acquire Oral Language Skills in Morphology

a. Identify and form plurals.

b. Use correct verb forms.

c. Use contractions.

d. Use compound words.

e. Use positive, comparative, and superlative forms of adjectives.

f. Use possessive forms of nouns and pronouns.

g. Use verbs to form agents.

h. Use inflected endings.

Sub-Category

C. Body Awareness

a. Identify body parts, surfaces, and functions.

b. Identify position and direction in space.

Sub-Category Division

1. Develop Visual Perception

a. Acquire visual discrimination.

b. Develop perceptual speed.

c. Develop sense of spatial relations.

D. Visual Skills

2. Develop Visual Memory.

3. Develop Visualization Skills.

E. Coordination Skills

1. Develop eye-hand coordination.

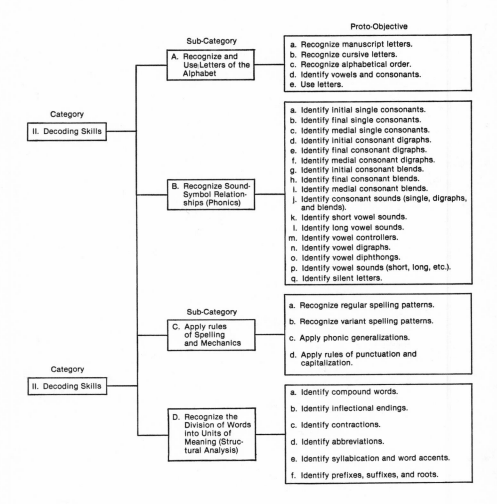

Proto-Objective

Sub-Category

A. Recognize and Use Letters of the Alphabet
a. Recognize manuscript letters.
b. Recognize cursive letters.
c. Recognize alphabetical order.
d. Identify vowels and consonants.
e. Use letters.

Category

II. Decoding Skills

B. Recognize Sound-Symbol Relationships (Phonics)
a. Identify initial single consonants.
b. Identify final single consonants.
c. Identify medial single consonants.
d. Identify initial consonant digraphs.
e. Identify final consonant digraphs.
f. Identify medial consonant digraphs.
g. Identify initial consonant blends.
h. Identify final consonant blends.
i. Identify medial consonant blends.
j. Identify consonant sounds (single, digraphs, and blends).
k. Identify short vowel sounds.
l. Identify long vowel sounds.
m. Identify vowel controllers.
n. Identify vowel digraphs.
o. Identify vowel diphthongs.
p. Identify vowel sounds (short, long, etc.).
q. Identify silent letters.

Sub-Category

C. Apply rules of Spelling and Mechanics
a. Recognize regular spelling patterns.
b. Recognize variant spelling patterns.
c. Apply phonic generalizations.
d. Apply rules of punctuation and capitalization.

Category

II. Decoding Skills

D. Recognize the Division of Words into Units of Meaning (Structural Analysis)
a. Identify compound words.
b. Identify inflectional endings.
c. Identify contractions.
d. Identify abbreviations.
e. Identify syllabication and word accents.
f. Identify prefixes, suffixes, and roots.

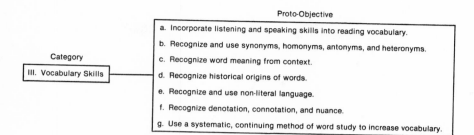

Proto-Objective

Category
III. Vocabulary Skills

a. Incorporate listening and speaking skills into reading vocabulary.

b. Recognize and use synonyms, homonyms, antonyms, and heteronyms.

c. Recognize word meaning from context.

d. Recognize historical origins of words.

e. Recognize and use non-literal language.

f. Recognize denotation, connotation, and nuance.

g. Use a systematic, continuing method of word study to increase vocabulary.

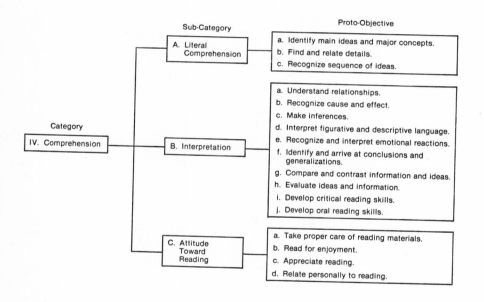

Sub-Category   Proto-Objective

A. Literal
   Comprehension

a. Identify main ideas and major concepts.
b. Find and relate details.
c. Recognize sequence of ideas.

Category
IV. Comprehension

B. Interpretation

a. Understand relationships.
b. Recognize cause and effect.
c. Make inferences.
d. Interpret figurative and descriptive language.
e. Recognize and interpret emotional reactions.
f. Identify and arrive at conclusions and generalizations.
g. Compare and contrast information and ideas.
h. Evaluate ideas and information.
i. Develop critical reading skills.
j. Develop oral reading skills.

C. Attitude
   Toward
   Reading

a. Take proper care of reading materials.
b. Read for enjoyment.
c. Appreciate reading.
d. Relate personally to reading.

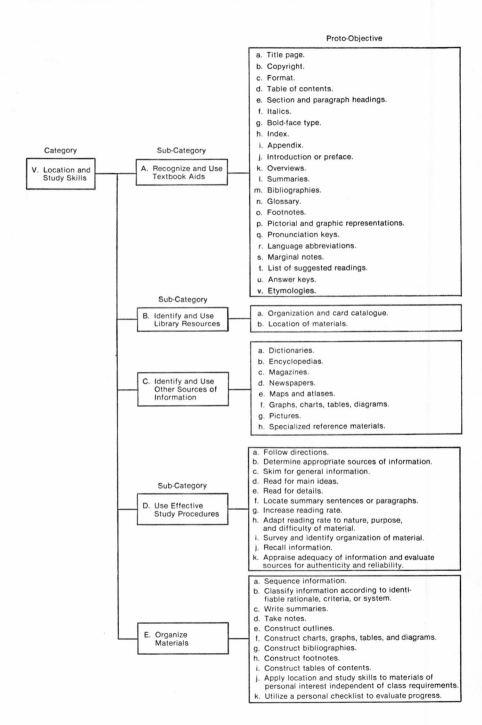

Proto-Objective

Category

V. Location and Study Skills

Sub-Category

A. Recognize and Use Textbook Aids

a. Title page.
b. Copyright.
c. Format.
d. Table of contents.
e. Section and paragraph headings.
f. Italics.
g. Bold-face type.
h. Index.
i. Appendix.
j. Introduction or preface.
k. Overviews.
l. Summaries.
m. Bibliographies.
n. Glossary.
o. Footnotes.
p. Pictorial and graphic representations.
q. Pronunciation keys.
r. Language abbreviations.
s. Marginal notes.
t. List of suggested readings.
u. Answer keys.
v. Etymologies.

Sub-Category

B. Identify and Use Library Resources

a. Organization and card catalogue.
b. Location of materials.

C. Identify and Use Other Sources of Information

a. Dictionaries.
b. Encyclopedias.
c. Magazines.
d. Newspapers.
e. Maps and atlases.
f. Graphs, charts, tables, diagrams.
g. Pictures.
h. Specialized reference materials.

Sub-Category

D. Use Effective Study Procedures

a. Follow directions.
b. Determine appropriate sources of information.
c. Skim for general information.
d. Read for main ideas.
e. Read for details.
f. Locate summary sentences or paragraphs.
g. Increase reading rate.
h. Adapt reading rate to nature, purpose, and difficulty of material.
i. Survey and identify organization of material.
j. Recall information.
k. Appraise adequacy of information and evaluate sources for authenticity and reliability.

E. Organize Materials

a. Sequence information.
b. Classify information according to identifiable rationale, criteria, or system.
c. Write summaries.
d. Take notes.
e. Construct outlines.
f. Construct charts, graphs, tables, and diagrams.
g. Construct bibliographies.
h. Construct footnotes.
i. Construct tables of contents.
j. Apply location and study skills to materials of personal interest independent of class requirements.
k. Utilize a personal checklist to evaluate progress.

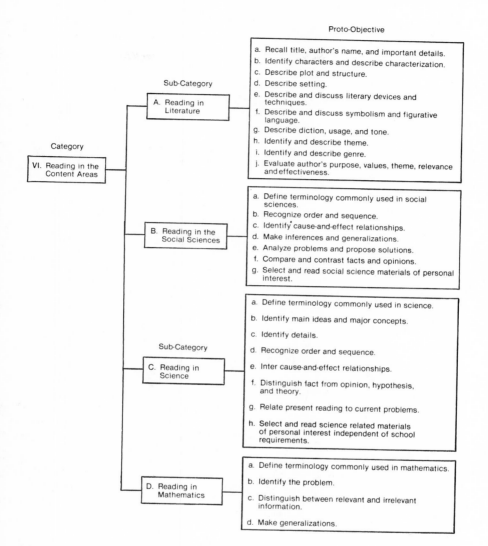

Proto-Objective

Sub-Category

A. Reading in Literature

a. Recall title, author's name, and important details.
b. Identify characters and describe characterization.
c. Describe plot and structure.
d. Describe setting.
e. Describe and discuss literary devices and techniques.
f. Describe and discuss symbolism and figurative language.
g. Describe diction, usage, and tone.
h. Identify and describe theme.
i. Identify and describe genre.
j. Evaluate author's purpose, values, theme, relevance and effectiveness.

Category

VI. Reading in the Content Areas

B. Reading in the Social Sciences

a. Define terminology commonly used in social sciences.
b. Recognize order and sequence.
c. Identify cause-and-effect relationships.
d. Make inferences and generalizations.
e. Analyze problems and propose solutions.
f. Compare and contrast facts and opinions.
g. Select and read social science materials of personal interest.

Sub-Category

C. Reading in Science

a. Define terminology commonly used in science.
b. Identify main ideas and major concepts.
c. Identify details.
d. Recognize order and sequence.
e. Inter cause-and-effect relationships.
f. Distinguish fact from opinion, hypothesis, and theory.
g. Relate present reading to current problems.
h. Select and read science related materials of personal interest independent of school requirements.

D. Reading in Mathematics

a. Define terminology commonly used in mathematics.
b. Identify the problem.
c. Distinguish between relevant and irrelevant information.
d. Make generalizations.

SAMPLE PERFORMANCE OBJECTIVES

I. Multisensory Readiness Skills

    A. Auditory Skills

        1. Acquire Auditory Discrimination

           a. Differentiate likenesses and differences in sounds

               1. Given pairs of sounds (e.g., environmental sounds, musical tones, familiar voices, words), the learner will identify those pairs that are identical and those that are not identical.

               2. Given pairs of sounds, the learner will identify those that are of the same or of different duration.

           b. Identify common environmental sounds

               1. Given familiar sounds (e.g., footsteps, baby crying, friend's voice), the learner will name the sounds.

           c. Differentiate directions and sources of sounds

               1. Given sounds from different sources, the learner will indicate the directions from which the sounds come.

           d. Distinguish among sound characteristics

               1. Given sounds (e.g., musical selections, noises, voices) of varying intensity, the learner will identify those that are loud and those that are soft.

               2. Given sounds (e.g., musical selections, tones, voices) of varying pitch, the learner will identify the higher and lower pitched sounds.

               3. Given pairs of sounds of different duration, the learner will identify the longer or shorter sound in each pair.

           e. Specify the number of syllables in words

               1. Given a word orally, the learner will specify the number of syllables it contains.

        2. Expand Auditory Memory

           a. Listen for a series

               1. Given a series of sounds, the learner will identify the sounds in the order presented.

               2. Given a series of numerals, words, or phrases, the learner will repeat them in the order presented.

               3. Given a short rhythmic sound pattern, the learner will identify the pattern (e.g., by tapping it out, circling a graphic representation).

           b. Recall and follow directions

               1. Given an oral direction, the learner will repeat it.

2. Given an oral direction, the learner will answer a question about it.

3. Given an oral direction, the learner will follow it.

4. Given a set of commands, the learner will follow them in the proper sequence.

5. Given the same set of directions twice, with one step omitted the second time, the learner will identify the omission.

6. The learner will give correct directions orally.

c. Listen for specific details

1. After hearing a two-line rhyme, the learner will repeat the words that rhyme.

2. After hearing a phrase or a sentence which is repeated with a word omitted the second time, the learner will identify the missing word.

3. Reproduce Auditory Stimuli

a. Imitate sounds

1. Given various sounds (e.g., the letter sounds), the learner will imitate or reproduce the sounds.

b. Repeat oral selections

1. After hearing a word, phrase, sentence, or familiar poem, the learner will repeat it.

c. Repeat variations in pitch, stress, and juncture

1. After hearing phrases, sentences, or short familiar selections of varying intonation, the learner will repeat the passage using the same intonation.

2. After hearing a declarative, exclamatory, interrogative, or imperative sentence, the learner will indicate the sentence type.

3. After hearing the teacher read a story with dialogue, the learner will imitate the intonation used by the teacher for different characters.

4. Acquire Listening Comprehension

a. Listen for main ideas

1. After listening to a selection, the learner will identify its main ideas.

2. After listening to a selection, the learner will construct an appropriate title.

3. After listening to a selection, the learner will name its main characters.

4. After a hearing a series of events from a familiar story, the learner will identify the story.

b. Listen for details

1. After listening to a sentence or selection, the learner will answer specific oral questions about its content.

c. Identify sequence

1. After listening to a story, the learner will identify the main events in the proper order.

d. Interpret descriptive language

1. After hearing descriptive words, phrases, or sentences, the learner will select from a series of pictures the event or object that was described.

2. After hearing a story, poem, or passage, the learner will describe what he hears.

e. Identify relationships

1. The learner will identify oral statements that are or are not related to a selection he has just heard.

f. Recognize emotions

1. After hearing a story, poem, or passage in which an emotion is depicted. the learner will describe the emotion.

B. Oral Language

1. Acquire Oral Language Skills in Semantics

a. Utilize a vocabulary appropriate to the learner himself, his home and family, his school and play activities, his community and environment

1. The learner will answer simple oral questions about himself, his family, school, play, the community, etc.

2. Shown familiar objects, or pictures of objects or activities, the learner will orally identify what he sees.

3. The learner will orally describe the functions of familiar objects (e.g., materials used at school).

4. Given orally the function of a familiar object, the learner will identify that object.

5. The learner will orally describe pictures of activities or situations.

6. Presented with a familiar object, the learner will describe it orally.

7. After hearing the description of an object, activity, landmark, community figure, etc., the learner will identify it.

8. Given a word or phrase orally, the learner will select from among several pictures the one that represents the word or phrase.

    b. Interpret, classify, and relate objects, pictures, and spoken words
1. The learner will classify several items into groups according to his own or a given rationale.
2. The learner will identify from among several items those that belong to a given class or set.
3. The learner will identify from among several items those that do not belong to a given class or set.
4. The learner will identify or explain similarities and differences of objects.
5. The learner will identify or describe the details of a picture.
6. The learner will identify or describe the main idea of a picture.
7. The learner will identify the meaning of symbols or objects (e.g., colors of a traffic light).
8. The learner will identify words, pictures, or objects representing similar concepts.
9. The learner will identify words, pictures, or objects representing opposite concepts.
10. The learner will identify phrases or pictures as fact or fantasy.
11. The learner will tell a brief story about a given picture or set of pictures.

    c. Utilize vocabulary appropriate to needs and emotions
1. Given a picture of a child expressing an emotion, the learner will orally describe the emotion.
2. Given a real-life or hypothetical situation, the learner will tell how he feels about it and why.
3. Given a series of pictures or objects relating to a child's needs and desires, the learner will choose the item which he most desires and state why he chose it.
4. Given a simple predicament, the learner will explain how he would solve the problem.
5. Given a statement about his wishes or desires (e.g., If I could do anything in the world, I would . . .), the learner will complete it.
6. Given a picture of a child expressing an emotion, the learner will explain what he thinks caused it.

    d. Interpret number concepts
1. The learner will count items.
2. The learner will count to a given number.
3. The learner will use ordinal numbers to indicate position.
4. The learner will identify numerals.

e. Compare diverse situations

   1. Given two similar pictures differing only in certain details, the learner will describe the differences.

   2. Given a story orally, the learner will describe an alternative possible ending for that story.

   3. Given two situations orally in which the same problem is handled in different ways, the learner will pick the one which he felt handled the problem best and describe why.

   4. Given two similar stories, the learner will identify their similarities and differences.

f. Establish and describe sequences of events

   1. Given pictures which portray a series of events, the learner will put them in proper sequence.

   2. The learner will describe the chronological or logical order of a series of events or activities.

g. Determine cause and effect and predict outcomes

   1. The learner will predict the consequences of a specific act or a given situation.

   2. The learner will identify the probable cause of a given situation.

   3. Given a selection without an ending, the learner will identify an appropriate ending.

h. Use new words

   1. Given a new word and a picture or definition of it, the learner will use it in a sentence.

i. Relate and interpret experiences

   1. The learner will retell a familiar story in his own words.

   2. The learner will compose fantasy with himself as the central character.

   3. The learner will describe a personal experience.

2. Acquire Aural-Oral Language Skills in Phonology

a. Identify, compare, and reproduce beginning consonant sounds (single, blends, digraphs)

   1. The learner will identify pairs of words beginning with the same consonant sound and those beginning with different consonant sounds.

   2. Given a set of words all beginning with the same initial consonant sound, the learner will reproduce the initial consonant sound.

   3. The learner will identify from given words or pictures those having the same beginning consonant sound.

4. Given words or pictures of objects, all but one beginning with the same consonant sound, the learner will identify the one having a different initial sound.

5. Given a word, the learner will state another word beginning with the same consonant sound.

b. Identify, compare, and reproduce final consonant sounds (single, blends, digraphs)

1. The learner will identify pairs of words ending with the same consonant sound and those ending with different consonant sounds.

2. Given a set of words all ending with the same consonant sound, the learner will reproduce the final consonant sound.

3. The learner will identify from given words or pictures those having the same final consonant sound.

4. Given words or pictures of objects, all but one ending with the same consonant sound, the learner will identify the one having a different final sound.

5. Given a word, the learner will state another word ending with the same consonant sound.

6. Given a word ending with a final consonant sound, the learner will substitute other final consonant sounds to make new words

c. Identify, compare, and reproduce medial consonant sounds (single, blends, digraphs)

1. The learner will identify pairs of words containing the same medial consonant sound and those containing different medial consonant sounds.

2. Given a list of words all containing the same medical consonant sound, the learner will reproduce the medial consonant sound.

3. The learner will identify from given words or pictures of objects those having the same medial consonant sound.

4. Given words or pictures of objects, all but one containing the same consonant sound, the learner will identify the one having a different medial consonant sound.

5. Given a word, the learner will state another word having the same medial consonant sound.

d. Identify, compare, and reproduce initial, final and medial consonant sounds (single, blends, digraphs)

1. Given a consonant sound and a word containing that sound, the learner will identify the position of the consonant in the word.

2. The learner will identify from a set of words those containing a given consonant sound in a specified position.

3. The learner will produce words with a specified initial, final, or medial consonant sound.

e. Identify, compare, and reproduce vowel sounds (short, long, digraphs, diphthongs)

1. The learner will identify pairs of words with the same vowel sounds and those with different vowel sounds.

2. Given words all containing the same vowel sound, the learner will reproduce the vowel sound.

3. The learner will identify, from given words or pictures of objects, those having the same vowel sound.

4. Given words or pictures of objects, all but one containing the same vowel sound, the learner will identify the one having a different vowel sound.

5. Given a word, the learner will state other words containing the same vowel sound.

6. Given a word containing a vowel sound, the learner will substitute other vowel sounds to make new words.

f. Identify, compare, and reproduce words and their phonograms

1. Given a set of words, the learner will identify those that rhyme.

2. Given a set of words, all rhyming but one, the learner will identify the one that does not rhyme.

3. The learner will identify pairs of words that rhyme and pairs that do not rhyme.

4. Given a rhyming couplet with an incomplete last line and a group of words or pictures of objects, the learner will select the word which best completes the rhyme.

5. Given a word, the learner will name words which have the same rhyme ending.

6. Given a series of rhyming words, the learner will reproduce the phonogram.

3. Acquire Oral Language Skills in Syntax

a. Identify and construct substitutions of parts of speech (nouns, verbs, pronouns, adjectives, adverbs) in simple sentences

1. Given two simple sentences which are identical except for one word, the learner will identify the different word.

2. The learner will substitute one word for another of the same syntactical function in a given simple sentence.

3. Given a sentence containing one or more nonsense syllables,

the learner will use one of the syllables to make a new
sentence, maintaining the syllable's grammatical function.

b. Identify and construct multiple substitution of parts of speech
(nouns, verbs, adjectives, and adverbs) in simple sentences

1. Given two sentences which are identical, except for two or
more words, the learner will identify the differences.

2. The learner will change a sentence by substituting two or
more of its words with two or more other words of the
same grammatical function.

c. Recognize and use complete sentences (past, present, and future
forms)

1. The learner will differentiate between phrases and complete
sentences.

2. The learner will construct complete sentences using past,
present, and future forms.

d. Identify and construct sentences with compound subjects, verbs,
adjectives, adverbs, or pronouns

1. Given a sentence with compound subject, verb, adjective,
adverb, or pronoun, the learner will substitute another compound of the same part of speech and grammatical function.

2. Given a compound subject, verb, adjective, adverb, or
pronoun, the learner will use the compound in a sentence.

e. Identify and use subordinates and coordinators

1. The learner will construct a sentence using a given subordinate clause.

2. The learner will expand a sentence by adding a subordinate
clause.

3. The learner will identify two simple sentences joined by a
coordinator.

4. Given two simple sentences, the learner will make a
compound sentence by adding a coordinator.

f. Identify and use prepositions

1. The learner will construct sentences using given prepositions.

2. The learner will expand a sentence by adding a prepositional
phrase.

g. Identify and use determiners

1. Given two identical sentences, except for the determiners,
the learner will identify the different determiners and
explain how they give the sentences a slightly different
meaning.

    2. The learner will construct sentences using given determiners.

  h. Use auxiliary words

    1. Given two sentences, identical except for the auxiliary, the learner will identify the different auxiliaries and explain how they give the sentences different meanings.

    2. The learner will substitute one auxiliary for another in a sentence.

    3. The learner will use given auxiliaries in sentences.

  i. Identify and construct transformations

    1. Given sentences, the learner will identify their types (declarative, interrogative, negative, etc.).

    2. Given a sentence, the learner will transform it into a specified type of sentence.

4. Acquire Oral Language Skills in Morphology

  a. Identify and form plurals

    1. Given words, the learner will identify those which are singular and those which are plural.

    2. Given the singular form of a word, the learner will give its plural form.

    3. Given the plural form of a word, the learner will give its singular form.

    4. The learner will describe objects or pictures using the correct singular or plural form.

    5. Given a sentence, the learner will repeat it, changing specified words from singular to plural or vice versa.

  b. Use correct verb forms

    1. The learner will use correct verb forms in daily speech.

    2. The learner will answer questions using the correct person and tense.

    3. The learner will complete or construct sentences using a given verb form.

  c. Use contractions

    1. Given a contraction, the learner will identify the two words used to form it.

    2. Given pairs of words commonly contracted, the learner will contract them.

    3. The learner will use given contractions.

  d. Use compound words

    1. The learner will identify the two parts of a given compound word.

    2. The learner will combine given words (or illustrations of objects) to form compound words.

    3. The learner will construct a sentence which contains a given compound word.

    4. Given words, the learner will identify those which are compound.

e. Use positive, comparative, and superlative forms of adjectives

    1. The learner will use correct positive, comparative, and superlative forms of adjectives.

    2. The learner will demonstrate understanding of the positive, comparative, and superlative forms of adjectives by answering questions which use these forms.

f. Use possessive forms of nouns and pronouns

    1. The learner will identify possessive nouns and pronouns in given phrases and sentences.

    2. The learner will construct sentences using given possessive nouns and pronouns.

    3. The learner will answer questions using appropriate possessives.

    4. The learner will answer questions using appropriate possessives.

g. Use verbs and form agents

    1. The learner will construct sentences containing agents.

    2. The learner will complete sentences by filling in the missing agent.

h. Use inflected endings

    1. Given a word and one or more of its inflected forms, the learner will describe how each inflection modifies the meaning of the word.

    2. The learner will complete or construct a sentence with specified inflections.

C. Body Awareness

  a. Identify body parts and functions

    1. Given the name of a body part, the learner will locate it on himself, another person, a doll, or a picture.

    2. Shown a body part on a person, a doll, or a picture, the learner will name it.

    3. Given the name of a part of the body, the learner will identify its function.

    4. Given a description of a part of the body, the learner will identify it.

5. The learner will identify missing body parts in incomplete illustrations.

b. Identify position and direction in space

1. The learner will identify right and left body parts.

2. Given a direction or position, the learner will identify it by pointing to it, moving toward it, etc.

3. Shown an object or person, the learner will describe its direction or position.

4. The learner will identify the direction or position of a specified object.

D. Visual Skills

1. Develop Visual Perception

a. Acquire visual discrimination

1. The learner will match items to illustrations of them.

2. Given items or illustrations, all identical but one, the learner will identify the one which is different.

3. The learner will identify a given visual stimulus from a background of competing stimuli.

4. Given a set of items or pictures, the learner will identify those that are identical.

5. Given complete and incomplete items or pictures, the learner will supply the missing part to make the items or pictures identical.

6. The learner will identify missing parts in incomplete pictures.

7. The learner will identify the differences in items or pictures which are identical except for details.

b. Develop perceptual speed

1. The learner will identify an item after a flash presentation of the item.

2. The learner will identify an item after a flash presentation of an incomplete sketch of the item.

3. The learner will identify identical items under timed conditions.

c. Develop sense of spatial relations

1. The learner will identify figures that are identical, though one is rotated.

2. Shown the same items from different angles or vantage points, the learner will identify them as the same.

2. Develop Visual Memory

    1. The learner will reproduce the arrangement of a set of items after the arrangement has been scrambled or removed from sight.

    2. Shown a group of items twice with an item added or removed before the second showing, the learner will identify the item that was added or removed.

    3. Shown an item briefly, the learner will identify that item from a set of distractors.

    4. The learner will describe an item after it has been removed from sight.

    5. The learner will reproduce an item after it has been removed from sight.

3. Develop Visualization Skills

    1. The learner will identify familiar objects by touch only.

    2. Given clues about the appearance of an item, the learner will identify the item.

    3. The learner will identify items which are conceptually similar (in different stages of development, represented in different forms, having various shadings, textures) as belonging to the same category.

    4. The learner will describe orally or in a sketch how he would visualize a given situation.

    5. The learner will complete a picture puzzle.

    6. Shown part of an item, or a picture of part of an item, the learner will identify the item.

E Develop Coordination Skills

Develop Eye-Hand Coordination

    1. The learner will hold a book properly, at a proper distance, and will turn the pages correctly.

    2. The learner will properly manipulate or operate toys, tools, and mechanical objects with coordination and dexterity.

    3. The learner will duplicate a given arrangement of items.

    4. The learner will duplicate a given sequence of steps in manipulating an object.

    5. The learner will properly hold and use a pencil or crayon to complete such tasks as drawing a simple picture, coloring within the boundary of an outline, copying a given illustration.

II. Decoding Skills

A. Recognize and Use Letters of the Alphabet

a. Recognize manuscript letters

1. Given upper- or lower-case letters in manuscript, the learner will identify each letter name.

2. Given an upper- or lower-case letter in manuscript, the learner will find it on an alphabet chart.

3. Given an upper- or lower-case letter, the learner will identify its corresponding lower- or upper-case form.

4. Given a set of upper- or lower-case letters, the learner will identify those that are identical and those that are different.

5. Given a set of upper- or lower-case letters, the learner will identify the letter that is named.

6. The learner will identify words written in manuscript that begin with a designated letter.

7. The learner will identify whether given letters are in upper- or lower-case.

8. The learner will name the letters in given words written in manuscript.

b. Recognize cursive letters

1. Given upper- or lower-case letters in cursive, the learner will identify each letter name.

2. Given an upper- or lower-case letter in cursive, the learner will find it on an alphabet chart.

3. Given a lower- or upper-case letter in cursive, the learner will identify its corresponding upper- or lower-case form.

4. Given a set of upper- or lower-case letters in cursive, the learner will identify those that are identical and those that are different.

5. Given a set of upper- or lower-case letters in cursive, the learner will identify the letter that is named.

6. The learner will identify words written in cursive that begin with a designated letter.

7. The learner will name the letters in given words written in cursive.

8. The learner will identify the cursive form of a given manuscript letter or the manuscript form of a given cursive letter.

c. Recognize alphabetical order

1. The learner will arrange given letters in alphabetical order.

2. The learner will identify the letters that immediately follow and precede a given letter in the alphabet.

3. The learner will arrange given words in alphabetical order.

d. Identify vowels and consonants

    1.   The learner will identify vowels in the alphabet or in words.

    2.   The learner will identify consonants in the alphabet or in words.

    3.   The learner will name the vowels from memory.

 e. Use letters

    1.   Given an upper- or lower-case letter in manuscript, the learner will write its corresponding upper- or lower-case form.

    2.   Given the name of a letter, the learner will write it in manuscript in upper- or lower-case.

    3.   Given an upper- or lower-case letter in cursive, the learner will write its corresponding upper- or lower-case form.

    4.   Given the name of a letter, the learner will write it in cursive in upper- or lower-case.

    5.   The learner will write in manuscript a familiar word after hearing it spelled.

    6.   The learner will write in cursive a familiar word after hearing it spelled.

    7.   Given letters in manuscript, the learner will write them in cursive and vice versa.

    8.   Given words in manuscript, the learner will write them in cursive and vice versa.

B.   Recognizing Sound-Symbol Relationships (Phonics)

 a. Identify initial single consonants

    1.   Given a word orally, or a picture of an object, the learner will identify its initial single consonant.

    2.   The learner will say a given written word, pronouncing the single initial consonant correctly.

    3.   The learner will generate other words that have the same initial consonant as a given written word.

    4.   The learner will identify from a set of written words those beginning with the same single consonant sound as a given word.

    5.   The learner will identify words beginning with a single consonant sound.

    6.   Given a word beginning with a single consonant, the learner will substitute other beginning consonants to create new words.

    7.   Given a written consonant and several pictures of objects, the learner will identify the object whose name begins with the given consonant.

 b. Identify final single consonants

    1.   Given a word orally, or a picture of an object, the learner will identify its final single consonant.

2. The learner will say a given written word, pronouncing the final single consonant correctly.

3. The learner will generate other words that have the same final consonant as a given written word.

4. The learner will identify from a set of written words those ending with the same single consonant sound as a given word.

5. The learner will identify words ending with a single consonant sound.

6. Given a word ending with a single consonant, the learner will substitute other final consonants to create new words.

7. Given a written consonant and several pictures of objects, the learner will identify the object whose name ends with the given consonant.

c. Identify medial single consonants

1. Given a word orally, or a picture of an object, the learner will identify its medial single consonant.

2. The learner will say a given written word, pronouncing the single medial consonant correctly.

3. The learner will generate other words that have the same medial consonant as a given written word.

4. The learner will identify from a set of written words those containing the same single medial consonant sound as a given word.

5. The learner will identify words containing a single medial consonant sound.

6. Given a written consonant and several pictures of objects, the learner will identify the object whose name contains the given consonant in the medial position.

d. Identify initial consonant digraphs

1. Given a word orally, or a picture of an object, the learner will identify its initial consonant digraph.

2. The learner will say a given written word pronouncing the initial consonant digraph correctly.

3. Given a written consonsant digraph and several pictures of objects, the learner will identify the object whose name begins with the given digraph.

4. The learner will generate other words that have the same initial consonant digraph as a given written word.

5. The learner will identify words beginning with a consonant digraph sound.

6. Given a word beginning with a consonant digraph, the learner will substitute other beginning consonant digraphs to create new words.

7. Given pairs of words, one of which begins with a consonant digraph, the other having the same initial consonants but a different pronunciation, the learner will pronounce the words correctly.

e. Identify final consonant digraphs

1. Given a word orally, or a picture of an object, the learner will identify its final consonant digraph.

2. The learner will say a given written word, pronouncing the final consonant digraph correctly

3. Given a written consonant digraph and several pictures of objects, the learner will identify the object whose name ends with the given digraph.

4. The learner will generate other words that have the same final consonant digraph as a given written word.

5. The learner will identify words ending with a consonant digraph sound.

6. Given a word ending with a consonant digraph, the learner will substitute other final consonant digraphs to create new words.

f. Identify medial consonant digraphs

1. Given a word orally, or a picture of an object, the learner will identify its medial consonant digraph.

2. The learner will say a given written word, pronouncing the medial consonant digraph correctly.

3. Given a written consonant digraph and several pictures of objects, the learner will identify the object whose name contains the given digraphs in the medial position.

4. The learner will generate other words that have the same medial consonant digraph as a given written word.

5. The learner will identify words containing a medial consonant digraph sound.

6. Given pairs of words, one of which has a medial consonant digraph, the other having the same medial consonants but a different pronunciation, the learner will pronounce the words correctly.

g. Initial consonant blends

1. Given a word orally, or a picture of an object, the learner will identify its initial consonant blend.

2. The learner will say a given written word pronouncing the initial consonant blend correctly.

3. The learner will generate other words that have the same initial consonant blend as a given written word.

4. The learner will identify words beginning with consonant blends.

5. Given a word orally with a beginning consonant blend, the learner will identify from a list of written words those with the same beginning consonant blend as the given word.

6. The learner will identify from words given orally or from pictures of objects those that begin with a given written consonant blend.

    Given a word beginning with a consonant blend, the learner will substitute other beginning consonant blends to create new words.

h. Identify final consonant blends

1. Given a word orally, or a picture of an object, the learner will identify its final consonant blend.

2. The learner will say a given written word, pronouncing the final consonant blend correctly.

3. The learner will generate other words that have the same final consonant blend as a given written word.

4. The learner will identify words ending with consonant blends.

5. Given a word orally with a final consonant blend, the learner will identify from a list of written words those with the same final consonant blend as the given word.

6. The learner will identify from words given orally, or from pictures of objects, those that end with a given written consonant blend.

7. Given a written word ending with a consonant blend, the learner will substitute other final consonant blends to create new words.

i. Identify medial consonant blends

1. Given a word orally, or a picture of an object, the learner will identify its medial consonant blend.

2. The learner will say a given written word, pronouncing the medial consonant blend correctly.

3. The learner will generate other words that have the same medial consonant blend as a given written word.

4. The learner will identify words with medial consonant blends.

5. Given a word orally with a medial consonant blend, the learner will identify from a list of written words those with the same medial consonant blend as the given word.

6. The learner will identify from words given orally or from pictures of objects those that contain a given written medial consonant blend.

7. Given a written word containing a medial consonant blend, the

learner will substitute other medial consonant blends to create new words.

j. Identify consonant sounds (single, digraphs, and blends)

1. The learner will complete a given written word by identifying its missing single consonant, digraph, or blend.

2. Given a word orally, or a picture of an object, the learner will identify its initial, final, or medial consonant letter(s), as indicated.

3. Given an oral word and a written consonant (single, blend, or digraph) from that word, the learner will identify whether the consonant is in the initial, medial, or final position.

4. The learner will generate words containing a given consonant, consonant digraph, or consonant blend in an indicated position.

k. Identify short vowel sounds

1. The learner will say a given written word, pronouncing the short vowel sound correctly.

2. The learner will say the short sound of given written vowels.

3. Given an oral word containing a short vowel sound, the learner will identify from a list of written words those containing the same short vowel sound as the given word.

4. The learner will identify the letter that represents the short vowel sound of words given orally or illustrated in pictures.

5. From a list of written words, the learner will identify those that have the same short vowel sound.

6. The learner will generate other words that have the same short vowel sound as a given word.

7. The learner will identify from given written words those containing short vowel sounds.

8. Given a word containing a short vowel sound, the learner will substitute other short vowel sounds to create new words.

l. Identify long vowel sounds

1. The learner will say a given written word, pronouncing the long vowel sound correctly.

2. The learner will say the long sound of given written vowels.

3. Given an oral word containing a long vowel sound, the learner will identify from among given written words those containing the same long vowel sound as the given word.

4. The learner will identify the letter that represents the long vowel sound of words given orally or illustrated in pictures.

5. From a list of written words, the learner will identify those that have the same long vowel sound.

6. The learner will generate other words that have the same long vowel sound as a given word.

7. The learner will identify from given written words those containing long vowel sounds.

8. Given a word containing a long vowel sound, the learner will substitute other long vowel sounds to form new words.

m. Identify vowel controllers

1. The learner will say a given written word, pronouncing the vowel and its controller correctly.

2. The learner will generate other words that have the same vowel sound and controller as a given word.

3. The learner will identify vowel controller in written words.

4. The learner will identify vowel controllers in oral words.

5. Given a word containing a vowel and controller, the learner will substitute another vowel or controller to create new words.

6. Given a vowel and controller, the learner will add letters to form complete words, maintaining the sound of the vowel and controller.

n. Identify vowel digraphs

1. The learner will say a given written word, pronouncing the vowel digraph correctly.

2. The learner will identify from given written words those containing vowel digraphs.

3. Given a word containing a vowel digraph, the learner will substitute other vowel digraphs to form new words.

4. Given a word orally or a picture whose name contains a vowel digraph, the learner will spell the digraph.

5. Given a vowel digraph, the learner will form words using the digraph.

6. Given a word containing a vowel digraph, the learner will identify the letter which represents the long vowel and the letter which is silent.

7. From a list of written words containing vowel digraphs, the learner will identify those with the same vowel digraph sound.

8. From a list of written words containing the same vowel digraph, the learner will identify those with different sounds.

o. Identify vowel diphthongs

1. The learner will say a given written word, pronouncing the vowel diphthong correctly.

2. Given a word orally containing a diphthong, the learner will identify from a set of written words those containing the same diphthong as the word specified.

3. Given pairs of written words, the learner will identify those containing the same diphthong sound and those containing different diphthong sounds.

4. The learner will identify from given words those containing diphthongs and those containing vowel digraphs.

5. Given a word orally containing a diphthong, the learner will spell the diphthong.

6. The learner will generate words containing a given vowel diphthong sound.

p. Identify vowel sounds (short, long, controllers, digraphs, diphthongs)

1. The learner will complete given written words by adding the missing single vowel, vowel digraph, or diphthong.

2. The learner will identify words containing the same vowel sound.

3. The learner will generate words containing a designated vowel sound.

4. The learner will identify designated types of vowels in given written and oral words.

5. Given a word containing a vowel sound, and a specific vowel sound to substitute for it, the learner will form a new word.

6. Given pairs of written words, identical except for a final "e" in one, the learner will pronounce the words correctly.

7. Given pairs of written words, identical except that one has a single and the other a double consonant, the learner will pronounce the words correctly.

8. Given pairs of written words, identical except that one has a final consonant, the learner will pronounce the words correctly.

q. Identify silent letters

1. The learner will select from written words those that contain a silent letter, and identify the silent letter.

2. The learner will identify rules governing the pronunciation of words with silent letters.

3. The learner will pronounce a given written word containing a silent letter.

C. Apply Rules of Spelling and Mechanics

a. Recognize regular spelling patterns

1. The learner will identify silent letters in words with regular spelling patterns.

2. The learner will correctly spell words with regular spelling patterns.

3. The learner will correctly pronounce written words with regular spelling patterns.

4. The learner will identify rules governing words with regular spelling patterns.

5. The learner will identify words with regular spelling patterns.

b. Recognize variant spelling patterns

1. The learner will identify silent letters in words with variant spelling patterns.

2. The learner will correctly spell words with variant spelling patterns.

3. The learner will correctly pronounce words with variant spelling patterns.

4. The learner will identify rules governing words with variant spelling patterns.

5. The learner will identify words with variant spelling patterns.

6. The learner will explain why a given word is considered variant.

c. Apply phonic generalizations

1. Given unfamiliar written words, the learner will pronounce them correctly.

2. Given words orally, the learner will spell them correctly.

d. Punctuation and capitalization

1. The learner will identify the beginning of each sentence in a given passage.

2. The learner will identify the ending of each sentence in a given passage.

3. The learner will identify the meaning of punctuation marks and capital letters.

4. The learner will supply missing punctuation marks and capital letters in given sentences.

D. Recognize the Division of Words into Units of Meaning (Structural Analysis)

a. Form compound words

1. The learner will identify the simple words making up a compound word.

2. Given words in random order that may be combined into compound words, the learner will form compound words.

3. The learner will generate compound words from a given simple word.

4. Given an unknown compound word composed of familiar simple words, the learner will identify the meaning of the compound.

5. Given a sentence containing one word of a compound word, the learner will use the context of the sentence to identify the missing part.

6. The learner will produce compound words.

b. Form inflectional endings

1. The learner will identify or write the possessive form of a given noun or pronoun.

2. The learner will write or complete a phrase or sentence using a possessive.

3. The learner will spell possessives correctly.

4. The learner will identify correctly and incorrectly used possessives in given phrases or sentences.

5. The learner will indicate whether written words ending in "s" are possessives, plurals or verbs.

6. The learner will write the plural form of given words.

7. The learner will write the singular form of given plural words.

8. The learner will explain when to use a plural form.

9. The learner will use the plural of a given word in writing phrases and sentences.

10. The learner will identify correct and incorrect uses of plurals in given phrases or sentences.

11. The learner will spell plural words correctly.

12. Given a sentence with a word missing, the learner will fill in an appropriate singular or plural word.

13. Given a familiar verb and a specified inflection, the learner will construct the designated inflectional form of the verb given.

14. Given a sentence with a verb missing, the learner will fill in the appropriate inflected form of a verb.

15. The learner will identify the tense of given sentences.

16. Given a verb with a specified inflection, the learner will write phrases or sentences using the designated verb form.

17. The learner will correctly spell inflected verb forms.

18. The learner will identify correct and incorrect uses of inflected verb forms in given phrases or sentences.

19. The learner will write the correct comparative and superlative form of given adjectives.

20. Given a written adjective which contains a comparative or superlative ending, the learner will write the positive form of the adjective.

21. The learner will identify comparative or superlative endings in written words.

22. The learner will write or complete a phrase or sentence using the comparative or superlative form of a given adjective.

23. The learner will correctly spell comparative and superlative forms of given adjectives.

24. The learner will identify correct and incorrect uses of comparatives and superlatives in given written phrases and sentences.

c. Form contractions

1. Given two written words normally contracted, the learner will identify their contraction.

2. Given a written contraction, the learner will identify the two words that form it.

3. The learner will correctly spell and punctuate contractions.

4. The learner will identify the letter(s) that the apostrophe represents in given contractions.

5. The learner will generate contractions from a given written word.

d. Form abbreviations

1. The learner will identify the abbreviations of given words.

2. Given an abbreviation, the learner will identify the word for which it stands.

3. The learner will identify instances where it is appropriate to abbreviate and where it is not.

e. Identify syllabication and word accents

1. The learner will divide given words into syllables.

2. Given a written word, the learner will identify the rule which governs the syllabication of that word.

3. The learner will identify the primary and secondary accented syllables and the unaccented syllables of given words.

4. Given pairs of written sentences which contain heteronyms, the learner will read each sentence pronouncing the heteronym correctly.

5. The learner will place accent marks on pairs of written heteronyms to show the different pronunciation.

6. The learner will identify the number of syllables in written words.

f. Identify prefixes, suffixes, and roots

1. The learner will identify the root, prefix, or suffix of a given written word.

2. The learner will add a prefix or suffix to a given root word, making appropriate spelling changes in the root when necessary.

3. The learner will identify from given words those with prefixes or suffixes.

4. The learner will supply a prefixed or suffixed word to complete a given incomplete sentence.

5. Given the definition of a prefixed or suffixed word and the word's root, the learner will use the definition to complete the word.

6. The learner will identify the meaning of given prefixes, suffixes, and roots.

7. The learner will correctly spell prefixed and suffixed words.

8. The learner will identify prefixed or suffixed words that mean the same as given phrases.

9. The learner will explain how the addition of a designated prefix or suffix changes the meaning of a given word.

10. Given a new word and the meaning of its prefix, suffix, and/or root, the learner will identify the meaning of the new word.

11. The learner will use given prefixed or suffixed words in sentences.

12. The learner will paraphrase given sentences, adding a prefix or suffix to a word in the original sentence (e.g., She is a beauty —She is beautiful).

13. The learner will explain how a knowledge of prefixes, suffixes, and roots helps him to understand the meaning of new words and to develop his vocabulary.

III. Vocabulary Skills

A. Incorporate listening and speaking skills into reading vocabulary

1. Given a new written word that is in his listening and speaking vocabulary, the learner will say it.

2. Given a new written word that is in his listening and speaking vocabulary, the learner will identify an illustration or object related to that word.

3. Given a written list of words, phrases, or sentences, the learner will identify the word or words in them dictated by the teacher.

4. Given illustrations and sets of descriptive written words, phrases or sentences, the learner will select the word, phrase, or sentence which best describes each illustration.

5. Given known words or phrases, the learner will locate them in a given reading selection.

6. Given a familiar written word, the learner will use it in an oral sentence.

7. Given a known word, the learner will identify its definition.

8. Given a definition, the learner will identify the word defined.

9. The learner will seek the meaning of new words he reads or hears.

B. Recognize and use synonyms, homonyns, antonyms, and heteronyms
1. The learner will identify synonyms in given pairs of words, lists of words, or reading selections.
2. The learner will identify antonyms in given pairs of words, lists of words, or reading selections.
3. The learner will identify homonyms in given pairs of words, lists of words, or reading selections.
4. The learner will generate synonyms for given words.
5. The learner will generate homonyms for given words.
6. The learner will generate antonyms for given words.
7. The learner will identify the definitions for a given pair of homonyms.
8. The learner will identify the definitions for a given pair of antonyms.
9. Given a pair of heteronyms, the learner will identify their definitions.
10. Given a pair of heteronyms, the learner will use each in a sentence.

C. Recognize word meaning from context
1. Given an unfamiliar word in context, the learner will use context clues to identify the meaning of the word.
2. Given an incomplete sentence, the learner will complete it by identifying a word or phrase suitable to the context of the sentence.
3. Given two or more sentences, each using the same multiple-meaning word in a different context, the learner will identify each different meaning of the word.
4. Given an unfamiliar word in a context sufficient to identify the word's meaning, the learner will identify the context clues that helped him derive the meaning.
5. Given a familiar word in context, used in a new or specialized way, the learner will use context clues to identify the new or specialized meaning of the word.

D. Recognize historical origins of words
1. The learner will identify in a given selection those words and phrases which have a different meaning today than they did when the selection was written.
2. Having identified words which have changed in meaning, the learner will identify both their original and their current meanings.
3. Given a new word in context and its etymology, the learner will identify the word's meaning as used in the context.
4. Given a familiar word or phrase, the learner will identify its origin.

E. Recognize and use non-literal language

1. The learner will identify specified figures of speech in reading selections.

2. The learner will identify examples of literal and non-literal phrases or sentences in given selections.

3. The learner will use figures of speech to complete or write sentences.

4. The learner will identify the definitions of designated figures of speech.

5. The learner will identify idioms in a list of phrases or in given sentences of passages.

6. The learner will use idioms to complete or write sentences.

7. The learner will identify colloquialisms in a list of words or phrases, or in given sentences or passages.

8. The learner will use colloquialisms to complete or write sentences.

9. The learner will identify onomatopoetic words in a given list of words, in sentences, or in passages.

10. The learner will identify onomatopoetic words to match illustrations or descriptive phrases.

F. Recognize denotation, connotation, and nuance

1. Given words with similar denotation, the learner will identify the differences in connotation or nuance.

2. The learner will choose from a list of words with similar meanings but with different connotations or nuances the correct word to complete a given sentence.

3. Given a set of words with similar meanings but different connotations, the learner will write sentences that illustrate the different connotations.

4. Given a word, the learner will use it in two or more sentences which reveal differences in connotation of that word.

G. Use a systematic and continuing method of word study to increase vocabulary

1. The learner will demonstrate a growing active and passive vocabulary as revealed in his speech, written work, and vocabulary tests.

2. The learner will actively engage in the process of vocabulary development by, for example, maintaining lists of unknown words, looking up their meanings in the dictionary, using the words in conversation, etc.

IV. Comprehension

A. Literal Comprehension

a. Identify main ideas and major concepts

1 The learner will select or write a title for an untitled reading selection.

2. The learner will identify the main ideas and major concepts of a selection.

3. The learner will summarize a selection or passage he has just read.

4. Given the main ideas of a selection, the learner will identify ideas subordinate to each main idea.

5. The learner will paraphrase a given passage.

6. Given a reading selection, the learner will identify key words, phrases, or passages important to the meaning of the selection.

b. Find and relate details

1. Given a passage or incident from a reading selection, the learner will identify the selection.

2. After reading a selection, the learner will answer specific questions or find detailed information.

3. Given a list of lines from a familiar selection, the learner will identify those which are main ideas and those which give detailed information.

c. Recognize sequence of ideas

1. After reading a given selection, the learner will identify its main events in proper sequence.

2. The learner will arrange a scrambled set of words or sentences in logical order.

3. The learner will explain why the sequence of events or ideas in a given selection is necessary or effective.

B. Interpretation

a. Understand relationships

1. The learner will identify related words or statements.

2. The learner will identify the relationship between given words, statements, or passages.

3. Given phrases or sentences, some of which are similar in meaning, the learner will indicate those which are similar.

4. The learner will identify the relationship between the elements compared in a given analogy.

5. The learner will identify the missing element in a given analogy.

6. Given class concepts, the learner will identify members belonging to each class.

7. Given class members (words or statements), the learner will identify class concepts.

8. Given class members, the learner will identify additional members in the same class.

b. Recognize cause and effect

1. Given a significant event from a reading selection, the learner will identify its cause.

2. Given a significant event from a reading selection, the learner will identify its consequences.

3. Given a hypothetical situation, the learner will select or write a probable cause.

4. The learner will select or discuss probable consequences of given situations.

5. Given a statement or passage involving cause and effect, the learner will identify the cause and the effect.

c. Make inferences

1. The learner will identify from several statements concerning a given reading selection, those which are directly quoted from the selection and those which can be inferred.

2. The learner will answer questions about a given hypothetical situation which require him to infer information not literally or directly stated in the situation as given.

3. Given pairs of statements or passages which are similar in meaning but contain differences in the feeling or attitudes conveyed, the learner will describe the differences.

4. Given an incomplete passage, the learner will select or write a sentence to complete it.

d. Interpret figurative and descriptive language

1. After reading a descriptive passage, such as a poem, the learner will indicate words or phrases evoking sensory images.

2. The learner will translate given examples of non-literal language.

3. Given a selection containing symbolism, the learner will identify or explain the meaning of the symbolism.

e. Recognize and interpret emotional reactions

1. Given a passage in which an emotion is conveyed, the learner will identify the emotion described in the passage.

2. Given a passage in which words are missing which express the feelings of characters in the passage, the learner will identify an appropriate word for each blank.

3. Given a passage in which an emotion is conveyed, the learner will identify the words or phrases conveying emotion.

4. The learner will interpret how a person would react to a given situation by identifying an appropriate emotion.

5. The learner will describe and interpret emotional reactions of characters in a given reading selection.

6. Given quotations from characters in a reading selection, the

learner will identify or describe the characters' feelings as implied by the quotations.

f. Identify and arrive at conclusions and generalizations

1. After reading several fables, the learner will describe the characteristics of a fable.

2. Given a work which conveys a moral, the learner will identify the moral.

3. Given statements of fact, opinion, and hypothesis, the learner will identify the characteristics of or define each type of statement.

4. Given a non-fiction reading selection, the learner will identify the author's conclusion.

5. Given several selections of the same type, the learner will identify the characteristics of that type.

6. Given two situations, arguments, or ideas which are the same but are expressed in different terminology, the learner will identify the similarity.

g. Compare and contrast information and ideas

1. Given several sentences, the learner will indicate which sentences are opposite in meaning.

2. Given a passage and a paraphrase of a statement appearing in that passage, the learner will locate the original statement in the passage.

3. Given two selections similar in certain respects, such as theme, mood, plot, or setting, the learner will identify the similarities and differences.

4. Given reading selections offering different interpretations of, or different points of view concerning the same issue, event or problem, the learner will identify or describe the differences and inconsistencies.

h. Evaluate ideas and information

1. Given a fantasy, the learner will identify events that could not happen in real life.

2. Given sentences, the learner will identify those that are realistic and those that are make-believe.

3. Given several statements, the learner will identify them as fact, opinion, or hypothesis.

4. The learner will locate in a newspaper or magazine an example of a well-documented and poorly documented article or editorial and give the reasons for each selection.

5. The learner will identify statements of fact, opinion, and value in a given article or editorial.

6. The learner will identify in a given article or editorial the author's opinions and one or more reasons or statements on which each opinion is based.

7. Given a reading selection, the learner will identify the opinions, philosophy, or values of the author.

8. After reading a given non-fiction selection, the learner will discuss how well the author substantiated his opinions with facts and references.

9. Given a reading selection, the learner will identify the author's purpose.

10. The learner will discuss why different newspapers or magazines often give very different accounts of the same event.

11. The learner will evaluate given articles, editorials, or other reading selections according to such criteria as accuracy in reporting facts, and care to exactness.

i. Develop critical reading skills

1. Given a selection expressing an opinion, the learner will discuss why he agrees or disagrees with the opinions and conclusions of the author.

2. Given a reading selection, the learner will state whether it is relatively biased or unbiased.

3. Given a reading selection, the learner will identify propaganda techniques such as persuasion, unstated assumptions, and emotionally charged statements.

4. Given a reading selection, the learner will identify evidence of illogical thinking such as inconsistencies in data, false assumptions, and fallacies.

5. Given several persuasive statements, the learner will identify the type of persuasive device used in each.

6. The learner will identify the type of persuasive device(s) used in a given article, editorial, advertisement, or speech.

7. The learner will explain the effects persuasive devices in a given selection or advertisement have on the reader.

8. The learner will report on a book he has read, giving his comments, criticisms, opinions, etc.

j. Develop oral reading skills

1. The learner will read given selections orally, with correct interpretation of punctuation and appropriate phrasing, speed, pronunciation, enunciation, and intonation.

2. The learner will read a selection orally without unnecessary sounds, movements, or tension.

3. The learner will read given poems orally with appropriate rhythm.

4. The learner will read a given selection orally with the expression, tone, and emotion appropriate to the selection.

5. After reading a selection orally, the learner will demonstrate comprehension by answering specific questions about its content.

C. Attitude toward reading

a. Take proper care of reading materials

1. The learner will not damage books (by writing in them, tearing or folding pages, etc.).

2. The learner will return classroom and library books to shelves after use.

3. The learner will return borrowed books to their owners and will return library books on time.

b. Read for enjoyment

1. The learner will explain what he liked and disliked about the stories or books he selected and read.

2. The learner will volunteer to read a favorite poem or selection to the class.

3. The learner will indicate that he enjoys reading activities in class.

4. The learner will recommend to others the reading selections he has particularly enjoyed.

5. The learner will indicate that he enjoys and reads many different types of reading materials.

6. The learner will indicate that he often reads in leisure time independently of school requirements.

7. The learner will indicate that he is acquainted with a wide variety of children's literature.

c. Appreciate reading

1. The learner will indicate that he appreciates the many values of reading.

2. The learner will indicate that he is developing a discriminating choice of reading materials.

3. The learner will select reading materials of a difficulty appropriate to his ability.

d. Relate personally to reading

1. The learner will identify the feeling or mood conveyed by a given selection.

2. The learner will describe how he would feel or what he would do if he were a designated character in a reading selection.

3. Given a descriptive reading selection, the learner will indicate the effects the mood and imagery have on him.

4. The learner will give his opinion concerning a current event or issue about which he has read.

5. The learner will answer questions in such a way as to indicate his frequent personal involvement in what he reads.

6. The learner will describe a specific instance in which his attitude or behavior was changed through reading.

7. The learner will report on his emotional response to a non-fiction reading selection.

V. Location and Study Skills

A. Recognize and Use Textbook Aids

a. Title page

1. The learner will locate the title page of a book.

2. The learner will identify the information a title page contains.

b. Copyright

1. The learner will locate the copyright in a book.

2. The learner will define copyright, giving its function and the information it contains.

c Format

1. Given a textbook, the learner will locate framed or boxed information.

2. The learner will explain why framed or boxed information is separated from the text.

3. The learner will locate symbols and colors in a given textbook.

4. The learner will identify the use or meaning of specified symbols or colors in a given text.

d. Table of contents

1. The learner will locate the table of contents of a book.

2. The learner will describe the information in a table of contents and its usefulness.

3. The learner will identify the chapters in a unit.

4. The learner will use the table of contents of a book to locate specific information or answer specific questions.

5. Given chapter titles and a list of unit titles from a textbook, the learner will classify the chapter titles under the appropriate unit title.

6. Given a reader, a novel, and a textbook, the learner will describe the similarities and differences in their tables of contents.

e. Section and paragraph headings

1. Given a chapter from a textbook, the learner will locate the heading of each section in that chapter.

2. The learner will locate a given section in a textbook chapter.

3. After reading a passage in a textbook, the learner will identify or write an appropriate section heading for the passage.

4. Given a section heading from a textbook, the learner will briefly explain what that section might be about.

f. Italics

1. The learner will locate italics in a given selection.

2. The learner will identify the uses of italics.

g. Bold-face type

1. The learner will locate bold-face type in a given selection.

2. The learner will identify the uses of bold-face type.

h. Index

1. The learner will locate the index of a given book.

2. The learner will identify the contents and uses of an index.

3. The learner will use the index to answer given questions or locate desired information.

4. Given a problem or question, the learner will identify the key word(s) he would look up in an index to find information related to the problem.

i. Appendix

1. The learner will locate the appendix of a textbook.

2. The learner will identify the contents in the appendix of a given textbook.

3. The learner will identify reasons why some books have appendices.

4. The learner will use the appendix of a book to find answers to given questions.

j. Introductory material

1. The learner will locate the introduction, foreword, or preface to a book.

2. The learner will describe the contents of an introduction, preface, or foreword.

3. The learner will describe the functions of introductions, forewords, or prefaces.

k. Overviews

1. The learner will locate the overview of a chapter.

2. The learner will explain the uses of chapter overviews.

3. After reading a chapter overview, the learner will describe what the chapter is about.

4. The learner will read a given chapter and write an overview for it.

l. Summaries
1. The learner will locate a chapter summary in a textbook.
2. The learner will identify the uses of chapter summaries.
3. After reading a chapter, the learner will summarize it.
4. The learner will read the overview and summary of a given chapter and explain their similarities and differences.

m. Bibliographies
1. The learner will locate the bibliography of a given textbook.
2. The learner will identify the uses of bibliographies.
3. The learner will identify each item of information in a given bibliographical reference.

n. Glossary
1. The learner will locate the glossary of a textbook.
2. The learner will identify the contents and uses of glossaries.
3. Given a word from a textbook, the learner will locate its definition in the glossary.

o. Footnotes
1. The learner will locate a footnote in a given book.
2. The learner will identify the passage to which a footnote refers.
3. The learner will identify the meaning of the symbols and abbreviations commonly used in footnotes.
4. Given a passage in a book with a footnote, the learner will identify the reason for the footnote and explain why it is not included in the text.
5. The learner will identify the uses of footnotes.

p. Pictorial and graphic representations
1. Given a graph, diagram, table, picture, or chart, the learner will summarize the information it provides.
2. Given a selection containing pictures, graphs, or diagrams, the learner will explain how a representation helps clarify the content of the selection.
3. The learner will locate in a text the pictorial or graphic representations matching given statements or descriptions of data.

q. Pronunciation keys
1. Given a dictionary, the learner will locate the pronunciation key.
2. The learner will describe the contents and uses of a pronunciation key.
3. Given an unfamiliar word, the learner will use a pronunciation key to pronounce the word correctly.

    4. Given a familiar word, the learner will use the symbols of pronunciation key to show how it should be pronounced.

r. Language abbreviations

    1. Given a list of words that can be abbreviated, the learner will use a dictionary to identify their abbreviations.

    2. The learner will use the table of abbreviations of a textbook or reference book to identify the words for which designated abbreviations stand.

s. Marginal notes

    1. Given a textbook, the learner will locate a marginal note.

    2. The learner will identify the contents and uses of marginal notes.

    3. Given a selection from a textbook without marginal notes, the learner will compose marginal notes for the selection.

t. List of suggested readings

    1. Given a book, the learner will locate its list of suggested readings.

    2. The learner will identify the contents and uses of a list of suggested readings.

    3. The learner will identify the types of books that might be in a list of suggested readings for a given chapter or book.

    4. The learner will describe the similarities and differences between a list of suggested readings and a bibliography.

u. Answer keys

    1. The learner will locate the answer key for a given chapter test in a textbook.

    2. The learner will explain how an answer key should be used.

v. Etymologies

    1. Given a dictionary, the learner will locate an example of an etymology.

    2. The learner will identify the contents and uses of etymologies.

    3. The learner will use the etymologies of a dictionary to find the origins of given words.

B. Identify and Use Library Resources

a. Organization and card catalogue

    1. Given a diagram of the floor layout of a library, the learner will identify the card catalogue, book stacks, periodicals section, reference desk and check-out desk.

    2. Given a library catalogue card, the learner will identify the author, title, subject, and call number of the book.

3. The learner will identify the use of the information on a library catalogue card.

4. The learner will correctly fill out a check-out card for a selected library book.

5. Given a book title, the learner will find its author and call number in the card catalogue.

6. Given the name of an author, the learner will find in the card catalogue the titles and call numbers of books by that author.

7. Given a topic, the learner will locate in the card catalogue the title, author, and call number of one or more books on that topic.

b. Location of materials

1. Given the call number of a book, the learner will indicate on a diagram of the floor layout of a library and section of the library in which the book can be found.

2. Given the title of a book, the learner will find the book in the library using the card catalogue and library floor layout.

3. Given a topic, the learner will use the card catalogue to locate one or more library books on that topic.

4. Given fiction books by different authors, the learner will return them to their correct place on the library shelf.

5. Given a chart of the book arrangement of a library using the Dewey Decimal System, the learner will identify the area in which a designated book or topic would be found.

6. Given the name of a periodical, the learner will use the card catalogue to indicate whether it can be found in the library.

7. Given a topic, the learner will find in the library a magazine article dealing with that topic.

8. Given a title of an article, the name of the periodical, and the number of the issue in which the article is found, the learner will locate the article in the library.

C. Identify and Use Other Sources of Information

a. Dictionaries

1. The learner will identify the various guides and sections found in a dictionary.

2. The learner will describe the use of each section of a dictionary entry.

3. Given a list of words beginning with the same letter or letters, the learner will arrange the words in alphabetical order.

4. Given a new word, the learner will use a dictionary to locate its definition.

5. The learner will use a dictionary to find a synonym or antonym for a new word.

6. The learner will identify a set of dictionary guide words and their function.

7. Given a set of guide words, the learner will identify from a list those words which would be found on a dictionary page having those guide words.

8. Given sets of sentences, each containing the same word but with variations in its meaning, the learner will use the context of the sentences and the dictionary to identify the meaning of the word in each sentence.

9. Given a sentence containing an unfamiliar multi-meaning word, the learner will select from the dictionary that meaning of the word appropriate to the context of the sentence.

10. The learner will use the dictionary to identify and add the diacritical marks and the accent(s) to given words.

11. The learner will use a dictionary to identify the meaning of diacritical marks.

12. The learner will use a dictionary to find the pronunciation of an unfamiliar word and pronounce the word correctly.

b. Encyclopedias

1. Given an encyclopedia, the learner will identify the types of information found in it.

2. The learner will indicate how the information in a given encyclopedia is arranged and how to locate desired topics.

3. The learner will describe the similarities and differences between an encyclopedia and a dictionary.

4. The learner will locate the index of an encyclopedia.

5. The learner will identify the information contained in the index of an encyclopedia.

6. The learner will use the index of an encyclopedia to locate the volume and page number of a given topic, illustration, or map.

7. Given names or topics with two or more words, the learner will identify which word he should use to find that name or topic in an encyclopedia.

8. The learner will use the encyclopedia to answer given questions.

c. Magazines

1. Given a magazine, the learner will locate the table of contents, the year the magazine was established, how often it is published, the name of the publisher and editor, the volume, and magazine number.

2. Given the names of various types of magazines, the learner will

identify the kinds of information that would be found in each type.

3. Given questions or topics, the learner will identify those which would profitably be researched in magazines.

d. Newspapers

1. Given a newspaper, the learner will identify the headline, caption, column, editorial, index, sports page, weather report, or classified ads.

2. Given the name of a newspaper section, the learner will describe the types of information found in that section.

3. The learner will use the newspaper to answer given questions.

4. The learner will find a newspaper article dealing with a given event or topic.

e. Maps and atlases

1. The learner will identify the kinds of information an atlas contains.

2. Given a location, the learner will use the index of an atlas to find a map on which the location would be found.

3. The learner will identify different types of maps.

4. The learner will explain the similarities and differences between maps and globes, and the advantages and disadvantages of each.

5. Given the name of a device used in map reading-legend, index, latitude and longitude lines, time zones, scale, compass, etc., the learner will find it on a map.

6. The learner will explain the meaning and use of map symbols, colors, keys, and other devices used in map reading.

7. The learner will use the symbols, colors, or keys of a map to answer specific questions.

8. Given a map and a location, the learner will find the location on the map.

9. Given a map and two widely separated points on the map, the learner will indicate the route he would take to travel from one point to the other.

10. The learner will draw a simple map of his school, community, state, or country including items and locations specified by the teacher.

f. Graphs, charts, tables, diagrams

1. Given a graph, table, chart, or diagram, the learner will summarize the information it provides.

2. Given a graphic illustration, the learner will use the legend or key to identify the meaning of designated symbols.

3. Given a graph, table, chart, or diagram, the learner will answer questions about its content.

4. Given a line, bar, or circle graph, the learner will identify it by type.

5. The learner will describe the functions and advantages of graphs, tables, charts, and diagrams in a text.

6. Given explanatory sentences or paragraphs, the learner will match them to the graph, chart, table, or diagram they describe.

7. The learner will identify the types of information each type of graphic illustration best provides.

8. Given a graph, table, chart, or diagram with missing information, and a reading selection containing the missing information, the learner will read the selection and complete the graph.

g. Pictures

1. The learner will find a designated picture in the picture file.

2. The learner will describe the functions and advantages of accompanying written materials with pictures.

3. The learner will locate in picture files, magazines, etc., pictures to illustrate reading selections, his own written work, or class projects.

h. Specialized reference materials

1. Given a specific reference work, the learner will describe its content and use.

2. Given a list of questions and a list of specialized reference materials, the learner will identify the reference which would provide the answer to each question.

3. The learner will locate an article about a given subject in the Reader's Guide to Periodical Literature.

4. Given an entry from the Reader's Guide, the learner will identify the meaning of each item of information in the entry.

D. Use Effective Study Procedures

a. Follow directions

1. The learner will correctly follow written instructions for tasks and hobbies.

2. The learner will correctly follow instructions and rules for indoor and outdoor games.

3. The learner will correctly follow the directions, written or oral, for taking quizzes, tests, and examinations.

4. The learner will correctly follow directions to complete textbook exercises, classwork, and homework assignments.

5. The learner will correctly follow instructions to fill out forms and applications.

b. Determine appropriate sources of information

1. Given a topic or problem, the learner will identify one or more appropriate sources of information on that topic or problem.
2. The learner will use appropriate study sources to complete assignments.

c. Skim for general information

1. The learner will define skimming.
2. The learner will identify when and why skimming is helpful.
3. After skimming a given reading selection, the learner will identify its main ideas or general content. (Timed)
4. After skimming a given reading selection, the learner will answer questions about it. (Timed)
5. The learner will skim a given reading selection to locate specific information. (Timed)
6. After skimming a reading selection, the learner will describe the way in which the material is organized and presented. (Timed)

d. Read for main ideas

1. The learner will locate in a given reading selection the sentence or paragraph containing its main idea.
2. After reading a textbook chapter or other factual selection, the learner will identify its most important facts without referring back to it.
3. After reading a selection, the learner will identify its main ideas without referring back to it.

e. Read for details

1. The learner will read a selection carefully to find specified information to answer specific questions.
2. Given a reading selection containing errors, the learner will proofread the selection and identify each error.

f. Locate summary sentences or paragraphs

1. Given a reading selection, the learner will locate its summary sentences or paragraphs.
2. The learner will describe when and why summary sentences or paragraphs can be helpful.

g. Increase reading rate

1. The learner will read with left-to-right eye movement.
2. Given a sentence or paragraph, the learner will divide it into phrases.
3. The learner will read silently without pointing to each word or

marking his place, and without visible head or lip movement.

4. The learner will demonstrate decreasing fixations per line without loss in comprehension as shown by periodic measures of number of fixations, and responses to questions on the content of a reading selection.

5. The learner will demonstrate increasing reading speed without loss in comprehension as shown by periodic measures of speed of reading of given selections, and responses to questions on the content of these selections.

6. The learner will read silently without subvocalization, as demonstrated by an absence of unnecessary movements of lips, tongue, or throat muscles.

h. Adapt reading rate to nature, purpose, and difficulty of material

1. The learner will explain when and why his reading rates should vary with different materials and purposes for reading them.

2. The learner will indicate appropriate reading rates and methods for designated materials and purposes for reading them.

i. Survey and identify organization of material

1. The learner will survey given reading materials, and answer questions on the organization and format of the materials and on the author's method of presentation.

2. The learner will explain the value of surveying materials before reading them.

j. Recall information

1. The learner will answer from memory, questions about the main idea, important facts, and general content of a selection he has read.

2. The learner will recite a given selection from memory.

3. The learner will identify study aids to help in memorization and recall.

4. The learner will write only major points or key words about a topic and use these notes to give an oral report on the topic.

5. Given a set of directions, the learner will follow them from memory in the proper sequence.

6. The learner will describe from memory a specified character, item, or event from a selection he has read.

7. The learner will paraphrase from memory a selection he has read.

8. The learner will identify from a list of events or ideas those contained in a previously read selection.

k. Appraise adequacy of information and evaluate sources for authenticity and reliability

1. Given a selection containing facts and conclusions drawn from those facts, the learner will explain whether or not the facts warrant the conclusions.

2. Given a passage with a quotation and its reference, the learner will locate the reference and explain whether it has been justly quoted or whether its meaning has been distorted by taking it out of context.

3. Given a selection followed by questions about its content, the learner will state whether the information given is adequate to answer each question.

4. Given statistical information (graph, table, census data, averages) and generalizations or conclusions drawn from the information, the learner will identify those which are warranted and those which are unwarranted or false assumptions.

5. Given a selection expressing an opinion, the learner will state whether the author adequately substantiates his opinion with facts or logic, and will justify his answer.

6. The learner will explain why it is often unwise to use one source or one type of source to obtain information on a current event, historical event, or controversial topic.

7. The learner will use more than one source when seeking information on controversial issues, doing reports, or writing research papers.

8. The learner will explain the criteria he would use for choosing sources from which to obtain specified information.

E. Organize Materials

   a. Sequence information

      1. The learner will arrange items (bibliography entries, index entries, etc.) in alphabetical order.

      2. Given a scrambled set of sentences which make up a paragraph or passage, the learner will arrange them in logical order.

      3. Given a list of items or events from a familiar reading selection, the learner will sequence them in the order of their occurrence in the selection.

      4. Given a scrambled list of dated or familiar historical events, the learner will put them in chronological order.

      5. Given an incomplete series of items, data, or events in sequential order, the learner will fill in the missing parts.

      6. The learner will arrange main ideas for an oral or written report in logical order.

   b. Classify information according to identifiable rationale, criteria, or system

1. Given class concepts, the learner will identify members.
2. Given class members, the learner will identify classes to which they belong.
3. The learner will classify data according to an identifiable rationale or system.

c. Write summaries

1. The learner will identify the main idea of a reading selection.
2. The learner will summarize the content of a reading selection.
3. The learner will summarize a class discussion or lecture.
4. The learner will summarize a school play, film, or program.
5. The learner will summarize a personal experience.

d. Take notes

1. The learner will identify the features of good notes (e.g., brief, clear, neat).
2. The learner will identify the meaning of certain techniques used in notetaking (e.g., underlining, circling, numbering).
3. The learner will take notes on a given reading assignment according to indicated criteria (concise, numbered, abbreviated, comprehensive, etc.).
4. During a class discussion, the learner will take notes according to indicated criteria.
5. The learner will explain the value of taking notes and reviewing them as soon as possible after they are taken.
6. After reviewing his notes on a subject, the learner will summarize them.

e. Construct outlines

1. Given a reading assignment and its major topics, the learner will write the appropriate subtopics under each.
2. The learner will identify the series of numbers and letters and the format commonly used in an outline.
3. The learner will describe the value and use of outlines as a study aid.
4. After taking lecture notes, the learner will put them in outline form.
5. The learner will write an outline of a reading assignment.

f. Make charts, graphs, tables, and diagrams

1. The learner will identify the most appropriate form for illustrating given data (table, chart, graph type, or diagram) and explain why.
2. The learner will use given data to construct a graph, table, diagram, or chart.

3. Given a single set of data, the learner will construct a bar graph, a circle graph, and a line graph.

g. Construct bibliographies

1. Given books, magazines, and/or articles, the learner will list them in bibliographical form.

2. The learner will prepare bibliographies to accompany his research reports and assignments, or for the class to use as a reference.

h. Construct footnotes

1. The learner will list given books as they would appear in a footnote.

2. The learner will include footnotes where appropriate in his papers and reports.

i. Construct tables of contents

1. Given a book, magazine, or pamphlet with the table of contents concealed, the learner will make an appropriate table of contents for it.

2. The learner will make tables of contents for his research reports, or collections of his compositions, book reports, or other works.

j. Apply location and study skills to materials of personal interest independent of class requirements

1. The learner will indicate that he uses the library card catalogue to locate materials.

2. The learner will often include graphs, charts, tables, maps, and/or diagrams to illustrate assigned research reports.

3. The learner will list and find the meaning of unfamiliar words.

4. The learner will volunteer to make wall maps, charts, graphs, tables, or diagrams for class projects or school activities.

5. The learner will indicate that he uses newspapers and magazines as a source of information.

6. The learner will indicate that he helps to read road maps when traveling by car.

7. The learner will indicate that he carefully reads and follows the directions given for games and hobbies.

8. The learner will indicate that he frequently takes notes during lectures and class discussions, from reading assignments, and when doing research for projects and papers.

9. The learner will indicate that he skims and surveys reading materials when appropriate.

10. The learner will indicate that he practices the speed reading techniques he has learned.

11. The learner will indicate that he applies the memory techniques he has learned.
12. The learner will indicate that he organizes personal items and school work systematically.
13. The learner will indicate that he uses the library frequently to find materials of personal interest and information on subjects being studied in class.
14. The learner will indicate that he independently uses reference materials for specific information, solutions to specific problems, verification of data when doubtful, and as an aid to study.

k. Utilize a personal checklist to evaluate progress
1. The learner will record on a chart or graph his progress in various school activities.
2. The learner will sum the hours he spends per week on sleeping, grooming, meals, classes, study, etc., and make a table or graph describing this information.
3. The learner will evaluate his chart of daily activities and explain whether or not he spends an appropriate amount of time on each activity.

VI. Reading in the Content Areas
  A. Reading in Literature
    a. Recall title, author's name, and important details
    1. Given a selection from a familiar literary work, the learner will identify the author or the title of the work.
    2. Given a selection from a familiar literary work, the learner will identify the speaker, the person spoken to, or the person or object being described.

    b. Identify characters and describe characterization
    1. Given the title of a literary work, the learner will identify the main character.
    2. The learner will write a character analysis of a selected main character from a given literary work.
    3. The learner will explain the importance of a selected minor character to a given literary work.
    4. The learner will explain how the traits of a selected character are revealed in a given literary work.
    5. The learner will define terminology associated with the study of characterization.
    6. The learner will explain why a specified character in a given literary work acted as he did in a specified situation, or why the character held certain attitudes.

7. Given two characters similar in certain respects from the same literary work or from different works, the learner will identify their similarities and differences.

c. Describe plot and structure

1. The learner will define terminology associated with the study of plot and structure.

2. The learner will write a brief plot summary of a given literary work.

3. The learner will identify the protagonist, antagonist, or the conflict of a given literary work.

4. The learner will identify or discuss specified structural elements of a given literary work.

5. Given the titles of two literary works with similar plots, the learner will identify their similarities and differences.

d. Describe setting

1. The learner will identify or discuss a setting of a given literary work.

2. The learner will identify the means used by the author to establish the setting of a given literary work.

3. The learner will define terminology associated with the study of setting.

4. Given the titles of two literary works with similar settings, the learner will identify their similarities and differences.

e. Describe literary devices and techniques

1. The learner will identify examples of syntactical or mechanical deviations from standard construction in given passages from a literary work.

2. Given a passage from a literary work with deviations from normal syntax or mechanics, the learner will explain the effects of the deviations on the selection as a whole.

3. The learner will identify the point of view used in a given literary work.

4. The learner will explain the effects of point of view of a given literary work.

5. The learner will identify regular and irregular patterns of sound in given poems.

6. The learner will explain the effects of a repetitive sound on a given poem as a whole.

7. The learner will identify important chronological, structural, or spatial techniques in a given literary work.

8. The learner will explain the effects of specified chronological, structural or spatial techniques in a given literary work.

9. The learner will define terminology associated with the study of literary devices and techniques.

f. Describe symbolism and figurative language

1. The learner will identify figures of speech in a given literary work.

2. The learner will explain the effects of the figurative language in a given literary work.

3. Given a literary work or a passage from a literary work in which one image dominates, the learner will identify the image and explain how it is developed throughout the work or passage.

4. Given a literary work whose theme or conflict is represented symbolically, the learner will explain the symbolism and how it operates in the work.

5. The learner will define terminology associated with the study of symbolism and figurative language.

g. Describe diction, usage, and tone

1. The learner will identify the tone of a given literary work.

2. The learner will explain how the tone of a given literary work is established.

3. The learner will explain how the diction of a given literary work or passage contributes to the work or passage as a whole.

4. Given a literary work or passage in which the level or levels of usage play a significant part, the learner will identify the level or levels and explain the significance of the usage.

5. The learner will define terminology associated with the study of diction, usage, and tone.

h. Describe theme

1. The learner will identify the theme of a given literary work.

2. The learner will explain how the theme of a given literary work is established and developed.

3. The learner will describe the similarities and differences in theme in two given literary works with similar themes.

i. Describe genre

1. The learner will identify examples of the major genres of literature.

2. The learner will identify examples of forms within the major genres, such as epics, ballads, and lyrics as forms of poetry.

3. The learner will describe the conventions of a given form.

4. The learner will define terminology associated with the study of genre.

j. Evaluate author's purpose, values, theme, relevance, effectiveness

1. The learner will describe the values expressed in a given literary work and the means by which these values are expressed.

2. The learner will state his personal judgment of the author's values in a given literary work.

3. The learner will state whether or not the author of a given literary work expressed his purpose effectively and will give reasons for his judgment.

4. The learner will state whether or not he agrees with the author's statement or theme as expressed in a given literary work and give reasons for his judgment.

5. The learner will state whether or not a given literary work was relevant or meaningful to him and will give reasons for his judgment.

B. Reading in Social Sciences

  a. Define terminology commonly used in social sciences

    1. The learner will define terms and abbreviations commonly used in the study of the social sciences.

  b. Recognize order and sequence

    1. The learner will identify the order in which a designated series of events occurred.

    2. The learner will identify the minor events which led to a major historical event.

  c. Identify cause and effect relationships

    1. Given a social passage about a major historical or current event, the learner will identify or discuss the causes which provoked or precipitated the event.

    2. Given a social science passage about an historical event or phenomenon, the learner will identify or discuss its effects.

    3. Given a passage, article, or editorial concerning a contemporary problem or recent event, the learner will identify or discuss possible outcomes or future consequences.

    4. Given reading material about a current issue or problem, the learner will identify the outcome he considers most favorable and explain why.

    5. The learner will discuss the difficulty in determining certain direct cause and effect relationships when studying social or historical phenomena.

  d. Make inferences and generalizations

    1. Given a reading selection such as a doctrine, law, or ammendment to the Constitution, the learner will identify its practical implications or applications.

  e. Analyze problems and propose solutions

1. Given current social, political, or economic problems, the learner will identify from among several solutions the one which he considers the best and explain why.

2. After reading about a current social, political, or economic problem or a controversial issue, the learner will propose a reasonable solution to the problem.

3. Given an article or editorial in which the author presents his views about how a current problem should be solved, the learner will explain why he agrees or disagrees with the author.

f. Compare and contrast facts and opinions

1. Given reading selections on an historical problem, event, or movement, and on a similar current problem, event, or movement, the learner will identify the similarities and differences.

g. Select and read social science materials of personal interest independent of school requirements

1. The learner will indicate that he regularly reads newspapers and news magazines.

2. The learner will indicate that he reads and enjoys historical books and novels.

3. The learner will indicate that he frequently reads and enjoys books and articles about politics, social issues, different peoples and cultures, etc.

C. Reading in Science

a. Define terminology commonly used in science

1. The learner will identify the meaning of terms commonly used in the study of science.

b. Identify main ideas and major concepts

1. Given a written description of an experiment, the learner will identify its main idea or purpose.

c. Identify details

1. The learner will identify in a given reading selection the observations or procedures made in testing or studying a designated hypothesis, prediction or problem.

d. Recognize order and sequence

1. Given a science reading selection about natural phenomena occurring in sequence, the learner will identify the sequence in which the phenomena occur.

e. Infer cause-and-effect relationships

1. Given a passage about a physical or biological phenomenon in which the causes of the phenomenon are only implied, the learner will identify these causes.

2. Given a list of explanations for various natural phenomena, the learner will identify those explanations which are based on superstition or folklore, and those which are scientifically sound.

3. Given a passage about a natural phenomenon in which the effects of the phenomenon are only implied, the learner will identify those effects.

4. Given a passage about the technological applications of a scientific discovery, the learner will identify the actual or possible effects of such an application.

5. Given a passage about experimental findings, the learner will identify the possible implications or consequences of the findings.

6. Based on information obtained in given reading selection, the learner will make a reasonable prediction about the outcome of an experiment.

f. Distinguish fact from opinion, hypothesis, and theory.

1. The learner will identify given statements as hypothesis, theory, or scientific law.

2. The learner will identify in a given magazine or newspaper an article on a recent scientific development or discovery, the hypothesis proposed, the facts it is based on, and the opinions of the scientist(s) involved.

g. Relate present reading to current problems

1. After reading about a recent scientific experiment or discovery, the learner will identify specific ways of applying this knowledge to improve our life style or to solve current problems in technology, medicine, ecology, etc.

2. The learner will apply knowledge gained in readings on science to identify or suggest possible solutions to current problems.

3. The learner will locate and discuss reading selections about how science and technology have contributed to the destruction or defacement of the environment or endangered human life.

4. The learner will locate and discuss reading selections about how the same scientific discovery can be used for both constructive and destructive purposes.

5. The learner will locate and discuss reading selections about discoveries in pure science and how they have contributed to applied science and improved our life style.

h. Select and read science related materials of personal interest independent of school requirements

1. The learner will indicate that he reads science news in periodicals and newspapers.

2. The learner will indicate that he frequently reads science-related materials independent of classroom requirements.

D. Reading in Mathematics

a. Define terminology commonly used in mathematics

1. The learner will define terms and symbols commonly used in the study of mathematics.

b. Identify the problem

1. Given a word problem, the learner will identify the mathematical concept involved.

c. Distinguish between relevant and irrelevant information

1. The learner will identify information which is essential and information which is unnecessary to the solution of a given word problem.

d. Make generalizations

1. Given a reading selection explaining a math concept, process, or principle, the learner will explain how the concept, process, or principle can be applied to solve math problems.

2. The learner will identify ways in which math can be useful in daily life.

The preceding pages have attempted to give the reader an understanding of the basic environmental, instructional, and organizational plans for teaching reading to secondary school-age youth with educational handicaps and chronically disruptive youth. Additionally, specific objectives related to the basic reading skills have been presented and operational performance objectives have been formed. It is hoped that the practitioner, regardless of the educational setting, will find utility in the approaches presented for educationally handicapped adolescents.

REFERENCES

Allen, R. L. "Better Reading Through the Recognition of Grammatical Relations." *The Reading Teacher* (December 1964).

Atkinson, R. C., and Fletcher, J. D. "Teaching Children to Read With a Computer." *The Reading Teacher* 25 (1972): 319.

Barbe, W. B. *Educators Guide to Personalized Reading Instruction.* Englewood Cliffs, New Jersey: Prentice Hall, 1961.

Bloom, B. S.; Hastings, J. T.; and Madaus, G. E. *Handbook on Formation and Summative Evaluation of Student Learning.* New York: McGraw-Hill, 1971.

Buchannon, C., and Sullivan Associates. *Sullivan Programmed Readers.* New York: McGraw-Hill Book Company, 1963.

Carroll, J. *Theoretical Models and Processes of Reading.* International Reading Association, 1970.

Cramer, W., and Trent, R. *Performance Objectives.* Cincinnati: Horizon Publishers, Inc., 1972.

Downing, J. *The Initial Teaching Alphabet Explained and Illustrated.* London: Cassell; and New York: MacMillan, 1964.

Dunn, L. M. "Special Education for the Mildly Retarded—Is Much of It Justified?" *Exceptional Children* 35 (1968): 5–22.

Ekwall, E. *Diagnosis and Remediation of the Disabled Reader.* Boston: Allyn and Bacon, Inc., 1976.

Ellson, D. G.; Harris, P.; and Barber, L. "A Field Test of Programmed and Directed Tutoring." *Reading Research Quarterly* 3 (1968): 307–368.

Fagen, S.; Long, N.; and Stevens, D. *Teaching Children Self-Control.* Columbus, Ohio: Charles C. Merrill Publishing Company, 1975.

Fox, G. A., and Fox, R. B. "The Individualized Reading Controversy." *The National Elementary Principal* 44 (September 1964): 46–49.

Gagne, R. M. *The Conditions of Learning.* New York: Holt, Rinehart, and Winston, 1965.

Glavin, J. P.; Quay, H. C.; Annesley, H. R.; and Werry, J. S. "An Experimental Resource Room for Behavior Problem Children." *Exceptional Children* 38 (1971): 131–137.

Guerriero, C. A., and Mauser, A. J. "A Life Roles Curriculum for Special Education Pupils." Unpublished paper, Northern Illinois University, 1974.

Hammill, D. D., and Bartel, N. R. *Teaching Children with Learning and Behavior Problems.* Boston: Allyn and Bacon, 1975.

Kerber, J. E. *The Tasks of Teaching Reading.* Worthington, Ohio: Charles A. Jones Publishing Co., 1975.

Mager, R. F. *Preparing Instructional Objectives.* Palo Alto, California: Fearon Publishers, Inc., 1962.

Mauser, A. J. "The Paraprofessional Panacea or Frankestein?" *Contemporary Education* 42 (January 1970): 139–140.

McCullough, C. "Reading and Realism." 1968 Convention Proceedings, International Reading Association, 1968.

McDonald, F. F. and Moorman, G. B. "Criterion Referenced Testing for Functional Literacy." *Journal of Reading* (February, 1974).

Montague, E. J., and Butts, D. P. "Behavioral Objective." *The Science Teacher* 35 (1968): 33–35.

Moore, O. K. "Autoletic Responsive Environments and Exceptional Children." *The Special Child in Century 21.* Edited by J. Hellmuth. Seattle, Washington: Special Child Publications, 1964, p. 95.

O'Reilly, R. P. *A System of Objectives in Reading.* Manual Draft, New York State Education Department, 1971.

Olson, W. C. *Child Development.* Boston: D. C. Heath and Co., 1949.

Reger, R. "What Is a Resource Room?" *Journal of Behavior Disabilities* 6 (1973): 15-21.

Rice, D. R. "Educo Therapy: A New Approach to Delinquent Behavior." *Journal of Learning Disabilities* 3 (January 1970).

Roman, M. *Reaching Delinquents Through Reading.* Springfield: Charles C. Thomas, 1957.

Sabatino, D. A.; Mauser, A. J.; and Skok, J. "Educational Practices in Correctional Institutions." *Behavioral Disorders* (1975): 21-26.

Sabatino, D. A. "An Evaluation of Resource Rooms for Children With Learning Disabilities." *Journal of Learning Disabilities* 4 (1971): 84-93.

Spache, G. *Investigating the Issues of Reading Disabilities.* Boston: Allyn and Bacon, Inc., 1976.

Veatch, J. *Individualizing Your Reading Program.* New York: G. P. Putnam's Sons, 1959.

Weiderholt, J. L. "Planning Resource Rooms for the Mildly Handicapped." *Focus on Exceptional Children* 5 (January 1974): 1-10.

Woodcock, R., and Clark, C. L. *Peabody Rebus Reading Program.* Circle Pines, Minnesota: American Guidance Service, 1969.

developing reading skills for nonreading youths

AUGUST J. MAUSER

The purpose of this chapter is to offer secondary teachers, special educators in high school programs, and correctional educators at all levels, specific word analysis strategies and reading comprehension skill approaches for teaching nonreading and functional nonreaders. Additionally, ideas related to basic reading instruction will be included along with suggestions for choosing reading materials for problem adolescents and chronic disruptive youth. The content of this chapter does not generally address the student reading above second grade level, although some of the word attack skills may be taught to readers in the second to ninth grade level. Any student reading with comprehension above the beginning fourth grade level is a functional reader and with remediation can succeed learning a technical reading vocabulary.

SEQUENTIAL OUTLINE OF WORD ATTACK SKILLS

Numerous texts and resource materials have provided extensive coverage of the content of structural and phonetic analysis and have discussed approaches to teaching structural and phonic analysis skills. Many teachers of educationally handicapped adolescents and chronic disruptive youths have indicated a need for a short summary of the most useful word identification generalizations, and for a sequential outline of word attack skills that would serve to guide their teaching. This section is intended to provide the teacher with both of these. Cramer, Dorsey and Mauser

(1975), in *How to be a Word Detective,* offer activities and procedures in word analysis skills suitable for problem adolescents and disruptive youth.

Heilman (1968) in his text, *Phonics in Proper Perspective,* points out that the teacher must understand that phonic analysis is one of several means by which children can "solve" words not known as sight words, and that they must note that phonics is related to, and interacts with, all other methods of word analysis—including: (1) Word Form or Configuration (All words can be said to have a unique configuration or to be unique in appearance; so while learning to discriminate word forms he notes such limited factors as the length of words or special features such as *tt, ll, oo,* or final *y*. As students expand their reading, these unique features become common to large numbers of words.); (2) Structural Analysis (identification of root words, prefixes, suffixes, and inflectional endings, i.e., structural changes which differentiate be-tween words having common roots); and (3) Context Clues (the context in which an unknown word appears is useful in suggesting what the word might be). Heilman (1968) offers the following principles which should guide the teacher's effort to provide students with a flexible approach to attacking new words.

1. For any student to profit from systematic instruction in phonics, he must have the ability to discriminate between similar speech sounds. To attempt to teach numerous phonic generalizations in the absence of auditory discrimination equal to the learning task is not only inadvisable from the standpoint of learning, but is often detrimental to the learner.

2. Auditory and visual training should be blended and taught simultaneously. Phonics (as it relates to reading) is teaching speech-sound equivalents for printed letters and letter combinations. Thus, a student must be able to recognize instantly and discriminate visually between printed letter symbols. For example, a student who can differentiate between the sounds of *bee* and *dee*, but cannot visually discriminate be-tween the printed symbols of *b* and *d*, cannot apply phonics in a reading situation which involves words containing these symbols.

3. Any instructional practice which produces a learning set, which in itself inhibits the development of reading for meaning, merits re-appraisal. If reading is "getting meaning," students should not be conditioned in beginning reading instruction to equate reading with sounding or word analysis. Practices followed in beginning reading instruction *do* inculcate a "set" in the learner. In the golden age of phonics, many children *did* develop the set that pronouncing words was reading. Sounding out words is a needed skill, but the facile reader will apply it

only when necessary; and the less analysis that is needed in a given reading situation, the more efficient and meaningful will be the reading.

4. All phonic facts and generalizations necessary for a student to become an independent reader should be taught.

5. For a student to learn to read, it is not necessary for him to learn phonic generalizations which may have extremely limited application. A teacher accepting this principle will have to arrive at a conclusion as to what rules actually fit under this classification. Individual teachers may resolve this problem by answering questions such as the following in regard to each phonic generalization they propose to teachers.

  a. What contribution will this generalization make in the "learning-to-read process"?

  b. Does this generalization apply to enough words which the child will meet in his current reading program to justify my teaching it *now*?

6. Instructional practice which leads to overreliance on one method of word attack is indefensible. In any reading situation, words appear in context; many words have prefabricated sound-sight units such as prefixes, suffixes, inflectional endings, and root words in compound words. To teach reliance on context clues alone would be equally indefensible. It is wasteful not to attack an unknown word simultaneously on every possible front.

7. All remedial teachers should be familiar with an entire phonics program. All teachers of reading, regardless of grade level, will probably find it necessary to teach certain phonic skills to some students. Thus, familiarity with all steps in phonics instruction is essential. (See the teacher phonics test and test yourself.)

8. A thorough and ongoing diagnosis of each child's needs and present knowledge is a prerequisite for following sound principles of teaching phonic skills. It is not desirable to teach more phonics than a given child needs or to omit teaching needed skills not yet mastered. Diagnosis is the key to achieving this proper balance.

9. Knowledge of phonic generalizations (rules) does not assure ability to apply these generalizations in reading situations. Both in teaching and learning, the process of sounding out words must be differentiated from learning rules. Some children can recite a given rule and yet not have the ability to apply or practice what it tells them to do. On the other hand, knowledge of phonic generalizations is useful. In general, material should be presented in such a way that the application of a given generalization evolves out of actual word study. At best, phonic

generalizations are a crutch which may have utility at certain points on the learning continuum. A reader who is continually groping for a rule to apply when he meets a word not known as a sight word is not a facile reader.

Phonic analysis

Phonics is a facet of reading instruction which teaches speech sounds of letters and groups of letters in words. Phonic analysis is the process of sounding letters and letter combinations to arrive at the pronunciation of words. Phonic analysis is concerned with: (1) consonants; (2) double consonants; (3) consonant digraphs; (4) consonant blends; (5) vowels; (6) vowel digraphs; (7) vowel diphthongs; and (8) vowels modified by consonants.

Consonants. Consonants may be identified by saying they are all the letters of the alphabet except the vowels. There are nineteen consonant letters and the two semi-vowels *y* and *w*. They are often classified as voiced, such as the consonant sounds heard at the beginning of *bat, done, gone, jam, very, there, zoo, many, not, lake, ran, you,* and *wit*; and unvoiced, such as those heard at the beginning of *put, two, keep, child, fat, think, shoot,* and *hop.*

Certain consonants are relatively consistent in the sounds they represent. For example, *f, j, m, n, r, v, y,* and *z* almost always represent the sounds heard in the initial part of the following words: *fell, jug, many, not, ran, veil, yes,* and *zero.* It should be noted, however, that the letter *f,* usually unvoiced as in *off,* is occasionally voiced as *v* in *of.*

The letter *y* is a consonant which records the sound heard in the initial part of words like *year* and *yourself.* In certain instances, generally at the end of a syllable, *y* represents sounds associated with vowels. For this reason, the request, "Name the vowels," is often answered by *a, e, i, o, u,* and sometimes *y. Y* may record the long or short *i* sounds as *my, cry,* or *myth. Y* may also represent the long *e* sound as in *merry* or *heavy.*

The consonants *b, h, k, l, p, t,* and *w* are also fairly consistent in the sounds they represent. They most often represent the sounds heard in the initial part of the words: *bird, hand, key, light, pan, top,* and *went.* There are instances, however, when the foregoing consonants are silent or represent phonemes other than the most common ones. For example:

B—When *b* follows *m* in a syllable, or precedes *t* in a syllable, it is silent (*climb, dumb, debt, doubt*).

H—When *h* is the first letter in a word, it most often sounds as it does in *hand,* but it is sometimes silent as in *hour.* The letter *h* is silent at the beginning of a word when it is preceded by *g, k,* and *r* (*ghoul, khan, rhetoric, ghetto, rhubarb*).

K—When a word begins with *kn*, the *k* is silent (*knife, know*).

P—The letter *p* is silent when it is the first letter of a word and is followed by *s* (*psalm, psychology*).

T—The letter *t* is silent when it precedes *ch* in a syllable (*pitcher, watch*). The letter *t* may represent *sh* when followed by *ion, ial, ious,* or *ient,* as in *portion, partial, cautious,* and *patient.* The letter *t* also represents *ch* when followed by *u* in *virtue, actual,* and *picture.*

W—When *w* is followed by *r,* the *w* is silent (*write, wrong*).

The other consonants, *c, d, g, s,* and *x,* are more varied in the sounds they represent. Actually, *c* and *x* are superfluous because they duplicate sounds already represented by other letters: *c = k* or *s*; and *x = ks.* In addition, the letter *q* is always written with a *u*; thus *qu = kw,* as in *quick.*

C—There are certain conditions under which each of the two sounds of *c* predominate. These are:

1. When *c* is followed in a syllable by *e, i,* or *y,* it usually has the sound associated with *s* or the soft sound, as in *cent, city, icy.*

2. When *c* is followed by other letters or is the final letter in a syllable, it usually has the *k* sound or the hard sound, as in: *camp, cup, arc, cat.*

G—Like *c,* the letter *g* also has sounds referred to as soft and hard. The letter *g* is usually soft (like *j*) when followed by *e, i,* or *y,* as in: *gentle, giant, gym.* When *g* is followed by any other letter or is the final letter in a syllable, it usually has its hard sound, as in: *go, ghost, rag.* Like some of the consonants referred to earlier, *g* can also be silent, for example, *gnat, reign.*

D—The letter *d* usually represents the sound heard in words like *did, do,* and *wanted.* Occasionally, however, when the consonant sound preceeding *d* in a syllable is that of a voiceless consonant, the *d* sounds like a *t* (*missed, kicked, puffed*). The letter *d* followed by *u* is sometimes like *j* (*individual*).

S—The letter *s* records the following sounds:

1. The unvoiced sounds as in: *see, ask, caps.*

2. The sound of *z* after a vowel or a voiced consonant as in: *goes, hers, pans.*

3. The sound *zh* or *sh* when followed by *u* as in: *sugar, sure, treasure.*

X—The letter *x*, like the letter *c*, does not have a sound of its own but represents the following:

1. The sound of *x* best represented by the letters *ks* as in: *box, axle.*

2. The sound of *x* represented by the letters *gs*, when *x* is preceded by an *e* and followed by a vowel: *exact, exertion.*

3. The sound of *x* at the beginning of a word: *xylophone.*

Double consonants. When a consonant is doubled, the first of the pair is usually sounded and the second is usually silent (*sitting, stirred*).There are two notable exceptions to this generalization. The first is when the letters *cc* are followed by *e* or *i*; the first *c* is hard and the second is soft, like *ks* (*accent, accident*). The second exception is when the letters *ss* are followed by *ion* and sounds like *sh* (*mission, passion*).

Consonant digraphs. The consonant digraphs are two-consonant combinations that represent one sound. The common digraphs are *ch, ck, gh, ph, sc, sh, th,* and *wh.* The more common sounds of these digraphs are:

ch as in chair, church

ch as *k,* as in chord, chorus

ck as *k,* in back, luck

gh when silent, as in high, taught

gh as *g,* in ghost, ghastly

gh as *f,* in rough, cough

ph as *f,* in phone

sc as *s* or *sh*, when followed by *e* or *i* (science, conscience)

sh as in she, wish

th as in their (voiced)

th as in then, with (unvoiced)

wh as *hw* in when, which, what

wh as *h* when followed by *o* (who, whole)

Consonant blends. Other combinations of consonants appear in our language so frequently that, even though the sound of each consonant is maintained, they are usually emphasized together as the blending of two.

ng sang	*pl* play
nk bank	*sl* sleep
bl black	*br* bring
cl clean	*tw* twin
sc scat	*str* strike
sk skin	*thr* three
sm smooth	*cr* cry
spl splash	*dr* dress
fl flag	*fr* frog
gl glow	*sw* swing
st stop	*gr* green
qu like (queen)	*pr* prince
squ like *skw* (square)	*tr* trip
sch like *sk* (school)	

Vowels. Vowels are speech sounds produced without obstructing the breath. The regular vowels are *a, e, i, o, u*. The letters *y* and *w* are semi-vowels. In phonics the particular sounds these letters represent are referred to as long vowel sounds, such as those heard in the initial part of the following words: *age, eat, ice, open,* and *use*.

The short sounds are those heard at the beginning of the following words: *ask, end, in, on, up*. Since these ten sounds are those most often represented by the vowels, they are given emphasis in phonics instruction. With each of the vowels having at least two sounds, it is important for the teacher to instruct children as to the conditions under which each sound predominates. Certain generalizations facilitate this instruction. In syllables which end with one or more consonants, the vowel is usually short: *sat, west, cup*. When there are two vowels within a syllable, the first is usually long and the second silent (silent *e* generalization: *cube, rage, keepsake*). The generalizations presented above, while helpful, will not always work. There are so many exceptions that other generalizations have been made about these exceptions.

1. The letter *i* is usually long when it is the only vowel in a syllable followed by *ld, nd,* or *gh* (*wild, find, sight*).

2. The letter *o* is usually long when followed in a syllable by *ld* (*old, behold, cold*).

3. The letter *u* is usually short when a syllable ends in *ous* (*jealous, dangerous*).

4. In the letter combination *ie*, the letter *i* is often silent and the *e* long (*field, piece*).

5. When the letter combination *ei* occurs in a syllable and does not follow *c*, it often represents the sound of long *i* (*height, feisty*).

Vowel digraphs. A vowel digraph is a two-vowel combination that represents one sound. Usually the first vowel is long and the second vowel is silent: *ea* (ē) *leap;* *oa* (ō) *boat;* *ei* (ē) *deceive.* Less commonly, the first vowel may be short or the second vowel may be sounded: *ea* (ā) *steak,* *eu* (u) *neutral.*

Vowel diphthong. A vowel diphthong is a succession of two vowel sounds that are joined in a single syllable under a single stress. Generally recognized are: *oi, oy,* (oy) *soil, toy; ou, ow,* (ou) *loud, cow.*

Vowel modified by consonant. There are three consonants which usually affect the sounds of vowels when they follow these vowels in a syllable. These consonants are *r, w,* and *l.* The most common modifications of the vowels when followed by *r* are illustrated below:

ar   arm
er   her
ir   thirst, girl, dirt
or   nor, order, forceful
ur   fur, curtsy, hurt

When *r* follows a vowel and is followed by *e*, other sounds result, as in the following:

ar   care
er   mere
ir   fire
ur   sure

When *w* follows *a, e,* or *o* in a syllable, it affects the sounds of these vowels:

aw   law
ew   few
ow   now

The letter *l* is more limited in its influence on vowels as it affects only the letter *a* as in *tall* and *hall.*

Vowels are also modified by certain consonants that precede them within a syllable, for example, when the letter *u* is preceded within a syllable by *d* or *t*, the resulting sound of the *du* or *tu* is a kind of sound represented by the letters *joo* or *choo* (*educate, gradual, mutual, punctuate*). When *i* is preceded within a syllable by *c, s,* or *t,* and is followed by another vowel, the *ci, si,* or *ti* is like the digraph *sh* (*facial, mission, action*).

A small number of generalizations about the relationship of sound to letter combination should be taught to children. These are generalizations that do not have an excessible number of exceptions. They offer best "first guesses" at word pronunciation. When using these generalizations on unknown words, children or adults may be incorrect, but still this approach offers an avenue for intelligent guessing at pronunciation. Generalizations recommended for teaching are:

1. When short words end in a consonant followed by *e*, usually the *e* is silent and the preceding vowel is long.

2. When two vowels come together in a word or syllable, usually the first is long and the second is silent.

3. The sound of a single vowel in a word or syllable ending in a consonant is usually short.

4. The sound of a single vowel in a word or an accented syllable, if it comes at the end of the word or syllable, is usually long.

Syllabication

Phonetic analysis of a word begins with the division of that word into syllables. Once a word is correctly divided, phonic generalizations may be applied to each syllable. The syllable thus functions as the unit of pronunciation. Some of the most helpful generalizations about syllabication are:

1. When two consonants appear between vowels, the division is normally between the consonants.

   num ber   *fan cy*   *scar let*
   In applying this generalization, it is important that consonant blends usually remain within the same syllable as in:

   a shamed   *ma chine*
   se cret   *rock et*

2. A single consonant between two vowels usually goes with the vowel following it.

   di vide   *se cure*   *u nite*

Accent

Accent is the emphasis given a syllable in a word (or a word in a sentence) that makes it stand out in comparison to adjacent syllables (or words). Some words may be accented in either of two ways with differences in meaning. For example, *absolutely* conveys more emphasis when the third syllable is accented than when the first syllable is stressed. Unfortunately, the stress patterns of American English words show much variation as to the sounds of the letters. In spite of these irregularities, however, generalizations regarding location of accented syllables are available. One of the most frequently reported generalizations suggests that the first syllable in two-syllable words is the accented syllable. This works well in many instances; but if the second syllable is also the root of the word, another generalization takes precedence: in derived or inflected forms of words, the stress usually falls on or within the root.

The following generalizations are commonly taught:

1. In most two-syllable words, the first syllable is usually accented.

2. In derived or inflected forms of words, the primary accent usually occurs within the root word.

3. In words containing a double consonant, the vowel preceding the double consonant is usually short and accented: *for bid′ den.*

4. Syllables containing long vowel sounds are often accented: *pa rade.′*

5. In multi-syllable words the first or second syllable has either a primary or a secondary accent: *su per vi′sion, re spon si bil′i ty.*

6. In words containing certain suffixes (*ion, ity, ic, ical, ian, ial, an,* and *ious*), the primary accent falls on the syllable preceding the suffix: *e qual i′ty, ter rif′ic.*

Guidelines for selecting and evaluating phonics material

Whenever an educational system or individual teacher desires to select materials which give emphasis to the teaching of phonics, it becomes readily apparent that there will be much material from which a selection can be made. The question immediately presents itself as to "Which material should be selected to produce the best results (quality) in line with good educational objectives?" A list of criteria for evaluation needs to be agreed upon by the selection committee. The seven guidelines listed below might be worthy of discussion in setting up a criteria or standards check-sheet.

1. The material should not develop skills which may handicap a student in later stages of learning.

2. The materials should be consistent with current research as to the way a student perceives printed symbols.

3. The materials should provide for extensive practice of the skills in normal reading situations where emphasis is given to the process using the printed page to stimulate thinking.

4. The materials should not force the child to become overly dependent on any one method of word-attack and thereby reduce his effectiveness as a learner.

5. The materials should introduce the skills at the academic skill level where the child is capable of learning them efficiently and successfully.

6. The materials should develop the skills inductively, proceeding from the known to the unknown and from the simple to the complex.

7. The materials should harmonize, not conflict, with the other materials used in the total reading program.

Structural analysis

Structural analysis is the means by which a reader identifies meaning units in words and sees relationships between inflected or derived forms and their roots. Structural analysis is concerned with:

1. *Roots Words or Stems.* A root word or stem is an original word base to which prefixes, suffixes, and inflectional endings (affixes) may be added. Generally the terms *root word* and *stem* are used interchangeably. In any case, the word base provides the essential meaning in the development of words through the addition of affixes. For example, *phone* is the root word for *telephone, brother* for *brotherhood, time* for *untimely,* and *jump* for *jumped.* One could list a very large number of English root words, but no attempt will be made to compile such a list here.

2. *Prefixes.* A prefix is a meaningful unit attached to the beginning of a word to modify its meaning. Actually, prefixes may give significant changes to the meanings of words. For example, the prefix *un* added to the root word *safe* makes the new word *unsafe,* which has an opposite meaning.

3. *Inflectional Endings.* Good definitions of inflectional endings have been given by numerous authorities. It is stated clearly and concisely as a meaningful unit which is attached to the ends of words "to

form plurals and the possessive case of nouns (*boys, churches, boy's*), the past tense, the third person singular, present indicative, and the present principle of verbs (*walked, walks, walking*); and the comparison of adjectives or adverbs (*bigger, biggest, sooner, soonest*)." Easily identified inflectional endings are *s, es, 's, s', ing, ed, er, est,* and *ly*.

4. *Suffixes.* A suffix is a meaningful unit attached to the end of a word to modify its meaning. A root word takes on a slightly different meaning when a suffix is added to it. For example, the meaning of the root *spect* is modified when the suffix *acle* is attached to make the word *spectacle*. A suffix may also serve a grammatical purpose. Examples of this occur when *er* is added to the verb *speak* to make the noun *speaker*, or when *able* is added to the verb *move* to make the adjective *movable*.

5. *Compound Words.* When two or more words are combined, a compound word is formed. The meaning of a compound word is different from the meaning of the first word plus the second. For example, the meaning of the compound word *masterpiece* is not the same as the meaning of the word *master* combined with the meaning of the word *piece*. A new and different word meaning results when the two words are joined together. A compound word may be written as a single word (*football*), as two words (*sport shop*), or a hyphenated word (*master-at-arms*).

6. *Contractions.* A contraction is composed of two words that have been shortened through the omission of certain letters. The following principles apply when adding affixes to root words:

I. A derivative or an inflectional form may be had simply through the addition of an affix (*refill, wordable, badly*).

II. When a root word ends in a single consonant, that consonant may be doubled before an ending is added (*fitting, dropped*).

III. When a root word ends in *e*, that *e* may be dropped before adding an ending that begins with a vowel (*emergent, advocating*).

IV. When a root word ends in *y*, that *y* may be changed to *i* before adding an ending (*dried, craziest*).

V. When a root word ends in *f*, that *f* may be changed to *v* before adding an ending (*shelves, wolves, calves*).

School books today are beautifully illustrated, and this helps the student understand the concepts presented in the written content of the book. Picture aids are helpful to the more advanced reader in understanding concepts that lend themselves to graphic illustration. Typical of this type of an aid is the science illustration.of the phases of the moon, or a social studies map of the United States. At all grade levels, the illustrations should clarify new reading vocabulary and enrich the pupil's concepts. The high school teacher must be careful in selecting picture material that reflects a limited reading vocabulary while not offensive to the more mature (chronologically older) but poor reader.

Configuration clues. The distinguishing shape or form of a word is called its configuration. Many words have distinctive configurations that serve as helpful clues to the reader in recognizing them. It is known that children characteristically have trouble with many small words that lack distinctive shapes, while they often learn with ease longer words such as *airplane* or *elephant*. The overall configuration of the word involves the length of the word, the height of certain letters, and the position of the letters that extend above and below the line. The position of initial and final letters is also important in determining word configuration.

The mature reader also uses configuration clues, but other word identification skills are very necessary. This is the case because the experienced reader has a much larger reservoir of words similar in general forms, and many words are similar in shape but very different in meaning.

Context clues. The use of context clues is an important technique used in the process of word identification. It is one of the many skills used by poor reading students, especially those of average or above intelligence. The mature reader uses context clues so frequently and effectively that he may not even be aware he is using them, nor is he aware of the valuable aid they serve in reading. The question "What word would it have to be to make sense?" is a common one teachers ask. Most teachers are aware that, like many other skills in reading, the use of context clues must be taught. They are not learned well through incidental teaching procedures. Research suggests that an average fourth grade student is able to use context clues to construct the meaning of a strange word about once out of each three opportunities. This indicates a need for thorough instruction in the use of context clues as a reading technique. The use of this method in reading is based on getting meaning from what is read and using this meaning to unlock the identity and meaning of unfamiliar words. In working with students, the teacher should exercise care in not allowing the use of context clues to degenerate to random "word guessing."

Although not exhaustive, the following clues are noteworthy:

1. *Definition.* The descriptive context defines the unknown word. (Tom and Dick lived next door. They were _____ _____.)

2. *Experience.* Children may rely on their past concrete experiences. (Jack gave his dog a _____ to chew.)

3. *Comparison with known idea.* The unknown word is compared to something known. (You do not have to ride; you can _____.)

4. *Synonym.* (When the captain gave up, the crew had to _____, too.)

5. *Familiar expression.* This requires an acquaintance with familiar patterns. (As they sat on the bank, Bill expected the fish to _____.)

6. *Summary.* The unknown word summarizes the several ideas that have preceded it. (Down the street they came. First there were the elephants, then the clowns, then the lions in cages, and then the performers. It was a circus _____.)

7. *Reflection of a mood or situation.* (The clouds were black. Scarcely any light came in through the windows. The whole house was dark and _____.)

Teaching the use of context clues should continue throughout all reading instruction. Many procedures may be used, but technical vocabulary in service, consumer education, career education, or vocationally related reading vocabularies are good examples of making a word meaningful through its context.

TEACHING WORD ATTACK SKILLS

The outline below presents a series of instructional tasks, and it is suggested that these tasks be taught in the order in which they are presented. The sequence presented is a logical one, although it is not the only defensible one. Also, it should be noted that the steps listed are only a bare outline of the major facets of instruction. For example, teaching consonant sounds is one step, but it involves at least two dozen separate steps, since some consonants have more than one sound. Teaching consonant, digraphs, and blends would include another thirty separate tasks. All steps must be taught, reviewed and taught again as needed. Diagnosis of individual pupil's progress will determine when, and how much, review or structured instruction is necessary. The teaching sequence is as follows:

1. Auditory-visual discrimination
2. Teaching consonant sounds
   a. Initial consonants
   b. Consonant digraphs (*sh, wh, th, ch*)

      c. Consonant blends (*br, cl, str*)
      d. Substituting initial consonant sounds
      e. Sounding consonants at the end of words
      f. Consonant digraphs (*nk, ng, ck, qu*)
      g. Consonant irregularities
      h. Silent consonants
      i. Sight-word, non-phonetic spellings
      j. Contractions

3. Teaching vowel sounds
      a. Short vowel sounds
      b. Long vowel sounds
      c. Long and short sounds together
      d. Exceptions to vowel rules taught
      e. Diphthongs

4. Syllabication
      a. Rules
      b. Prefixes and suffixes
      c. Compound words
      d. Doubling final consonants
      e. Accent

Sight word recognition

Sight words are usually those words which cannot be taught by the previously presented techniques. Sight words may also refer to the many short words of similar configuration which a reader must recognize by sight in order to read quickly and smoothly. Many of these words are taught in beginning reading but any word may be taught by the sight word method or methods in the classroom, or in remediation settings.

Methods

1. Usually the word is introduced by the teacher who uses it in a sentence to teach the meaning. The sentence is written on the board or on a chart. The word can then be underlined, framed, or circled. The students are encouraged to look at the word carefully while they say it. Next the word may be presented in phrases with other known words. Immediate practice in meaningful content is essential for both word recognition and comprehension.

2. When possible, present a new word in connection with a picture which enhances the meaning. The picture and the words are

presented together and the student may be asked what he thinks the word is. He is told if he does not guess it. He may refer back to the picture if he forgets the word. The picture is used to enhance the meaning and not as a crutch. Again, practice of the word in meaningful material is essential.

3.   Unusual configuration of sight words may be pointed out to aid in recalling them. Students seldom have trouble with words such as *elephant* or *grandmother* simply because of their appearance. Pointing out double letters in words such as *moon* or *button* may aid in recalling them. Words such as *went, want,* and *said* are too similar and are not taught by configuration clues.

4.   For students with poor visual memories, it may be necessary to add tracing to the above procedures. The student is helped to trace the word as he says the whole word. Tracing very large on the board, in the air, or on worksheets may be helpful with certain students having difficulty acquiring a sight vocabulary.

5.   The student dictates sentences to the teacher using words from the sight word pile that he is having difficulty remembering. The teacher writes the sentences on a chart or types them for the student. The student tries to read what he has said. The words being taught are again emphasized by circling, underlining, etc. This activity can begin with very short sentences or even phrases and go on to complete stories. Visual-Motor Word Study approach could be used with students having extreme difficulty in gaining an adequate sight vocabulary. The teacher could proceed as follows:

a.   The teacher chooses a few words with which the students are having difficulty. A word is presented on the board in a meaningful sentence which is read by the teacher.

b.   The teacher holds up a card with the word printed on it. The teacher pronounces the word and the students repeat the word softly to themselves several times.

c.   The student closes his eyes and tries to visualize the word. He opens his eyes and looks again at the word.

d.   The card is removed and the student tries to write the word from memory.

e.   The student compares his word with the original card noting differences if he is incorrect.

f.   The above process is repeated until he can reproduce the word accurately from memory.

g. Give immediate practice in meaningful context of the words so learned.

6. The kinesthetic method adds another dimension to the Visual-Motor approach. The word to be taught is presented in blackboard-sized script and pronounced. The student pronounces the word slowly as he traces it with his first or second two fingers. The letters are not named or sounded out. Then he tries to write the word from memory, saying it slowly as he writes. If it is incorrect, it is obliterated and he returns to tracing it again. Incorrect letters are not erased or corrected. The word is learned as a whole. A copy of the word may be put in a file to be referred to when needed in writing. The words learned are incorporated into his own stories. He never copies the word, but traces it, turns it over, and tries to write it. Gradually he will begin to remember the words and will no longer need to trace them. (The two methods presented above are slight variations of the method developed by Grace Fernald.)

Techniques

The following short drill type activities may be use to enhance the word recognition skills and should be used in conjunction with conventional reading material to develop word meaning and comprehension.

1. Write five sight words on the chalkboard. Read each one aloud and then ask the students to close their eyes. Erase a word and ask, "What is missing?" Continue until all words are erased. Then ask the students what the five original words were and write them again on the board. See who can read the entire group. Work in small groups.

2. In a pile of assorted words, write all difficult sight words in red for danger to alert the student that he must recall the word by memory.

3. Sort words according to whether they are sight words or words that can be sounded out. In a pile of flash cards that can be sounded out such as *cat, man, pin*, put some sight words such as *father, could, what, want*. Have the student sort them according to those which can be sounded out and those that must be remembered by sight. Provide a category tag for each group—a picture of an eye or an ear.

4. Place word cards needing more practice face down on the table. Each student draws a card and if he knows it, he may keep it. If he does not, he must return it to the pile. Then the next student has a turn. The student having the most cards is the winner. Discourage attempts to try to sound out the words or subvocalize. Set a time limit to

speed it up. Either the student recognizes the word immediately or he is guessing.

5. Use Dolch's Group Word Teaching Game for additional practice in recognizing basic sight vocabulary.

6. The teacher prepares a tape, reading the most common sight words. The student listens to the tape through earphones and follows a worksheet. The teacher's voice says "Number 1 is *guess*, Number 2 is *could*," etc. To test a child, give him a word list without numbers and let him mark the worksheet as follows: "Put number 1 in front of *guess*. Put number 2 in front of *could*," etc. Check by using a prepared key.

7. Use the Flash-X device to give rapid exposure of basic sight words.

8. Use the Language Master to teach new words or review those previously taught. Use the blank cards to program the most persistently miscalled words.

9. Ditto a sheet with groups of words with similar configurations such as: *went, want, kind, mind; am, an, at, me.* Direct the child to circle the word you read. The tape recorder could be used here to free the teacher to help another student.

10. Sight words used in phrases are put on oaktag strips. Games played with flash cards can be adapted using the phrase cards. Ready-made small phrase cards by Dolch can be purchased.

11. Have students fold a large piece of paper into squares. Write a word on the board and have the students write it in a square. Continue until all squares contain a word. Have the students illustrate the words. Teachers might have difficulty illustrating words such as *what* and *guess* but the students won't. A little pondering about the words will be beneficial. Let them tell about their pictures. This also develops their oral language and could be carried on to written language.

12. The teacher and students can make this game. Give each student a 5" × 8" card marked off into 25 blocks. The teacher writes a word on the board and each student writes it in any block on his card. Each card should have the same words but in different places. The teacher says, "Put a marker on a word beginning with *b*. If there is more than one word, put a marker on just one word." When a student has five in any row covered, he calls "Sight-O." He is a winner if he can read back the words he has covered. The game may be extended to two in a row or to blackout where the entire card is covered. One card can be used to call the words.

13. Picture dictionaries can be helpful in learning words and associating meaning. Encourage students to make their own dictionaries with either magazine pictures or their own illustrations.

COMPREHENSION OF READING MATERIALS

Factors effecting comprehension

According to Kaluger and Kolson (1969), the degree of comprehension achieved by a reader depends on several factors. First, the *physical condition* of the reader will affect comprehension level. It is obvious that a person with a migraine headache or a severe toothache will be unable to concentrate on the material sufficiently enough to attain a high level of comprehension, but it is just as certain, though less obvious, that minor physical anomalies can affect the degree of the reader's comprehension. Those people in a captive audience at a testimonial banquet who have fastened their belt too tightly and must sit passively through a speech, generally hear little of what the speaker says and comprehend nothing. The student with a sensitive nervous system or a defective perceptual process will find it hard to concentrate on what he is supposed to be studying and comprehending.

A second factor affecting the degree of comprehension is the *interest* of the reader in what the reading matter is about. Interest affects attention which in turn affects comprehension. Almost every college student in their academic life has had to take a course in which he was not interested but also antagonistic toward that particular subject. Reading for that cause was distracting and served as an excuse to stop reading. That attitude is what the functional nonreader faces in every reading assignment.

The third factor that affects comprehension of reading materials is the *level of difficulty* of the materials to be read. The authors of the material to be read generally make assumptions about the background of the reading audience. The book that you are now reading, for example, is for those with a college level reading ability. Additionally, it must be assured that the interest and enthusiasm of students is provided in any method or material selected.

The reader's *purpose* is the fourth factor that may affect reading comprehension. The good reader generally has the ability to modify the amount of comprehension needed to fulfill his personal objectives for reading the material. If the purpose is to be entertained, then the level of comprehension may be merely to identify oneself with a specific character and to escape from reality by vicariously experiencing his activities.

If, however, one is reading to pass a comprehensive examination, he will read carefully and try to assimilate the main ideas and their supportive data.

Sequence of comprehension skills

As with all reading skills, comprehension skills run from the simple to complex. Materials specifically designed for one skill should be used for maximum efficiency in mastery of that skill. Reading specialists generally accept these eight skills (Kaluger and Kolson, 1969):

1. Ability to locate answers. To become proficient at this task the reader must be able to distinguish relevant information from irrelevant information, and to skim to find pertinent paragraphs.

2. Ability to follow a sequence. Cause-effect relationships must be understood if the reader is to reproduce the story or events in order.

3. Ability to grasp the main idea. Basic to many other comprehension skills is the ability to skim the material in order to glean a total impression. Grasping the main idea gives the reader the scope and tone of the material to be read.

4. Ability to note details. Indepth studies require the use of this skill. Until the reader has mastered this skill, he is unable to see the relationship of details to the main idea.

5. Ability to determine organization. To fully comprehend factual material the reader must recognize elements such as introduction, body, conclusion, headings, subheadings, paragraph organization, and topic sentences.

6. Ability to follow directions. This skill is the amalgamation of noting details, determining organization, and grasping sequence.

7. Ability to read critically. Here the reader must engage the material in a dialogue in which he compares this printed material with other material or with the total conceptual background he possesses. He must be able to recognize and resist subtle persuasions (propaganda). It is an investigation calling for reason.

8. Ability to organize and summarize. This highest skill involves all other skills.

Specific comprehension skills

Additional skills related to comprehension of reading materials are listed below. These skills should be incorporated into the reading lessons designed for problem adolescents and chronic disruptive youths.

—Following instructions
—Classifying things and ideas
—Understanding sequence
—Comparing and contrasting
—Visualizing characters, settings, events
—Discriminating phrases, sentences, paragraphs
—Selecting the right meaning of words
—Understanding adverb and pronoun references
—Using punctuation as an aid in meaning
—Suggesting titles for a story
—Finding part of story for a specific purpose
—Making and using questions
—Distinguishing narrative from conversation
—Identifying declarative and interrogative sentences
—Finding major thought units
—Finding details for support of main ideas
—Recalling information for objectives
—Recognizing relevant and irrelevant parts
—Generalizing on given information
—Identifying time and place
—Discerning literal vs. figurative
—Finding main idea of a paragraph
—Deciding on subtitles
—Understanding diagrams
—Understanding maps
—Understanding graphs
—Understanding schedules
—Making inferences
—Predicting outcomes
—Drawing conclusions from ideas
—Using imagination
—Relating cause and effect
—Relating general and specific
—Classifying things
—Recognizing parts and wholes
—Recognizing relative sizes
—Sensing relationships between people
—Recognizing story plots

—Analyzing characters

—Identifying with story characters

—Recognizing emotional reactions

—Reacting to moods

—Relating story to personal experience

—Distinguishing fact from opinion

—Weighing facts and opinions

—Deferring judgment on inadequate evidence

—Passing judgment on evidence

—Obtaining ideas from many sources

—Perceiving analogous situations and ideas

—Evaluating content in terms of author's purpose

—Relating past and present

—Judging validity by author and recency

—Recognizing backgrounds for points of view

Rationale for teaching comprehension skills

Secondary-level educationally handicapped adolescents and chronic disruptive youths, like others, are concerned with relevance of materials and activities. The following are some examples of in-school and out-of-school purposes related to teaching comprehension skills to secondary level educationally handicapped students.

Functional Reading Purposes (in-school)

to understand what is asked for in math problems

to follow the sequence of a science department

to see cause-effect relationship of historical happening

to understand the questions on a teacher's test

to understand the questions on a standardized test

to detect subtlety in a poem

to interpret the constitution of a club

to learn the new cheer that has been printed and distributed before a big game

to learn the school song that has been printed and given to all new students

to follow directions for registering to use a tennis court

to read the pamphlets distributed by the guidance office

to read a report to the class of a project done independently

to report on current events in the newspaper

to participate in choral reading for the Christmas program

to read training rules for school athletics

to draw a picture about a story as one part of a group reading project

to find dates of the Civil War

to find names of famous black scientists

to find out what siestas are and why they are popular with Latin Americans

Functional Reading Purposes (out-of-school)

to read a menu in a restaurant

to follow directions for assembling or operating a Christmas present

to read the note left by some member of the family

to follow a recipe

to interpret signs for automobile drivers and pedestrians

to read the advertisement that came in the mail

to interpret the questions in the driver's test

to find who is advertising to give puppies a good home

to follow the map to a new friend's house

to read the instructions for operating the automatic washer and dryer

to learn the regulations for use of the YMCA swimming pool

to read a blueprint

to follow directions for using a popular car wax

to learn the fishing regulations for an inland lake

to find a number in the phone book

to order from a catalogue

to learn the new regulations for newspaper carriers

to read the instructions left by a neighbor for a Saturday cleaning job

to learn the material of an article of clothing on a shopping trip

to read the *caution* message on a dangerous product

Ideas related to teaching comprehension in reading

The following are a few classroom activities that can be used in developing skills related to comprehension for secondary-level educationally handicapped adolescents and chronic disruptive youths.

Memory.   Recognizing or recalling information as given in the passage.

a. Facts

Who did _____?

When did _____?

How many _____?

What are _____?

b. Definitions of terms used, and perhaps explained, in text

What is meant by _____?

What does _____ mean?

What meaning did you understand for _____?

Define _____.

Explain what we mean by _____?

c. Generalizations—recognizing common characteristics of a group of ideas or things

What events led to _____?

In what three ways do _____ resemble _____?

How did _____ and _____ effect (cause) _____?

d. Values—a judgement of quality

What is said about _____? Do you agree?

What kind of a boy was _____?

What did _____ do that you wouldn't?

Translation. Expressing ideas in different form or language.

Tell me in your own words how _____?

What kind of a drawing could you make to illustrate _____?

How could we restate _____?

Could we make up a play to tell this story? How?

What does the writer mean by the phrase _____?

Write a story pretending you are _____.

Interpretation. Trying to see relationships among facts, generalizations, values, etc.

a. Comparative—are ideas the same or different, related or opposed?

How is _____ like _____?

Is _____ the same as _____? Why not?

Which three _____ are most alike in _____?

Compare _____ with _____ in _____.

How does _____ today resemble _____ in _____?

b. Implications.   Arriving at an idea which depends upon evidence in the reading passage.

What will _____ and _____ lead to?

What justification for _____ does the author give?

If _____ continues to _____, what is likely to happen?

What would happen if _____?

c. Inductive thinking. Applying a generalization to a group of observed facts.

What facts in the story tend to support the idea that _____?

What is the author trying to tell you by _____?

What does the behavior of _____ tell you about him?

What events led to _____? Why?

d. Quantitative.   Using a number of facts to reach a conclusion.

How much has _____ increased?

What conclusions can you draw from the table (graph) on page _____?

How many times did _____ do _____? Then what happened?

How many causes of _____ can you list?

e. Cause and effect.   Recognizing the events leading to a happening.

Why did the boy _____?

How did the boy make ＿＿＿＿＿＿＿ happen?

What two things led up to ＿＿＿＿＿＿＿?

When the girl ＿＿＿＿＿＿＿, what had to happen?

Why did ＿＿＿＿＿＿＿happen?

Application.   Solving a problem that requires the use of generalizations, facts, values, and other appropriate types of thinking.

How can we show that we need a traffic policeman at the crossing at the south end of our school?

If we want to raise hamsters in our classroom, what sort of plans will we have to make?

John has been ill for several days. What could we do to help him during his illness to let him know how you think of him?

Analysis.   Recognizing and applying rules of logic to the solution of a problem; analyzing an example of reasoning.

Discuss the statement, "All teachers are kind and friendly."

Some people think that boys can run faster than girls. What do you think?

John was once bitten by a dog. Now John dislikes all dogs. Is he right or wrong in his feelings? Why?

Synthesis.   Using original, creative thinking to solve a problem.

What other titles could you think of for this story?

What other ending can you think of for this story?

If John had not ＿＿＿＿＿＿＿, what might have happened?

Pretend you are a manufacturer of pencils who wishes to produce a much better pencil. Tell what you might do.

Evaluation.   Making judgements based on clearly defined standards.

Did you enjoy the story of ＿＿＿＿＿＿＿? For what reasons?

What do you think of ＿＿＿＿＿＿＿ in this story? Do you approve of his actions?

In the textbook, the author tells us that ＿＿＿＿＿＿＿ felt ＿＿＿＿＿＿＿. Is this a fact or the author's opinion? How do you know?

This story has a very happy ending. Should all stories end happily? Why or Why not?

The author of our textbook apparently believes that the American colonists were right in their actions. Do you agree? What do you suppose the British said about the colonists?

Write a short story about your favorite person in history. Tell why this person is your favorite.

Suggested guide for a reading lesson

The following suggestions are primarily designed for teachers of secondary-level educationally handicapped adolescents and chronic disruptives preferring to follow a lesson plan. Once the materials to be used in the lesson are decided upon, the teacher may proceed accordingly. Remember, these are not rigid instructions but suggestions of how to stimulate the student's interest and to get him to think.

Discuss the title. What does the student think it means and what does he think it tells him about the story?

Discuss the pictures. Are the figures, places, or items depicted unfamiliar to the student? If so, they should be discussed. Ask him what the pictures mean to him, and if they give him a clue to what the story is about.

Check vocabulary. Be sure the student can pronounce key words in the story. Does he know their meaning? Can he use them in sentences? Can he get their meanings from context? If a word has more than one meaning, try to explain the other meaning, and then ask how the word is used in the story. If, when reading, he makes a mistake or cannot read a word, supply the correct word but keep a record of each error.

Oral or silent reading. Ask him to read aloud or silently, whichever he prefers. When teaching him to read silently for independent reading, try to set a purpose and suggest that he read to himself to see if he can find the answer. Then he can read it aloud. He can read a paragraph, a page, or more at a time, depending on the teacher's feelings about his ability to understand.

Check comprehension. With the reading materials closed, ask questions such as:

1. What is the story talking about?
2. What is the most important idea in the story?
3. Do you think the title was a good one, or would you have chosen another?
4. What makes you think . . . . .?
5. How do you know it is true? Why is it so?
6. What do you think will happen next?

Check for factual information. Ask questions of specific details such as, the color of something, the age of someone, the size of something, when something happened, who did something.

Help to skim read. If the student cannot answer questions, have him look back in the story to find the answer and read it aloud. If he has trouble, help him find the answer.

1. Ask whether it was at the beginning, middle or end.
2. Tell him the page the answer is on.
3. Tell him the paragraph the answer is in.
4. Give clue words to help find the answer.

List of words missing. For the next session, work out some little exercise or game using the words missed in the reading.

Give me a word that rhymes with _____. (Offer word that rhymes with missed word.)

What is the opposite of _____?

Give me a word that begins with _____. (Name the initial sound.)

Look at the story and find _____. (Name missed word.)

Enrichment/Overlearning activities. To insure that the student retains the basic concept from the selection, each lesson or session should include a variety of practice and enrichment activities. These might include teacher-made exercises or drills related to word analysis skills, field trips, guest lectures, or simulation or role playing activities related to the content of the materials read by the students.

Summary of needs to conduct a good lesson in reading are:

1. Know the ability level and specific deficit and strength areas of the student.
2. Determine the primary and secondary objectives for the reading lesson.
3. Determine and have ready all the materials needed to conduct the reading lesson.
4. Describe the step by step procedure to carry out the lesson. Be able to task-analyze those activities that give undue difficulty to the student.
5. Determine and have available those reinforcers that will motivate the students to initiate or continue the teacher-assigned tasks related to the reading lesson.

6. Evaluate the degree of effectiveness of each lesson presented to the student. Note specific problem areas and revise teaching strategies accordingly until success occurs.

The reading lesson is not to be presented in total and carried out in one session. Multiple sessions may be needed to progress through the total reading selection. The teacher may be required to progress through stages such as those listed below.

Stage I (first session)

—Introduction section through discussion of title, pictures, etc.

—Check vocabulary and introduce new vocabulary.

—Seat-work activities related to above.

Stage II (second session)

—Review previous session's activities.

—Read selection silently and have student respond to comprehension types of questions and check for factual information.

—Seat-work activities related to above.

Stage III (third session)

—Oral reading of selection. If selection is of great length, use a "sampling" technique whereby the student(s) read(s) orally selected paragraphs or pages. After doing this the student(s) can read the total selection to another student or into a tape recorder.

—Evaluation of progress in terms of stated objectives and enrichment types of activities.

Material selection

This section will aid the teacher of problem adolescents in selecting reading materials and aids relevant to efficient programming for such students. When selecting materials to be used in a program for secondary-level educationally handicapped students with reading disabilities, the teacher must consider five principal factors.

1. *Need.* Does the material meet the student's specific reading needs? Does he understand his needs and how these materials will help meet them?

2. *Interest.* Will these materials be of sufficient interest to sustain his motivation and attention? If he finds the materials boring, he is not likely to do well with them, and they could do more harm than good.

3. *Reliability.*   Are the materials too difficult for this student, and will he, as a result, experience failure? The difficulty level of these materials should be such that the student can realize success with them.

4. *Novelty.*   Has the student used this material or this type of material before? If so, it should not be used now if he has already experienced failure with it. Materials which are new to the student should be chosen when possible.

5. *Length.*   Can the student handle the materials in a time span which will not create frustration? The length or "time-expectancy" of the materials and lessons should be geared to the student's attention span. If assignments are too lengthy, the student may just give up.

Other evaluative criteria which may need to be taken into consideration where budgeting is concerned are adaptability, cost, durability, and consumability.

Determining the difficulty level of printed materials

As a teacher of secondary-level educationally handicapped adolescents attempts to locate suitable materials that are published, or writes and develops his own materials, it is important that he be able to determine the difficulty or readability level of the materials. There are several readability formulas that the teacher of educationally handicapped adolescents can use to find the approximate grade level score of written materials. In many cases, he will see utility in readability formulas in determining which of two different books having similar content is the easier to read. In this case, the teacher is more accurately comparing the relative difficulty of materials. There are two basic characteristics that appear whenever one considers any of the available formulas to determine readability levels of materials: (1) word difficulty—the greater the number of long or unusual words that the selection contains, the harder the selection is likely to be: and (2) sentence length—the longer and more complex the sentences are, the more difficult the selection is likely to be.

Different readability formulas when utilized on the same materials may oftentimes arrive at different readability levels. The difference occurs because word difficulty is defined differently in different formulas. Oftentimes sentence length is defined and determined differently. Flesch (1948) states that a word is difficult or easy according to the number of syllables it contains. The more syllables a word has, the harder it is. No attempt will be made to fully describe the Flesch formula here, but it basically involves counting the number of syllables in each 100-word passage associated with selected reading materials. Fry (1963) also proposes a practical readability formula. His formula includes these directions:

1. Select three 100-word passages from near the beginning, middle, and end of the book or materials in question.

2. Count the total number of sentences in each 100-word passage. Estimate to the nearest 10th of a sentence. Average these three numbers (add together and divide by 3).

3. Count the total number of syllables in each 100-word sample. There is a syllable for each vowel sound, e.g., cat—1, black-bird—2, continental—4. Do not be deceived by word size, e.g., polio—3, through—1. Endings such as -*y*, -*el*, or -*le* usually make a syllable, e.g., ready—2, bottle—2. Average the total number of syllables for the three samples. (See Table 7.1.)

4. Plot on the graph the location of these two points to determine the grade level of the material. (See graph presented.)

5. Choose more passages per book if great variability is observed and conclude that the book has uneven readability. According to the author, few books will fall in the gray area, but when they do, grade level scores are invalid.

Table 7.1. AVERAGE NUMBER OF
SYLLABLES OF THREE
WORD SAMPLES

Example	Syllables	Sentences
1st 100 words	124	6.6
2nd 100 words	141	5.5
3rd 100 words	158	6.8
Average	141	6.3

Factors that influence the difficulty of printed materials as they relate to readers of such materials definitely include the reader's interest in the content of the materials. His background of information as it relates to the content is also a factor. The familiarity of the reader with the kind of language which is used—in terms of syntax, semantics, and organizational patterns—are all prime considerations. Section and paragraph headings, illustrations, type, size of print, kind of paper, and even the cover of the materials may readily influence the readability of any material. Selecting the right and most important reading materials for secondary-level education-ally handicapped adolescents is one of the teacher's most important jobs. If the teacher gives the student materials that are too hard, the student will become bored with it and stop reading. Proper material selection and development is a great challenge for the teacher of problem adolescents.

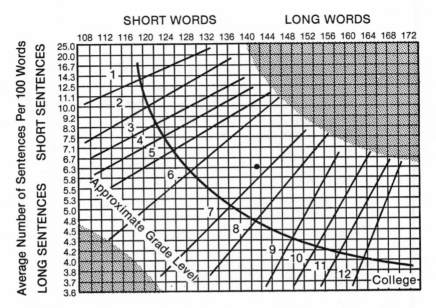

Figure 7.1 Average Number of Words and Sentences per 100 Words of Each Grade Level

High-interest, low-vocabulary reading

A list of selected reading materials purporting a high-interest, low-vocabulary rationale is presented at the end of this chapter. Teachers of educationally handicapped adolescents are encouraged to experiment with those materials listed. Selection, of course, will depend on the teacher's knowledge of the student's specific interests and dislikes. Previous experiences of failure with the items listed will also influence selection or rejection of the materials presented.

The books and materials are only some of the commercially produced items useful for secondary-level educationally handicapped adolescents with problems in reading. However, all these things cost money which may or may not be available. Therefore, additional activities will be suggested that could be used by the teacher of problem adolescents. These activities will aid instruction, but they will not depend on a cash outlay for materials. Many more such activities could be created by the teacher and put to equally good use.

Hip dictionaries are quite popular with students of all ages. If the student uses a lot of "hip" talk or a special language, let him make a "hip" dictionary. Every time he uses one of his rich colorful words, put it on a card, ask him what it means, look in the dictionary for words which might mean the same thing, and record the English definition for his word as well as some of its synonyms. Most students are excited about using new words that no one else will be able to understand.

Comic strips may be cut from newspapers and used for a variety of activities. Select those comic strips which contain an entire story each day (*Blondie, Nancy, Peanuts,* etc.)—not continued stories. The teacher reads the comic strip aloud, then cuts the strip into sections and asks the student to put the sections in order. Cramer (1973) offers excellent suggestions in using the total newspaper as a teaching device.

Hum *television commercials* and ask the child to guess the words. Words to a favorite television commercial could be written down and read by the student later—a type of language experience approach.

Popular songs may be used in the same way. Words to the student's favorite song could be written for him to read—another language experience approach.

Picture cards can be made by the teacher or the student. One card could have a picture and a word on it, and the student would match this card with another card that has only the word printed on it. The more sophisticated student would match a word card with a picture card (no word under the picture).

Scrapbooks can be made from a number of things and for a number of reasons. One student may cut articles from newspapers or magazines about a particular topic that interests him. He might read these articles or the teacher could read them to him if the words are too difficult. However, the student might learn some of the key words which have the most meaning for him.

Maps may be made by the student. He could make a map of the area he knows best—the area between his home and the school. The important things in his neighborhood should be put on the map. If the teacher and the student go on some kind of field trip the student could map out the trip.

Word games may also be played with the student, and he will learn new words without much effort. One type of word game includes choosing categories such as automobiles, or four-legged animals, or certain categories of athletes such as baseball players. Each person names as many words as he can for the category. This game can be played orally, or the words may be written down.

Another game might be one in which the first person gives a word such as *kangaroo* and the next player must think of a word that begins with the last letter in that word. He might think of *okay*. Some help may have to be given to young students who don't know what the last letter of the word is, but students love to try to stump adults with words that end in *x*.

"I'm thinking of a word that begins with the same sound as the word *bell*." In this game additional clues are given until the player gets the answer. "It is something we use in school." When the student guesses *book*, then he thinks of a word.

Teachers of problem adolescents can think of many more games which can be played for various types of skill development. Students often know some games of this type, too. Thus, not all instructional materials need to cost money. But what about the ones that do cost money? Where can the teacher of secondary-level educationally handicapped adolescents get some additional instructional materials?

One of the best ways to discover what kinds of materials appeal to the student would be to borrow some materials on a trial basis. If a particular book, game, or series of books has great interest, it may be worth purchasing. Materials might be borrowed from the public library, school administration curriculum libraries, university reading center libraries, and private homes. Visits to some of these places would be rewarding just because teachers might see what kinds of materials are available.

Community sources might be investigated for donations of materials. Local service organizations, and government agencies could be approached for donations of funds of specific materials. Locating materials for a successful reading program for problem adolescents takes time, but the results will be worth it. Don't overlook any possibilities.

SUMMARY

This chapter intended to aid the practitioner in developing specific strategies to teach secondary-age educationally handicapped children skills in independent word analysis and comprehension. Basic commercially produced materials are cited as tentative suggestions and alternatives to those materials developed personally by teachers working with this student population. A great void in available materials is quite evident. It is hoped that the next decade will provide the needed systems and materials that are critical to quality programming for such students.

MATERIALS FOR THE DEVELOPMENT OF WORD ATTACK SKILLS

Academic Therapy Publications
How To Be a Word Detective (Clues on how to unlock words as familiar as sight words.)

Allyn and Bacon, Inc.
Happy Times with Sounds Series (Complete phonics course, four books, grades 1–6.)

American Book Company
Reading Skillbooks (Two workbooks, word recognition and comprehension, grades 7–9.)

Beckley-Cardy Company
Beckley-Cardy Aids for Teaching Phonics (Series of workbooks, grades 1–6.)

Hayes Mastery Phonics Workbooks (Complete phonics source, six books, grades 1–6.)

Bureau of Publications, Teachers College Press
Reading Aids Through the Grades (Three hundred activities for grades 1-8 in remedial programs.)

Continental Press, Inc.
Reading-Thinking Skills (Spirit masters on comprehension skills, grades 1-6.)

Economy Company
Phonetic Keys to Reading (Basal phonic series, grades 1-3.)

Educational Developmental Laboratories
Word Clues (Filmstrips, tests, flash sets, grades 7-13.)

Educational Publishing Corporation
A to Z Phonics Charts (Twelve charts, basic elements, all grades.)

Educator's Publishing Service
A Phonetic Reader Series (Six phonics books, titles, grades 1-8.)

Educator's Publishing Service
Improving Word Skills (Workbook for intermediate grades—phonics methods.)
Word Attack Manual (Manual to be used for junior high pupils.)

Follett Publishing Company
Read Aloud Books (Forty-one books, book titles, grades 1-3.)
Turner-Livingstone Reading Series (Occupational reading workbooks, remedial, grades 7-12.)

Ginn and Company
Building Pre-reading Skills; Kit A and B (Complete set of visual materials—Prereading-first grade.)

Grolier Educational Corporation
Reading Attainment System (One hundred twenty remedial reading selections, grades 3-4.)

Harcourt, Brace and World
Speech-to-Print Phonics (Readiness programs, pads, cards, lessons, grades 1-2.)

Word Attack: A Way to Better Reading (Remedial reading text, see page 68 for high school.)

D. C. Heath and Company
Reading Caravan Series (Comprehension skills, remedial, grades 7-9.)

Holt, Rinehart and Winston, Inc.
Reading Skills (Texts, booklets, shutter cards, junior high level.)

Hough Community Project, Cleveland, Ohio
A Practice Workbook on Phonetic Instruction (Phonic workbook, see page 67 for junior high school.)

Kenworthy Educational Service
I Learn to Read (Two workbooks, grades 1-4.)

J. B. Lippincott Company
Basic Reading (Highly phonetic, workbooks, filmstrips, grades 1-8.)

Lyons and Carnahan
Phonics We Use (Phonics program for grades 1-8.)

McCormick-Mathers Publishing Company
Building Reading Skills (Set of six phonics workbooks, grades 1-6.)

Modern Curriculum Press
Phonics is Fun (Six books for grades 1-3.)

F. A. Owen Publishing Company
Instructor Basic Phonics Course (Five sets of materials, grades 3-5.)

Phonovisual Products, Inc.
Phonovisual Skill Builders (Charts, boards, filmstrips, etc., grades 1-4.)

Reader's Digest Services, Inc.
Reader's Digest Skill Builders (Independent comprehension builders, grades 2-8.)

Science Research Associates
Lift-Off to Reading (Basic phonic program, grades 1-6.)
Reading in High Gear (Workbooks for culturally disadvantaged, grades 7-12.)

Steck-Vaughn Company
Reading Essentials Series (Skills-comprehension building, grades 1–8.)

Systems for Education, Inc.
Reading A (Doman and Delacato's program, giant cards, films, grades 1–2.)

Teachers College Press
Word Attack Series (Workbooks for grades 1–4.)

Webster Division, McGraw-Hill Book Company

Conquests in Reading (Structural-phonic skills workbook, grades 4–6.)
Time for Phonics (Workbooks, grades 1–3.)

Webster Publishing Company
Webster's New Practice Readers (High-interest readers, grades 2–8.)
Keys to Your Reading Improvement (Work-text, phonic methods, grades 6–12.)
It's Time for Phonics (Four workbooks, phonics, grades K–3.)
Eye and Ear Fun (Phonics program workbooks, grades 1–6.)

MATERIALS FOR THE DEVELOPMENT OF COMPREHENSION

Acoustifone
Reading Achievement Program (Filmstrips and printed materials for junior high students.)

Allyn and Bacon, Inc.
Breakthrough (Series of four books with teacher's manual for vocabulary and comprehension.)

Bobbs-Merrill Company
Traxler High School Reading Test (Measures rate of reading and comprehension, grades 10–12.)

Bowmar
Bowmar Language/Communication Program (Book and dictionary series for general language skills.)

California Test Bureau (a division of McGraw-Hill Book Company)
California Reading Tests (Designed to test vocabulary and comprehension. The junior high edition is for grades 7–9 and the advanced test is for grades 9 to college.)
Comprehensive Tests of Basic Skills (An achievement test series for evaluating comprehension and reading vocabulary. Level 4 is designed for use with grades 8–12.)

Committee on Diagnostic Testing
Diagnostic Reading Tests (Contains a Survey Test which is useful for grades 7 through college and evaluates vocabulary, comprehension, and rate. Seven forms available.)

Developmental Reading Distributors
Maintaining Reading Efficiency (Exercises in reading skills, grades 7–12.)
Audio Reading Progress Laboratory (Set of tapes, progress books, and teacher's guide for junior high use.)

Educational Testing Service
Cooperative English Tests (Contains a section on comprehension. Four forms for grades 12–14 and three forms for grades 9–12.)

Encyclopedia Britannica Press
Language Experiences in Reading, 1 (Three books, word recognition skills, grades K–1.)

Field Educational Publications, Inc.
Checkered Flag Series (Books with high-interest, low-vocabulary range for reluctant secondary readers.)

C. S. Hammond and Company
Building Reading Confidence (Text-

book, comprehension skills, word attack, grades 5-6.)

Harcourt Brace Jovanovich, Inc.
Kelley-Greene Reading Comprehension Test (Group test which is designed to test listening comprehension of students on various subject areas, grades 9-13.)

Laidlaw Company
New Horizons through Reading and Literature (Comprehension skills, outlining, grades 7-9.)

Learn, Inc.
Rapid Comprehension Through Effective Reading Program (Series of three study books, tests, time and practice logs, paperback books.)

Lippincott
Reading for Meaning (Series of workbooks for junior and senior high use.)

Macmillan
Advanced Skills in Reading (Hardcover books and graded practice exercises.)

McCormick-Mathers Publishing Company
Building Reading Skills (Word recognition, phrase and sentence meaning, grades 1-6.)

Charles E. Merrill Company
Modern Reading Skill Text Series (Three books on comprehension, clues. tapes, grades 7-12.)

The Psychological Corporation
Davis Reading Test (Measures level and rate of comprehension and is composed of Series 2 for grades 8-11, and Series 1 for grades 11-13 with four forms for each series.)

SUGGESTED READING MATERIALS: HIGH-INTEREST, LOW-VOCABULARY

Key: R.L. - reading level
      I.L. - interest level
      P.P. - pre-primer
      P. - primer

Allyn and Bacon

  Adventures in Science with Judy and Joe (R.L. 1 I.L. 6)
  Breakthrough (R.L. 6)
  Winners Circle
  Beyond the Block
  This Cool World
  The Big Ones

Amsco School Publications, Inc.

  More Powerful Reading
  Vocabulary for the College-Bound Student
  Vocabulary for the High School Student

Audio Teaching Center

  The Imperial Junior High School (Grades 7-9)
  Reading Lab (Sold only as a set)

Bobbs-Merrill Company, Inc.

  Folk Tales Around the World Series (R.L. 4 to 6)

Book Lab Inc.

  The Hip Reader (R.L. Beginning to 6)
  Young Adult Sequential Reading Action Program (R.L. 6)

Children's Press, Inc.

  Presidents, Pitchers and Passers (R.L. 4 to 6)
  Open Door Series (R.L. 5 I.L. Jr. and Sr.)

Coronet Learning Programs from Coronet Instruction Films

Figures of Speech (R.L. 10–12)
How to Research and Write a Report
(R.L. 10–12)
*Vocabulary Growth, Divide and
Conquer* (R.L. 10–12)

Dell Publishing Co., Inc.
Yearling Books (R.L. 2 to 6)

Developmental Reading Distributors

Developing Reading Efficiency
(R.L. Jr. and Sr. High)
Maintaining Reading Efficiency
(R.L. Jr. and Sr. High)

The Economy Company

Guidebook to Better Reading (R.L.
Remedial Jr. & Sr.)
Six Supplemental Readers (R.L.
Remedial Jr. & Sr.)

Educational Activities, Inc.

*Developing Reading Efficiency (De-
velopmental)* (R.L. 7–10)
*Maintaining Reading Efficiency
(Diagnostic)* (R.L. Jr. & Sr. High)

Educational Developmental Laboratory
Study Skills Library
Science D to I (R.L. 4–9)
Social Studies, EE, FF, GG (R.L.
5–7)
Reference, FFF (R.L. 6)

Educators' Publishing Service

*Language Training for Adolescents
Teacher's Guide* (R.L. High
School)
*Reading Comprehension in Varied
Subject Matter*
Workbooks (R.L. 3–12)
Efficient Study Skills
Study Manual, Methods and Habits
*Spelling Workbook for Corrective
Drill*
Work Attack Manual
The Structure of Words
Vocabulary Builder Series

Pearon Publishers

Pacemaker Books

To Be a Good American
In your Family (R.L. 3.3)
In your Community (R.L. 3.6)
In your State (R.L. 3.9)
In your Country (R.L. 3.9)
Pacemaker Story Books (R.L. 2)
Adventures in Snow
A Bomb in the Submarine
Devils Rock
Island Adventure
The Haunted House
Mystery at Camp Sunshine
*Fourteen Remedial Reading
Methods* (R.L. 1–12)

Field Educational Publications, Inc.

The Americans All Series (R.L. 4.4
I.L. 3–8)
Chum Boy
The Magic Door
China Boy
Stranger at Cherry Hill
Free to Read (R.L. High School)
World of Ideas (R.L. High School)
Jim Forest Readers (R.L. 2–3)
Checkered Flag Series
Wheels (R.L. 2.4 I.L. Jr. & Sr.)
Scrambler (R.L. 3.0)
Riddler (R.L. 2.5)
Flea (R.L. 3.5)
Bear Cat (R.L. 2.5)
Grand Prix (R.L. 4.0)
Smash-Up (R.L. 2.6)
500 (R.L. 4.5)
Reading-Motivated Series
Desert Treasure (R.L. 4.5 I.L.
4–10)
The Mysterious Swamp Rider
(R.L. 4.7)
The Secret of Lonesome Valley
(R.L. 4.7)
Adventures in Apacheland
(R.L. 5.3)
*Cyclo-Teacher Learning Aid School
Kit*
Language Arts
Work Attack Skills
Vocabulary Syntax

Pronunciation
Spelling
Study Skills
Reference Materials
Reading and Understanding Maps

Follett Publishing Company

Interesting Reading Books Series
(R.L. 3 I.L. Jr. High)
Adventure in Space
Buried Gold
First Adventures at Sea
First Men in Space
Great Moments in American
History
The Indian Fighters
Mystery of Broken Wheel Ranch
Ten Great Moments in Sports
High-interest Easy to Read Books
(R.L. PP–3)
The Turner-Livingston Reading
Series
Slow Learners' Program (R.L.
7–12)
Vocational Reading Series
Turner Career Guidance Series
The Turner-Livingston Communi-
cation Series
Study Lessons in Map Reading
Social Studies-Study Lessons in Our
Nation's History
World History Study Lessons (R.L.
Jr. and Sr. High)
American History Study Lessons
Senior high slow learners
Study Lessons in Civics (R.L. Jr.
and Sr. High)
Study Lessons in General Science
(R.L. Jr. High)
English Learning Lang. I (R.L. Jr.
High)
English Learning Lang. II (R.L. Jr.
High)
Success in Language and Literature
Set A, Set B (R.L. 7–12)
Adult Education Programs
Reading for a Viewpoint
Systems for Success

Getting Started, Communications I,
II, III

Foster and Futernick Co., Inc.

Special Developmental Reading
Series (R.L. 7 and 8)
Adventures of Huck Finn
Anne Frank: Diary of a Young
Girl
April Morning
Around the World in 80 Days
Beany Malone
Because of Madeline
(52 other titles)

Garrard Press

Basic Vocabulary Series (R.L. 2
and 3)
Discovery Books (R.L. 2)
First Books (R.L. 1)
Folklore Books (R.L. 3)
Junior Science Series (R.L. 2)
Pleasure Reading Series (R.L. 3)
Reading Shelf (R.L. 1 and 3)
Indians (R.L. 3)
Scouting (R.L. 3)
Holidays (R.L. 3)
Sports (R.L. 4)
American Ace Books (R.L. 4)
Creative People Books (R.L. 5)
Creative People in the Arts and
Sciences (R.L. 5)
Defenders of Freedom (R.L. 5)
Legends and Folktales (R.L. 4)
Rivers Series (I.L. 4–7)
Century: Makers of World History
(R.L. 6 I.L. 4–8)

Ginn and Company

Discovery Through Reading (R.L. 7)
Achievement Through Reading
(R.L. 8)
Exploration Through Reading
(R.L. 9)

Globe Book Company

Modern Literature Series (R.L. 6)
Adapted Classics (R.L. 4–8 I.L. Sr.
High)

Social Studies for the Slow Learner
(R.L. 5.5 I.L. Sr. High)
Exploring World History (R.L. 5.5
I.L. Sr. High)
Exploring American History (R.L.
6.1 I.L. Sr. High)
Exploring Our Nation's History
(R.L. 5.5 I.L. Sr. High)
The Afro-American in U.S. History
(R.L. 5.5 I.L. Sr. High)
For the Slow Learner
   *Myth and Folk Tales Around the
   World* (R.L. 4)
   American Folklore and Legends
   (R.L. 4)
   Stories for Teen-agers
      Book A (R.L. 4)
      Book B (R.L. 4)
      Books 1 and 2 (R.L. 5-6)
   Stories for Today's Youth (R.L.
   4-5)
   Great Americans (R.L. 6)
   Great Lives (R.L. 6)
   Great Adventures (R.L. 6)
   Programmed Reading (R.L. All
   Levels)
   Better Reading (R.L. 5-8)
   Stories for Teenagers (R.L. 6)

Grolier Educational Corp.

Reading Attainment Series (R.L.
3-4)

Grosset and Dunlap, Inc.

An Early-Start Preschool Reader
Easy Reader Books (R.L. 2)
Signature Books (R.L. 6)
We Were There Books (R.L. 6)
Young Readers Bookshelf (R.L. 6)
How and Why Wonder Book Series
(R.L. 4-6 I.L. 7-9)
Illustrated Books (R.L. 4-6 I.L. 7-9)
Illustrated Junior Library (R.L. 3-9
I.L. 7-12)

E.M. Hale and Company

All About Books (R.L. 4 to 6)
Beginner Books (R.L. 1 and 2)
Easy to Read Books (R.L. 3)

Easy to Read Science Library
(R.L. 3)
Landmark Books (R.L. 5 and 6)
Zarra
Digging into Yesterday
From Kite to Kittyhawk
Insect Builders and Craftmen
Just So Stories
The Mystery Key
The Secret of Smugglers' Cove
Desert Dog
Mystery of the Black Diamonds
The Twenty-Six Letters

Harcourt Brace Jovanovich

Adventures in Literature Series (R.L.
7-12)
Design for Good Reading (R.L.
Developmental for high school)

Harper and Row

Scope Series (R.L. High School)
Workbooks for English
Creative Writing Series (R.L. Jr.
High)

Harr-Wagner Publishing Company

Checkered Flag Series (R.L. 2)
Deep Sea Adventures (R.L. 2-5)
Jim Forest Series (R.L. 2 and 3)
Morgan Bay Mystery Series (R.L.
3 and 4)
Reading Motivated Series (R.L. 4)
The Time Machine Series (R.L. PP
to 3)
Wildlife Adventure Series (R.L. 4
and 5)

D.C. Heath and Co.

Our Animal Story Books (R.L. 1)
Walt Disney Story Books (R.L. 1
and 2)
Teen-Age Tales (R.L. 5 and 6)
It's Fun to Find Out Story Books
(R.L. 3 and 4)

Houghton-Mifflin

Easy to Read Series (R.L. 2)
Piper Books (R.L. 4)

North Star Books (R.L. 6 and 7)
Riverside Reading Series
  Shane (R.L. 7-12)
  Good-bye, Mr. Chips
The New Riverside Literature Series
  Standard Classics
Trouble Shooter Workbooks
  Spelling Skill
  Spelling Action
  Word Attack
  Word Mastery
  Sentence Strength
  Punctuation Power
  English Achievement

Imperial International
Imperial Junior High School Aural
  (R.L. 7-12)
Reading Laboratory

Laidlaw Brothers
Reading for You (R.L. 5-6 I.L.
  7-8-9)
  Used with Inner city school

Learning Materials, Inc.
The Curriculum Motivation Series
  Better than Gold and other Stories
    (R.L. 3.6 and I.L. 5-7)
  Three Green Men and other
    Stories (R.L. 4.1 I.L. 6-8)
The Literature Sampler, Secondary
  Edition
  144 book previews about 2,000
    words in length
  Includes reading aids, discussions
    (R.L. 5-11)

J.B. Lippincott Company
Reading for Meaning (R.L. 7-9)

Lyons and Carnahan
The Bond Classmate Readers
  Basal remedial reading program,
    skillbooks available for each
    book
  Stories to Remember (R.L. 4.0
    I.L. 6)

A Call to Adventure (R.L. 5.0
  I.L. 7)
Deeds of Men (R.L. 5.5 I.L. 8)

MacMillan Co.
Aviation Readers (R.L. P to 3)
MacMillan Readers Unit Books
  (R.L. PP to 3)
Sports Readers (R.L. 2 and 3)
Book 9-Roots Middle English and
  Modern English (R.L. 9-12)
Book 10-American English Dialects
  (R.L. 9-12)
Book 11-Linguistic Geography (R.L.
  9-12)
Book 12-Dictionaries and the Lan-
  guage (R.L. 9-12)

Malfex Associated, Inc.
Citizens All Series (R.L. 1-3)
The Magpie Series (R.L. 1-3).

McGraw-Hill Book Company
Reading for Concepts (R.L. 3-12)

Charles E. Merrill Books Inc.
Building Reading Power
  15 sequential programmed units in
    three series
  Boxed kits (R.L. Jr. High)
    Context clues
    Structural Analysis
    Comprehension Skills

William Morrow and Company, Inc.
Morrow's High Interest/Easy Read-
  ing Books (R.L. 1-8)

Noble and Noble Publishers, Inc.
Crossroads
  Reading selections, graphics,
    supplementary records and dis-
    cussion ideas.
  Tomorrow Won't Wait (R.L. 3)
  Breaking Loose
  In Others' Eyes
  Playing it Cool
  Loves Blues (R.L. 2)
  Me, Myself, and I

Dreamers of Dreams
He Who Dares
Supplementary Texts
Specially abridged and edited
"best sellers" carefully adapted
to minimize reading difficulties,
special teacher's notes prepared
for each title.
Karen
Fail-Safe
Times 4
April Morning
West Side Story
Laurel Leaf Books (I.L. Inter.
and Jr.)

Perma bound
Pyramid Hi-Low Series (R.L. 3–8
I.L. 5–12)

Portal Press, Inc.
Springboards Reading Lab I (R.L.
3–6)

Prentice-Hall, Inc.
Be a Better Reader (R.L. 4–12)

G.P. Putman and Sons
Horse in No Hurry (R.L. 3)

Quality Educational Development, Inc.
Planning and Evaluation Kit

Reader's Digest Services, Inc.
Pegasus Story Books (R.L. 2 and 3)
Self-Help Reader (R.L. 7–10)

Benjamin H. Sanborn & Co.
Famous Story Series (R.L. 6)
Sanborn Readers (R.L. p to 3)

Scholastic Magazine and Book Service
The Action Library 1 (R.L. 2.0–2.4)

Science Research Associates
Reading Laboratory Series (R.L.
1–12)
SRA Pilot Library Series (R.L. 2–12)
Kaleidoscope of Skills: Reading
(R.L. 5–6–7)

Dimensions—We are Black
Reading level 2.6; recommended
for secondary pupils. Boxed kit.
Papertexts Series
For use in an individualized pro-
gram in high school;
Library-8 and 9

Scott Foresman and Company
Special Reading Books (R.L. 3 to 6)
Reading for Independence (R.L. 2
and 3)
The Galaxie Program (R.L. 7–11)
The Basic Reading Program (R.L.
7–8)
Tactics in Reading (R.L. 9–10–11)
What's Happening (R.L. 8–10)
The Open Highways Program
Book 7
Book 8 (Below average)
Activity-Concept English Ace 301
Lowest track Grade nine student

Charles Scribner's Sons
Social Learning Readers (R.L. 1
and 2)

Silver Burdett Company
Success in Reading (R.L. 6–9)

Steck-Vaughn Company
Easy Readers (R.L. pp to 4)
Treasure Books (R.L. 5 and 6)

Teaching Resources, Inc.
People Profiles (R.L. 3.0–3.5)

United States Department of the Inte-
rior, Bureau of Indian Affairs
Publication Service
Navajo Series (R.L. 3 to 5)
Pueblo Series (R.L. 3 to 5)

Franklin Watts, Inc.
Reading books-large type editions
Catcher in the Rye
The Fire Next Time
Great Expectations
Good-bye, Mr. Chips

Games People Play
Profile in Courage

Webster Division, McGraw-Hill Book Company
Everyreader Series (R.L. 4)
Junior Everyreader Series (R.L. 3)
+4 Reading Booster (R.L. Middle Grades below Grade 4)
Reading Incentive Series (R.L. 3–7 I.L. 7–12)
Mystery in the Sky
Swamp March
Full Speed Ahead
Venus Bound
Go Climb a Mountain
Reading Shelf I (R.L. 4–6 I.L. 7–12)
Webster Classroom Reading Clinic Remedial materials (R.L. 4–9)
New Practice Readers (R.L. 6–9 I.L. 2–8)

Albert Whitman and Company
Action-packed high interest sports stories by Joe Archibald (R.L. 5–8 I.L. 7–12)

Xerox Education Publications
Know Your World (Newspaper Form) (R.L. 3–5)
Pal Paperback Kits
Kit A—Yellow Series (R.L. 1.5–2.5)
Kit A—Red Series (R.L. 2.5–3.5)
Kit B—Blue Series (R.L. 3.5–4.5)
Kit B—Green Series (R.L. 4.5–5.5)
Theme: True Life Adventures
Man-Killer—Yellow Series and other stories of real danger (R.L. 1.5–2.5)
Amazing Adventures—Red Series (R.L. 2.5–3.5)
Real Life Adventures—Blue Series True Tales of Courage (R.L. 3.5–4.5)
Nine Daring Adventures—Green Series (R.L. 4.5–5.5)

Theme: Science Fiction/Supernatural
The Monster Fly—Yellow Series (R.L. 1.5–2.5)
The Weird Watches Spell—Red Series (R.L. 2.5–3.5)
Strange Happenings—Blue Series (R.L. 3.5–4.5)
Eight Haunted Stories—Green Series (R.L. 4.5–5.5)
Theme: The World of Sports
Sports Stars—Yellow Series (R.L. 1.5–2.5)
Sports Action—Red Series (R.L. 2.5–3.5)
Champions All—Blue Series (R.L. 3.5–4.5)
Sports Greats of the 70's—Green Series (R.L. 4.5–5.5)
Theme: Teen Problem (Girls)
Don't Dye Baby—Yellow Series (R.L. 1.5–2.5)
The Sacrifice—Red Series (R.L. 2.5–3.5)
Ten Top Favorites—Blue Series (R.L. 3.5–4.5)
Just for Kicks—Green Series (R.L. 4.5–5.5)
Theme: Teen Problems (Boys)
Wild Tales—Yellow Series (R.L. 1.5–2.5)
Pay off in the Park—Red Series (R.L. 2.5–3.5)
High and Mighty—Blue Series (R.L. 3.5–4.5)
The Junkie—Green Series (R.L. 4.5–5.5)
Theme: Cars and Cycles
The 'Vette—Yellow Series (R.L. 1.5–2.5)
Varoom!—Red Series (R.L. 2.5–3.5)
The Handy Kid—Blue Series (R.L. 3.5–4.5)
Speed Kings—Green Series (R.L. 4.5–5.5)
Theme: Famous Persons and Events
America's Bad Men—Yellow Series (R.L. 1.5–2.5)

Great Disasters—Red Series (R.L. 2.5–3.5)

Against All Odds—Blue Series (R.L. 3.5–4.5)

Events that Shook the World—Green Series (R.L. 4.5–5.5)

Theme: Jokes and Tricks

Laugh it Up—Yellow Series (R.L. 1.5–2.5)

Jokes on You—Red Series (R.L. 2.5–3.5)

Would You Believe?—Blue Series (R.L. 3.5–4.5)

The Trick Book—Green Series (R.L. 4.5–5.5)

Theme: Beyond the Natural

Living Monsters—Yellow Series (R.L. 1.5–2.5)

True Ghost Stories—Red Series (R.L. 2.5–3.5)

Earth's Hidden Mysteries—Blue Series (R.L. 3.5–4.5)

Outer Limits of the Mind—Green Series (R.L. 4.5–5.5)

READING LABORATORIES

Addison-Wesley Publishing Co.

Reading Development Kit B (K) (R.L. 4–6 I.L. 5–adult)

Reading Development Kit C (K) (R.L. 7–10+ I.L. 7–adult)

Allied Education Council

Comprehension Series 601–604 (WBs) (R.L. 5–7 I.L. 4–12)

Mott Basic Language Skills Program Classroom Series 600 Series (WBs) (R.L. 5–8 I.L. 4–12)

Classroom Series 900 Series (WBs) (R.L. 8–10 I.L. 6–12)

Semi-Programmed Series 1607–1610 (WBs) (R.L. 5–6 I.L. 4–12)

Semi-Programmed Series 1911–1914 (WBs) (R.L. 7–10 I.L. 6–12)

American Education Publications

Reading Success Series 1–6 (WBs) (R.L. 2–6 I.L. 5–12)

Amidon and Associates

Listen: Hear; Tapes on variety of skills response booklets, grades 4–9

Systems 80; Grades K–12

Barnell Loft, Ltd.

Specific Skill Series
Complete Specimen Kit (K) (R.L. 1–6 I.L. 1–12)

Benefic Press

Mystery Adventure Series (B) (R.L. 2–6 I.L. 4–9)

Space Science Fiction Series (B) (R.L. 2–6 I.L. 4–9)

World of Adventure Series (B) (R.L. 2–6 I.L. 4–9)

D.C. Heath

Teenage Tales Books 1, 2, 3, (B) (R.L. 5–6 I.L. 7–12)

Educational Developmental Laboratories

EDL: Study Skills Library; Science, social studies and research kits, grades 4–9.

Grolier Educational Corporation

Reading Attainment System 2 (K) (R.L. 5–6 I.L. 7–12)

Hoffman Information Systems, Inc.

Hoffman Gold Series; Ten albums, four filmstrips, and two records. Vocabulary, comprehension rate, grades 3–9.

Houghton Mifflin

Reading Skills Laboratory
Level 3
Box A = Diagnostic tests (R.L. 6 I.L. 4–6)

Box B = Lab books (K) (R.L. 6 I.L. 7–12)

Learning Materials, Inc.

Literature Sampler; Previews of 144 books on reading levels 4–9.

MacMillan Co.

The Reading Spectrum; Non-graded, multilevel skills program, grades 2–8.

McGraw-Hill Publishing Co.

EDL: Listen and Read Program; Tapes and workbooks for junior and senior high.

Random House

Criterion Reading (WB) (R.L. K–12+ I.L. K–12+)
Random House Reading Program Reading Pacemakers (BO) (R.L. 1–12 I.L. 2–12)
Random House Reading Program Skilpacers (K) (R.L. 1–12 I.L. 2–12)

Reader's Digest

Adult Readings (K) (R.L. 4–9 I.L. 7–12+)
Help Yourself to Improve Your Reading (WB) (R.L. 7–10 I.L. 6–12+)
Reading Skill Builders New Reading Skill Builders (WB) (R.L. 2–8 I.L. 2–12+)
Reading Skill Practice Pads (WB) (R.L. 1–6 I.L. 1–6)
Reader's Digest Readings (WB) (R.L. 1–6 I.L. 7–12+)
Science Readers (WB) (R.L. 3–6 I.L. 3–9)

Scholastic Book Services

Scope/Skills (WB) (R.L. 4–6 I.L. 7–12)
Scope/Visuals (WB) (R.L. 4–6 I.L. 7–12)

Science Research Associates

SRA Advanced Reading Skills Program; Twenty-four lessons on reading skills, grades 9–12.
Dimensions in Reading—An American Album (K) (R.L. 3–8, 9 I.L. 4–12)
Dimensions in Reading—Manpower and Natural Resources (K) (R.L. 4–11, 9 I.L. 7–12)
SRA Graph and Picture Study Skills Kit; Reading charts, diagrams, cartoons, grades-intermediate.
Pilot Library IIb (K) (R.L. 3–8 I.L. 4–6)
Pilot Library IIc (K) (R.L. 4–9 I.L. 5–9)
Pilot Library IIIb (K) (R.L. 5–12 I.L. 6–12)
Reading Laboratory IIIa (K) (R.L. 3–11 I.L. 7–12)
Reading Laboratory IIb (K) (R.L. 2–8 I.L. 4–6)
Reading Laboratory IIIb (K) (R.L. 5–12 I.L. 7–12)
Reading Laboratory IIc (K) (R.L. 3–9 I.L. 4–9)
Reading Laboratory IVa (K) (R.L. 8–12+ I.L. 9–12+)
Reading for Understanding Laboratory; Four thousand selections for grades 3–12 covering a wide variety of reading skills.
Vocabulab^{tm} III (K) (R.L. 4–9 I.L. 7–9)

Scott Foresman and Co.

Tactics in Reading, I and II; Box exercises for grades 9–10.

The Reading Laboratory

Reading Improvement Skill File; Box of 180 selections at several reading levels for junior and senior high use.

Steck-Vaughn Company

New Goals in Reading; Remedial

worktext remedial word attack, grades 4-6.

Teachers College Press

McCall-Crabbs Standard Test Lessons in Reading; Paperbacks, reading rate, and comprehension, grades 2-12.

Gates-Peardon Reading Exercises; Skills: significance prediction, directions, details, grades 1-7.

Conquests in Reading; Remedial workbook, word attack, comprehension.

Reading for Concepts (WB) (R.L. 1-6 I.L. 3-12)

Sullivan Reading Materials; Programmed reading materials for remedial work.

Webster Classroom Reading Clinic; Reading skill cards, questions, word wheels, grades 2-8.

Webster Publishing Company

The Everyreader Series; Corrective reading program for grades 3-6.

New Practice Readers; Comprehension skills, word analysis, grades 2-8.

J. Weston Walch, Publisher

Keys to Your Reading Improvement; Word attack skills, comprehension, grades 7-12.

MECHANICAL DEVICES

Audio-Visual Research

AVR Reading Rateometer

AVR Eye-Span Trainer; Plastic, hand-controlled shutter, grades 3-12.

AVR Flash Tachment; Attachment converts filmstrip projector to tachistoscope.

Bell and Howell

Language Master Cards Vocabulary (OM) (R.L. 4-12 I.L. 4-12)

Carlton Films

Rheen-Califone Percepta-matic Tachistoscope; grades 1-8.

Craig Research Inc.

Craig Reader

Cenco Center

Cenco Pacer; Pacer with 14 rolls, used with slow reader.

Educational Developmental Laboratories

Controlled Reader; Controlled Reader, Jr.

Flash - X Discs:

Advanced Accuracy (R.L. 9-adult I.L. 9-adult)

Letters and Numbers (R.L. 9-adult I.L. 9-adult

EDL Tach - X Tachistoscope; Projected images filmstrips, words flash in and out of focus.

Field Education Publications

Checkered Flag
    Classroom Audio-visual Kit A and B (K) (I.L. 6-12)
    Kaleidoscope Readers (WB) (R.L. 2-9 I.L. 7-12)

Genco Educational Aids

Reading Pacer

Keystone View Company

Keystone Standard Tachistoscope Flashmaster; Use on overhead projector, 5 fractional speeds.

Keystone Reading Pacer; Uses a pointer with speeds from 50 to 1,000 words per minute. Pointer must be reset on each page.

Lafayett Instrument Company

Electro-Tach; Near-point instrument,

controlled exposures, training cards of letters, words, phrases *T-ap;* All Purpose Tachistoscope attachment *Tachistoscope;* Exposures of 1/100 to 1 second. Adaptable to all filmstrip projectors.

Learning Through Seeing, Inc.

Tachist-O-Viewer, Tachist-O-Flasher; Grades 1–12.

Psychotechnics, Inc.

Shadowscope Tachomatic 500 Reading Projector; Level K–adult.

Reader's Digest

Reading Skills Library

Builders Audio Lessons (K) (R.L. 1–10 I.L. 1–12)

The Reading Laboratories, Inc.,

Prep-pacer; Electrical paċer using disk.

Phrase Flasher; Manually operated, designed for individual use.

Science Research Associates

SRA Reading Accelerator Synchroteach M_3X^{tm} IIIa (OM) (I.L. 7–12)

Tachisto-Flasher; Attaches to filmstrip projector shutter mechanism

Society for Visual Education, Inc.

SVE Speed-I-O-Scope; Grades 1–6.

ADDRESSES OF PUBLISHERS

Academic Therapy Publications
1539 Fourth Street
Sun Raphael, CA 94901

Acoustifone Corp.
20149 Sunburst Street
Chatsworth, CA 91311

Addison-Wesley
2725 Sand Hill Road
Menlo Park, CA 94025

Allied Education Council
P.O. Box 78
Galien, MI 49113

Allyn Bacon
310 West Polk
Chicago, IL 60607

American Book Co.
1015 West Euclid Avenue
Arlington Heights, IL 60004

American Education Council
1 DuPont Circle
Washington, D.C. 20036

American Guidance Service
Publishers Building
Circle Pines, MN 55014

Amidon & Assoc.
1035 Plymouth Bldg.
Minneapolis, MN 55411

Amsco Book Co.
315 Hudson Street
New York, NY 10013

Audio Teaching Center
137 Hamilton Street
New Haven, CT 06511

Audio-Visual Research
1509 Eighth Street
Waseca, MN 56093

Barnell Loft, Ltd.
958 Church Street
Baldwin, N.Y. 11510

Beckley Cardy Co.
1900 North Narragansett Street
Chicago, IL 60639

Bell and Howell
7100 McCormick Road
Chicago, IL 60645

Benefic Press
10300 West Roosevelt Road
Westchester, IL 60153

Bobbs-Merrill Co., Inc.
1720 East 38th Street
Indianapolis, IN 46218

Book Lab Inc.
1449 37th Street
Brooklyn, NY 11218

Borg Warner Education System
7450 North Natchez Avenue
Niles, IL 60648

Bowman
622 Rodier Drive
Glendale, CA 91201

Bureau of Publications,
  Teachers College
Columbia University
New York, NY 10027

California Test Bureau
Del Monte Research Park
Monterey, CA 93940

Carlton Films
Beloit, WI 53511

Cenco Center
2600 South Kostner
Chicago, IL

Children's Press Inc.
310 South Racine Avenue
Chicago, IL 60607

Committee on Diagnostic Testing
Mountain Home, NC 28798

Continental Press
Elizabethtown, PA 17022

Coronet Instructional Films
65 East Water Street
Chicago, IL 60601

Craig Research, Inc.
3410 South LaCienega Blvd.
Los Angeles, CA 90016

D.C. Heath
1815 Prairie Avenue
Chicago, IL 60616

Dell Publishing Co.
750 Third Avenue
New York, NY 10036

Developmental Reading Distributors
1944 Sheridan
Laramie, WY 82070

Doubleday and Co.
Garden City, NY 11530

The Economy Co.
24 West Park Place
Oklahoma City, OK 73103

Educational Activities, Inc.
Freport, L.I., NY 11520

Educational Developmental Laboratory
Huntington, NY 11743

Educational Progress Laboratory
8538 East 41st Street
Tulsa, OK 74145

Educational Publishing Corporation
Darwin, CT 06820

Educator's Publishing Service
15 Moulton Street
Cambridge, MA 02139

Educational Testing Service
20 Nassau Street
Princeton, NJ 08540

Encyclopedia Britannica Press
425 North Michigan Avenue
Chicago, IL 60611

Fearon Publishers
2165 Park Blvd.
Palo Alto, CA 94306

Field Educational Publications, Inc.
609 Mission Street
San Francisco, CA 94105

Follett Publishing Co.
1010 West Washington Street
Chicago, IL 60606

Foster & Futernick Co., Inc.
44 Bryant Street
San Francisco, CA 94107

Garrard Press
1607 North Market Street
Champaign, IL 61820

Genco Educational Aids
Chicago, IL

Ginn and Co.
205 West Wacker Drive
Chicago, IL 60606

Globe Book Co.
175 Fifth Avenue
New York, NY 10010

Grolier Educational Corp.
Dept. RA-7
845 Third Avenue
New York, NY 10022

Grosset and Dunlap, Inc.
51 Madison Avenue
New York, NY 10010

E.M. Hale and Co.
1201 South Hastings
Eau Claire, WI 54701

C.S. Hammond & Co.
515 Valley Street
Maplewood, NJ 07040

Harcourt Brace & World, Inc.
7555 Caldwell
Niles, IL 60648

Harcourt Brace Jovanovich
757 Third Avenue
New York, NY 10017

Harper and Row Publishers
2500 Crawford Avenue
Evanston, IL 60201

Harr-Wagner Publishing Co.
29 Columbine Drive
Palatine, IL 60067

Hoffman Information Systems
2626 South Peck Road
Monrovia, CA 91016

Holt, Rinehart & Winston
5641 Northwest Highway
Chicago, IL 60646

Hough Community Project
Cleveland, OH 44101

Houghton-Mifflin
1900 South Batavia Avenue
Geneva, IL 60901

Kenworthy Service
c/o John Green
411 West Sixth Street
Covington, KY 41011

Keystone View Co.
Dept. Rt. 93
Meadville, PA 16335

Lafayette Instrument Co.
North 26 Street and 52 ByPass
P.O. Box 57
Lafayette, IN 47901

Laidlaw Brothers
Thatcher and Madison
River Forest, IL 60305

Learn Inc.
21 East Euclid Avenue
Haddonfield, NJ 08033

Learning Through Seeing, Inc.
Sunland, CA 91040

Learning Materials Inc.
100 East Ohio Street
Chicago, IL 60611

J.B. Lippincott Co.
333 West Lake Street
Chicago, IL 60606

Lyons and Carnahan
405 East 25th Street
Chicago, IL 60616

MacMillan Co.
60 Fifth Avenue
New York, NY 10011

Mafex Associated Inc.
111 Barron Avenue
Johnstown, PA 15906

McCormick-Mathers Publishing Co.
1440 East English
Wichita, KS 67211

McGraw-Hill Book Co.
4655 Chase Avenue
Lincolnwood, IL 60646

Charles E. Merrill Books, Inc.
1300 Alum Creek Drive
Columbus, OH 43209

William Morrow and Co., Inc.
425 Park Avenue South
New York, NY 10016

Modern Curriculum Press
P.O. Box 9
Berea, OH 44017

Noble and Noble Publishers Inc.
750 Third Avenue
New York, NY 10017

F.A. Owen Publishing Co.
Daneville, NY 14437

Perma Bound
Division of Hertzberg New Method
  Inc.
Vandalia Road
Jacksonville, IL 62650

Phonovisual Products, Inc.
P.O. Box 5625
Washington, D.C. 20016

Portal Press, Inc.
369 Lexington Avenue
New York, NY 10017

The Psychological Corporation
304 East 45th Street
New York, NY 10017

Psychotechnics, Inc.
105 West Adams Street
Chicago, IL 60603

Prentice-Hall, Inc.
Educational Book Division
Englewood Cliffs, NJ 07632

G.P. Putman and Sons
200 Madison Avenue
New York, NY 10016

Quality Educational Development, Inc.
Washington, D.C.

Random House
201 East 50th Street
New York, NY 10022

Readers Digest Services, Inc.
Pleasantville, NY 10570

The Reading Laboratory, Inc.
Developmental Research Institute, Inc.

500 Fifth Avenue
New York, NY 10017

Benjamin H. Sanborn and Co.
249–259 West Erie Blvd.
Syracuse, NY 13201

Scholastic Magazine and Book Services
50 West 44th Street
New York, NY 10036

Science Research Associates
259 East Erie Street
Chicago, IL 60611

Scott Foresman and Co.
433 East Erie Street
Chicago, IL 60611

Charles Scribners Sons
597 Fifth Avenue
New York, NY 10017

Silver Bordett Co.
460 Northwest Highway
Park Ridge, IL 60068

Society for Visual Education, Inc.
1345 Diversey Parkway
Chicago, IL 60614

Systems for Education, Inc.
612 North Michigan Avenue
Chicago, IL 60611

Teaching Resources, Inc.
100 Boylston Street
Boston, MA 02116

Franklin Watts, Inc.
575 Lexington Avenue
New York, NY 10022

Webster Division
McGraw Hill Book Co.
Manchester Road
Manchester, MO 63011

Webster Publishing Co.
1154 Reco Avenue
St. Louis, MO

J. Weston Walch, Publisher
Box 658
Portland, ME 04104

Albert Whitman and Co.
560 West Lake Street
Chicago, IL 60606

Xerox Education Publications
55 High Street
Middleton, CT 06457

REFERENCES

Cramer, W. *Reading Beyond the Headlines.* Portland, Maine: J. Weston Walch, 1973.

Cramer, W.; Dorsey, S.; and Mauser, A. J. *How To Be A Word Detective.* San Rafael, California: Academic Therapy Publications, 1975.

Ekwall, E. *Diagnosis and Remediation of the Disabled Reader.* Boston: Allyn and Bacon, Inc., 1976.

Flesch, R. "A New Readability Yardstick." *Journal of Applied Psychology* 30 (1948): 221–233.

Fry, E. *Teaching Faster Reading.* New York: Cambridge University Press, 1963.

Heilman, A. W. *Phonics in Proper Perspective.* Columbus, Ohio: Charles E. Merrill Publishing Company, 1968.

Kaluger, G., and Kolson, C. *Reading and Learning Disabilities.* Columbus, Ohio: Charles E. Merrill Publishing Co., 1969.

Spache, G. *Investigating the Issues of Reading Disabilities.* Boston: Allyn and Bacon, Inc., 1976.

8

mathematical programming for problem adolescents

LES STERNBERG AND ROBERT A. SEDLAK

This chapter discusses diagnosis and remediation of arithmetic difficulties in norm-violating institutionalized and public school youths. It presents information related to past educational practices in this area, the academic achievement characteristics, learner aptitudes, and needs assessment regarding this population as they interact with the essential components of a mathematics program. Each of these components is described so that a mathematics program can be implemented in practice by the reader. The emphasis is on a workable scheme for ameliorating the academic difficulties that problem adolescents face in this achievement area.

PROGRAMMING MODELS FOR PROBLEM ADOLESCENTS

Although one may find an enormous amount of literature pertaining to curricular programming for elementary, primary, or intermediate aged children, there are very few academic programs designed for the problem adolescent who shows considerable variance in basic academic skills. This paucity of academic programs may be due, in part, to differing philosophies or models through which the problem adolescent is viewed and treated. Rhodes (1972) has described several of these philosophies or models. The first is the *biological-medical* model which views the youth's behavior as being caused by specific inherent (genetic, neurological) processes. Treatment in this case emphasizes a direct attempt at eliminating these causes of behavior (such as drugs).

Education, then, is viewed as an after-the-fact methodology once treatment has been initiated. The second approach is the *rational-affective* model which supports the supposition that thoughts and feelings cause a youth's behavior. The basic approach used to deal with children in this case is one that attempts to discover the inward emotions which are responsible for the individual's behavior (for example, through psychotherapy). Again, education is looked upon as a post hoc phenomenon. Third is the *behavioral* model which views the child as behaving because of some consequences of that behavior. The child learns an undesirable behavior because in the past it has been reinforced. The importance of this model is that it leads directly into specific teaching strategies. Treatment and education, then, are linked together into one educational framework. The fourth and last approach is the *ecological* model which views the child within a total environment milieu. While environment change is the key to this model, many educators view this model as too complex in working with children in that environment itself is too complex.

Kauffman (1974) contrasts the educational model with the treatment model and states that the issue is no longer one of value of education to behaviorally disordered youth, but one of curricular designs. He cites a number of key approaches to use in the education of these types of youth. Two extremely important alternatives are as follows: (1) *relevant experience curricula,* where emphasis is on the application of a curriculum to practical or applied situations, the purpose being to teach functional academics and social skills development in real life situations; and (2) *specially designed curricula* for behaviorally disordered youth. These two alternatives exist because past curricular approaches have dealt with a modification of the standard curricula program based on the similarities that exist between the learning of disturbed youth and normal youth.

Hunter (1972) stresses the need for a specialized curriculum and has outlined three categories of innovative practices to be used in the classroom: structure (school and classroom organization); content (subject matter); and process (socialization or interaction). Hunter makes the following statement:

> . . . The possibilities inherent in any innovation in content or structure cannot be duly realized without accompanying changes in the third area, that of process. Furthermore, . . . what is currently most needed in our schools is, in fact, process change. (Hunter, 1972, p. 15)

Hunter then describes a number of needed process innovations. One is the interaction between pupil and teacher which requires the pupil to display imaginative rather than simple memorization. Another is the interaction between pupil and teacher which emphasizes the sequential development of necessary skills. Still others are decision-making (both teacher and pupil), cooperation instead of competition, and cooperative success (pupil-to-pupil).

Dimensions of an academic program

Based on the preceding discussion of the academic characteristics of problem adolescents and program models for treating this population, a total academic program would need to accommodate the following six components: (1) flexibility; (2) relevance to the real world; (3) diagnostic/prescriptive format; (4) concept and skill emphasis; (5) social skill development; and (6) management and/or treatment free. These six elements would need to be considered regardless of the curricular area being planned. An operational definition of these six elements is provided.

Flexibility. This component mandates that the curriculum provides the teacher with a variety of options or procedures for presenting information to a learner and, in addition, provides the learner with a variety of ways to respond. Since many problem youths are extremely poor readers, the curriculum should be designed so that being a nonreader will not penalize learning mathematical concepts.

In regard to traditional math programs, usually the *flexibility* aspect, which would accommodate learner needs, is absent. Traditional basal text programs follow an age-in-grade model. This means a 13-year-old in the eighth grade is expected to perform in all academic areas as most other 13-year-olds. If a particular 13-year-old is reading at a fifth or sixth grade level, he may be unable to read his eighth grade math book. He is penalized in learning math due to a reading problem. A sad characteristic of most traditional basal mathematics programs is that from grade level to grade level, all aspects of the texts become more involved (for example, math, reading, vocabulary, sentence structure, etc.). A flexible curriculum would need to provide ways to circumvent the problems associated with increasing reading difficulty throughout the program.

Relevancy. As Kauffman (1974) has stated, the content of the curriculum needs to provide useful types of experiences for the learner. True-to-life simulations and examples are to be preferred to the storybook types of activities found in many conventional mathematics programs. Dropping the learner down to a level where he is able to understand the material may not be fruitful because the interest value of the material changes considerably.

Diagnostic/prescriptive format. A diagnostic/prescriptive format means that the assessment is directly aligned with specific objectives and content in the curriculum. The plan for instruction for each learner is based on the results of preassessment tests that are criterion referenced. Global achievement tests are not designed to provide the type of information that is needed to plan for short-term instructional goals. There are few commercially available instruments that are designed for this purpose. Several that are available which operate from a diagnostic/prescriptive base will be reviewed later in this chapter. For the most part, however, the instruments will have to be teacher-constructed.

Concept and skill emphasis. Rote memorization of facts and principles may satisfy short-term needs of a learner; but if the expected end product is for that learner to make use of what he has learned after he leaves school, the material must have meaning. Students can be taught "tricks" to get the correct answers to verbal problems or to solve complex mathematical computations. These tricks usually cannot be successfully implemented in the real world. The focus of the curriculum, then, should be built upon the development of concepts that will help a learner function satisfactorily after he leaves school.

Enhancement of social skills. Adjudicated youths quite obviously have exhibited, in the past, behaviors that are socially unacceptable. Activities which develop decision making, discrimination, social responsibility, cooperation, sportsmanship, etc., can be built into a curriculum.

Independent of management procedure. Described earlier in this chapter were four models for treating behaviorally disordered youth (biological-medical, rational-affective, behavioral, and ecological). It is desirous that the curriculum not come into conflict with the management model being adhered to since most institutions operate their treatment procedures based on one of these four models. Some math curricula contain specific management procedures. For example, the use of Direct Instructional Systems for Teaching Arithmetic and Reading (DISTAR) would be very compatible with an institution following a behavioral model, but may run into conflict with a biological-medical model operation.

CONTENT COMPONENTS OF A MATHEMATICS PROGRAM FOR NORM-VIOLATING YOUTH

Bartel (1975) has reviewed and evaluated a number of commercially available math programs that might be useful with youths who have behavioral problems. She has also modified and summarized the Mathematics Content Authority List: K–6 (Primes, 1971), which delineates relevant math concepts and skills which would constitute a comprehensive set of content for most mathematics programs. The list is a good beginning point for building a math curriculum. The five dimensions discussed in the preceding section need to be interfaced with content, and modifications made accordingly.

Interfacing content with dimensions

One of the most crucial dimensions discussed previously when planning an academic curriculum was to allow for flexibility. Cawley and Vitello (1972) have described an instructional system in mathematics that effectively incorporates this flexibility component into the curriculum. The mechanism for accomplishing this feat is called the Interactive Unit (IU). (See Figure 8.1.) The IU describes the interaction which takes place between the teacher and pupil and emphasizes the affective component of mathematics instruction. The IU graphically shows the four ways a teacher may present material to the learner, and the four ways in which the learner may respond to or interact with the teacher. In presenting a mathematical task to the student, a teacher can *construct* something, *present* a picture or prearranged set of something, *say* something, or *write* something. The pupil, in terms of interacting with the teacher, can construct something, identify something, say something, or write something. There are, therefore, sixteen possible instructional interactions between teacher and pupil. This provides the student with the opportunity to demonstrate acquisition of a specific arithmetic concept through a number of interactive channels. Even with a student who is a functional nonreader, there are twelve options available to the teacher for presenting the information and getting a response. The teacher would stop presenting material that required reading to the youth.

Interactive Unit Model

*Input (Teacher)	constructs	presents	states	graphically symbolizes (writes)
Output (Student)	constructs	identifies	states	graphically symbolizes (writes)

*In certain instances, another student may provide input.

Figure 8.1.

Another component of the mathematics system (Cawley and Vitello, 1972) is the flexibility principle which verbal problems can be systematically prepared to control for a variety of crucial variables (such as reading level, computational difficulty, distracting information, etc.). A discussion of how this can be attained will be described later in the chapter.

A third and a fourth component of the Cawley-Vitello model which meet the flexibility requirement are the learning unit and the cognitive processing unit which describe several factors: (1) different types of learning and learning styles; and (2) cognitive processes that are inherent in different kinds of instructional strategies. The instructional systems component basically outlines different types of materials or methodologies to be employed in the curriculum. Also, an emphasis is placed on the evaluation of student performance within the instructional systems. For a more indepth discussion of alternative instructional strategies which can be used with learners who exhibit difficulties in mathematics, see Sternberg and Mauser (1975).

Diagnosis

A shortcoming of most evaluation systems in mathematics is their failure to correlate student performance in a program with student performance on an assessment battery. The following section provides an overview of diagnosis as it pertains to mathematics programming.

It is imperative that diagnosis be looked on as one segment of a continuous process leading toward effective instructional programming in mathematics skill development for norm-violating youth. Teachers are usually faced with results from various diagnostic batteries, usually in the form of achievement tests, that give supposed indications of where a student is presently functioning. Results are often stated in grade equivalent or age equivalent scores. Occasionally, a student's performance is reported in terms of how he compares with others of his same age (scaled scores or percentile ranks). The obvious teacher's question stemming from such reports is, "What should I now teach the student?" Any report of a student's performance on a diagnostic test or inventory related to attained mathematical skills is basically useless unless some type of preferred instructional programming is recommended. To state a student's grade or age equivalent score or his scaled score indicates where he stands in relation to the norm group. However, this statement does not permit real direction as to the teaching process. What is needed, then, is a specification of a student's individual academic-related then, is a specification of a student's individual academic-related behaviors so that prescriptive instruction based upon those behaviors can ensue.

Another consideration must be given to an explanation of what generates the results of most diagnostic tests. The essential question is what *performances* or *behaviors* are being measured to justify the score? Too often the assumption is made that this is not a necessary question. In the past, the emphasis in diagnosis of mathematical abilities has been in the area of computation. It seemed all that was necessary to measure a student's achievement level in mathematics, and to diagnose his strengths and weaknesses within this area, was to measure how well he could compute with whole numbers and fractions, and how well he could use computation to solve basic verbal problems. To design a diagnostic instrument based on this assumption was indeed a very easy task.

It seems rather obvious that there is much more to mathematical ability than mere computation and its use. To show that a student can add, subtract, multiply, and divide does not necessarily show that a child understands these operations. He could be simply following a rote computational habit without any regard to the rationale or reasoning encompassing that operation. Care must be taken, therefore, in selecting or developing instruments that give a much more indepth analysis of covert abstract conceptualizations and reasoning skills leading toward overt behavioral performances indicating correct usage of these covert processes.

What is being recommended, then, is the use of diagnostic instruments that (1) provide a depiction and delineation of specific mathematical behaviors through behavioral or performance objectives; and (2) indicate or prescribe instruction based upon a student's performance on a given formal or informal instrument or behavior observation device. At the present time, norm-referenced diagnostic tests or achievement tests do not meet these two requirements. The only appropriate path to follow seems to be in the use of criterion-referenced and concept-referenced tests or inventories. The former measure the acquisition of specific behaviors, prescribe instruction toward those behaviors, and then test acquisition of the behaviors; while the latter measure a behavior, then relate successful performance of that behavior to various instructional concepts related to that behavior. See Figure 8.2 for examples of these two methods.

A basic premise of the diagnostic/prescriptive teaching model has been that the contents of tests used in the assessment procedure should be directly correlated with instructional alternatives. The following section will deal with four innovative diagnostic/prescriptive systems that attempt to ameliorate some of the problems existing in current mathematics programs. Each is an attempt at not only making mathematics meaningful but also meeting specific nonacademic needs of the youngster.

Fountain Valley Teacher Support System in Mathematics (FTSS)

The Fountain Valley Teacher Support System in Mathematics, developed by Richard L. Zwieg, Associates, Inc., provides a direct link between a learner's performance on a series of diagnostic math tests and the materials that a teacher could use to teach the skills the learner lacks.

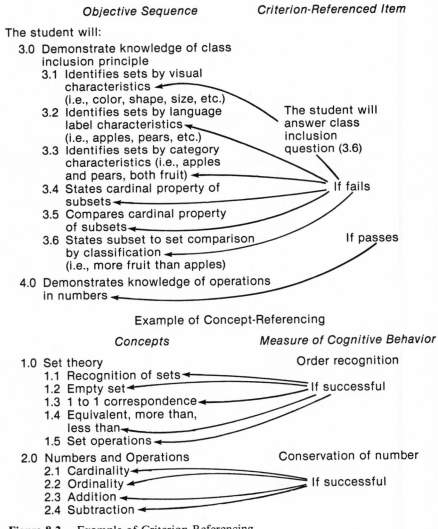

Figure 8.2. Example of Criterion-Referencing

The FVTSS in Mathematics contains a series of criterion-referenced diagnostic tests which cover 785 behaviorally stated mathematics objectives suitable for grades K–8. The mathematics objectives cover nine distinct math strands: (1) numbers and operations; (2) geometry; (3) measurement; (4) applications of mathematics; (5) statistics and probability; (6) sets; (7) functions and graphs; (8) logical thinking; and (9) problem solving.

The direction for each of these tests is recorded on audio cassette tapes so that they may be used by groups or individuals. Each test is on a two-part sealed piece of paper designed to be self-scoring. Number codes on the correction sheet indicate the objective each item is intended to measure. The teacher merely notes the number codes for the items a learner missed and records the information on an Individual Continuous Pupil Progress Profile. The teacher then consults the Teacher's Manual for a further explanation of the objective code or the Teaching Alternatives Supplement to the Teacher's Manual if he or she desires to know which basal mathematics texts or supplementary audio-visual programs cover that specific objective. The major basal tests and audio-visual supplements have each been analyzed in terms of the 785 objectives and cross-referenced with page numbers in the texts back to each item on the tests. The end result is a direct link between the test and the instructional options.

The system allows for a great deal of flexibility on the part of the teacher. It permits the teacher to build an individualized program for learners with disabilities in mathematics. The cost for each level of the system (of which there are nine) is about $135.

The Basic Educational Skills Inventory in Math (BESI)

The Basic Educational Skills Inventory is a component of, and used in conjunction with the Prescriptive Materials Retrieval System (PMR, Select-Ed, 1972). BESI contains 433 items that have been divided into 20 sections. Each of the items is cross-referenced on the scoring sheet with a PMR System number and descriptor. A student doing poorly in a section of the inventory might qualify for additional testing or be taught the skills he or she did not demonstrate to criterion. To locate materials that are aligned with the particular skill which each item or cluster of items is measuring, the teacher needs to go to the descriptor card file and locate the materials that are available for teaching the needed skill(s). If the teacher wishes to impose further restrictions on the type of material needed, an additional card can be pulled from the descriptor card file (95 descriptors in mathematics) and superimposed on the content card. For example, the teacher may wish to specify that the material be in a workbook format. The descriptor card listing all workbook materials would then be pulled.

These two cards could then be placed upon the code reading light box to determine how many materials are available which meet the two requirements the teacher has specified. This is an innovative aspect of PMR in that most rational systems can only specify one variable at a time. The teacher next copies down the acquisition numbers of the materials and reads a description of each material meeting the two requirements by consulting the Material Analysis Sheets.

The teacher can then acquire the materials from a distributor or on loan from a materials library. Approximately 55% to 65% of the materials cataloged in the PMR system are readily available in any well-equipped school district. If the materials are not available, they might be borrowed. The cost of the PMR System is about $2,000. Periodic updates of the system are available at a cost of about $200.

Key Math (American Guidance Service)

Key Math (Connolly, Nachtman, & Pritchett, 1971) is an individually administered diagnostic arithmetic test that contains fourteen subtests organized into three major areas—Content, Operations, and Applications. Historically, diagnostic tests in mathematics have stressed the area of computation. Key Math has broadened this limited focus on math diagnosis and included math concepts and applications. Key Math has grouped the computational aspects of math under the rubric of Operations. Under the area of Content, the authors have incorporated items that deal with the concepts of numeration, fractions, and geometry and symbols. Applications deal with word problems, missing elements, money, measurement, and time. Each of the subtests is made up of items which are arranged in order of increasing difficulty. Certain subtests require paper-and-pencil responses (the four subtests dealing with fundamental computations). All of the other subtests require oral responses.

Key Math provides the following information to the teacher: (1) a grade equivalent score which indicates how well the student performed on the entire test; (2) a profile delineating the student's relative performance in each of the fourteen skill areas; and (3) a description of each item's content as well as an indication of the student's performance on that item.

Evaluation.   Key Math is functional in content. It is very appropriate to use with students who are experiencing specific learning problems. It requires almost no reading or writing ability. The administration format is extremely easy to follow and gives the teacher the opportunity to be involved in relevant diagnosis. The manual also presents instructional implications based upon the students' performance on the various subtests. The authors have cross-referenced each of the items on the test with specific behavioral objectives. They have included this information in Appendix A of the manual. The authors also encourage the teacher to examine the item-by-item performance of the learner for the purpose of planning additional testing or a corrective program. The Diagnostic Profile makes it very easy to see a student's item performance at a glance.

Development of the instrument was initiated in 1961. Field tests have involved over 2,900 pupils in 20 states. Item analysis was conducted related to the performance of 951 subjects in grades K-8. Normative data were gathered on 1,222 subjects in grades K-7. Correlations range from 0.94 to 0.97. Median subtest reliability falls in the range of 0.64 to 0.84.

Validity. The selection and sequencing of content in Key Math was based on an analysis of 10 major mathematics programs. The Key Math Diagnostic Arithmetic Test has no upper limit for individual remedial use. It does not neglect the diagnosis of computational areas. However, by measuring other mathematical concept skill development, it supports the supposition that diagnosis of other reasoning processes is crucial in the determination of a student's mathematical ability. The approximate cost of Key Math is $25.

Pattern Recognition Skills Inventory (PRSI)

The PRSI developed by Sternberg (Hubbard Scientific Co., 1976) is a measuring tool and a diagnostic device. It is designed to help educators and other specialists make certain determinations about students, including levels of readiness for functioning in language and mathematics, levels of development of reasoning skills, and appropriate curricular approaches. The inventory is arranged in four equivalent sets, each set consisting of 24 pattern tasks. Only one set (random selection) is presented to the subject. As the teacher presents each task, he or she instructs the subject to (1) view the model pattern sequence; (2) view the four-choice array of pattern sequences; and (3) make a choice from this array. Each student's response is recorded on a response evaluation sheet. The response evaluation sheet provides information related to three areas: (1) pattern task performance; (2) stimulus dimension performance; and (3) pattern performance. The author has related these performance areas to basic instructional implications in language and mathematics. The implications (concepts) are listed in figures that are present in the Teacher's Manual. PRSI can also be used to develop pattern recognition skills. The teacher presents one set as a pre-test, uses another two sets for instruction, and uses the remaining set as a post-test.

Evaluation. This instrument has been under development since 1972. During this time four research studies have been conducted involving the testing of over 500 students. Normative data were gathered on normal subjects (preschool through fourth grade) and handicapped students (primary, intermediate, and junior high school).

The PRSI is a concept-referenced tool which attempts to take a specific behavior (pattern recognition) and relate it to other conceptual areas (language and mathematics). It requires no reading on the part of the student. It was expressly designed for use by teachers. The instructional implications figure pertaining to mathematics provides concepts listed in developmental order. The real emphasis of the PRSI is in instructional implications. Since the inventory is comprised of four equivalent yet different task sets, the teacher may use the materials, if so desired, to teach pattern recognition, a prerequisite skill to language and mathematical skill development. The approximate cost of PRSI is $85.

Verbal problem solving

To satisfy the relevancy dimension of the curriculum model described previously and also the concept development emphasis, a verbal information processing component is essential.

Verbal problem solving deals with mathematical problems that are embedded in verbal phrases. In the past, problem-solving instruction was conducted in a very unsystematic fashion. The following discussion outlines a procedure for diagnostically teaching problem solving to norm-violating youth so as to systematically control the variables present in word problems. It also shows how to minimize computational and reading difficulties and maximize the active processing of information on the part of the learner.

A verbal problem is a statement or statements accompanied by a question, presented orally or in written form, that *should* require reasoning and quantitative thinking on the part of the learner to arrive at the correct answer. In addition, a verbal problem is person, time, and event specific. The following examples should clarify this point.

Determining how much interest $100 will earn at 6% compounded semi-annually may be a problem for a fourth grade boy, but it certainly would not be a problem for a certified public accountant. This is an example of a person-specific problem. For the certified public accountant, supplying the correct answer might merely involve the application of a rule or the recall of factual information, and therefore would not be a problem. In several years, the preceding example may cease to be a problem for the boy who is in fourth grade in that he has gained certain basic skills that have become an ingrained part of his behavioral repertoire.

An example of an event-specific problem is one in which a person is asked to find the floor area of a square room. The child may experience no difficulty in solving this problem. However, by presenting the same child with a floor plan of a room that has one or several offsets, he or she may be unable to provide a solution. What we have done is change the events or stimulus conditions.

A time-specific problem can be shown by a person's inability to solve a problem at an early age, but finding no difficulty solving the same problem when he or she is older. Once a person has successfully solved a problem and is able to successfully complete similar problems in a consistent fashion, the task ceases to be a problem for the person. Solving a problem requires something more than the rote application of a rule.

Understanding a little bit about person variables, time variables, and event variables will help a great deal in diagnostically teaching verbal problem solving to norm-violating youths.

Since verbal problems are person, time, and event specific, students within any given class will be operating on a variety of levels in terms of being able to solve word problems that appear in their textbooks or that are teacher-made. Being able to supply different students with a variety of problem types should be a great aid to facilitate the problem-solving process. However, to do this indiscriminately may not help the teacher to determine the reason for an incorrect response on the part of the learner. For this reason, any problems that are given to a learner to solve should be analyzed in terms of their component parts or parameters. In other words, the teacher should construct problems in a systematic fashion so that he or she is aware of what factors are operating within the framework of the verbal problem.

To write word problems which systematically vary on significant parameters of components requires that a model (procedure) be used to write the word problems. The procedure advocated in the following presentation will be that of a matrix.

The basic idea for using a matrix as an organizer of verbal problem characteristics was originally proposed by Cawley (1972). Each cell within the matrix represents a problem that is composed of certain characteristics. These characteristics may be language-related, reading-related, computationally-related, content-related, operation-related, information load-related, etc.

Table 8.1. UPS MATRIX FOR INDIRECT VERBAL PROBLEMS

| Operation | Reading Vocabulary Level | | | Number Size |
	3	4	5	
Addition	1	2	3	Decimal money
Subtraction	4	5	6	2-digit. No cents. (e.g., $10.00, $57.00)
Addition	7	8	9	Decimal money
Subtraction	10	11	12	2-digit. With cents. (e.g., $10.15, $55.37)

Table 8.1 depicts a matrix for indirect verbal problems. The dimensions or components of importance in this particular matrix are number size, reading vocabulary level, and problem type. Problem 3 in the matrix would have the following characteristics: fifth-grade reading vocabulary, computation of decimal money with values from $10.00 to $90.00, and operation of addition. A problem that might fall into this cell would look as follows:

> George, the carpenter's helper, had just been paid today. He decided to go out and pay all his bills. He had $63.00 left after spending $42.00. How much money did he start with?

Problem 6 would be an indirect subtraction problem and would fall directly beneath the problem we just indicated in the matrix. An example of this type of problem is as follows:

> Frank Wilson now has $37.00 in his wallet. He had won $27.00 of it from Fred in a poker game. How much money did he start out with?

Essentially, the primary difference between the two problems is one of arithmetical operation; one is addition and the other is subtraction. Number size for the two problems has been controlled as well as vocabulary. The key to the teaching of problem solving is systematic dimension control of problem components. If two components of a problem are changed simultaneously, it is unclear as to which of the changes in the problem facilitated or inhibited the correct response being made by the learner. By making only one change at a time the source of the difficulty can be isolated.

Math labs

Up to now we have described how four of the five dimensions of a curriculum can be accommodated in mathematics. The final dimension (enhancement of social skills) can be accomplished through the mechanism known as the math lab.

The general purposes of a math lab are to allow a student to explore his environment and make discoveries based on quantitative relationships. They can, however, be designed to enhance social skills. Mathematics labs usually revolve around a basic idea or theme. One component of the mathematics lab requires that the student use certain arithmetical skills which he has previously mastered. The purpose of a lab, in our view, is not for developing new math skills but rather to expand a student's understanding of the physical environment. The topics for math labs can be in the areas of economics, science, geography, history, and even language arts. Schminke, Maertens, and Arnold (1973) suggest several criteria that can be applied to assess the potential of various environmental arrangements for conducting a mathematical laboratory. These are as follows:

1. Does the choice really promote mathematics as a system of ideas?

2. Does the choice stimulate personal initiative and self-reliance?

3. Does the choice encourage a unique teaching style and unique learning style in the group of children?

4. Does the choice accommodate discussion and exploratory responses?

5. Is the choice generally appropriate for the desired learning?
    (Schminke, Maertens, & Arnold, 1973, p. 81)

Cawley (N.D.) suggests that the purposes of a mathematical laboratory are as follows:

1. To provide the learner with an opportunity to practice selected number skills in real and vicarious experiences.

2. To provide the instructor with an opportunity to develop experiences that will extrapolate the learning activities over a period of time.

3. To develop in the learner selected quantitative- and quantity-related skills specific to a particular cognitive strand.

4. To provide a combination of experiences that will elicit quantitatively-related principles and roles.

5. To provide a socially responsible or interactive experience in which to reinforce quantitative and behavioral characteristics.

Essential components of math laboratories

It appears as if math labs must concentrate on three distinct areas: (1) social responsibility development; (2) arithmetic skill utilization; and (3) arithmetic concept development. For norm-violating youth, probably the most essential component is that of social responsibility. One purpose of math labs is to have students apply mathematics to specific real-life situations. Therefore, each student must be made aware of his or her behavioral responsibilities within the group for completion of the activity. For example, every student participating in a math lab will not necessarily be doing the same thing. One student's responsibility might be to plan a sequence of tasks. Another might be required to collect and collate specific data that are obtained from the daily math lab activities. Still another might be asked to perform some specific mathematical operation on the data so as to have a basis for the next day's activities. The key point here is that each student has a task to do, a social responsibility to the rest of his or her group. The requirements are that each student is made aware of these responsibilities and understands that meeting them will aid not only that specific student but also the rest of the group participating in the math lab.

The second area of the math lab is arithmetic skill utilization. This refers to the prerequisite abilities that a student must have in order to complete the laboratory. These skills must also be carefully delineated by the teacher so as to afford her the opportunity of instructing the students in specific mathematical skill development if these are lacking. Also, as stated previously, given individual student's mathematics concept development, not all students will be required to demonstrate the same utilization of arithmetic skills. This allows for extreme flexibility as well as individualization of programming.

Arithmetic concept development refers to the specific mathematical principles that hopefully the student will understand as a result of the mathematics laboratory. In essence, the concept is a result of the application of the arithmetic skill to a real situation. For example, a student may bring the arithmetic skill of averaging numbers to the lab. He then applies the skill to a specific situation (that is, average number of garbage cans in front of each house in a suburban area versus an inner-city area). Combined with other variables (that is, average amount expended by a homeowner per garbage can), the concept that is hopefully developed is an environmental area-rate structure-cost interaction based on the question: Who receives the best sanitation service?

The following is an example of a Mathematics Laboratory.

Math Lab 25

Lab: Prices Over Time in Newspaper Food Ads
Length: Four to Six Weeks   Level: Senior

Social Skills to be Developed:

1. An increased feeling of responsibility by collecting the newspaper ads each week and bringing them to class when required.

2. A greater skill in communicating with peers by presenting the findings to them.

3. A greater ability to make decisions by choosing certain products to examine.

Arithmetical Concepts to be Developed:

1. Sequence of days, months.

2. Comparison of prices over time.

3. Simple chart and graph construction.

Skills Needed for Lab:

1. Reading newspaper ads.

2. Reading money notation—dollars and cents.

Introduction:

Part I. The key behavior in this part is the collection of the newspaper ads during the weeks that the lab takes place. This must be done so that the rest of the lab can be done.

Part II. The behavior to be stressed in Part II is deciding on certain items to chart and doing this each week. Part II must be done so that the learners can present their findings to the others.

Part III. The important behavior in this part of the lab is the presentation of each learner's findings to the class. Stress to the learners that their presentations should be brief but should convey the important information necessary to make a comparison of prices over time in various supermarkets.

Instructions:

Part I—Have the learners:

1. Look in newspapers for the supermarket food ads.

2. Collect ads each week for four to six weeks for one supermarket chain.

3. Bring these ads to class at the end of the four to six weeks' period. Date each ad.

4. Choose different supermarkets for comparison.

Part II—Have the learners:

1. Examine their ads and note at least five different items which are advertised every (or almost every) week.

2. Make a chart listing these items and their prices for each week that ads were collected; for example:

	Prices Each Week		
Item	*May 20*	*May 27*	*June 3*
1 qt. milk	.40	.40	.41
1 doz. eggs	.85	.88	.87

3. Graph the prices over the weeks; for example:

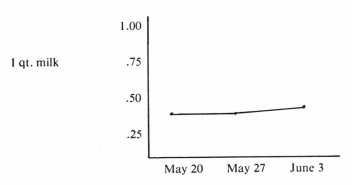

Part III—Have the learners:

1. Present their results to the other learners.
2. Discuss the findings.

Probe Questions:

Was the trend in food prices over the week steady?

Did the prices rise?   Did they fall?

What products seemed to have the greatest rise in prices?

Did any of the supermarkets raise their prices more than others?

What are some reasons for the rise or fall in food prices?

REFERENCES

Bartel, N. "Problems in Arithmetic Achievement." *Teaching Children with Learning and Behavior Problems.* Edited by D. Hammill and N. Bartel. Boston: Allyn and Bacon, Inc., 1975, pp. 61–88.

Cawley, J. F. "Teaching Arithmetic to Mentally Handicapped Children." *Strategies for Teaching Exceptional Children.* Edited by E. L. Meyer, G. A. Vergason, and R. J. Whelan. Denver, Colorado: Love Publishing Co., 1972, pp. 250–263.

Cawley, J., and Vitello, S. "A Model for Arithmetical Programming for Handicapped Children: A Beginning." *Exceptional Children* 39 (1972): 101–110.

Connolly, A. J.; Nachtman, W.; and Pritchett, E. M. *Key Math Diagnostic Arithmetic Test Manual.* Circle Pines, Minnesota: American Guidance Service, Inc., 1971.

Feldhusen, J. "Prediction of Delinquency Adjustment and Academic Achievement over a Five-Year Period with the Kvaraceus Delinquency Proneness Scale." *Journal of Educational Research* 65 (1973): 375–381.

Fountain Valley Teacher Support System in Mathematics. Huntington Beach, California: Richard L. Zweig, Associates, Inc., 1974.

Hunter, E. *Encounter in the Classroom.* New York: Holt, Rinehart, and Winston, Inc., 1972.

Kauffman, J. "Conclusion: Issues." *Teaching Children with Behavior Disorders.* Edited by J. Kauffman and C. Lewis. Columbus University: Charles Merrill Publishing Co., 1974, pp. 275–286.

Prescriptive Materials Retrieval System. Olathe, Kansas: Select-Ed, Inc., 1972.

Primes: Mathematics Content Authority List: K-6. Harrisburg, Pennsylvania: Pennsylvania Department of Education, 1971.

Rhodes, W. *A Study of Child Variance: Conceptual Project in Emotional Disturbance.* Ann Arbor: University of Michigan, 1972.

Schminke, C.; Maertens, N.; and Arnold, W. *Teaching the Child Mathematics.* Hinsdale, Illinois: Dryden Press, Inc., 1973.

Sternberg, L., and Mauser, A. J. "The LD Child and Mathematics." *Academic Therapy* 10 (1975): 481–488.

Index

subject index

author index